MORALITY AND UNIVERSALITY

THEORY AND DECISION LIBRARY

AN INTERNATIONAL SERIES
IN THE PHILOSOPHY AND METHODOLOGY OF THE
SOCIAL AND BEHAVIORAL SCIENCES

Editors:

GERALD EBERLEIN, *University of Technology, Munich*
WERNER LEINFELLNER, *University of Nebraska*

Editorial Advisory Board:

VOLUME 45

MORALITY AND UNIVERSALITY

Essays on Ethical Universalizability

Edited by

NELSON T. POTTER

*Department of Philosophy, University of Nebraska,
Lincoln, Nebraska, U.S.A.*

and

MARK TIMMONS

*Department of Philosophy, Illinois State University,
Normal, Illinois, U.S.A.*

D. REIDEL PUBLISHING COMPANY

A MEMBER OF THE KLUWER ACADEMIC PUBLISHERS GROUP

DORDRECHT / BOSTON / LANCASTER / TOKYO

Library of Congress Cataloging-in-Publication Data
Main entry under title:

Morality and universality.

Bibliography: p.
Includes index.
1. Ethics—Addresses essays, lectures. I. Potter, Nelson T.,
1939– . II. Timmons, Mark, 1951– III. Title:
Ethical Universalizability. IV. Series.
BJ1012.M63545 1985 170 85-19282
ISBN 90-277-1909-8

Published by D. Reidel Publishing Company,
P.O. Box 17, 3300 AA Dordrecht, Holland

Sold and distributed in the U.S.A. and Canada
by Kluwer Academic Publishers,
190 Old Derby Street, Hingham, MA 02043, U.S.A.

In all other countries, sold and distributed
by Kluwer Academic Publishers Group,
P.O. Box 322, 3300 AH Dordrecht, Holland

Printed in The Netherlands

TABLE OF CONTENTS

v

ACKNOWLEDGEMENTS

There are many people to acknowledge in connection with this collection of essays. We can begin with all of our contributors, who assisted us in many ways, including finally an exhibition of the virtue of patience. There are some others who require to be singled out for acknowledgement, notably those who helped us with secretarial and bibliographical matters at our two institutions, Arlene Rash, Verda Schweitzer, Beth Hettinger, Patricia Kelly, Sandy Taylor, and Elizabeth A. Kelly.

The last acknowledgement is the most important, however. Marcus Singer not only wrote an essay for inclusion in our volume; he also encouraged us from the beginning, gave us many good leads on possible additional authors, and helped us significantly with the bibliography at the end of this volume. His support and assistance through the long process of bringing this book to print were invaluable, and we have appreciated them greatly.

N.T.P.
M.T.

NELSON POTTER AND MARK TIMMONS

INTRODUCTION

In the past 25 years or so, the issue of ethical universalizability has figured prominently in theoretical as well as practical ethics. The term, 'universalizability' used in connection with ethical considerations, was apparently first introduced in the mid-1950s by R. M. Hare to refer to what he characterized as a logical thesis about certain sorts of evaluative sentences (Hare, 1955). The term has since been used to cover a broad variety of ethical considerations including those associated with the ideas of impartiality, consistency, justice, equality, and reversibility as well as those raised in the familar questions: 'What if everyone did that?' and 'How would you like it if someone did that to you?'

But this recent effloresence of the use of the term 'universalizability' is something that has deep historical roots, and has been central in various forms to the thinking about morality of some of the greatest and most influential philosophers in the western tradition. While the term is relatively new, the ideas it is now used to express have a long history. Most of these ideas and questions have been or can be formulated into a principle to be discussed, criticized, or defended. As we discuss these ideas below this principle will be stated on a separate numbered line.

The concepts of justice and equality were closely linked in Greek thought. These connections between these two concepts are apparent even in two authors who were hostile to the connection, Plato and Aristotle. They attempted to defuse the connection by emphasizing that justice or equality requires treating unequals unequally (see Vlastos, 1973). Aristotle writes:

Now if the unjust is unequal, the just must be equal; and that is, in fact, what everyone believes without argument . . . the just involves at least four terms: there are two persons in whose eyes it is just, and the shares which are just are two. Also, there will be the same equality between the persons and the shares; the ratio between the shares will be the same as that between the persons. If the persons are not equal, their [just] shares will not be equal; but this is the source of quarrels and recriminations, when equals have and are awarded unequal shares or unequals equal shares.[1]

This discussion could be condensed into the following principle.

(1)   Treat equals equally, unequals unequally.

Nelson Potter and Mark Timmons (eds.), Morality and Universality, ix–xxxii.
© 1985 *by D. Reidel Publishing Company.*

Jesus in the *New Testament* gives an influential statement of what has long been called the "Golden Rule", but which is more often discussed by philosophers under the title of a moral principle of reversibility:

(2)   Do unto others as you would have others do unto you.

There seem to be problems with the Golden Rule when we attempt to use it to determine what our obligations in specific circumstances are. It is because of these difficulties that, as is remarked below, philosophers, when they get their hands on this principle tend to turn it into a non-substantive principle (see Singer, 1963; Gewirth, 1978). Another course is followed by Narveson in the lead essay of this anthology, who considers its claims as a moral principle in a variety of different formulations and rejects them all. Apart from such specific difficulties, part of the basic insight of the Golden Rule remains alive in those philosophers such as Kurt Baier who make significant use of such related notions as reversibility or reciprocity.

One of the most influential of moral philosophers ever, Immanuel Kant, proposed several different formulations of what he called "the categorical imperative". And he called the categorical imperative the "supreme principle of morality". This latter phrase apparently means that he believed that this principle was the only *moral* principle needed to determine our moral obligations in any particular circumstance (i.e., with reference to any given maxim). Other statements used in arriving at such conclusions about our moral obligations would be one and all non-moral statements. According to this view, any other correct moral principles or rules, such as "Don't tell lies", or "Be beneficent", would be a subsidiary principle or rule arrived at using only a single moral principle, the categorical imperative itself. What is often called the "first formulation" of the categorical imperative is a version of what we will shortly be referring to as a substantive universalizability principle. Here are two different statements of it:

(3)   Act only on that maxim through which you can at the same time will that it should become a universal law.

(4)   Act as if the maxim of your action were to become through your will a universal law of nature (Kant, 1785, AK., IV, 421).

The differences between these two versions are important for its application, but for our present purposes we may refer to either statement indifferently as versions of what we will call, following the usual practice, the "first formulation" of the categorical imperative. Both versions contain the key phrase "universal law" which makes it clear that Kant's attempt is to use a substantive universalizability principle as the basis of his entire moral theory. This is the most ambitious claim ever made for a principle of ethical universalizability.

Henry Sidgwick, writing about a century ago, kept a notion of universalizability alive within the utilitarian tradition:

(5)   [I] f a kind of conduct that is right (or wrong) for me is not right (or wrong) for someone else, it must be on the ground of some difference between the two cases, other than the fact that I and he are different persons (Sidgwick, 1901, p. 379).

Another formulation which seems likely to yield quite similar results to Sidgwick's principle is one that has been mentioned by more than one recent writer; here it is given in a formulation from a recent book by an author who is a contributor to the present volume, Wlodzimierz Rabinowicz:

(6)   Moral properties of things (persons, actions, states of affairs, situations) are essentially independent of their purely 'individual' or 'numerical' aspects (Rabinowicz, 1979, p. 11).

Another direction has been taken by another much discussed writer who also contributes to this volume, Marcus Singer:

(7)   If the consequences of everyone's doing some action x would be undesirable, then no one ought to do x (Singer, 1961, p. 66).

In another recent influential essay Bernard Williams imagines a world in which we have the power to control, alter, and improve all of people's personal qualities to the point where each is brought up to the level of all the others in qualifications. He writes,

In these circumstances, where everything about a person is controllable, equality of opportunity and absolute equality seem to coincide; and this itself illustrates something about the notion of equality of opportunity (Williams, 1962, pp. 128–9).

The idea of absolute equality appears to be one of the more radical theses that a concept of universalizability could yield: the idea that all persons should be treated in exactly the same way period.[2] Such an idea has had few if any defenders, but as the present quotation from Williams indicates, its existence as a possible ideal may be used to help clarify by contrast other related conceptions. Williams' thought may be formulated in the following principle:

(8)   Where all differences between persons are controllable, equality of opportunity and absolute equality coincide.

The connections with universalizability are also clear in the statement of the first part of John Rawls' principle of justice:

(9)   [E]ach person is to have an equal right to the most extensive basic liberty compatible with a similar liberty for others (Rawls, 1971, p. 60).

The connections with universalizability are to be found in the words "equal" and "similar".

The above nine principles aim to represent both the history and the possible scope of concepts of ethical universalizability. There are some who think that it is not a single concept that has such a scope, but at best a family of concepts that exhibit family resemblance, and at worst a miscellaneous assortment of ideas arising from various puns on key words such as "equal" and "universal". And we wish to regard these questions about the unity of the concept of universalizability and about the importance or soundness of the concept in its applications (the Nakhnikian issue) as open ones.

Singer, though not exactly a "sceptic" in either of the senses just specified, remarks in his paper below that not only has 'universalizability' been used to cover a variety of distinct theses, but '. . . the . . . term has been so promiscuously generalized as to cover a variety of only tenuously related matters'.

These points raise questions about the connections, however tenuous, among these principles, which in turn raise more fundamental questions about their meaning, justification, and application. The papers contained in this anthology represent some of the most recent thinking about these fundamental questions regarding universalizability principles and related matters. In editing this volume, we have sought to arrange the papers according to what seems to us as a helpful way of distinguishing among types of universalizability principles. In what follows, we shall introduce our scheme of organization and explain how the papers fit into this scheme.

We have found it convenient to classify universalizability principles of the sort listed above according to whether they are *non-substantive* or *substantive*. What we mean in calling a principle 'non-substantive' is, roughly, that such a principle does not entail, either alone or together with other non-moral premises, any moral conclusions of the sort that something (some action, person, state of affairs) has a certain moral property. Rather, it is only in connection with a moral judgment or statement to the effect that a thing of a certain sort has a certain moral property that a non-substantive principle can be used to derive any moral conclusions. By contrast, a 'substantive' ethical principle is one which, either alone or together with other non-moral premises, can be used to derive moral conclusions.

This distinction between non-substantive and substantive moral principles is the basis for what seems to be a main division between two types of universalizability principles. Thus, the so-called 'principle of universalizability', alternatively expressed by the first two principles on the above list, is typically interpreted as a principle of ethical consistency, which as one author has put it: 'may be seen as a purely hypothetical thesis. According to it, a certain moral claim applies to an object *only if* similar moral claims apply to similar moral objects' (Rabinowicz, 1979, p. 14). The idea is that in order to derive a moral claim about (for example) the moral quality of some action in a certain situation, this principle must be taken in conjunction with a moral claim about the possession of the same moral quality by a similar action in a similar situation. By contrast, substantive universalizability principles, such as Kant's categorical imperative and Marcus Singer's generalization argument, are not hypothetical in this sense; rather they set forth a standard or test for determining in connection with other non-moral information, the moral acceptability of something. In the case of the categorical imperative, those actions whose maxims cannot be willed consistently as universal laws of nature are unacceptable. The generalization argument on the other hand (If the consequences of everyone's doing some action x would be undesirable then no one ought to do x without a reason) sets forth a standard forbidding those actions the general doing of which would produce undesirable consequences.

Reflection on important differences between the principles of Kant and Singer in particular, and on the differences between two of the main normative ethical traditions in general, viz., the Kantian and utilitarian traditions, suggests a further subdivision within the class of substantive universalizability principles. Thus, if we use the term, 'consequentialist', in a general way to denote not only utilitarian principles, but also those associated, though strictly speaking non-utilitarian, principles,[3] then we can distinguish between Kantian and consequentialist universalizability principles.

Of course, this scheme for dividing universalizability principles is only intended to provide a rough means for classifying such principles, one which though useful, does not seem to make mutually exclusive divisions. For example, Jonathan Harrison, in his contribution to this volume, seems to be proposing a consequentialist moral theory, though one incorporating considerations of Kantian universalizability. Moreover, some principles are not clearly classifiable as either substantive or non-substantive, e.g., the Golden Rule. In its most common formulation 'Do unto others as you would have them do unto you', it appears to set forth a test or criterion for morally acceptable action. Gewirth has put it this way. 'This criterion consists in the agent's desires or wishes for himself qua recipient: what determines the moral rightness of a transaction initiated or controlled by some person is whether he would himself want to undergo such a transaction at the hands of another' (Gewirth, 1978, p. 133).

Now the problems with the Golden Rule so interpreted have been recorded many times, going back at least as far as Kant (see Kant, 1785, AK, IV, 430n). In attempting to preserve the spirit of this principle, if not the letter, many philosophers have sought to find an acceptable formulation of the rule. And what is interesting is that some, though not all, of these attempts have in effect transformed it from an apparently substantive principle into a non-substantive principle (see Singer, 1963, and Blackstone, 1965).

With these points in mind, let us turn to some of the specific issues that have been raised in connection with each of these types of universalizability principles and briefly indicate how the papers in this collection are related to such issues as well as to each other.

ETHICAL UNIVERSALIZABILITY: A VARIETY OF THESES

We placed Jan Narveson's paper at the head of the anthology because it provides a broad survey of some of the main theses that have been discussed or might be discussed under the title of 'universalizability'. This survey to some extent cuts across the distinctions embodied in the arrangement of the rest of the essays in the present volume, so that there is scarcely another single appropriate place for it in our table of contents. It also provides an excellent introduction to the present state of discussions of universalizability. The range of Narveson's discussion is great, emphasizing a point we have already made in this introduction, that the term 'universalizability' is today used to cover quite a large family of ideas. Some of these theses when they are considered as the only contribution that the concept of universalizability has to make to morality, make the contribution of that concept rather peripheral. Others, when considered by themselves, make universalizability to be close to the essence of morality. After taking us on a tour of some of the more peripheral conceptions, Narveson zeroes in on some of the more important conceptions, the ones in which he finds himself the most interested.

In the course of his discussion he criticizes certain formulations of the Golden Rule and other reversibility criteria as causing problems seemingly no matter how they are formulated. He does not distinguish sharply between U-formulations that are utilitarian or consequentialist and those that are not. In fact it is an interesting surprise to find this well-known defender and explicator of utilitarianism to be indicating some doubts about certain aspects of utilitarianism (see especially note 31) and to be defending the view that universalizability is close to the essence of morality. His final formulation is:

U16 R is an acceptable moral rule only if there is sufficient reason in terms of their own values, for all moral agents who have reason to decline the ruleless state to accept R.

The qualification referring to those who "have reason to decline the ruleness state", would omit or exclude only those who prefer or at least have no reason on balance to reject the Hobbesian state of nature. Fortunately such a person would be both rare and unusual. Apart from this exclusion, which we have every reason to expect is insignificant, the point is that there are certain rules which everyone will have an interest in everyone's following. Such a skeleton of rules for social relations, if they are fairly well in place, can give us assurance in dealing with others. Many of these rules, as we may expect, would be negative rules of non-interference. And since U16 refers to "all moral agents", it puts aside golden rule issues about whether agent or patient preference should be followed.

U16 is then finally a principle that is not merely proposed abstractly for our decision-making; it is instead based on a conception of what morality is for (regulating the skeleton of all personal relations so that individuals can within this structure accomplish their own goals). And it places one specific concept of universalizability at quite a central location in the structure of morality.

UNIVERSALIZABILITY AND ETHICAL CONSISTENCY

If an action is right (or wrong) for one agent in a certain
circumstance, then it is right (or wrong) for any similar
agent in similar circumstances.

This is one formulation of a non-substantive principle of ethical universalizability that has been given various labels: the Principle of Universalizability; the Generalization Principle; the Principle of Justice; the Principle of Impartiality; to mention the most common. In one variant formulation or

another, this principle enjoys widespread acceptance among moral philosophers despite the fact that there is not widespread agreement about its
meaning (and hence correct formulation); or about its justification (or how it
should be "accounted for"); or about its implications, not only in connection
with practical moral issues (i.e., concerning its practical application) but
also in connection with other moral principles. These and associated issues
are taken up in the papers by Singer, Rabinowicz, Nielsen, Olafson, Gorr,
and Lycan and are thus grouped together in the anthology. In order to
indicate how these authors approach these issues, it will be useful to provide
brief sketches of their articles (though we have refrained from engaging in
detailed exegesis and criticism).

The paper by Marcus Singer, 'Universalizability and the Generalization
Principle', touches on a number of the above-mentioned issues concerning this
principle of ethical consistency. In particular, Singer considers its justification
and various criticisms that have been leveled against it. The paper is divided
into five sections. In Sections I and II, Singer considers certain important
theses advanced by R. M. Hare concerning the principle's interpretation and
justification. Hare prefers the label 'Principle of Universalizability' for the
principle in question, and has argued on a number of occasions that, owing
to important differences in meaning between 'universal' and 'general', it is
incorrect and misleading to speak of ethical generalization, or to use the label
'The Generalization Principle' (Singer's label) either for the principle in question or for associated ideas in ethics. In the first section of this paper Singer
examines Hare's arguments for this claim and, finding them inconclusive,
defends his use of 'generalization' for the idea and principle in question.

Hare has also advanced an account or explanation of the truth or validity
of the principle of universalizability. According to Hare, singular moral
judgments (e.g., 'It is right (wrong, obligatory) for me to tell the truth in
these circumstances') are universalizable in the sense that they commit the
person making the judgment to a corresponding universal judgment ('It is
(right, wrong, obligatory) for anyone who is relevantly similar to me in
relevantly similar circumstances to tell the truth'). The entailment relation
between singular and universal moral judgments holds because the principle
of universalizability holds and the truth or validity of this principle is to be
explained by reference to descriptive meaning rules that govern (at least
in part) the meaning of such singular judgments. The central idea is this.
On Hare's view, singular moral judgments in which such evaluative terms
as 'right', 'wrong', and 'obligatory' occur as predicates are analogous to
ordinary singular descriptive judgments in which descriptive terms occur

as predicates (e.g., "This is red"). The meanings of such predicates (both evaluative and descriptive) are governed by descriptive meaning rules—rules which, so Hare explains, "lay it down that we may apply an expression to objects which are similar to each other in certain respects". He adds, "It is a direct consequence of this that we cannot without consistency apply a descriptive term to one thing, and refuse to apply it to another similar thing (either exactly similar or similar in the relevant respects)" (Hare, 1963, p. 13). So, on Hare's view, the universalizability of moral judgments (or the principle of ethical universalizability) is to be explained or justified in a way analogous to the way the universalizability of singular descriptive judgments is to be explained, viz. by appealing to descriptive meaning rules.

In Section II, Singer criticizes this account of the principle of universalizability, charging that it leads not only to triviality but "leads [Hare] to move from his theoretical account of its basis – in descriptive meaning rules – to otherwise sensible judgments inconsistent with the original account".

In Section III, then, Singer turns to his own account of the validity of this principle, reaffirming the view he offered in his *Generalization in Ethics*, according to which it is the inferential character of singular moral judgments – a feature that makes them analogous to "because" judgments in general and to causal and probability judgments in particular – that accounts for the validity of the generalization principle.

Turning to Sections IV and V, Singer (Section IV) considers the use Alan Gewirth has made of the generalization principle in the context of his own moral theory. Gewirth attempts to deduce what he claims to be the supreme principle of morality – the so-called principle of generic consistency – in an argument one of whose premises is the generalization principle. Singer considers Gewirth's use of the principle and critically discusses some of the claims Gewirth has made about the generalization principle, in particular that it is neither a substantial nor a moral principle and that it "set no limits on the criteria of relevant similarity or the sufficient reasons for having the right to perform various actions" (Gewirth, 1978, p. 106). Singer argues in the first place that, when properly understood, this principle is both substantial and moral (as well as being logical) and furthermore, that "when properly understood [it] illuminates the concept of a genuine moral reason and what can count as one and what cannot, and shows that it is not open to anyone to invoke its form in justification of what is unjustified". Section V again takes up and considers further the criticism that the generalization principle sets no limits on what can count as a genuine moral reason.

The above formulation of a universalizability principle with which we began our discussion of the papers in this section makes reference to the notion of *similarity*. In fact, this notion which is absolutely crucial in this and related principles, admits of two different interpretations, one in terms of *exact* similarity, and the other in terms of *relevant* similarity. Each has special problems. The problem with the exact similarity formulation is that together with the Leibnizian thesis that indiscernability (exact similarity) entails identity, the principle turns out to be trivial. That is, together with Leibniz's principle, the ethical principle of universalizability thus interpreted reduces to: If an action is right (or wrong) for one agent, then it is right (or wrong) for *that* agent. On the other hand, the relevant similarities variant of the principle encounters the vexing (and, according to some, insurmountable) problem that the notion of relevance is unclear. Thus, we have what Rabinowicz calls the 'universalizability dilemma': embracing either of the only two alternative formulations seems unacceptable.

Rabinowicz's paper, 'The Universalizability Dilemma', offers a way out of the dilemma. Making use of set-theoretic models and defining the principle of universalizability as a condition on a model, Rabinowicz employs, in addition to the concepts of exact similarity (copyhood) and relevant similarity, the concept of a *universal aspect* of a situation. Taking this newly introduced concept as primitive, Rabinowicz formulates a universalizability condition on a model that he claims is not trivialized by the Leibnizian principle and does not make use of the problematic concept of relevant similarity.

In 'Universalizability and the Commitment to Impartiality', Kai Nielsen is concerned with the rationalist program of seeking "the foundations of justice and sometimes the whole of morality in an *a priori* or formal principle *of Universalizability*". Nielsen denies that this program can be carried out and illustrates his claim by considering the attempts to go from the principle of universalizability (either directly or together with other considerations of logic and rationality) to an impartiality principle of the following sort: 'All human beings have an equal right to the fulfillment of their interests'.

Nielsen begins by making the same distinctions we have seen in Rabinowicz between the *exact* and the *relevant* similarity variants of the principle of universalizability. Working with the latter variant, Nielsen points out its two important limitations. First, it "does not tell us *what* is right or wrong, good or bad, or *what* ought or ought not be done. It says rather *if* one thing is right, good or ought to be done, then another thing relevantly similar to it is too." In other words, the principle is non-substantive. Second, Nielsen claims that the principle itself does not specify or set forth any criteria for determining what counts as being relevantly similar from the moral point of view. So, in order to go from the principle of universalizability to the principle of impartiality, one would have to judge first that some human being has a right to have his or her interests fulfilled and second that all human beings are (in general) relevantly similar. Since such additions do not follow directly from the principle in question and do not seem to be matters of logic, one can, without being inconsistent or irrational, affirm the principle of universalizability yet deny the principle of impartiality. (Nielsen reaches the same conclusion as a result of analysing Paul Taylor's claim that from the principle of universalizability one can derive the following principle of impartiality: 'If it is wrong for another to discriminate against him (the agent) on the ground of a difference he (the agent) does not acknowledge to be relevant, it must also be wrong for him (the agent) to discriminate against another on the ground of a difference the other does not accept as relevant.')

The upshot, at least if Nielsen is correct, is that doubt has been thrown on the rationalist strategy of using an apparently formal principle as a foundation on which to base substantive moral principles.

The papers by Olafson and Gorr are concerned with this general upshot of Nielsen's paper. Both papers consider the use of universalizability as a formal foundation (or at least as part of one), on which to base substantive moral principles.

As we have already noted, although Hare and Singer seem to disagree over the correct account or justification of the principle of ethical consistency, they do agree that this principle admits of a "logical" justification – one that makes essential reference to the logic of moral terms (see e.g., Singer, 1961, p. 34, and Hare, 1963, p. 30). We have also just noted Nielsen's argument that from such a formal, logically based principle, either alone or together with considerations of logic and rationality, it is not possible to derive any substantive moral principles or judgments. In particular he argues that it is not possible to derive a principle of impartiality. The paper by Frederick Olafson, 'Reflections on a Passage in Mill's *Utilitarianism*', offers an account of the principle in question that stands in sharp contrast to these views of Hare, Singer, and Nielsen.

Beginning with a suggestive passage from Mill's *Utilitarianism*, Olafson is concerned to defend a certain thesis concerning our allegedly rationally based commitment to a principle of impartiality (or what Olafson calls 'intersubjective reciprocity'). According to Olafson, "Mill's argument appears to postulate a direct connection between our social natures and a relationship to at least some other human beings in which we acknowledge an operative equivalence between their situation and our own". Olafson's elaboration of this argument in Mill goes as follows. We are essentially social creatures having a "social nature" involving, among other things, entering into agreements (both explicit and implicit) with other human beings. Such agreements presuppose "a set of conceptual instruments that function in a neutral manner as far as differences between persons and their points of view are concerned". This implies that in cases of conflicting interests, we must at least implicitly acknowledge the idea that, in general, no one person's interests occupy a special or privileged position. In other words, reflecting on our social natures reveals that we implicitly if not explicitly assent to the idea that, generally, the interests of all human beings are to be weighed equally. Therefore, a person who, as Olafson explains, takes or tries to take an egocentric point of view failing to weigh interests equally, "will not be able to persist in this course of conduct without feeling the strain of contradiction within the policies by which that conduct is governed". Thus, all conduct involving interpersonal transactions is governed by a set of presuppositions that make any social interaction possible, one of which is that of according equal weight to the interests of others. An egocentric line of conduct, however, denies this presupposition.

The relevance of all this for ethical universalizability, as Olafson explains, is that if we consider this principle in the "true context of ethical reflection . . . that of an ethical community in which human beings stand to one another in determinate relationships that register the actual needs and circumstances and multiple forms of interdependency that in fact characterize our lives . . . the requirement of universalizability is not simply an isolated logical thesis but widens into an immensely intricate and powerful dialectic of actions and persons". Thus, Olafson might agree with Nielsen that if we consider the principle of universalizability on its own as a logical thesis, then there is no contradiction involved in assenting to it yet denying a principle of impartiality. After all, as Nielsen points out, neither the principle itself nor considerations of logic and rationality entail the crucial judgment that all human beings are relevantly similar. However, analysis of "the pragmatic context" reveals that in general no one person's interests occupy a position of privilege vis-à-vis the interests of others, i.e., in general all human beings are relevantly similar when it comes to the satisfaction of their interests. This condition is a requirement that we are bound to accept on pain of contradiction, and, together with considerations of universalizability, it entails a principle of impartiality: In general, the interests of all other human beings are to be weighed equally. Thus, it is Olafson's contention that when interpreted in the proper context, and not simply as a logical thesis, the principle of universalizability does entail substantive conclusions.

In some of his recent writings, including *Moral Thinking: Its Levels, Point and Method*, R. M. Hare has attempted to accomplish what Nielsen argues cannot be done, viz., go from considerations of universalizability (together with non-moral principles of rationality) to a substantive moral principle. Hare's view is that "the requirement to universalize our prescriptions generates utilitarianism" (Hare, 1981, p. 11). In 'Reason, Impartiality and Utilitarianism', Michael Gorr investigates the connection in Hare's work between 'universal prescriptivism' (the name generally given to Hare's metaethical views) and utilitarianism.

Hare's argument for a kind of preference utilitarianism based on two formal properties of singular moral judgments — universalizability and prescriptivity — is roughly the following. The formal or logical properties of universalizability and prescriptivity impose certain formal rules for reasoning from the moral point of view. In particular, such features require what Gorr calls the "full reversibility test". That is, in judging from the point of view of morality one is to determine whether one can prescribe acting in accordance with a universal principle which, as Gorr explains, involves determining "whether one would actually choose to perform that action if one knew that one would have to play, in a series of possible worlds otherwise identical to the actual world, the role of *each* person (including oneself) who would be affected". Furthermore, one is not "simply to imagine oneself with one's *own* interests, in the place of other persons", but, rather, to imagine "having in turn *their* interests and desires". This thoroughgoing impartiality requirement taken together with a Bayesian account of rationality entails the claim that a rational and fully informed universal prescriber would inevitably adopt and act on utilitarian principles. So, on Gorr's reconstruction, Hare's argument is this.

1. A rational person will always seek to maximize his expected utility. (Bayesian principle)
2. Utility = preference satisfaction.
3. Adopting the moral point of view is equivalent to deciding how to act as if one had (or were going to have) all the preferences of all those who would be affected by one's action. (Full Reversibility Test)
4. Therefore, a rational person who adopts the moral point of view will always seek to maximize the total expected utility of the group of all persons who would be affected by his action.

This move from universal prescriptivism to utilitarianism via the full reversibility test is, of course, hard to reconcile with Hare's well-known claim in *Freedom and Reason* that the thesis of universal prescriptivism is "normatively neutral" in the sense that it does not entail any moral theory or principle. However, as Gorr points out, there are traces of Hare's more recent views on the matter in *Freedom and Reason*, and, in the first part of his paper, Gorr suggests an explanation of why, in that earlier book, Hare held apparently inconsistent views on the question of the normative neutrality of universal prescriptivism. His suggestion is that there are two interpretations of the full reversibility test to be found in Hare's earlier writings (the "in *propria persona*" and "ideal observer" interpretations) which Hare did not clearly distinguish and which led him to opposing views on the normative significance of his metaethical views. What Gorr points out is that, in *Moral Thinking,* Hare has made clear that he now accepts the second interpretation of the full reversibility test and that this in effect ensures that principles chosen by rational and informed universal prescribers will be utility maximizing.

In the remaining sections of his paper, Gorr considers the plausibility of Hare's view that such a strong impartialism is constitutive of morality (premise 3 of the above argument) and argues for the following claims: (1) The contention that a person might be motivated by a desire to be fully impartial is incapable of a non-circular explication; (2) Hare's claim that a strong impartiality condition is a formal requirement of morality is counterintuitive; and (3) Hare's metaethical theory does not entail such a strong impartiality requirement. If Gorr's objections go through, serious doubt has been cast on Hare's attempt to go from metaethical considerations concerning the logic of moral judgments (particularly the principle of universalizability) together with constraints on rationality to a substantive moral principle.

We have claimed that the principle under consideration is non-substantive in the sense that it does not alone (or even together with non-moral judgments) entail any substantive moral judgments. But to say this is not to say or even imply that this principle is useless or pointless or inapplicable in the context of practical moral issues.[4] Its use in such a context is illustrated by William Lycan in 'Abortion and the Civil Rights of Machines'. In fact it is one of Lycan's main contentions that an argument based on universalizability considerations is perhaps the best we may be able to do in making headway on the abortion issue. Lycan begins by claiming that because the fetus is a being of a "uniquely exceptional sort", we have no clear intuitions about the putative rights of such beings. Moreover, no further analysis of personhood or further fact finding is going to help us move closer to clarifying our intuitions on this matter. Thus, Lycan proposes that we explore this issue via a rather indirect route that involves reflecting on the status and rights of certain sorts of hypothetical machines. Lycan's proposed exploration proceeds roughly as follows.

Assuming that a materialist account of human beings is correct (that human beings have only physical attributes among their irreducible attributes) and in addition that it is technologically possible to (someday) construct a machine — a robot — that not only looks but behaves like an ordinary human being, Lycan claims that we could justifiably infer that such beings were conscious. Of course, given that consciousness of a certain complexity (involving certain cognitive and conative capacities) is sufficient for personhood, Lycan concludes that such sophisticated machines would be clear cases of persons. Lycan then goes on to consider the case of certain hypothetical machines — "proto-machines" — which do not yet possess those conceptual and conative capacities that are morally significant, but which are of a "highly individual basic design (which determines the personality it will have when it is finished)". We are to consider further the hypothetical case of the proto-machine plugged into a "fully developed" mother machine and "ask whether it would be wrong for the technician to interrupt the mother-robot's activity at an early stage (with its concurrence if it is a person), unplug the proto-machine from the mother, take it off the workbench and dismantle it". Lycan reports no feelings of disapproval at the technician's actions and argues that since the proto-machine and the fetus appear to be relevantly similar, then by the principle of universalizability, we may conclude that at least early on in fetal development there is nothing morally wrong with aborting the fetus.[5]

KANTIAN UNIVERSALIZABILITY

The "universal law" formulation of Immanuel Kant's categorical imperative has already been cited in two different versions as Principles 3 and 4 near the beginning of this introduction. It was noted there that Kant made just about the most ambitious possible claim for this version of a universalizability principle, viz., that it is "the supreme principle of morality". Kant's view has been enormously controversial since it was first proposed, and issues of its interpretation and of its correctness have each generated an immense literature. The provocativeness of Kant's claim is added to by the fact that he believes that the principle is in no way a consequentialist one; he condemns all teleological, and hence all consequentialist views as "heteronomous" theories of morality. The papers in the present volume that center upon explicit discussions of Kantian universalizability are three. Onora O'Neill defends Kant s claims. George Nakhnikian finds them (and just about any other substantive universalizability principle) lacking. And Jonathan Harrison attempts a rapprochement between the historically hostile Kantian and utilitarian views; his paper could have been placed with equal appropriateness in either the section on Kantian or the one on consequentialist generalization.

The essay entitled 'Consistency in Action' by Onora O'Neill is a defense of the Kantian first formulation of the categorical imperative. She begins her essay (as does Nakhnikian) with an extended discussion of the Kantian concept of "maxim". This is surely a key move for any would-be defender of Kant, for in the Kantian concept of the maxim as the formulation of the inner principle of action is where we find hope, if anywhere, of replying to objections that actions can be described in an indefinitely large variety of ways for the purpose of universalizing them. Any given individual action can be made to turn out to possess the quite different and incompatible moral qualities depending on the description one arbitrarily chooses to universalize. The idea is that the *maxim* state a fundamental description under which the agent performs the action and this, at least when it can be formulated clearly and uniquely, provides the correct description of the action for the purposes of moral evaluation. O'Neill also makes the point that for Kant the primary moral quality of any action is an inner one of moral worth rather than an outward one of conformity with the requirements of external action. O'Neill, like Nakhnikian, emphasizes that there is a variety of ways in which maxims can be impossible or self-defeating prior to any consideration of their potential universalizability; but such difficulties must be cleared aside before a properly moral evaluation of the maxim can even begin. O'Neill states the intuitive idea behind the categorical imperative as being that " . . . if we are to act as morally worthy beings we should not single ourselves out for special consideration or treatment" (p. 172). Actions which the universality test shows wrong are shown to result when we attempt to universalize acts or practices such as deception, coercion, and abrogation of autonomy. She states that much of the anti-Kantian literature here assumes that it is possible to state the proposed maxim of action in such a way that the action is described in quite a narrow fashion; but her earlier discussion of the nature of maxims has undercut this objection. The kinds of inconsistencies involved in Kant's "contradiction in the will" examples are also discussed. A point that is emphasized throughout O'Neill's essay is that Kant is not some sort of generalized utilitarian; the latter sort of view would be, according to Kant's terminology, a heteronomous moral theory. "The interest of an autonomous universality test is that it aims to ground an ethical theory on notions of consistency and rationality rather than upon consideration of desire and preference" (p. 182).

In a lengthy and thorough essay, George Nakhnikian considers very seriously the claim of the first formulation of the categorical imperative ("K1") to be what Kant calls it, "the supreme principle of morality", and finally rejects the claim. He looks with more favor upon the second formulation, which draws moral consequences from the fact that human beings are to be regarded as absolute ends who are not to be treated as mere means, and the third, "kingdom-of-ends" formulation which mentions as essential the peer status of moral agent-legislator-subjects. But our main interest in the present discussion is in Nakhnikian's thesis that "K1 does not work" (p. 189).

As we consider this claim more closely we find that what Nakhnikian has to say has an interest quite far beyond issues of the exegesis of Kant. From its Kantian beginnings, his discussion becomes a much broader and more general discussion of the possible modes of universalizability, in a sense attempting to cover the range of possible universalizability theses in the same thorough way that Narveson does, though as it turns out the possibilities that he discusses are mostly rather different from those discussed by Narveson. Thus for example, he discusses logically and physically impossible practical situations, and physically possible practical situations that cannot be universally practiced, and those that can be, but that in various ways we could not will to be universal practice.

The difficulties that Naknikian finds in Kantian and related versions of universalizability revolve around a set of counterexamples first stated on pp. 202–203, those of patenting an invention, visiting a sick friend in the hospital, publishing Icelandic jokes in a journal, and lying only in cases where no-one will find out.

Many discussions of universalizability criteria of morality have been carried on in terms of alleged counterexamples. Marcus Singer's *Generalization in Ethics* (1961) mentions a wealth of such proposed counterexamples and attempts to respond to them, and a fair amount of the literature discussing Kant on the application of the categorical imperative does the same. There is a large literature discussing Kant's famous four examples in the *Grundlegung zur Metaphysik der Sitten* (1785), the arguments for the wrongness of suicide, making a lying promise, and the obligation to develop one's talents and to render aid to another. These are not "counterexamples" to universalizability, at least certainly not so far as Kant's intentions were concerned! But Kant's

application arguments have seemed to a number of writers either so inade-
quate or so obscure that for these people they have come to be regarded as
counterexamples to Kant's claim to be able to apply the first formulation
(the "universalizability" formulation) to moral situations to obtain unique
correct answers to the question "Is an action of sort S morally correct or
not?"

Nakhnikian sees his proposed counterexamples as not just showing the
first formulation of the categorical imperative to be seriously defective.
His conclusion is more general: it is that any such universalizability criterion
must exhibit the same defects, must fall to the same counterexamples. Such
scepticism about purely "formal" criteria of morality dates back at least
to Hegel, who has some of his own proposed counterexamples.

On the other hand there also seems to be a perennial attractiveness about
some concepts of universalizability, for they have their defenders today,
as can be seen by examining the contributions to the present anthology by
Narveson, O'Neill, and Singer, among others.

The counterexamples that Nakhnikian proposes call for further detailed
discussion, something that is beyond the scope of this introduction. One
large class of counterexamples to Kantian universalizability deal with the
alleged arbitrariness of the description of actions for the purpose of moral
evaluation. Singer's discussion of the concepts of "invertibility" and "reiterability" in *Generalization in Ethics* (1961) is one important attempt to
deal with this problem. Potter (1973) also discusses this issue in its Kantian
context. There are no doubt also other classes of counterexamples that result
from other kinds of problems with universalizability, such as questions about
the relevance or irrelevance of the wants, wishes, or likely actions of others.
(Is it right to perform an action that is such that if many performed it, we
could not accept the consequences, just in case very few others are likely
to want to perform such an action? Is it obligatory to render aid to another
when others are failing to do their part in rendering aid, and this makes it
either likely or certain that my own attempt to render aid will be unsuc-
cessful?) Another kind of issue arises when we are considering cases of
actions based on false beliefs, a kind of case that Kant never mentions, and
still different cases arise from puzzles concerning competition, in which,
necessarily, not everyone can win (O'Neill discusses these in her paper).

CONSEQUENTIALIST UNIVERSALIZABILITY

As has already been remarked, the paper by Jonathan Harrison, though placed by us in the division on consequentialism could equally well have been placed in the section on Kantian universalizability. Harrison's main aim is to show that there are large areas of agreement between Kantians and utilitarians, and in particular that many of Kant's criticisms of teleological ethics do not apply as sound criticisms to utilitarianism.

The version of utilitarianism that Harrison defends is a version he calls "cumulative effect utilitarianism", to distinguish it from rule utilitarianism, and a kind of "ideal" utilitarianism which is prepared to allow that Kantian moral virtue might be something good in itself, an admission that would of course be incompatible with the hedonism of classical utilitarianism. Here are some of the Kantian objections that in Harrison's view do not have proper application to utilitarianism: (1) Kant thought that teleological theories all appeal to the agent's own inclination, but utilitarianism, which demands that we seek for the good of all, does not. We are not likely to have an inclination to bring about the good of all, and it is also clear that our having the utilitarian obligation does not presuppose our having the inclination. (2) It is quite possible and reasonable to develop a version of utilitarianism which does not have the rightness or wrongness of acts depend on actual consequences, but instead has such moral qualities of acts depend on intended consequences and the qualities of character which tend to produce certain kinds of facts. Such a version of utilitarianism is closer to Kant's view. (3) Kant thought that duty, as a modal notion, implied a kind of necessity, and he thought that teleological ethics was incompatible with morality properly conceived. Harrison in response tries to sort out the kinds of necessity which moral judgments do and do not have, mentioning some of the possible confusions that may arise concerning such issues. He concludes that Kant may have been guilty of certain confusions, and that in any case Harrison's version of utilitarianism is not incompatible with the proper kinds of necessity attaching to moral judgments.

Meanwhile, Harrison does have some criticisms of Kant: (1) He thinks that Kant exaggerated the goodness of good will. Even if it is allowed as *a* good in itself, it is not the only good in itself, nor is its good infinitely greater than other kinds of goodness. (2) On the matter of greatest interest in this anthology Harrison says that Kant's universal law formulation of the categorical imperative marks "the point at which utilitarianism has to be modified in order to fulfill Kant's requirements". The modification arises in cases such as promise-keeping, where the utilitarian would recommend failing to keep promises in certain individual cases; if such recommendations were commonly followed by bad consequences – the cumulative consequences of a large number of promise-breakings — would follow. So the individual is well advised not to follow the utilitarian's advice, not because his maxim would be self defeating if universalized (this fact has no relevance to the moral quality of the act in Harrison's view), but because there would be bad consequences. Harrison recognizes that this point does not quite mean that he is accepting Kant's first formulation, but he thinks it comes rather close.

The papers by Cork and Gillespie concern Marcus Singer's generalization argument:

> If everyone were to do that, the consequences would be undesirable, therefore no one ought to do that.

The principle corresponding to this argument,

> If the consequences of everyone's doing that would be undesirable, then no one ought to do that

functions in Singer's theory as the supreme moral principle and thus "serves as a test or criterion of the morality of conduct, and provides the basis for moral rules" (Singer, 1961, p. 9).

Now Singer offers an argument or deduction of this principle (GA, hereafter) of the following sort.

(1)   If the consequences of A s doing x would be undesirable, then A ought not to do x. (The principle of consequences, C.)

(2)   If the consequences of everyone's doing x would be undesirable, then not everyone ought to do x. (The generalization from the principle of consequences, GC.)

(3)   If not everyone ought to do x, then no one ought to do x. (The generalization principle, GP.)

(4)   Therefore, if the consequences of everyone's doing x would be undesirable, then no one ought to do x. (GA.)

Premise (2) is said to be a generalization from (1) — the latter taken to be necessary — and (4) is supposed to follow from (2) and (3).

This argument has been the subject of a good deal of criticism, perhaps the most common being the so-called 'collective-distributive' criticism which can be explained as follows. The term 'everyone' can be construed *collectively* as referring to the whole of a class of (relevantly similar) agents or *distributively* as referring to each and every particular member of that class.

Accordingly, GC admits of two interpretations depending on how 'everyone' is understood in the consequent.

> If the consequences of everyone's doing x would be undesirable, then it ought to be that someone not do x. (The collective interpretation.)
> If the consequences of everyone's doing x would be undesirable, then there is someone who ought not to do x. (The distributive interpretation.)

The problem is this. On the collective interpretation, the argument is invalid since as Singer makes clear 'everyone' in the antecedent of GP (Premise 4) is to be read distributively. However, on the distributive interpretation, GC is susceptible to counterexamples of the following sort. Although if no one stands guard duty on a particular occasion, the consequences would be undesirable, it does not follow that there is someone about whom we could say that *he* ought to stand guard duty and could be punished for not doing so (Nakhnikian, 1964, p. 446)

Charles M. Cork, in his 'The Deontic Structure of the Generalization Argument', develops a formalized version of Singer's argument that attempts to avoid this collective-distributive problem. His new version involves an analysis of the consequent of GC ('it ought to be the case that someone not do x') that allows a transition to a distributive claim about the members of the relevant set of agents but "not to those flesh and blood relevantly similar agents ... to whom we can point, but to logical constructions of agents (blanks, as it were), into which the former can be filled ...". In other words, instead of distributing the collective obligation to avoid undesirable consequences to identifiable persons (which then raises the embarrassing question of *who* is forbidden to perform the action in question), on Cork's analysis, such obligation is distributed to "*arbitrary members* of a set ... defined here as those about whom we make no assumptions other than their membership in the set".

If successful, Cork's analysis of this argument not only solves the collective-distributive problem but helps make clear how the various alleged counterexamples to the generalization argument can be handled by Singer's theory.

Antecedent to the publication of David Lyons' *Forms and Limits of Utilitarianism*, it was generally thought that so-called *general* utilitarianism (a label used to characterize Singer's generalization argument) was immune to certain apparently devastating criticisms besetting analogous forms of *simple* or act utilitarianism. The claim was that a principle like Singer's is able to account for our obligations concerning generally accepted moral rules that are troublesome on the act utilitarian view. This alleged difference between analogous forms of these two sorts of theory was challenged by Lyons who argued persuasively that despite appearances, analogous forms of simple and general utilitarianism are really extensionally equivalent – they yield the same substantive judgments when applied to the same cases. In other words, according to Lyons once we bring into consideration all of the relevant facts and utilities bearing on a particular case, "it matters not whether we ask 'What would happen if everyone did the same?' instead of 'What would happen if this act were performed?' " (Lyons, 1965, p. 119), the results of these two tests will be the same.

Our final article, Norman Gillespie's 'Moral Reasons and the Generalization Test in Ethics', concerns Lyons' extensional equivalence thesis. In particular, Gillespie considers Lyons' explanation of the relevance of the behavior of others in describing actions for purposes of applying the generalization test which is the key to the reductive thesis. Gillespie distinguishes two readings of the generalization test – the *de dicto* and the *de re* – and argues that it is Lyons' *de dicto* reading of the test that leads him to mistaken conclusions about the relevance of the behavior of others in applying the test. According to Gillespie, once the test is interpreted *de re*, which "is the appropriate one for capturing its moral force", we can see not only that the extensional equivalence thesis fails but that the test is not strictly utilitarian. In fact, as Gillespie explains, "The *moral* point of the generalization test in ethics is *not* that your act will, either incidentally or as part of a general practice, produce undesirable consequences, but that it is unfair".

CONCLUSION

The aim of the present volume is to show that recent philosophical thought on universalizability is multifaceted and alive, and is making advances. This has been done by presenting a wide variety of work by authors who are among the best of those currently working on these issues. This introduction has aimed to present the main points of our authors in summary form, exhibiting some of their relationships to each other.

Now that we have briefly discussed the papers included here it can be seen that they each have an important role to play in further discussions of this general topic. The pieces by Singer, Gillespie, and Cork discuss and reassess one of the major works on this aspect of moral philosophy, Singer's own *Generalization in Ethics*. O'Neill, Nakhnikian, and Harrison take views each opposed to the other on the interpretation of Immanuel Kant's view on universalizability. Kant is surely the single most important historical writer on this topic in ethics. Michael Gorr takes up a recent important new work by another major contemporary figure in the literature of universalizability, the man who created the term, R. M. Hare. Nielsen considers (and rejects) connections with the seemingly related concept of impartiality. Lycan considers a problem arising in the application of certain universalizability principles, viz., that some kinds of moral issues seem to be unique, and thus, frustratingly, to allow of no clearcut moral analogies with other issues that could be used to alleviate our moral perplexity. Rabinowicz discusses a closely related issue that is also discussed in various ways by O'Neill and others, the problem of how to interpret the universalizability principle so as to avoid the Scylla of the banal useless truism, and the Charybdis of an unuseable notion of "ethical relevance". The issue is that of the relativity of descriptions of action that are to be evaluated morally, the multiplicity of available descriptions, and the seeming arbitrariness of choosing one description over another.

The essay by Frederick Olafson, which chooses as its text an interesting and neglected passage from an important classic of moral philosophy, J. S. Mill's *Utilitarianism*, illustrates the ways in which utilitarian and deontological themes often intermingle in discussions of universalizability. The same point is illustrated in different ways in the work here by Harrison, Gillespie, and Narveson. "Unfairness" considerations are surely best understood as non-consequentialist if not Kantian in their appeal. The fact that (if Gillespie is correct) Singer's theory, which has been taken by most readers to be consequentialist, contains, when properly understood, an important appeal to the deontological characteristic of "unfairness" illustrates the complex interplay of consequentialist and Kantian moral characteristics which we have also seen in other papers.

In fact it is often difficult to discern when a conception of universalizability is purely consequentialist as opposed to when it contains appeals only to deontological elements. Likewise it is sometimes difficult to discern whether a universalizability principle is merely "logical" and hence non-substantive, or whether it may in fact have some important element of extra-logical substance.

The distinctions on which we based the organization of this volume of essays, though important ones, are often overlooked or overridden by actual philosophical practice. This present introduction is not intended as a brief for philosophical purity with respect to such distinctions. The common presence of "impurity" surely reflects something important about the moral phenomena that are under discussion.

There is no common theme or new consensus that emerges from this collection. Any attempt to achieve consensus or to unify under a common theme is surely premature. In no case, we think, does an essay in this collection resolve and thereby close off further philosophical discussion. The usefulness of the essays is much more likely to lie in a different direction — in the direction of providing advances upon previous current discussion and thereby not closing off but rather opening up these issues and providing a stimulus to further discussion.

NOTES

[1] Aristotle, *Nicomachean Ethics* (Ostwald translation (Indianapolis: The Bobbs-Merrill Company, Inc., 1962, p. 118), Book V, Chapter 3, 1131a13–23).

[2] An even more radical thesis would be that of giving the treatment that will yield equal results (compensating equality). For a discussion of this sort of equality see Onora O'Neill s essay, 'Opportunities, Equalities, and Education' (*Theory and Decision,* 7 275–295, October 1976).

[3] Without involving ourselves in the task of defining what counts as a consequentialist moral theory or principle, suffice it to say that we are using the term in a general way intended to cover utilitarians of all varieties as well as, e.g., Singer's theory which, as he correctly insists, is not, strictly speaking, utilitarian (see Singer, 1977).

[4] On this point see Sid B. Thomas (1968).

[5] As Lycan admits, the analogy here needs some adjusting which he attempts to supply and, moreover, this particular argument is only persuasive (if at all) when considering the proto-machine at an early stage of construction development.

PART I

ETHICAL UNIVERSALIZABILITY: A VARIETY OF THESES

JAN NARVESON

THE HOW AND WHY OF UNIVERSALIZABILITY

1. INTRODUCTION

It is widely, if not quite universally, accepted by moral philosophers that morality involves — somehow, some way — some such requirement as universalizability. Some writers make more of this than others, but there is a considerable tradition that puts universalizability at the very heart of morality: Kant, obviously, but one can cite Hobbes, Hume, the classical utilitarians, and many modern writers — Hare, Marcus Singer, Bernard Gert, myself, and recently Alan Gewirth, among many others, who belong to this tradition. Still, different writers characterize this requirement quite differently, and make quite different claims about its status. Indeed, the differences are such that they are really different doctrines altogether, different restrictions on the possible or acceptable content of moral principles which lead to markedly different moralities. Furthermore, there has been question about the status of universalizability restrictions: are they supposed to be "formal", or not? Is it to be supposed that any of several mutually incompatible moralities could all pass the tests imposed by universalizability? Or are we to take it that once the dust has cleared, there will turn out to be only one morality? And if so, is this morality supposed to be rationally demonstrated by this very test?

The point of view informing the present essay is that these last two questions are, in principle, to be answered in the affirmative. On this view, universalizability, if we can only properly spell it out, is the very essence of morality, and if all goes well there should emerge one basic moral principle or set of principles which has the strongest rational claim on our acceptance. At very least, the idea that universalizability is "purely" formal in a sense that implies no restriction at all on the possible content of morality is entirely mistaken.

The plan of this essay is to survey, in a fairly comprehensive if also sketchy way, the field of universalizability theses. In each case, we shall consider the proposed universalizability thesis first in the somewhat dim light of intuitive plausibility: does this seem like the right sort of thing? But as we proceed, we will also be addressing ourselves to the question of whether the

Nelson Potter and Mark Timmons (eds.), Morality and Universality, 3–44.
© 1985 *by D. Reidel Publishing Company.*

proposed requirement can be made sense of in relation to a coherent and powerful account of the nature of morality.

2. 'MORALITY'

Before proceeding to our main task, it may be helpful to explain what the subject of this paper is. I am taking it that a 'morality' is a set of requirements, restrictions, and recommendations about behavior, but that not just any old set is a morality. How to identify which of these possible sets of restrictions, etc., is a 'morality' and which is not is no easy matter, and a good deal of the answer is properly left to the content of the following essay. However, it seems that the term 'morality', or at least the term 'moral', is ambiguous, and is so in a way quite pertinent to our subject. For some people, I think, really would label "just any old set" of restrictions on behavior as 'moral'. On this usage, it seems, whenever anyone does something "as a rule" or "on principle", he is ipso facto acting on a moral rule or principle. But if we consider the use of the term 'morality' as it occurs in such contexts as 'the morality of the Ashanti', or 'contemporary Western morals', clearly many of the former "principles" would simply be irrelevant. Now, I am certainly not proposing to identify morality in general with the morality of some particular group; nor (as will be evident later) am I advocating moral relativism of some kind. But I am concerned with that sense of the term 'morality' in which the social codes of behavior so called are the sort of thing that I have in mind. Let us call the codes in question moralities in the "positive" sense of the term 'morality', the point of the qualifier being to leave open the question whether any particular morality in that sense may not also be criticized as living up to or failing to live up to some relevant rational standard. The universalizability theses we shall be considering are proposed standards of that kind.

It may be thought that I have here begged a question, the question whether morality is "individual" or "social". But for one thing, it is quite obviously both, as will be explained, or at any rate argued, below. And in part, if the term 'moral' really is, as I am somewhat inclined to think, ambiguous, then the effect of the preceding paragraph is simply to make clear which of its senses I have in mind. The point is not to *reject* purely personal principles as immoral, nor as "amoral" − that would seem to be nonsense in any case, as will also be seen below − but rather to identify the subject of this paper. In short, this is partly stipulative.

3. TESTS FOR TRUTH OR TESTS OF SINCERITY?

We shall be considering universalizability theses as tests, or conditions, on proposed moral rules. In most cases, they will be stated as imposing necessary conditions on the "acceptability" of such proposals. The question will arise in many readers: acceptability as what? On some views, and the view will be more plausible in the case of some of the theses we will examine than in others, they are in effect tests of sincerity: unless the rule in question meets the condition in question, R cannot even be intelligibly considered to be one of the proposer's moral rules at all, much less a correct or true one. That idea about universalizability makes these tests "formal", in the sense that mutually incompatible proposals of moral rules could satisfy the conditions raised. At the extreme, universalizability would be an utterly trivial test: it would rule out nothing at all. Morality could have any "content" whatever. At the opposite extreme, universalizability would be so powerful a test that only one unique set of fundamental moral principles would emerge intact. It would then be a test not just of consistency or sincerity, but of truth, or whatever is analogous to the notion of truth in the moral field.

It would be a waste of time to try to "decide" this issue, if indeed it is one.[1] In the first place, there is no such thing as a completely contentless test of moralities. No matter how 'formal', all will effectively rule out some conceivable prescriptions for behaviour and recommend others. And secondly, the question whether somebody *sincerely* holds R *as a moral rule* is, surely, the question whether he really thinks that R is a true, correct, or acceptable moral rule. "This is my moral principle, though of course I agree that it's false!" is a nonsense statement in the moral area, just as it is in any other. It is also nonsense to say that morality is not susceptible to any kind of truth, anything analogous to it.[2] We must look for a true theory, a theory about when a proposed moral principle is acceptable and when it isn't; we may not find it, but to reject the question is absurd. Accordingly, all of our tests will be construed as tests of "acceptability", meaning by this to refer to what a rational person should accept – that there is good reason to accept what is thus acceptable. Most of our tests, of course, are in the form of necessary conditions on acceptability, so the effect of most of them is to tell us what to reject rather than what to accept. The point is that acceptability is what is at issue, and not just sincerity.

Now it is part of the leading idea of universalizability that consistency is what is fundamentally at issue – consistency in *some* sense. I follow Kant in this; the idea is to see whether some rule for all is authorized by the moral agent himself, somehow. Just how, of course, is what is in question. The conclusion of the essay suggests, rather sketchily, an answer to it.

Even so, there is, of course, no way to prevent disagreement. Very likely, no matter how we frame our notion of consistency, and even if that notion generates in principle a single universal morality, there will be disagreement among different thinkers as to whether a certain sort of activity does or does not display the kind of consistency in question. It is not reasonable to expect to come up with a theory that is immune to such disagreement. What matters is whether or not there is something to disagree *about*, or whether the appearance of disagreement is purely illusory. And, of course, there might be acceptable principles for accommodating practical disagreement at lower levels of generality. Agreement to disagree is often possible.

With all this in mind, then, we proceed to my classification of Universalizability theses.

4. SIX CLASSES OF UNIVERSALIZABILITY THESES

When I first contemplated writing on this subject, I had thought to come up with a comprehensive list of universalizability theses; but I eventually gave it up as hopeless. Philosophers have a habit of assuming that if there are more than about three of something then there are an infinite number of them, but I don't wish to make the lavish claim that there are an endless number of possible universalizability ideas – only that there are probably more than crop up on the following list. I hope, however, that this contains the most important ones, and enough to lend weight to the conclusions of this essay.

My list of roughly fifteen theses is marshalled under six headings, derived more or less from Kant – as seems appropriate. The Kantian general recipe, it will be recalled, goes like this: "Act only on that maxim that you can at the same time will to be a universal law!"[3] Fortunately, this is not an essay in Kantian exegesis, and I shall therefore feel free to take whatever liberties I like with Kant's famous formula without defending them via his texts. The formula as it stands makes, to begin with, explicit use of the term 'universal'. In admonishing us to act only on maxims that "can be willed to be" universal laws, it plainly entails that moral principles must be "universal laws", and the first question is, just what does that mean? My first heading, then, is (1) Universality, under which I discuss what I shall call (a) Supervenience, (b) Generality, and (c) Universal Applicability. Kant's formula also uses the word 'can', and indeed, it is that word that raises the main and still unsolved problems about what the formula as a whole means. However, we may at least take it that one could not, in the relevant sense of 'could', *will* a certain rule to be a universal law unless that rule could at any rate *be* a universal law. My next category, then, is (2) Universal Possibility, under which I discuss the proposals that it must be (a) possible for everyone to "follow" the rule in question, (b) *logically* possible for everyone to *do* what the rule requires them to do, and (c) "materially" possible for them all to do what it requires. (The distinction is made especially in order to afford some discussion of the sense in which morality does or does not presuppose substantive factual claims, and what difference those claims might make to the content of morality; Kant, it will be recalled, sometimes talks as though morality were utterly abstract at its core, and even as though factual considerations would subvert ethics.) As a variant, or possibly an extension, of (2), we have the suggestion that a rule can be a moral rule only if the *consequences* of its general adoption, or its general adherance (or ...) would be of one kind or another. This gives us (3) Universalized Consequentialism, which has a horde of species depending on whether what is universalized for purposes of assessing consequences is (a) the universal adherance to the rule, (b) the universal adoption of the rule, (c) the universal attempt to get the rule adopted, or others; and whether the consequences in question are to be (i) non-disastrous, (ii) maximal, or (iii) optimal, as determined by some possibly nonaggregative criterion of assessment. (It is thought, with some encouragement from the Kantian texts, that Kant meant to rule out any such appeals to consequences, but I include category (3) not only because this essay is not, as I say, one of Kantian exegesis anyway, but also because those who think that are, I suspect, confused and in any case in error.)[4] Be that as it may, we next have the subject of "willing universally". Here we have two versions to consider: (4) Willing Universally: (a) would the person whose principles are in question will that everyone do the act whose requirement is contemplated? Or perhaps (b) would he will it if, at any rate, he met some condition of adequate or perhaps full knowledge of just what he would then be willing? But then perhaps we need (c), Would he *rationally* will it? Further conditions on this, however, are often proposed, and these I marshall under heading (5) Universal Patient Willing: (a) would the subject will this rule if he were on, so to speak, the receiving end of the acts in question? (This is the classic Golden Rule, approximately.) Or perhaps (b) would the subject will this rule if he actually were any of the others affected by it? Finally we have (6) Universal Rational Agent Willing: would it be *rational* for every moral agent to will such a rule? Does reason require us to "will" the rule in question?

My discussion of many of these options will necessarily be sketchy in this modest essay; but it would not do simply to omit ideas that have been seriously advocated in this connection. The hope, as I say, is that we will emerge with a clear rationale for accepting some, rejecting others, and ending up with a fairly clear picture of the basic structure of morality.

5. FIRST GROUP: GENERALITY

(a) *Supervenience*

It has long been accepted that ethical predicates, along with other evaluative predicates, have a property known as "supervenience".[5] To say that a predicate, F, is supervenient is to say that it is conceptually impossible for anything to exemplify F unless it also exemplifies some *other* predicate, G. The metaphysics (or "logic", if you like) of this is obscure. Whatever F may be, can anything exemplify F unless there are at least some other properties also possessed by it? However, supervenience is at least somewhat stronger than that: if F is supervenient on G, then G somehow *explains F*. If x is good, for instance, then the property G upon which it is supervenient is what "makes" x good. But "makes" it, how? This is not an easy question. If some version of ethical Naturalism is correct, then the answer would seem to be at hand: what makes x good is the properties of x on account of which it has that natural property signified by the word 'good'. The connection would presumably be causal. But naturalism is not generally accepted. Are there other reasons for accepting supervenience?

Intuitively, the case for supervenience is, I think, overwhelming. For to deny supervenience is to assert that it is logically possible that two cases, x and y, might be identical in all of their nonevaluative properties, yet differ in value. And this seems impossible — though the plot begins to thicken when we consider, to take a popular example, two pictures that are indistinguishable visually. Could one be a good painting, the other bad or indifferent or less good? Well, suppose that one of them is the original, painted by Rembrandt, and the other an incredibly good copy. Despite their visual indistinguishability, we may be sure, a collector would pay handsomely for the original, modestly for the copy. To the collector, the difference in "value" is enormous.

But would the collector claim that one was a *better* painting than the other? Likely not. It seems to me that he would be inclined to say that they were the *same* painting. In effect, he would say (but probably not in these terms) that the aesthetic objects were identical, but the "historic objects", as we might call them, were not. And between the historic objects, of course, there *is* a difference: one of them is three hundred years older than the other, and they are the products of different hands. We do not, after all, have a case of identical objects with nonidentical values, but rather two cases: one of identical objects with identical values, the other of nonidentical objects with nonidentical values. And I conjecture that in every proposed counterexample, we would be able to find a plausible explanation of some such type as that. But whether or not this conjecture is correct, let us move on; for we shall find other and more important reasons for affirming the related thesis on the moral level.

(b) *Generality and the Exclusion of Proper Names*

There is a connection between the thesis of supervenience, which is expressed as a restriction on predicates, and *generality*, which is expressed as a restriction on principles. If no two cases that are otherwise identical can have different values, then it must follow that for any singular predication of value, some generalization underlies it. Suppose that what *makes* x F is the fact that x is G. Then it seems that there must be a true generalization to the effect that all G's are F. Immediate qualification: there will be such a generalization with a rider of the "other things being equal" variety. The need for such a rider is easily shown in any nonexotic case; watertight evaluative generalizations in ethics are exceedingly hard to come by. Meanwhile, what we have is an appreciation that ethics is susceptible of generalization. If someone rates a certain case as good or bad, right or wrong, etc., then that someone is making a judgment to which it is relevant to respond by considering *other* cases. "But Norbert did it last week, and you said it was O.K.!" is *relevant*: the speaker must come up with a relevant difference. And thus there lurk, implicitly, in the background of singular value judgments, generalizations, if rebuttable ones. As Hare has noted, the speaker may be very hard put to come up with generalizations that he'd be willing to stick by, and we certainly can't say that every intelligible judgment of value is one whose maker has ready to hand the principle upon which he has made it. Often, indeed normally, he has none, and if he does offer one, any moderately competent Socrates will be able to make short work of it until refuge behind ceterus paribus clauses and, likely, "normal conditions" enables the speaker more or less gracefully to avoid offering a fully worked out Moral Philosophy. Nevertheless, if the intuition that particular cases cannot differ *only* in their evaluative predicates is right, then we are committed to there being, somehow and somewhere, principles.[6] And thus begins the quest for universalizability.

Professor Rawls has laid it down as one of the "Formal Constraints of the Concept of Right" that principles should be general, explaining this as follows: "That is, it must be possible to formulate them without the use of what would be intuitively recognized as proper names, or rigged definite descriptions."[7] This is clearly right. As Sidgwick says, "If a kind of conduct that is right (or wrong) for me is not right (or wrong) for someone else, it must be on the ground of some difference between the two cases, other than the fact that I and he are different persons."[8] The question is whether this restriction is in some very pallid sense "logical". It is tempting to say so, certainly. If we consider the example of two playings of the very same record of some musical work, it is surely just unintelligible to claim that one was a better or worse *performance* (though again, one could easily enjoy it much more the one time than the other, especially if they were played one right after the other).

But turn, for a moment, to the "rigged definite descriptions" part of Rawls' Constraint. These, after all, are not literally proper names; yet so long as they were evidently equivalent to proper names, the unsatisfactoriness of making some significant moral distinction turn on them is equally evident. But so indeed is the trouble with bringing in a great variety of utterly arbitrary considerations, even though they are perfectly universal, perfectly devoid of proper names *or* definite descriptions. "Always throw salt over your left shoulder before going out", if offered as a *basic* principle of morality, would surely leave any rational mind quite blank, just as much as would 'maximize the well-being of Elwood D. Thuringer of 99 Gable Street, Olney, Saskatchewan'. Considerations could be marshalled, in conceivable circumstances, that would cause us to take seriously the practice recommended in the first of these two proposed "principles"; but then, so too could they in the second. It *could* turn out that Elwood T. has uniquely some extremely important characteristics upon which the rest of us depend for our very lives, just as with the throwing of salt over one's shoulder. But if offered as *basic* principles, surely the one is as much of a nonstarter as the other.

Thus we have Universalizability Thesis One:

U1:   *R* is an acceptable fundamental moral rule only if *R* contains no proper names, or what amount to proper names, in its Agent Scope specification.

(c) *Universal Applicability*

The restriction on proper names and the like seems very promising at the level of particular individuals. But what about tribes, for instance? Many tribal codes have, it seems, differentiated very sharply between proper behavior with respect to fellow tribespeople and proper behavior in relation to outsiders. Indeed, one supposes that some tribal moralities have simply left a blank so far as outsiders are concerned. Now 'Zuni', I suppose, is essentially a proper name, though that of a group rather than an individual. It is unlikely that the Zuni, supposing that they have a morality of one of the above types, explicitly base their moral theory on the importance of possessing certain properties that happen to be unique to the Zunis. Do we say, then, that the morality of the Zuni stands convicted of a *logical* defect?

This brings up the question of what the force of 'logical' is here. It's not as though the Zuni had some principles of the form "square one circle before every breakfast", after all. We would unhesitatingly refer to their code as a moral code. In fact, I can think of some people who would probably not regard it as defective at all. Perhaps moralities *should* be "tribalistic"! And if they should not, then we need to come up with some good reason why they should not. The reason, "but that simply is not a 'morality' at all' is unlikely to carry much weight. Or if it does, then that will have to be because it has been antecedently established that what is so called is something weighty, *and* that it precludes tribalism. We shall return to this later in this essay.[9]

We come face to face here with the question of just what the 'universality' of morality consists in, and why. Sorting this out is no fussy little logical exercise. There would, we may be sure, have been far fewer wars if every tribe and nation were persuaded that the lives of foreigners were no more dispensable than those of one's children or neighbors. And what about the questions of animal rights, or abortion? Questions about the scope of morality loom large in both.

(d) *'Application'*

A logical question: just what does it mean to say that a certain rule, R, "applies to" everyone, whereas another, R', does not? Intuitively, we are inclined to suppose that a tribal morality, for example, has a restricted scope of application. Yet the statement 'All Zunis are to do x' is, as we know, logically equivalent to the statement, "Everyone, if a Zuni, is to do x."

Indeed, even particular directives may be translated into statements nominally directed at all: "Everyone, if identical with John L. Smith, is to do x." This brings up a problem which I do not claim to have a completely satisfactory solution to. But perhaps for present purposes it is enough to say some such thing as this: that there are some types of action which virtually any moral agent, or at least any human moral agent, can perform, in a significant sense of 'can' (stronger than logical possibility, e.g.); whereas there are others that by definition could not, or could not because of the special properties required, properties that many people lack. Now we can suggest that the idea that moral principles should be "universally applicable" is roughly the idea that the act-descriptions in those principles should be such that it is significantly possible for all moral agents to perform acts of those kinds. Or perhaps we need to say "all *human* moral agents"? And even so, perhaps we must qualify this too: "all normal agents", or even, throwing in the towel, "virtually all human agents", to allow for the possibility that some persons simply *could* not do anything properly described as killing, lying, or cheating, for instance. Once we have principles whose contents are possibly observable by (virtually) all, we can then readily spot principles whose scope is restricted. Not everyone is or can be a Zuni, a woman, a member of a hereditary aristocracy, etc. That the fundamental principles of morality must be unrestricted is, therefore, an idea with a reasonably clear content even if it is hard to nail it down precisely.

Thus we have the second Universalizability thesis:

U2: R is an acceptable fundamental moral rule only if R is significantly applicable to all moral agents.

6. A NOTE ABOUT MORAL RULES AND PRINCIPLES: REQUIREMENTS, PERMISSIONS, AND RECOMMENDATIONS

We shall be construing universalizability theses, henceforth, as imposing conditions on the admissibility of proposed moral rules, or principles. It is essential for the success of any such treatment that we won't be missing anything by talking as if there were only one kind of thing in a morality, that thing being sufficiently characterized as a "rule" or "principle". In this section, I will partly argue and partly stipulate that this apparent restriction is nevertheless acceptable. I shall do so by making what I hope are all the main distinctions and showing how all can be well enough marshalled under this single heading.

(a) *'Rule' vs. 'Principle'*

Moral "rules" are, I think, intuitively thought of as relatively concrete and specific; principles, by contrast, are relatively abstract and, especially, fundamental. Such philosophically famous examples as the Principle of Utility or Kant's Categorical Imperative mention no acts: before one can know what to do on the basis of either of those principles, one would need more information — characterizations of acts which relate them to the concepts employed in those principles. Nevertheless, both purport to tell us what to do, to guide behaviour by distinguishing, at however high a level, between those possible acts that we should do, those we should not, and perhaps those which it would be desirable versus those which it would be undesirable, to perform. In what follows, 'rule' will ordinarily be used to cover this whole range.

(b) *Fundamental and Nonfundamental Rules*

However, there is one stipulation about the range of 'rule' in the following which should be made here. It is assumed here that some rules are more fundamental than others, and that ultimately there are rules or principles which are simply and unqualifiedly fundamental — at least, within any particular full theory of morality. A rule R is more fundamental than another, R', if R' is deducible from R (together with suitable definitions and nonmoral premises) and not vice versa; and R is unqualifiedly fundamental if there are no further moral rules, R_f, such that R_f is more fundamental than R. The various universalizability theses which we shall be examining will in general apply primarily to proposed *fundamental* rules. Where the thesis proposes a necessary condition on moral rules, this should be understood as meaning that in the case of *non*fundamental rules, R', the thesis applies in the sense that any such rule must be based on a fundamental one which met the condition proposed. In short, the assumptions being made here about the conceptual structure of a morality are old-fashioned; I shall not attempt to defend them in detail against possible objections.

(c) *Requirements and Permissions*

A more serious question about my proposed marshalling is whether there aren't two quite distinct sorts of things in the way of "rules", namely: (a) Requirements, rules saying that such-and-such must be done (or avoided), and (b) Permissions, "rules" to the effect that such-and-such is O.K., permitted. Now anything which is required is, presumably, permitted as well, but there remains a — hopefully very large — class of acts that is neither required nor forbidden (neither it nor its negation is required). Some theorists have apparently thought that the category of "rules of permission" demonstrates the untenability of the prescriptivist account of morality, since permissive rules neither prescribe nor forbid.

But wrongly. The idea that there are fundamentally distinct "permissive" rules of morality is, upon deeper reflection, unintelligible. In what sense would a sentence of the form '*A may* do *x*' express a "rule" if it neither required nor forbade any behavior on the part of anybody? But if it is a moral rule, it does require or forbid, indeed. To say that a certain act *x* is morally allowable, permitted, is to direct the behaviour of *other* persons besides the agent of the permitted act. It is to tell those other persons that they are to refrain from preventing the actions in question, or from criticizing in certain ways. One who says, "I *may* do *x*", "It is morally O.K. for me to do *x*" is saying "You must *allow* me to do *x*!" When such claims are made, of course, there are generally background circumstances envisaged, as well as other background rules which might well authorize restrictions on various particular cases of doing *x*, but the general thrust of the statement, nevertheless, is to make a claim on the behaviour of others, and that claim takes the form of a directive. *All* meaningful moral statements direct behaviour in one way or another. It is on this understanding that "permissive rules" are cited or admitted as values of the variable *R* in the theses we consider below.

There are subsidiary respects in which permissive rules might also direct behaviour. Sometimes the point of a permissive rule is to explicitly rescind a restrictive rule assumed in context to have been previously operative, or contemplated as possibly operative in the context. Such permissive rules direct those who administer the restrictive rule in question to refrain from administering it (the effect of the permissive rule is "Lay off those who are attempting to do *x*!"). Again, permissive rules sometimes are framed deliberately with a view to fixing the limits within which the agent may operate: "you may do *x*" often means, "and you may *not* do *more* than *x*", where *x* is the sort of thing that indicates a degree of something. But we need not labour this point further.

(d) *Requirements and Recommendations*

Some moral rules are intended to state a flat restriction or prohibition. But others merely recommend, specifying a kind of action as desirable or undesirable but not necessarily strictly required or forbidden. This distinction, I take it, has to do with the degree and kind of reinforcement to be employed with respect to the kind of action in question. Requirements and prohibitions envisage negative reinforcement, viz., preventing people from doing what is forbidden or from not doing what is required, and/or punishing them for failure to do or refrain. Recommendations in general envisage encouragement for doing rather than punishment for nondoing. Further, they envisage the exercise of discretion on the part of the agent: they tell him, in effect, to attach a certain weight to the doing of the kind of act (or achieving of the kind of result) in question, but do not insist that nothing else could outweigh it; they even allow that the personal interests of the agent might well be enough to outweigh on many or most, or even all, occasions when the doing of x is in question. Still, a recommendation is a prescription, a directing of behaviour, and we may allow recommendational rules as values of our variable R as well.

(e) *Virtues and Vices*

Perhaps the most serious alleged counterexamples to my general assumption that everything we are concerned with can suitably be marshalled under the heading of moral rules are our concerns with dispositions and qualities of mind and character. Respected thinkers have insisted that here, in fact, lies the essence of morality. We should, they say, be concerned not with "rules", which they regard as cut-and-dried and often irrelevant, but with dispositions and such — with virtue and vice, in short, rather than right and wrong.

This challenge cannot be adequately dealt with here. It seems to me clear that a virtue or vice is a disposition, and a disposition is a disposition to do or avoid various things. Why cannot those things be the subjects of rules? Indeed, could they possibly *not* be, if the disposition to do or avoid them is so important? And one can remind these theorists that the most famous "rule" theorist, Immanuel Kant, thought that the object of all these rules was to promote the Good Will. My inclination, in short, is to deny the envisaged opposition of virtue and rule. So the defense rests.

7. UNIVERSALITY: AGENT AND PATIENT

We need a distinction. Normative sentences are intended to direct conduct. Some are addressed to particular individuals, some to various groups, and some to everyone at large. Let us call those whose conduct is capable of being directed by normative considerations Agents. When normative sentences are said to "apply" (or fail to apply) to some or other set of persons, it is usually persons *qua* agent that are in question. There is, due to the structure of any normative sentence, the question of whose conduct is to be directed by it. Let us call this the question of *Agent Scope*. Kant's Categorical Imperative directs us to perform an operation on the agent scope of normative sentences. We begin with what he calls a Maxim, a "subjective principle of action", the agent scope of which is confined in the first instance to the agent himself: "When in circumstances *C, I* will do *x*". The Categorical Imperative directs us to replace the constant 'I' with a universal quantifier: "When in circumstances *C, everyone* will do *x*." This new sentence is the one on which the further tests of consistency, or whatever, are to be performed.

But there is another question of scope concerning every normative sentence. The sentence directs some agent to perform some action or actions (or: to perform some action in some special way, or possibly with some special attitude — we will ignore such differences in this essay). But these actions will, or might, *affect* some person or persons. They might also affect some individuals which we do not consider as "persons", e.g. animals. Perhaps also they will affect some entities that are not 'individuals' or not, at any rate, sentient. When an agent performs any action, we presume that it is intended to affect someone or something, and to do so for better or worse (normally, at least himself, for the better). Let us call what is thus affected the *Patients* with respect to those actions.[10] When a normative sentence directs agents to perform an action, it usually does so with a view to affecting some or other class of patients. Considerations of what happens to the patients of those actions are very often what supply the rationale of the actions. They will include, for example, the following: bringing about improvements in the situations of certain persons; bringing about improvements in the situation of the agent; worsening the situations of certain agents (at least in some respects — punishment, for instance); improving the situations of animate nonpersons (or the reverse); improving (or the reverse) the "situations" of some inanimate objects. Among the most important and basic questions about morality are those concerning the bearing on our actions of considerations of the wellbeing of (a) other persons than the agent, (b) animate nonpersons, and (c) inanimate entities. Should we ever act ultimately for the sake of any considerations about (c)? Or (b)? Or even (a), for that matter?

Now, universalizability theses can be brought to bear on Patient scope as well as Agent scope. Some of them admonish the agent to refrain from performing an action if its intended or expected effects on its intended or likely patient could be expected to be of a type such that, if the agent himself were in the patient-position in respect of those effects, he would object, dislike it, or manifest some other putatively relevant reaction. There is a strong tendency, among agents, to confine their interest in patients to certain particular ones: themselves, most prominently, but also their friends, loved ones, or fellow participants in some common endeavors. Some theorists believe that the main point of morality, or perhaps its essence, is to broaden those interests so as to include "everyone", on some basis or other. We shall be examining some proposals of that kind below. Meanwhile, the point is that whether universality is to be observed with respect to patients, agents, or both, is evidently going to be a serious question.

It should be noted that principles urging freedom of action as a prominent consideration, which are naturally thought of as essentially "agent-oriented", nevertheless treat agents as patients in a prominent respect. For if agent A is urged to *permit* B to act in certain ways, then it is in virtue of certain possible effects of A's actions *on* B that A is urged to act or refrain. Why should the fact that other persons are agents make any difference to any particular agent? We shall have occasion to touch on that question below. Meanwhile, let us move on to the second class of universalizability theses to be considered.

8. SECOND GROUP: UNIVERSAL POSSIBILITY

Let us suppose, for the present, that some reason will be found for insisting that the Agent scope of moral principles, or at least of fundamental ones, must be universal, understanding this to mean that they reach significantly to all moral agents. Among the questions we could ask about a proposed rule or principle of this form is the question whether it is *possible* for all agents to follow that rule or principle. If the point of a normative statement is to direct the actions of some set of agents, then it will clearly not be able to achieve that point if what it directs them to do is such that they cannot all follow the directions. Seriously to issue such a norm is to invite a charge of incoherence, a failure of practical reason.

In my classification, I referred to three kinds of universal possibility, with by implication three kinds of attendant failure. Let us consider each.

> U3: R is a moral rule only if it is possible for everyone to *try* to adhere to R.

This is scarcely a restriction at all, it would seem. For provided we don't worry about failure, it is surely always going to be possible for everyone to try to live up to rule R, no matter what R may prescribe. This is so even if what R prescribes is logically impossible for all to do, or even for any to do, one might suppose. But not quite. At some point, it will be incoherent to describe someone as even trying to do a certain thing. Suppose the subject simply doesn't understand what R is supposed to be asking him to do? In that case, he cannot even *try* to do it. He can't set himself in the direction R purports to be steering him in, because he has no idea which direction that is.

However, the restriction on moral rules that this brings with it would not seem to have anything special to do with universalizability, as such. It is not through generalization that some kind of paradox or incoherence is generated, but rather because the purported rule is ill-formulated or because the individual whose behaviour we hope to affect by it is not capable of understanding the rule and thus unable to control his action in the light of it. Neither of these failings has anything in particular to do with universalization in the logical sense.

But it may have to do with universal applicability in an important empirical sense. For suppose that typical people could not learn R, not because R was incoherent but merely because it was very difficult or complicated, employing concepts beyond the capability of the normal intellect. This, surely, would bar us from considering R to be one of the basic rules of morality.

The point here interacts with a question about Agent Scope. Kant held that morality was for all rational beings. But *how* rational? If we could simply play around with the agent scope variable to our heart's content, we could make the above R a fundamental rule of morality, applying to all five of the rational beings who were capable of understanding it; the rest of humanity would simply be declared beyond the pale of morality. This, surely, would not do. But *why* not? We shall address ourselves to this question below. Meanwhile, we have

> U4:   A rule, R, requiring everyone to perform an act, x, is a moral rule only if it is logically possible for everyone to *succeed* in doing x.

Formula U4 imposes a genuine restriction of moral interest. Consider, for example, what we may call the Maxim of the Poor Sport: "I will play only if I win." But competitive sports or games are such that it is *logically impossible* for everyone to win (or anyway, many of them are): in order for me to be said to have won at chess, there must be an opponent who has lost. Everyone could certainly *have* this maxim; it passes test U4 readily enough. But since necessarily not all could succeed, the rule "everyone plays only if he wins" is unrealizable, except in the uninteresting case that nobody plays.

In fact, I should not say that this is "uninteresting". One who knows that he is a poor sport could refuse to play on that very ground. Others could look on him with pity or contempt, but they would not have the same kind of complaint as those who, upon winning a game with the Poor Sport, faced bitter allegations of misconduct; or for that matter as those who discovered that Poor Sport would only play with persons much inferior to himself in ability, eschewing competition with his equals or superiors.

Possibly another example is that of Kant's Lying Promise. This example has long been contentious among interpretors of Kant. The difficulty is that, as Kant frames the case anyway, it seems as though it is an empirical question whether everyone could operate on the maxim of borrowing things on condition that the loan will be repaid, yet having no intention of repayment. It seems that gullibility on the part of the lender is the relevant variable: if everyone is gullible enough, the agent's credibility will never be impugned. But this is surely unsatisfactory, both to Kant's intentions and in itself. We don't suppose that the wrongness of false promises is contingent on the perceptiveness of those being bilked by them.

But we may look at it this way. Let us suppose that we have a case of genuine borrowing, in the sense that the lender would not have supplied the borrower except on condition that it be returned; more generally, that where A falsely promises B to do x in return for B's doing y, B would not intentionally do y unless he believed that A would do x. Now if A's promise is false in the full sense that he is misleading B into believing that he will do x, though in fact not intending to, then A is into the following shabby game: A *intends* (i) that B does y only if A does x, and (ii) that A not do x. Why does he intend (i)? Because he is *borrowing*, not asking for a handout. To do that is to give others to believe that one is accepting B's act with the condition on it that A will do what he said he would do. And so A brings about a situation in which someone *must* be frustrated: B, if A gets away with it, and A, if he doesn't. It is not logically possible for everyone to succeed in doing what a "rule" of lying promises would permit.

But not every case of failure of universal possibility will be logical, even in the broad sense of 'logic' in which the aforementioned examples are so. Thus we have

U5:   A rule, R, requiring everyone to perform an act, x, is a moral rule only if it is *materially* possible for everyone to do x (successfully).

Here the term 'materially' is not meant to distinguish cases where the relevant agents know about the facts making it materially impossible from those where they do not know them. Rather, I am distinguishing between logical or conceptual necessity and possibility on the one hand and causal, nomological possibility on the other. But the distinctions are perhaps related to each other, in the following way. If we suppose that morality is to apply to "all rational beings" — something we'll be considering further below, but will assume to be somewhere near the mark at the moment — then it seems part of the idea of such a being that he be able to discern the logical implications of his proposals, but not part of the idea that he have all the material facts at his disposal. So we might take it that we can hold people responsible for failings of the former sort when we perhaps cannot do so for failings of the latter sort.

Nevertheless, it is surely a relevant test of a moral rule that it be possible, not just logically but really, for everyone to do what that rule requires (or avoid what it forbids). If someone can establish that a particular proposed rule fails this condition, then that is a relevant criticism. And again, therefore, it will follow that the proposed moral rule in question cannot do what it purports to do: viz., direct the behavior of all to whom it is addressed. The expectation that all conform to that rule is unreasonable. That is the sense in which failures on this score can be called "practical inconsistencies", or "contradictions", and in which we could apply Kant's rubric of 'contradiction in the will'. That "contradiction" is present "in the will" of those who know the facts that make for material impossibility; for those who do not, of course, the problem is in what they will, not simply in their willing it.

The big question from this point of view is whether we are to countenance "psychological" impossibilities. Consider the command, "Love ye one another!" This has been held by many people to be a, or even the, fundamental requirement of morality. But it has often been objected to by theorists as quite mad: it is unreasonable to require universal love, they insist, because it is impossible for everyone to do so. Either love cannot be commanded at all, or (more pertinently to the present context) the capacity for love of most or perhaps all people is simply too limited to permit of its extension to all and sundry. It is unreasonable to demand that everyone love everyone, because it is impossible for everyone to love everyone, and perhaps because it is impossible for anyone to love anyone *on command*. It is unnecessary for us to settle the question of fact at issue here. It is, for that matter, not entirely clear that what is at issue here *is* mainly a question of fact — we shall return to that point later on. But it is surely clear that it is relevant to consider this question if an ethical requirement of universal love is envisaged.

Where considerations of universalizability proper come into it via the formula of material possibility is, especially, in that broad class of cases in which, owing to various facts, everyone's attempting to live up to the rule in question would be incompatible with everyone's succeeding even though there is no particular person who must meet with failure if that person tries, and even though sizable subgroups could also succeed. Here we come upon the phenomenon of nonlinearity: the effects of action are not a linear function of the number of attempts.[11] Beyond some number, for the kind of act and in the circumstances in question, attempts become incompatible with general success. The supply of gasoline becomes exhausted, or life on earth gets wiped out, or whatever.

When there is such a nonlinearity, what do we do? To start with, the rule in question is thereby shown not to be satisfactory, in just that form anyway. But it is mistaken enthusiasm to conclude immediately that no acts of that type are acceptable. In principle, two kinds of supplementary restrictions need to be brought in. First, one can come up with a new rule requiring persons to attempt the act only if in the circumstances not more than n other persons are doing likewise. Some reasonable way to fix the relevant value of n is then needed, including in the criterion of 'reasonableness' that it will be possible for typical persons, among those needing to be reached, to ascertain (readily enough for the purposes at hand) whether they in fact are in those circumstances. And second, some way of allocating the right to attempt to a suitable group of relevant persons, in case there should be more applicants for that right than there are spaces to allot, will need to be incorporated. In the latter, we are likely to encounter considerations of fairness; indeed, the rule as a whole is likely to be seen as a rule of fairness. What the structure of such allocative rules should be is plainly important, and just how we construe the requirement of universalizability will importantly affect this matter.

Meanwhile, nonlinearity considerations loom still larger in the next kind of universalizability formulae to be considered, namely appeal to the consequences of general performance, adoption, or suchlike. So let us move on to them.

9. THIRD GROUP: UNIVERSALIZED CONSEQUENCES

"But what if everyone did that?" Some proposals about the essence of morality make this the central question.[12] One might even think of the preceding group as a subclass of the present one, since the particular case where the consequences of a universal attempt to do x make the universal doing of x impossible might be held merely to be a special case of the consequences of such universal attempts being merely undesirable. But there is a reason for not thinking of it that way. For the special case of impossibility is one which cannot be dismissed as irrelevant by the proponent of a rule whose general observance would lead to that, whereas there is a significant question about this if what's wrong with the generalized consequences is merely that they are "undesirable". The question will be, undesirable according to whom? And how does one justify the proposed criterion of assessment of consequences? These questions are an embarassment if the idea is to propound a fundamental principle of morality that is independent of "subjective" considerations. And that this may be the idea is an important possibility. But since it will be considered below, we shall table that matter for the moment. Meanwhile there is the question of just what *about* the rule is supposed to generate the consequences in question. And in addition, we have the question what *level* of consequences is sufficient to disqualify the rule from acceptance. Let us tackle the former question first.

> U6:   A proposed moral rule is unacceptable if the consequences of its general *observance* would be undesirable.[13]

Clearly there will be a problem of determining whether to blame the *rule* for possible undesirable consequences or something else. And of course there will be a problem about the other moral rules (or other nonmoral rules, for that matter) forming the background in which we have observed the operation of this particular one. But putting aside such admittedly difficult issues, it is impossible to see how one could shuck off the present proposal, provided that the criterion by which one assesses consequences is relevant. The point of issuing a prescription is to get it followed. But what is the point of getting it followed, if not to make things (relevantly) better? Or at least not to make them worse?

It might be thought that "Let justice be done, though the heavens fall!" is a slogan that counterexemplifies this criterion. But that is not clear. It depends on what the proponent is proposing to entertain in the way of criteria of assessment of consequences. Presumably he thinks that that aspect of the situation resulting from the observance of his rule in which its "justice" consists outweighs any other consequences that might be undesirable. Whether the slogan is plausible depends on whether that assessment is plausible. If it is not, then why shouldn't we conclude that the proposed principle is not universalizable?

Like the other formulae considered thus far, this one is stated as imposing a necessary condition on a proposed moral rule. It might be thought that it also implies a sufficient condition: if the consequences of general adherance would be good, then the rule is to be accepted. But that, again, is not clearly so. As stated, the formula contains a subjunctive: if R were adhered to, the consequences would be good. But suppose that there isn't the slightest chance that R would be adhered to? Such reflections suggest a modified version:

U7:   A proposed moral rule is unacceptable if the consequences of its general *adoption* would be undesirable.[14]

The difference between U6 and U7 is that there could be slips between the cup of adopting a rule and the lip of actually doing what it tells us to do. Suppose that if people adopted the rule, the difficulty of adhering to it would be so great as to cause enormous psychological pain? And in any case, that its adoption would not lead to a very great degree of adherance in practice? The present criterion is broader than the first, for if adoption would lead to adherance, and adherance itself would, as in U6, be undesirable, then surely we could count those consequences as consequences of adoption as well. But on the other hand, even if the consequences of adherance would be good, they could be outweighed by the evils engendered in the attempt to adhere to it, or in an "adoption" which didn't even lead to serious attempts to live up to it. A morality whose costs are too great to bear is surely to be rejected on that very count.

But now another distinction looms before us. A principle whose consequences, if adhered to, would be good might be nevertheless bad because of the consequences of its adoption. But why stop there? Should we not also concern ourselves with the consequences of attempting to *get* it adopted? Thus we have a third version (or class of versions, really):

U8:   A proposed moral rule is unacceptable if the consequences of attempting to get it generally adopted would be undesirable.[15]

In speaking of 'undesirable consequences' here, I intentionally choose a description that could take in either those "undesirable" consequences which stem from lack of success in getting R adopted, or other consequences engendered in the process of trying to do so, consequences which might even be encountered in the course of success in one's efforts at "moral education" or whatever we wish to call the procedure in question. Now, academics such as those who will undoubtedly form the lion's share of readers of this article will tend to ignore such considerations at first, since we think of the adoption or rejection of an ethical principle as essentially a rational procedure: if we are convinced that the principle is correct, we adopt it; if not, we reject it. But even if that really is the way we proceed − which may be doubted! − what about five-year-olds? Or persons brought up with a very strong faith in some incompatible religious belief? Or persons from powerful cultures quite alien to the proposed rule? Notoriously, the consequences for the person who attempts to preach his new morality to such persons are apt to be pretty severe! But might they not additionally be severe for the people themselves? Suppose that we can foresee both that our efforts to inculcate a new principle would be quite successful, *and* that the result would be alienation, rootlessness, and despair for the next couple of generations?

Consideration of these further versions of generalized consequentialism suggests a further distinction. Surely we should be loathe to conclude that the very fact that Christ and Socrates met their ends as they did showed that their *principles* were in error. What they may show is only that they were perhaps overly zealous in their efforts to get them adopted. We could distinguish, then, between the intrinsic correctness of a principle and its practicability, between "ideal" and "realistic" moralities. It might then be suggested that moral theorists are properly concerned more nearly with the first sort, but practical moral agents with the second.

But is there really any such distinction? Can a moral principle be right, and yet wrong to preach?[16] An example illustrates the problem here, as well as neatly illustrating the threefold distinction explored above: consider the case of pacifism. The proponent of pacifism might argue that if everyone were to be pacifist, the consequences (viz., universal nonviolence) would be highly desirable. But his opponent might insist that although that would indeed be a desirable state of affairs (we shelve the very different view that it wouldn't even be that), yet the consequences of pacifism would in fact be much less desirable than those of a principle allowing violence when it was necessary in order to prevent aggressive violence. By formula U6, the two principles are presumably identical; but by formula U7, even, they diverge: for those who fail to live up to their pacifist principles and opt for a life of violence would now have the way open to them, since none of those who did live up to those principles would be able to offer effective resistance. And note that if the opponent is correct in this claim, he makes a claim that it would be hard for the proponent to ignore, since the consequences are being evaluated by the very same criteria as the proponent is apparently employing. But the divergence is still greater by formula U8, for it is surely not realistic to expect that very many people would adopt pacifism anyway, no matter how enthusiastically it might be preached. And in a world with both criminals and pacifists, the considerable majority of persons, who are both law-abiding and yet nonpacifist, would be stuck with the defense not only of themselves but of the pacifists as well! Or so it could plausibly be argued.[17]

Now I submit that *if* the facts are as the opponent claims, then the argument goes very strongly against pacifism not only "in practice" but "in principle" too. Or at least, it raises the issue of just what this distinction is supposed to be all about. Perhaps the solution is to relativize: a moral principle is one which it would be right to advocate *to A* (a person or group) only if the consequences of advocating it *to A* would on the whole be desirable (bearing in mind that we have yet to consider how to appraise desirability).

But now we come to the other question: what is the relevant level of unacceptability? How bad would the consequences have to be before the proposed rule is shown to be unacceptable? I have distinguished three in my proposed list: A moral rule is unacceptable if its consequences would be: (i) "disastrous", (ii) non-maximal, or (iii) non-optimal, in a sense to be explained.

If we start with the first two of these, I believe the decision is simple. For let us suppose that the consequences of proposed rule R would be, not disastrous but merely less desirable than those of an alternative, R'. Surely it would be nonsense to urge that either of these might still be perfectly acceptable, if (a vital 'if', but one we are always assuming for this discussion) the right criterion of desirability is employed. The maximality criterion would have it that a rule is unacceptable if its consequences are less good than some *available* alternative. Insofar as we are accepting the kind of considerations advanced in formulae U7 and U8 above, "availability" is obviously a crucial consideration. One alternative which, I take it, is always available is to have no rule at all; so a rule's being the best of a bad lot *of rules* would not make it acceptable by this test. But its being the best of a bad lot, when no rule would be still worse, would make it acceptable (or at any rate would keep it from being unacceptable, which in the special case in question might come to the same thing).

Why should some have thought otherwise? Due, I think, to a misunderstanding. We have thus far been speaking loosely of moral rules as "requiring" acts or imposing "restrictions" on acts. But now we must be more subtle. If a rule *forbids* an act, in the sense of actually declaring that act to be morally wrong, merely on the ground that the *act* was nonmaximal, then there is very good reason to think that the *rule* in question would be nonmaximal. For what one loses in the way of restricting of freedom, for instance, would surely much outweigh what one gained in the way of slightly better performance in the area of the particular acts in question, e.g., a rule *forbidding* people to give goods to their own children when possession of those goods by the poor, or by needy strangers, would produce more net happiness in the world, can reasonably be argued to cause more harm than good. But it might produce more net good in the world for people to harbor a pro-attitude toward the giving of goods to needy strangers in preference to one's own kin or friends, i.e., to regard that kind of benevolence as a virtue. And if it would, why should not a theorist who thought that the net happiness of all is what counts in morality insist that that would be the right attitude to harbor, and to foster?[18]

Criterion (iii), non-optimality, is a different kettle of fish, however. The term is selected in order to distinguish it from an aggregative criterion, rather than to pick out a different level of consequences within the aggregative sphere. The question whether the utilitarian idea, to evaluate on the basis of consequences computed impartially overall, is the right *idea* for moral purposes, is a deep one, about which something will be said below. Meanwhile criterion (iii) would have it that a moral rule is unacceptable if an alternative (available) rule would be such that some would be better off and none worse off. As between such a pair of alternatives, one morally dominates the other: that is the idea of criterion (iii). Bearing in mind that we are tentatively accepting the need to consider costs of advocacy and, so to speak, "moral overhead" (what Rawls calls "the strains of commitment"[19]), as in U7 and U8 above, it seems clear that provided we are using the appropriate criterion of evaluation, a proposed moral rule that was dominated by an available alternative should be rejected.

Our tentative conclusion regarding consequential universalizability is that it offers a useful further insight, but raises crucial questions which await resolution. Most prominent among these is the question of what we are to use as a criterion for assessment. If there is a single such criterion that can be shown to be the correct one for all to employ, fine: but what if that happy situation does not obtain – as seems very likely? And even if it did, would an aggregative criterion be the one to use? The formulae we have considered here are incapable of handling these questions as they stand,

and it is an important question whether any procedure making universalizability the central consideration in ethics can do so. We shall return to these
matters. They will come into focus as we turn to the remaining two groups
of formulae, those which crucially employ the idea of "willing" the proposed
moral rule whose acceptability is in question.

10. FOURTH GROUP: WILLING UNIVERSALLY

We now come to the question of just what "willing" has to do with morality.
If R is a moral rule, must it be the case that any particular agent wills R? That
is obviously implausible on the face of it. But it is less implausible to suggest

U9:   If R is one of A's moral principles, then A must "will" that
        everyone follow R.

Here we have a formula that might well be held to be true by definition.[20]
Bearing in mind the question about who "everyone" is for moral purposes,
it is plausible to hold that a (true, fundamental) moral rule must be a rule
for the direction of everyone's behaviour. Now suppose that A professes
to believe that R is a moral rule. Now, if moral rules are indeed *rules*, they
contain the idea of directing people, telling them to do whatever the rule
says to do. In that sense, seriously to believe that R is a moral rule is ipso
facto to "will" it: it is to accept a sentence of the form, "so-and-so is to do
x", which is tantamount to saying "so-and-so, do x!" And since by definition,
we have said, 'so-and-so' is in this case understood to be 'everyone', it follows
that anyone who accepts that R is a moral rule universally wills that people
do whatever R directs them to do.

Note that 'willing' here does not have the same force as 'wanting'. I may
want you to do so-and-so without directing, urging, or otherwise telling you
to do it: I may merely hope that you will. The idea of a moral rule or principle, however, seems to require something stronger than that. Or perhaps
different, rather than "stronger": for conceivably I may not even want you
to do what I direct you to do − consider the case of an officer doing his
distasteful duty. Morality can certainly be like that; indeed, in the case where
one directs oneself to do something on principle, we should expect it to be
frequently, even typically, that case that one wants to do what one directs
oneself not to.

Clearly the test as proposed, however, is neither necessary nor sufficient
for R's being, in very truth, one of "the" principles of morality (if there are
any such). For if there are true moral rules (in some appropriate meaning

of 'true'), it surely does not follow that anyone in particular knows or even believes any of them; and plainly someone's believing something does not in general make it true. Further, obviously different people seem to be able to accept contrary moral rules or principles, and if they are indeed contrary then they cannot both be true, if 'true' has any meaning at all here.

But is willing R universally a sufficient condition of R's being one of the willer's moral principles? It seems not, intuitively, for two different reasons. For one thing, the willing in question might be whimsical, fleeting, irrational. That is hardly enough, we suppose, to credit the agent with a moral principle. But this is easily taken care of, by adding or perhaps understanding it to be part of the notion of 'willing' here that it be a relatively firm disposition to will; as discussed below, there may also be a rationality condition to apply. But, secondly, it seems that one could will that everyone do something without having any intention of being committed to the idea that the act in question be morally obligatory on all. Mightn't I will that everyone eat a certain brand of pancakes every day, just because I think that would be cute?

It seems plausible at this point to invoke two sorts of restrictions. In the first place, we can add the idea that morality is to be "overriding"; in particular, that it is intended to override individual inclinations or interests. Do I not only want everyone to eat Auntie Jones' pancakes, but want them to do so whether they like them or not?[21] Secondly, there is the matter of whether and how the proposed rule is to be "enforced". Do we not only want everyone to act this way, but also want everyone to condemn those who do not, perhaps even inflict punishment on violators? Do we want people to be brought up from an early age confirmed in the habit of doing what R bids them do? If not, it is not as a moral requirement that our agent is invoking R.[22]

It is not clear that these suggestions get us all the way to sufficient conditions for R's being regarded as a moral principle or rule by an agent. But even if they do, it is clear that they don't identify the "true", correct, or acceptable moral principles. Quite outlandish or ridiculous rules could be "willed". Perhaps more knowledge on the part of A would fix things up:

U10: R is an acceptable moral rule for A to act on if A would continue to will R given full knowledge of R's implications and effects.

Long ago (1952) R. M. Hare proposed that when pressed for a justification of a decision, an agent could do no better than specify the general principles underlying it, together with an account of the effects of observing those principles, thus leading ultimately to "a complete specification of the way of life of which it is a part. ... If the inquirer still goes on asking 'But why should I live like that?', then there is no further answer to give him. ... "[23] But did Hare mean that when the person has done that, then his decision *is* justified? It is not clear whether he did, though the language suggests it. But consider how implausible it is to suppose so. Surely we could intelligibly reply, to many such "complete specifications", if that is all that is produced, "I don't see how *that* shows that you did the right thing." Perhaps at the time Hare thought that the production of such a specification would at any rate end the discussion, and that that is the best we can do. But of course it would not end it, in any sense other than that it would show the original speaker to be pig-headed. That a "way of life" was so admired by the agent that he wanted everybody to conform to it hardly shows that everyone ought to conform to it. To make progress in the direction of a criterion of accept-ability, we must — and here I merely recapitulate the history of ethics in the past thirty-odd years — move to formulae invoking notions of *reason*.

Just "willing" a universal behavioral constraint isn't enough to make it an acceptable moral principle, even if we add a condition that it is willed given lots of information about its implications. But suppose we add a rationality requirement of a suitable kind? By anticipation, I will suggest that this must be the right way to go. Why so? Because we are identifying morality with a general system of behavioral requirements, and because the object of our search is the one that has the "force of reason" behind it. Let us distinguish *de facto* morality, morality in the anthropologist's sense of the term, from "true" morality. The former is the system of such rules actually deferred to, invoked, inculcated, and in general employed in the society whose morality it is. But philosophers, and I think also ordinary people, are either clear-headed (in one view) or presumptuous (in another) enough to believe that *de facto* moralities could be in error, in one way or another. Let us leave it undecided, for the moment, whether there is a Platonically true set of moral rules or principles whose truth has nothing to do with what rational persons would construct in the way of behavioral constraints, or whether instead morality is in some important sense an artifice. In either case, the set of principles or rules in question must be rational, either because simply true, and truth is the object of reason; or because the very essence of critical morality is that there are good reasons for accepting something other than what we have, or accepting what we in fact have. The question is not whether "ideal" or "true" morality is rational, but rather just how rationality comes into it, indeed what rationality in ethics consists in. I shall take it that the several formulae considered next, which include the most celebrated versions of ethical universalizability, are attempts to spell out precisely what a rational ethics is to be like. We start with the simplest idea:

U11:   *R* is an acceptable rule for A to follow if it would be *rational* for A to will that everyone accept *R*.

Whether this formulation is satisfactory depends on how one understands the details. But on the face of it, it surely will not do. One could have good reason to *want* everyone to act in a certain way, yet it could be recognizably immoral for people to act that way, or even to want them to do so. Wanting is not willing, as noted above; but in the absence of special understandings about that, it seems also possible to quite rationally will that all do *x*, yet the requirement that they do so be immoral or at very least arbitrary. In the face of this fairly obvious criticism, we should want to impose some further restriction.

11. UNIVERSALIZATION IN THE PATIENT SCOPE

It seems that if we are to come up with a plausible formulation, we must look in a different direction. One direction in which to look for a suitable restriction is toward those on the receiving end of the actions — what I have called the "patient class" of the proposed rule. The feeling that A might will universal acceptance of an arbitrary or immoral rule is no doubt in considerable part due to the thought that A simply may not take into account, or take properly into account, the interests, wishes, happiness of those affected by the actions licensed by *R*. The cure is to insist that A look at it from their points of view. Thus we have the classic moral formula known as The Golden Rule. In its classic form, this rule calls upon all of us to "Do unto others as you would have them do unto you." Translated into the technical terminology adopted above, we would have:

U12:   *R* is an acceptable moral rule for A to act on only if A would accept *R* even if A were in any patient-position of actions permitted or required by *R*.

One question immediately raised by such formulae is just what is meant by "acceptance", and what is supposed to determine acceptance by some affected person. We will consider that question a little later. Meanwhile, there is another criticism specific to this formula, one that has been widely advanced: Suppose that A has quite different tastes, interests, desires or values than those of the particular patient whose position he is now imagining himself to be in? A might be delighted to be acted on as R prescribes, though B would be horrified or discomfited.

The cure for this particular complaint is ready enough at hand. It is not enough to require only that A imagine himself in B's *situation* or *position*. Those terms suggest an "external" characterization, such that the "situation" is a kind of slot that might be occupied by anybody, or at least a wide range of persons. But the nub of the matter is to get the point of view of the particular individual being affected into the picture. So we put A not only into B's "shoes", as R. M. Hare puts it,[24] but we put him into them with B's desires, interests, and so forth − in short, with B's psychology. Thus:

U13: R is an acceptable moral rule for A to act on only if A would accept R even if A were in any of the patient positions of R and had the psychology of that patient.

The effect of this idea is drastic and far-reaching. To see how far, let us consider for a moment the question "immediately raised" above and tabled. Just what is the "acceptance" idea contemplated in the formula? At first sight, it seems reasonable to assume that the Golden Rule envisaged a kind of board meeting on the subject of proposed rule R. Everyone affected is a member of this board, each has a vote, and the condition imposed by our formula U12 was that R has to get unanimous approval before it is passed. But if that is so, the question of just how the various members are to deliberate before casting their votes is evidently important. In fact, it is absolutely crucial. May the members act irresponsibly, whimsically, on impulse? Indeed, mightn't they be *biased*? It could be urged that it was precisely that possibility that motivated the move from U12 to U13: A might, naturally enough, look at R only from his own point of view, that is, in the light of his *own* desires, interests, and values. Formula U13 heads off this tendency, indeed. But if A is required to look at things from the point of view of those affected by R, and as dictated by *their* psychologies, then although A's actions will not be determined solely by his own desires, he will nevertheless, one might suppose, have traded them in for the perhaps equally biased and narrow motivations of the others affected. And since each of these persons has in effect a veto on R's acceptability, this would seem to run the danger of putting morality into the hands of the whimsy of others. But it seems eminently reasonable to think that for at least some persons A, and some patients B, the result of this procedure will not be very promising as candidates for basic principles of morality.

A move in a slightly different direction might cure this difficulty. If the problem is that each of the relevant positions might be ruled by whim or mindless passion, etc., then we can require that the set of desires/interests/values of each patient be subjected to rational scrutiny before "voting":

U14:   R is an acceptable rule for A to act on only if A would accept R even if A were in any of the patient positions of R and had the psychology of that patient, but with the desires, interests, and values of the patient subjected to rational purification.

The purificatory procedure envisaged here might, for instance, be R. B. Brandt's "cognitive psychotherapy".[25] Clearly this new move raises further important questions. Rules passing test U14 are, in effect, rules made in the *best* interests of all parties, rather than simply in their interests *simpliciter*. But what if the agent and that party should be in disagreement as to what constitutes his best interests? Should A act in the light of his own best judgment of B's best interests? Or should he instead act in the light of B's judgment?

12. PATIENT-ORIENTED MORALITY AMD UTILITARIANISM

The above discussion may have struck the thoughtful reader as rather unreal in the light of the fact that our new fomulae have been requiring the proponent of a proposed moral rule to consider it not only from the positions of those affected, but also as if he had their psychologies. The effect of this requirement, we should now realize, is drastic. What is intended is that we take on the decision-making apparatus of the other person. But this includes his beliefs, desires, interests, purposes, and so on. Nor can that be all. Consider for example, the short person who proposes a rule that all doors have a five foot height. In response to U13 or U14, he considers this rule from the point of view of the sevenfooter who would, plainly, be quite put out by it. Does U13 invite him to imagine that he remains but five feet tall but, oddly, suddenly endowed with the *belief* that he is seven feet? If so, perhaps U14 would cause him to shed that belief — after all, it would be plainly irrational. But of course that is not the idea. The requirement amounts to the requirement that we imagine ourselves to *be* that other person, with his (or her) physical as well as psychological properties. To say that we must act as if we were in the other person's position and with his practical psychology is simply to say that his desires, etc., count as they stand. If so, however, then how can it be the case that A's estimate of what is good for B might conflict with B's? Does not our formula require him to act, in effect, on B's estimate?

In fact, the answer is no, though we must make a further distinction here. Consider U14's requirement that desires, etc. be rationally criticized. Such a requirement is possible only if such criticism can influence people's actions; we are clearly assuming that they can. But if they can, then we should note that not only can A normally choose between acting on B's desires as they are and his desires as they would be if criticized, but *so can B*. A may therefore face the problem of which to follow even if A is imagining himself to be B.

Now let us relate this point to the other question, concerning the precise character of the decision procedure for our "board meeting" regarding rule R. If everyone has a veto at this "meeting", why should we expect any rule, if it affects many persons, to pass? In democracies, it is hard enough to get clear majorities, let alone unanimity: why should it be any different here? And what do we do if we don't get unanimity?

An important possibility is this.[26] When any individual makes a decision, he is likely to have different desires and interests, pushing him in different directions. In order to choose coherently, he must decide which of the various desires has greater "weight"; or which action among those possible would optimally satisfy the greatest net total of the interests in question. No interest has, of itself, a "veto", in other words. Now if A is assuming the viewpoint of each affected party, and doing so in so thoroughgoing a way that it is as if he actually were each of those parties in turn, then it is reasonable to assume that our procedure will call upon A to determine the weights of the various desires and interests of each such party and then try to satisfy the greatest net total of all of those interests. In effect, on this view, every desire counts, impartially considered, in proportion to its intrinsic "weight". And thus it is not as though every board member has a veto. Rather, each has a vote — in fact a vote which he may split among several policies with various weights. And the decision of the whole board will be arrived at by computing the net vote for each possible policy being considered.[27]

On that view of the matter, what U13 leads to is Utilitarianism. And what U14 may seem to lead to is the "Ideal Utilitarianism" of, say, Hastings Rashdall,[28] as distinguished from the "hedonistic" Utilitarianism of Bentham. If this was the choice, which should we take? I have previously considered this issue,[29] and argued in favor of a view that may be distinguished from both Rashall's and Bentham's. Sidgwick, it will be recalled, thinks that the good for any individual is maximal satisfaction of his set of reasoned desires or interests, the reasoning in question being consideration in the light of full information.[30] But suppose that A attempts to consider B's desires that way, and comes up with a different critical view from that of B after going through a similar consideration. Which is A to act on, given formula U14? I suggested that he is to act on *B's*. This conclusion is motivated by what I take to be central to that idea of ethics that would make universalizability the heart of the matter: no one, I assume, would willingly subject himself to a scheme of values that he found alien even after careful consideration.[31]

The more fundamental question here, however, is not just which form of utilitarianism we should go for, but whether we should go for *any*. Formulae such as U13 and U14 require an extreme kind of impartiality, it seems. We are to assign as much weight to the desires of any person affected as we do to our own similar desires. But, waiving questions on the score of whether it is possible for people to do this, and whether the requisite cardinal comparisons of utilities make any sense, there is also the question whether we *should* do this. In particular, it must be questioned whether a rational morality would give the kind of dominance to the viewpoint of patients that is evidently involved in golden-rule ethics.

In order to answer this question, we must have a view of what ethics is *for*. The "how" of universalizability cannot be settled until we know the "why" of it.

13. UNIVERSALIZATION FOR RATIONAL AGENTS

Let us go back, for a moment, to formula U11: *R* is an acceptable moral rule for A if it would be rational for A to will that everyone accept *R*. Whether this formula is satisfactory, I suggested, depends on the details. We now consider the said "details". They include the basic story about morality.

First, why "will" any sort of general rules at all? Why *general* rules? And why general *rules*? That there are reasons for having standing policies of action for oneself is not likely to be much disputed. An element of generality is essential if one is to do any planning, any rational deciding of anything whatever. It is possible to be at cross purposes with oneself, and then one has problems. But they are a different kind of problem from those encountered in the course of dealing with other agents. We may say that a rational agent, at least insofar as rational, will not have purposes wholly inconsistent with themselves or with other major purposes he may have. But other agents, alas, may quite rationally have such purposes. We cannot simply assume that the other person and ourselves will share fundamental unity of purpose; and insofar as these collide, life will be more difficult. But when the other party is a rational agent, we have a possible avenue for dealing with him that is not available when relating ourselves to nonrational agents or entities. This avenue is practical reasoning: we may be able to *talk* the other party into adopting courses of behavior more satisfactory to ourselves. But talk, of course, is not just making noises, the example of too many politicians to the contrary notwithstanding. The noises (or scratches) are to some purpose: they address the practical reasoning of the other party; and this fact makes a radical difference to the situation. Superior force, in the form of superior technology perhaps, might sometimes enable one to bypass the reasoning powers of others with whom we must deal; but this, to put it mildly, is not the typical case. And it is never the case when what one wants *is* that others do certain things voluntarily, deliberately, and even wholeheartedly. In those cases, which are likely to be frequent when one thinks of it, there is no alternative to persuasion other than the special case in which there is a natural, antecedent unity of purposes. And that *is* a special case. Some few persons − one's children, perhaps, persons with whom instant mutual love somehow flourished (the list is so short that one is hard put to add any cases, and both of those listed are quite dubious anyway as any parent or lover must know!) − just might have this high level of natural harmony with you or me, but what about the rest of mankind?

Now we do not deal daily with "the rest of mankind". We do, however, deal daily with many persons falling outside the very special class mentioned. And nowadays, of course, we are apt to deal with persons falling well outside even the class of those enjoying sameness of nationality, social class, color, or some few other sources of insubstantial unity. For our dealings with all such persons, we need some source of reliability of behavior. If we have no reason at all to assume that we won't be knifed in the back the moment we turn it, there is simply no question of "dealings" with others at all. What gives this point particular weight is that the problem isn't confined to cooperative dealings in the usual sense of the term; for it extends to *any* activities that might be adversely affected by the other party's actions, including those in which all that we require from him is that he leave us alone.

Such reflections enable us to see why pure, unadulterated ethical relativism is virtually a non-starter at the practical level. The resolution to allow every person to act in accordance with his own principles no matter what they are is one that can't long be entertained by any rational agent. Likewise the resolution to allow any member of a group, G, to act in accordance with G's principles *no matter what they are*, can only be entertained at all because we are fairly confident that either we won't have to worry about encountering any of the more refractory sorts (head-hunters, perhaps?), or that there won't in fact be any truly refractory sorts, sorts that make dealings with them quite impossible. In high theory, however, we must consider all possibilities, and we need not dream long to come up with tribal codes that would have that characteristic. And simply to throw up one's hands at the level of basic theory is to declare that in principle nothing could be done in such cases. But that's absurd. Obviously intransigence can and does happen, but why frame one's theory so as to guarantee it?[32]

That is why there must be (some) *general* rules, rules reaching to just any agents one might have to deal with, and covering the vast variety of particular dealings one might have with them. Such rules will, of course, also be "general" in the sense of rather thin and abstract, providing only the skeleton for further relations. Our specific dealings with our fellows, in all their diversity, call forth all sorts of understandings and arrangements, the particular substance of which we should not expect to be dictated by the basic rules of morality. And the reason there must be general *rules* is that rules are internalizable guides to intentional, deliberate conduct; and that is the kind of conduct we can possibly reach by the methods of persuasion, reasoning – in a word, words. Any activities lying quite beyond the reach of such methods are, by definition, beyond the reach of morality (except in the sense that the things *we* may do to cope with such activities may fall within its reach).

Now consider the project of getting proposed rules accepted by these others whom we have reason to want to reach. The proposed rules are to govern their behavior – that is why we propose them. But since they are rules, "governing" their behavior rather than blindly causing it, there has to be a basis in reason for their adoption of them. The basis has to be in *their* reason. It cannot simply be in one's own. A might be happy to have everyone adopt as his sole ultimate rule of conduct, "Everything for A!"; but if A is rational, he will quickly reflect that no other person in the universe has any real *reason* to adopt a rule of that form. Or perhaps we should say that each has a reason to adopt a rule of that *form*, but with a different content: "Everything for B!", responds B! A worldful of people propounding *such* "rules" is not a worldful of *rational* agents. The need for rules universalized at the agent level is not far to seek: there is simply no point in any agent's adopting rules if the costs of the rule are all borne by himself, the benefits all going to others.[33] There is no need to assume, in any very narrow sense, that the object of every voluntary action is some good of the agent. It is enough to note that agents have all sorts of purposes, all sorts of values, and that we have no a priori guarantee that these will be in harmony with the purposes of other agents. An agent assesses his actions in the light of his values, whatever they may be. If a proposed rule of action simply doesn't fit into this scheme, he will with reason reject it. Morality must, then, be "for the good of everyone alike", as Baier[34] puts it — understanding, of course, that 'for the good' means 'at least contrary to the evil' of all.

What is the nature of the 'must' in question? In particular, is it, as Kant held, "categorical"? Or is it, as Mrs. Foot argues,[35] hypothetical? ("Merely" hypothetical, as some would say.) It is easy enough to see why one would be tempted to claim that it is "categorical", that is, not ultimately grounded in the well-being of the agent at all. Morality is an internalized behavioral control system. It is internalized: ordinarily it has to be instilled by others, rather than growing naturally without social reinforcement. It is, then, contrary, as Kant says, to inclination. That is essential to it: were our inclinations naturally in utter harmony, there would be no need for morality, and no recognizable morality. But inclinations can, as we all know from having once been children and, most of us, are still re-reminded daily, be overruled in one's own interest. But what about the overruling of one's most strongly held life-values? Can morality reach to that? Could a morality that was not consistent with what is deepest and most passionately desired have any power over us?

The answer to this question can be held to be a matter of definition: No. If, that is to say, one's deepest goals and so forth are inconsistent with morality, then of course *they* will move the subject to action, and not morality. But this, as I say, is a matter of definition: those goals and values are 'deepest', by definition, simply by virtue of having more power over the soul than anything else, and so if morality is inconsistent with them, then morality will lose. And it is surely evident that in many cases, morality, unhappily, *does* lose. But in a great many others, it wins. There is no necessity about this, one way or the other, at the level of metapsychology. Where necessity comes into it is in the framing of the moral project. Rational agents issue restrictions on behavior that all must have good reason to acknowledge, and these restrictions are meant to restrict. There is no room for the idea that just because your "projects" (as Bernard Williams calls them)[36] mean so very much to you, you therefore get to go about, for example, killing people in the course of getting them accomplished. Roughly, the point is this: there is no reason why the rest of us should let you do this, and you know that perfectly well — don't you?

But suppose you don't? Then what? The formula for ethics we are currently contemplating, after all, goes something like this:

U15:   R is a sound moral rule only if all moral agents have good reason, in terms of their own values, to accept R.

Note that I have now dropped qualifiers of the 'for A' type from this formula. The reason, of course, is that they are superfluous: if there is good reason for *all* agents to adopt R, then there will be no difference between A's case and anyone else' on the score of R's acceptability. The snag we are considering now is the possibility that some person, undoubtedly an agent, might *not* have good reason in terms of *his* values to accept R, and this for any R one can name. What to do about this? How can we suppose that ethics is possible at all if it requires universalizability of roughly the above kind? It will not do to redefine the term 'moral agent', for example, so that some agents just don't count. But without some such maneuver, isn't the project doomed?

I think not. But we do need a maneuver. The maneuver I suggest is an interpretation of the State of Nature a la Hobbes. In that State, it will be recalled, all bets are off — indeed, no "bets" are ever made. There is, Hobbes says, neither justice nor injustice because there are no rules. What Hobbes says about this, it seems to me, is in essence correct; but we must be careful. The question is not one of historical fact, of course. Is it, perhaps, one of psychology? I think not. It is rather one of what we may call practical logic. We are contemplating the possibility of an agent, A, with a value, V, such that other agents could not, in terms of their values, allow the pursuit of V. The question is: what does A want of us? Is he trying to insist that the pressing and transcendent importance of V is such that the rest of us ought to allow him to get on with it, even though it is perceived by us (and reasonably so perceived) to be utterly incompatible with our pursuits of our differing values? Is that his argument? Well, is it *an* argument?

Here we have, I believe, the essence of the State of Nature. If we construe A's case *as* an argument, then it is, like any practical argument, an effort to convince us to do something, in this case to refrain from preventing A from doing something. But it is an argument with an *a priori* guarantee of failure, under the circumstances. Each person reasons in terms of values he accepts. Should others press new ones upon him, the agent may be persuaded of them, or he may not. In the present case, one of the premises is that he is not. If that is so, then our hypothetical plaintiff A simply has no case. He is asking for the rest of us to permit him a course of action which is, by hypothesis, in terms of our values impermissible. A, we suppose, *knows* this. Need we say more? We need not. Those who "argue" as we are supposing have no argument; they may as well forget it. But the consequences of "forgetting it", note, are that there are *no* rules as between us and A, and we may therefore treat A as we please. The 'may' and the 'therefore' are the nub of it. Should we treat A very badly, in his terms, what *complaint* can he have? What complaint, that is, that we have any reason to accept?

We shall therefore make the following slight modification:

U16:   *R* is an acceptable moral rule only if there is sufficient reason, in terms of their own values, for all moral agents *who have reason to decline the ruleless state* to accept *R*.

Is this actually "slight"? For after all, it explicitly recognizes the possibility that some rational agents may not accept morality. But though this is true, I think that it really *is* slight. First, because the number who would choose to stay in a "state of nature" must be extremely tiny, once they realize what's involved. And second, we may make another dialectical maneuver of use here by declaring that "Anything goes in the State of Nature" is itself a Moral Rule. Thus Hobbes spoke of the "Right of Nature", and claimed that this, in the circumstances of the State of Nature, gave everyone a right to everything, "even one another's bodies".[37] But obviously this is no "right" in any interesting sense of the term: for it gives the "rightholder" no protection — indeed, it denies him any and every protection. Except one: there can be no complaint of treatment at the hands of fellow members of the State of Nature. From such complaint, we are logically "protected" — much good may it do us!

Why should we suppose that virtually no one will choose to remain outside the pale of morality? The answer to this is that nobody is invulnerable to the possible depredations of his fellows, and virtually no conceivable plan of life, as well as absolutely no recognizable plan of life, is immune to the effects of such depredations. Given the Hobbesian state of nature as the sole alternative, we can be certain that no human we shall ever have occasion to come across would *rationally* choose the rule-free condition, even though we adopt no prescriptive notion of rational behavior. In terms of his own values, whatever they may be in the actual world we know about, any agent will do better to accept some rules.

It is misleading, actually, to speak of "the" State of Nature. For if by this we mean the state of rulelessness, then it is reasonable to think of that as a contextual matter: in many situations we exist without rules for that situation, and sometimes find the rule-free state preferable. Even when there would seem to be something to gain for all concerned by having rules, the sheer making and administering of them might be too much trouble to bother. However, those rules that crop up on codes of morality are the ones that govern very basic and pervasive aspects of life. It is rulefreeness on even the most elementary levels, regarding such things as life and death themselves, that we have in mind when we talk of "The" State of Nature; and if other states of nature are only inconvenient or somewhat disadvantageous, the state of nature on the fundamental level contemplated by Hobbes and by us above is reasonably argued to be as intolerable as Hobbes said it was.

Finally, a note about "accepting". The level of acceptance at which we can count on the rational agent's participation in morality is that of lip service: the agent will verbally support R, appraise the behavior of others in terms of R, and when readily possible assist in inculcating R into the souls of the impressionable.[38] But can we also count on the rational agent's actual *compliance* with R? Would it were so! But alas, we cannot be sure, except in the case of special persons we know and trust. As for the rest, we of course can expect; we can insist; and ordinarily we will have good reason to be quite confident of at least decent performance. In terms of almost any reputable coinage in the world of values, morality pays, in both the long and the fairly short run. It cannot be shown to pay in the shortest run, for that is precisely the run in which it almost certainly will not. Nor, I think, can we genuinely demonstrate, to all and sundry, that it must pay that individual person in the long run. If everyone does his bit, everyone will come out a great deal better off than if nobody does, and will usually come out better off than he would if even only a healthy majority do theirs. But it remains between the individual and his own soul whether a lifelong commitment in action to those rules which can be seen to be for the good of all if all comply will afford the best life for him. All we can do is hope so, and encourage people to think so, especially by doing our own parts well.[39] But any stronger result than this must fall outside the realm of sheer reason; indeed, it must run a danger of losing grip on the facts.

14. CONCLUSION

This survey of universalizability principles and ideas has, in part, been intended to bring home the fact that there is not just one concept of it, nor even just a few. Several are compatible with each other, and indeed in the course of the above discussion I have urged acceptance of several of the theses considered. But I have argued that a definite point of view about the nature of morality and its foundations, a point of view incorporated, in essence, in the final formula, accounts for what is acceptable in the ones I have proposed that we should accept, and also explains the unsatisfactoriness of some, including the classic version of the Golden Rule, on the other. It is a point of view inherent in all substantial universalizability theses that the principles of morality emerge from within, in particular from within the soul of the moral agent. It is necessary that they do so, for moral agents are voluntary beings who act in the light of their ideas; there is no "external" source of morality. And it is necessary that we have moral rules, for we live in a world in which we encounter our fellows, and especially those of our fellows whom we do not personally know. Thus I have formulated the various universalizability formulae as tests on the acceptability of proposed moral rules, proposals for the status of universal self-enforceable canon of behavior. This general conception will serve, I believe, as a basis for generating moral rules; but of course I have said very little about the likely content of the set of rules that would be thus generated. Many philosophers currently are working on that in one way or another, and if the arguments of this paper are sound, perhaps we may say that all moral philosophers, indeed everyone concerned to reflect on and attempt to reshape the rules by which we live, is doing so. Or is, if done wisely.

Department of Philosophy
University of Waterloo, Canada

NOTES

[1] Peter Singer, "The Triviality of the Debate Over 'Is-Ought' and the Definition of 'Moral' ", *American Philosophical Quarterly*, January 1973 gives some reasons for this with which I sympathize.

[2] Even Charles Stevenson accepted this, I believe. See his *Facts and Values* (Yale, 1963), Essay 11, Sect. 8 (pp. 214 ff.).

[3] For the reason given in the succeeding sentence, and to avoid being pedantic, I will not in general footnote my sometimes high-handed statements about Kant. The main source, of course, is his *Foundations of the Metaphysics of Morals*, but one can learn considerably about his understanding of the Imperative from his other major writings on moral philosophy as well.

[4] See in this connection Onora O'Neill (formerly Nell), *Acting on Principle* (New York: Columbia University Press, 1975), pp. 70–71 especially.

[5] I am not sure who invented this term for this purpose, but the substance of it is discussed interestingly by G. E. Moore in "The Conception of Intrinsic Value", in his *Philosophical Studies* (London: Routledge & Kegan Paul, 1922), 259 ff. Hare discusses

it in many places, among them *The Language of Morals* (Oxford, 1952), pp. 80 ff. In his later writings, Hare uses the word 'universalizable' as a synonym for 'supervenient', e.g., *Freedom and Reason* (Oxford, 1963), p. 10, and his recent *Moral Thinking* (Oxford, 1981), p. 7, among many other places. It is interesting that Professor Hare seems to think that supervenience is a property which moral predicates *share* with "descriptive" ones (*Freedom and Reason*, p. 10); this on the ground that "If a person says that a thing is red, he is committed to the view that anything which was like it in the relevant respects would likewise be red" (*op. cit.*, p. 11). But that is not supervenience at all; it is merely generality. Any predicate logically applicable to more than one thing behaves like that. But with '*x* is red', the "relevant respect" in which another thing would, if like it, also be red, is simply redness itself − the *same* property, not a different one. What is interesting about value predicates in this regard is that they seem to be genuinely supervenient: two things which are *otherwise* identical cannot differ in value.

6 Here, of course, I follow Hare, see, e.g., Ch. 3, "Principles", in *Freedom and Reason*. Some have objected strenuously to this general line. For example, cf. John Hartland-Swann, *An Analysis of Morals* (London: Allen & Unwin, 1960), who objects to "The Dogma about Universalizability" (pp. 84−89), pointing out that it would be very difficult to specify any nontrivial principle that must be the back-up for such judgments as 'You ought to be kinder to your wife.' "But . . . the issuer of the injunction might not have been at all concerned with the general behaviour of husbands to wives, but only with the nature and circumstances of this particular wife and this particular husband" (88). Of course he may only have been concerned with that; but how does this show that he needs no significant principle here?

7 J. Rawls, *A Theory of Justice* (Harvard, 1971), p. 131.

8 H. Sidgwick, *Methods of Ethics*, 7th Edition (London: Macmillan, 1907, 1962), p. 379.

9 Here, I presume, I am differing from Hare, who holds that universalizability is a matter of "logic". But (as usual, perhaps) we come out at the same place in the end, for Hare agrees that one must justify using moral language at all, where 'moral language' has a very heavy burden on it, such as the analytic requirement that morality be non-tribal.

10 I take the term 'patients' for this purpose from David Gauthier ("Reason and Maximization", in *Canadian Journal of Philosophy*, **IV**.3 (March 1975), p. 424). Gauthier's work has been the major stimulus for my own work along such lines as those taken in this essay, as will be apparent to those who know it well. Alan Gewirth (*Reason and Morality*, Chicago, 1978) uses the term 'recipient'. Cf. pp. 129 ff, especially. 'Patient' seems a bit more neutral and general.

11 Perhaps the first source in print in which this factor is noted and made much of is David Lyons' *Forms and Limits of Utilitarianism* (Cornell, 1965).

12 Cf. Marcus Singer, *Generalization in Ethics* (New York: Alfred Knopf, 1961). His central argument, The Generalization Argument, has the form "If everyone were to do *x*, the consequences would be disastrous (or undesirable); therefore no one ought to do *x*" (p. 60) Despite several chapters devoted to ifs, ands, and buts, this remains the nub of it for Singer. Cf., among other sources, Narveson, *Morality and Utility* (Baltimore: John Hopkins Press, 1967), pp. 129−41 for one discussion of this.

13 One early source of this view is in Jonathan Harrison's "Utilitarianism, Universalization, and Our Duty to be Just", *Proceedings of the Aristotelian Society*, 53 (1952−3), pp. 105−34.

[14] This is roughly the view advocated in R. B. Brandt's "Toward a Credible Form of Utilitarianism", in H-N. Castaneda and G. Nakhnikian, *Morality and the Language of Conduct* (Detroit: Wayne University Press, 1963), pp. 107–44. The difference between U6 and U7 is discussed in Lyons (*op. cit.*, note 11).

[15] This approximates the view proposed in Brandt's later paper, "Some Merits of one Form of Rule Utilitarianism", *University of Colorado Studies in Philosophy*, No. 3, 1966. This and the paper cited in note 13 by Harrison are both to be found in S. Gorovitz's *Mill: Utilitarianism, Text and Critical Essays* (Indianapolis: Bobbs-Merrill, 1971).

[16] An interesting case in point is Sidgwick's discussion of whether a Utilitarian might not sometimes have the duty not to preach Utilitarianism; *Methods of Ethics*, pp. 489–90, e.g.

[17] Cf. R. L. Holmes, "On Pacifism", *Monist* 57, No. 4 (1973), pp. 489–506; and my own brief discussion in the chapter "Violence and War" (Sect. 14, pp. 122–24) in T. Regan, ed., *Matters of Life and Death* (New York: Random House, 1980).

[18] There has been much literature on this matter. J. O. Urmson's "Saints and Heroes", in A. I. Melden, *Essays in Moral Philosophy* (Seattle: University of Washington Press), pp. 198–216, started a good deal of it. It motivated the treatment in my *Morality and Utility* (*op. cit.*, note 12); the matter is discussed more closely still in "Aesthetics, Charity, Utility and Distributive Justice", *Monist*, 56, No. 4 (1972); and the essays by myself, Lyons, Harrison, Copp, and especially Sumner in the *Canadian Journal of Philosophy* Suppl. V (1979), *New Essays on John Stuart Mill and Utilitarianism* are also very pertinent here.

[19] Rawls, *Theory of Justice* (*op. cit.*), Sects. 25, 29, 76 especially.

[20] The discussion of prescriptivism and moral weakness, backsliding, etc., in R. M. Hare's *Freedom and Reason*, Chs. 4 and 5, seems to me plausible in this connection. The sense in which I claim that U9 is true by definition is, however, not the same as Hare's. He thinks universalizability part of the meaning of 'ought' in general, and that this is an important truth about it. My own definition of 'morality' is, as I say, partly stipulative.

[21] Hare has taken overridingness also to be part of the notion of 'moral', a position reconfirmed in his new book, *Moral Thinking* (Oxford, 1981); cf. pp. 55–61, e.g. But Hare, I think, understands overridingness in such a sense that it becomes difficult to see how a person could, logically, go against his own moral principles. My account (see Sect. 13) doesn't. Compare Baier here, in *The Moral Point of View* (Cornell, 1958), p. 309.

[22] Such accounts are to be found in Mill, *Utilitarianism*, Ch. V; following him are, for instance, myself (*Morality and Utility*, Ch. VI), David Richards (*A Theory of Reasons for Action*, Oxford, 1971, Ch. 7), and many others. Cf. again the sources mentioned in note 18.

[23] Hare, *The Language of Morals* (Oxford, 1952), pp. 68–69.

[24] *Freedom and Reason* (Oxford, 1963) p. 126.

[25] *A Theory of the Good and the Right* (Oxford, 1979).

[26] It seemed clear to me that Hare was going in this direction at the end of the 1960's; the tendency is fully confirmed in *Moral Thinking*: cf. Ch. 7.

[27] An important discussion, distinguishing three concepts of universalizability, is to be found in Robert Fullinwider, "Fanaticism and Hare's Moral Theory", *Ethics*, January 1977 (87, 2), especially p. 166. See also my further discussion of Fullinwider and Hare

in "Liberalism, Utilitarianism, and Fanaticism: R. M. Hare Defended", *Ethics* April 1978 (88.3), pp. 250–259.

[28] Hastings Rashdall, *The Theory of Good and Evil* (Oxford: Clarendon Press, 1907) especially Ch. VII. G. E. Moore, *Principia Ethics* (Cambridge, 1903) Chs. 1 and 5 especially.

[29] *Morality and Utility*, Ch. 3.

[30] *Methods of Ethics*, Bk. I, Ch. IX, Sect. 3 especially (7th Edition, pp. 106–109).

[31] This is, I think, the nub of the objection to utilitarianism urged by Bernard Williams; cf. his part of *Utilitarianism: For and Against* (Cambridge, 1973), esp. Ch. 5, "Integrity". It is the nub of most other theorists' theoretical objections to it as well, including myself in recent years.

[32] This is a consequence which any form of moral relativism, if thoroughgoing, must have. I include, for instance, such supposedly sophisticated brands as that of Gilbert Harman ("Moral Relativism Defended", *Philosophical Review*, January 1975). Harman appeals to an "implicit agreement": but is the idea that we ought, all of us, to keep such agreements? Presumably. And if not, where are we?

[33] Thus defenders of egoism must either look very absurd or must identify a different segment of practical theory as the domain of their accounts. For example, Jesse Kalin ("Ethical Egoism as a Moral Theory", *Canadian Journal of Philosophy*, 5, No. 3, November 1975) makes a distinction between 'ethical' and 'moral', where 'moral' carries with it connotations of interpersonal application (as in my usage above) and of acting for the general interest (which my usage does not include as a matter of logic, though materially it will, in a general sense, end up that way). Then Kalin's argument is that ethical reasons are superior to moral ones. But superior for what? Presumably for individual decision-making; but for that it is true by definition, as I suggest a little later in this paper. If offered as a social canon, however, it is practically a non-starter.

[34] *Moral Point of View* (1958), Ch. 8, Sect. 4, pp. 200–203.

[35] "Morality as a System of Hypothetical Imperatives", *Philosophical Review*, 81, No. 3, July 1972.

[36] Williams, *loc. cit.*, note 31.

[37] *Leviathan*, Ch. XIV. David Gauthier, in *The Logic of Leviathan* (Oxford, 1969), insists that the right of nature is "merely permissive" and that it "entails no correlative duties". In a sense, I accept this: for if everyone has a right to do anything, then he has a right to do what a correlative duty might have been a duty to avoid, whatever it might be. But that is in regard to what we might call substantive actions. However, there *is* a correlative duty regarding *verbal* actions and *attitudes*: if everyone has the right to *do* anything, then we may not *blame* them for doing it, we cannot *complain* if they do it.

[38] Bernard Gert, in *The Moral Rules* (New York: Harper & Row, 1966, 1970), made this a chief point in the justification of moral rules. I have been much influenced by Gert's account here. Cf. P. 75 in particular.

[39] J. R. Lucas, reconstructing Plato, makes what I feel to be the right point about this: "There will be an inevitable dissonance between the line he [the unjust man] shoots to the world and the truth he hears in his own heart, and this will destroy the harmony of his soul." *On Justice* (Oxford, 1980), p. 260.

PART II

UNIVERSALIZABILITY AND ETHICAL CONSISTENCY

MARCUS G. SINGER

UNIVERSALIZABILITY AND THE
GENERALIZATION PRINCIPLE

Without generalization foreknowledge is impossible. The circumstances under which one
has worked will never reproduce themselves all at once. The observed action then will
never recur; the only thing that can be affirmed is that under analogous circumstances
an analogous action will be produced. In order to foresee, then, it is necessary to invoke
at least analogy, that is to say, already then to generalize.*

How does universalizability relate to what I have called generalization in
ethics? Is it just a matter of different terminology or is there a difference of
substance? On the present occasion I think it appropriate to say a few words
on this. What follows, however, will be about the generalization *principle* and
will not extend over the whole range of generalization in ethics. In particular
it will not deal with the generalization *argument*, nor will it be about the
generalization question, the generalization test, the generalization criterion,
or the generalization thesis (whatever these last things are).

The generalization principle, called in other uses the Principle of Justice,
states that what is right for one person is right for any similar person in
similar circumstances, and correspondingly for what is wrong, for what one
ought to do, for what one has a right to do, and so on through the whole
series of normative terms used in the evaluation or judgment of conduct. The
Generalization Argument is the argument pattern that, since the consequences
of everyone's doing some act would be undesirable, no one has the right (or
ought) to act in that way without a justification. The Generalization Question
is the question "What if everyone did that?", and the generalization test
is the test the generalization argument provides or is supposed to provide of
conduct. But "test" is a very misleading expression; it suggests something
like a litmus paper test of conduct, and there can be no such test of conduct.

The generalization question is a generalization, of sorts, of the Reversibility
Question, "What if someone were to do that to you?" The exact relations
between the reversibility question and the generalization question, like the
exact relations between the Golden Rule and the generalization principle,
pose an interesting question that has not yet been definitively answered,
and that must here be put off still further.[1]

Generalization in Ethics was first published in 1961,[2] and there has since
been considerable discussion of a number of the ideas contained in it and

47

Nelson Potter and Mark Timmons (eds.), Morality and Universality, 47–73.
© 1985 *by D. Reidel Publishing Company.*

related to it, especially of the closely related — if not identical — idea of Universalizability. Indeed, the discussion of the latter idea had already been going on for some years prior to that. Such ideas were in the philosophical air since at least 1952. The bulk of the discussion of course has tended to be about, not generalization in ethics, but universalizability. This has been in large part due to the writings and the influence of R. M. Hare, though there were other stimuli as well, and the bulk of the discussion has tended to center around Hare's numerous writings on the subject. Hence the term "universalizability" has tended to predominate. Nonetheless there are, as we shall see, some serious problems with it, both with the term and the elusive concept. At the same time, there has been considerable discussion of what has been called, following Lyons (though some prior writers, such as Harrod and Harrison, were also responsible for the identification),³ utilitarian generalization (or general utilitarianism). Utilitarian generalization, so-called, has thus by some writers come to be identified with the generalization argument. This has had some curious consequences. One of them is that no one has spoken of utilitarian universalizability (or universal utilitarianism). Another is that the Kantian Categorical Imperative, a principle of universalizability par excellence, so profoundly anti-utilitarian, can come to be thought of as akin to or as a form of utilitarianism. But I cannot in this place do more than notice this, and I plan to pay my respects to this notion elsewhere.

Now the generalization principle has been variously criticized as:

(a) trivial — utterly, absolutely, shatteringly, and otherwise;
(b) tautological — hence trivial;
(c) unusable, useless, idle — because of (a) or (b);
(d) not substantial, merely formal — hence (c) or (a) or (b);
(e) not a *moral* principle, but rather (i) a merely logical or (ii) a merely linguistic principle — hence having no moral implications, hence not substantial, useless, trivial;
(f) false;
(g) restricted, having exceptions.

Some of these charges, such as that it is trivial and is "bare tautology", and that it has no moral implications, were dealt with in GIE (pp. 18, 46). Others are new, if not in import then in formulation, and even the earlier ones have now been reargued in new ingenious ways. I take up some of these complaints in what follows. One I will admit here and now, though I will have to deal with it in another place, is that the Generalization Principle is restricted in the sense that it does not apply universally in all circumstances of life or on all occasions of action.[4] This is one reason, indeed, for speaking of it under the heading of *generalization* rather than that of *universalizability*, since "universal" suggests, though it does not entail, the absence of restrictions. But all the others are, in my considered and reconsidered judgment, false. In particular, I will consider again the claim that the generalization principle is merely formal and that it is not a moral principle but a merely logical or linguistic one and hence without moral import.

It is worth noting at the outset that I deliberately introduced the expression "the generalization principle" for a principle that has been present in the tradition for a long long time and has always been thought of as a moral principle, even if a formal and very abstract one. Sidgwick called it the principle of justice, for what he regarded as good reason (see *GIE*, pp. 5, 50, 343). I called it the "generalization" principle to emphasize its procedural and formal aspects and its relationship to other principles that it must go along with. But that a principle has procedural and formal aspects does not entail that it is merely formal, and in its substantial and moral aspect it is still the principle of justice — though even yet we may not have got it straight.

I. GENERALIZATION VS. UNIVERSALIZABILITY

As was just noticed, in recent writings — especially British, following Hare — the generalization principle, or something very much like it, has come to be called the principle of universalizability. And on more than one occasion Professor Hare has lectured me in print on the importance of distinguishing between "general" and "universal" and the consequent importance of speaking of universalization instead of generalization in ethics.[5] I agree that there is some distinction, do not think it marked in just the way Hare does, will here explain why.

Hare construes "general" as the opposite of "specific" and "universal" as the opposite of "singular"; and on the premise that "specific" and "singular" mean different things he concludes that "general" and "universal" must have different meanings. What is singular is that he thinks this illuminating. As he actually recognizes, universality and generality "are often enough used interchangeably" (*FR*, p. 39). It is true enough that "general" and "universal" are used in the way Hare demarcates, but they are also used in other ways and have other opposites. The term "particular", for instance, is a true antonym of both "general" and "universal". And a rule or principle can be general – indeed, a rule or principle *must* be general – and specific at the same time.

Hare points out also that generality is a matter of degree, while universality is not. This is true, but its import is hollow. For, this being true, it is generality that has more importance for our topic, generally. And the implication is off. The question is whether "generalization" or "universalizability" is more apt for our topic, and these points of difference between the terms "general" and "universal" do not decide the matter.

The term "general" – and so with generality – actually has many opposites, because it has many senses. "A is more general than B" can mean any one or more of the following:

 (i)   A is vaguer, or less definite, than B;
 (ii)   A is more abstract than B;
 (iii) A is more fundamental, more basic, than B;
 (iv)   A is more comprehensive, extends over a wider range of cases, than B (cf. vi);
 (v)   B is deducible from A, or can be derived from A;
 (vi)   A includes or implies B (cf. iv).

Correspondingly, generality can mean vagueness, abstractness, etc. Furthermore, (vii) "A is general" can mean that A is universal.

It is true that there are occasions on which "more general than" is used to mean "less specific than", but this is not the primary use of the term. And the opposite of "specific" is not necessarily "general"; "generic" would be closer to the mark. A specific generalization can be contrasted with a *broad* generalization; the latter is not necessarily more general; it is only less specific, less detailed.

Hare's contrast of "general" with "specific" suggests that he is thinking of "general" as meaning the same as "vague", and so indeed we find him so speaking. Thus he says, in his first foray on this subject, that:

it is . . . impossible to propound . . . principles which have both a high degree of generality and a high degree of precision. We can speak generally if we are content to speak loosely and to admit the possibility of exceptions; but of matters which are complex and various we cannot be both general and precise" ("Universalizability", *PAS*, pp. 311–12).

But "general" does not mean the same as "vague"; though it may be admitted it is occasionally used as if it does, it is only confusion to confuse generality with vagueness. Hare's idea that *the* opposite of "general" is "specific", which in turn can be taken to mean "precise", may account for this misidentification. The point is that a generalization, or a general statement or principle, need not be vague or indefinite. And the following paraphrase makes just as much sense and is just as accurate as the original: "We can speak universally if we are content to speak loosely and to admit the possibility of exceptions; but of matters which are both complex and various we cannot [read: should not] be both universal and precise."

Hare observes that though a moral principle does not have to be "highly general or simple ... it has got to be universal" (*FR*, p. 47). Here he is confusing being *general* with being *highly general*. What is true is that a moral principle must be general; it may not be specific or particular, though it can be specific on some details; but it *does not have to be universal*. To put it another way, a moral principle or rule has not got to be highly or greatly universal or extend universally to absolutely everyone irrespective of circumstances or conditions, but it has got to be general, in the sense that it is not a particular judgment, a judgment about a particular or specific action, event, situation, or person.

Hare thinks that "the difference between the two pairs of terms" (generality and specificity; universality and singularity) can be put "quite simply by means of examples". Thus:

The moral principle 'One ought never to make false statements' is highly general; the moral principle 'One ought never to make false statements to one's wife' is much more specific. But both are universal; the second one forbids *anyone* who is married to make false statements to his wife. It should be clear from these explanations that the thesis of universalizability does not require moral judgements on the basis of highly general moral principles of the copy-book-heading type (*FR*, p. 40).

This last statement is unexceptionable. It is quite true that a moral judgment need not be made through the conscious and explicit application of some general rule or principle, and if this were all the disagreement between us were about it could end here, could have ended long ago. But it is not. The term "general" need not be restricted to copy-book examples of the type Hare is trying to exemplify. For the second principle, as Hare calls it, is *not universal*, because it applies only to males, not to females, only to men, not to women. Hare says that "it forbids *anyone* who is married to make false statements to his wife", which suggests, since only males can have wives, that only males can be married. So the second "principle" (call it *W*) is not as universal as the first (call it *F*). *F* applies to *everyone* without exception (at least to everyone who is a moral agent, which does, it is true, imply some exceptions). But W does not have this range of application; it applies only to males, and indeed only to married males. In not extending to females, nor to unmarried males, it is not universal. Consider now "One ought never to make false statements to one's husband" (call it H). H is presumably the other side of this matter. Is H implied by F? Without knowing the reason for the restriction W places on F, we cannot tell. If one in asserting F meant to include both W and H, then why not put it this way: "One ought never to make false statements to one's spouse – or, husband or wife, as the case may be"? (Call this S.) Now S follows from F, as do W and H alike. But what is the reason for asserting S – or W or H – *independently*? Its independent assertion suggests (though it does not entail) that it is all right to make false statements to other people, not one's spouse – to someone else's spouse, for instance, or to anyone who is unmarried. To the degree that the suggestion is misleading so is the original example. In any case it thus seems false that universality is never a matter of degree, and it would seem closer to the truth to say that it is hardly ever a matter of degree.

I conclude from this brief survey that Hare's repetitious insistence on just the distinction between generality and universality that he feels inclined to emphasize is not compelling and provides no good and certainly no conclusive reason for preferring the term "universalizability" to the term "generalization" in ethics. Now let us look at the matter more independently.

I first used the term "generalization" and spoke of generalization, – not universalizability – in ethics, not because I was somehow confusing generality with universality – and their alleged opposites, the specific with the singular – but for quite different reasons entirely, and yet for reasons. It was in fact largely by analogy with generalization in mathematics and logic and the process of generalization in language. "Universalize" is a term of art, hence artificial, and it struck me as a singularly inappropriate term for a process that is more akin to abstraction, as generalization is. Furthermore, in ethics universality is almost always restricted; hence "generality" is better than "universality", since, notice, it makes perfectly good sense to say "it holds generally but not universally". This is one perfectly proper, ordinary, and legitimate contrast between generality and universality, and this is thus more the concept wanted.

The analogies with the process of generalization in mathematics seemed – and are – so great and so illuminating as to make the term "generalization", and its cognates "generalize" and "generalizable", irresistible. And so is the analogy provided in the passage from Poincaré used above as a motto. "Universalizability", on the contrary, is a term only philosophers would use. It was in use of course well before 1952, but it was used solely in reference to Kant's moral philosophy and its basic principle. Of the many references that could be given, I give just one, to G. C. Field's *Moral Theory* (1921),[6] where we find reference to "the possibility of being universalized" (p. 25), "seeing whether they can be universalized or not" (p. 35), "actions . . . which could not possibly be universalized" and "attempts to universalize" (p. 38; see also pp. 43, 82), but solely in reference to Kant's first moral principle (as Field himself called it in a later essay), commonly called the principle of universality. It is common currency that Kant's first moral principle, his first formulation of the Categorical Imperative, puts forward a test of universalization and it is but a short step from that to "universalizable" and "universalizability". Even writers and critics who got the principle and the test all wrong − as, in my judgment, G. C. Field did, and that in no unique or original albeit in an interesting way − were right to speak of it under the heading of universalizability.

But if this is the correct term for Kant's principle and test, only confusion can follow − and it has − from generalizing universalizability, as Hare and Hare-followers have done. Another reason I chose to speak of *generalization* was to distinguish the generalization principle (and argument) from the Kantian principle of universalizability. Only by keeping the terms distinct could the question even be stated of how generalization relates to the categorical imperative, the principle of universality. To have used the terminology of "universalization" at the outset would have begged these crucial questions − indeed, might have kept them from being raised.

Finally, generalization in ethics is not and need not be literally universalization. "Generalization" is hence a wider and therefore more general term, because universality is always − or almost always, at least where valid − restricted (cf. *GIE*, pp. 68ff.).

II. UNIVERSALIZABILITY IN KANT AND HARE

But there is no doubt that "universalizability" has caught on, as the standard term for the topic. That has the merit, however, of reserving "generalization in ethics" as a term for my own theory, instead of its being generalized to cover a variety of different though related ones, a fate that has overtaken "universalizability". Indeed, the latter term has been so promiscuously generalized as to cover a variety of only tenuously related matters.

Some of the problems of continuing to favor the term "universalizability" are brought home by contrasting the concepts in Kant's ethics and in Hare's.

Kant's ethics is the original home of the concept of universalizability. Not that Kant used the term himself. He did not. He did, to be sure, talk about universal law and the universal imperative of duty, and he made other and numerous references to universality. And he advanced a principle or criterion or test that has come to be called that of universalizability, albeit Kant himself did not actually use the term.

On Hare's view of the matter, the characteristic of universalizability "is common to all judgements which carry descriptive meaning" (*FR*, p. 10), "any singular descriptive judgement is universalizable" (*FR*, p. 12), and "this characteristic . . . is common to all judgements which carry descriptive meaning" (p. 10). Hence, on his view, "Any judgement which has descriptive meaning must be universalizable, because the descriptive meaning-rules which determine this meaning are universal rules" (p. 39). And, he adds later, "by calling a judgement universalizable I mean only that it logically commits the speaker to making a similar judgement about anything which is either like the subject of the original judgement or like it in the relevant respects" (p. 139).

Thus, for Hare, the thesis that any singular descriptive judgment is universalizable, and, indeed, that any descriptive judgment, singular or not, is universalizable, means that "it commits the speaker to the further proposition that anything exactly like the subject of the first judgement, or like it in the relevant respects, possesses the property attributed to it in the first judgement" (p. 12). And for Hare this thesis though "apparently trivial [is] at any rate unobjectionable". Let me merely note here for the discussion to come that on this last point I disagree: it is objectionable.

The example Hare chooses to illustrate this thesis is the statement, taken to be "a descriptive judgement", "This is red."

'This is red' entails 'Everything like this in the relevant respects is red' simply because to say that something is red while denying that some other thing which resembles it in the relevant respects is red is to misuse the word 'red' . . . (p. 11).

The example is objectionable, though, happily, illuminating. For the moment, however, let us observe only that, on the view being put forward, universalizability is common to descriptive and evaluative (including moral and aesthetic) judgments, and is not shared by imperatives, decisions, or desires (*FR*, pp. 36, 56, 71, 57). Thus, to repeat, on Hare's view any descriptive judgment is universalizable, and this "feature of value-judgements" which Hare calls "universalizability is simply that which they share with descriptive judgements; namely the fact that they both carry descriptive meaning"

(p. 15). Hare maintains that "descriptive judgments are universalizable in just the same way as . . . moral judgements are" (p. 16).

Now on Kant's theory it is a *maxim*, not a judgment and not a descriptive statement, that is either universalizable or not universalizable, and not every maxim is universalizable. A maxim is universalizable if and only if it can be willed, without self-contradiction, to be a universal law – that is to say, if and only if one could be willing, without inconsistency in the will, to have everyone adopt and act on that maxim. Some maxims are universalizable and some are not, and universalizability, in the sense defined – the only sense it has in Kant's ethics – is the test of the moral acceptability of a maxim of action, and consequently of conduct.

For Hare, universalizability – at the outset, at any rate – holds of all singular descriptive judgments, hence of all descriptive judgments, that is, of all judgments that have descriptive meaning, in virtue of their descriptive meaning, and hence of all moral, value, and aesthetic judgments. It is not a test of the moral acceptability of anything, either of a judgment or of conduct. If some judgment or statement is not universalizable, it is simply not a judgment (statement) of the prescribed class, or else the speaker is guilty of misusing some word. But if this guilt is not found, it is something else – a desire, a decision, or an order perhaps, but its moral status is not in the least affected.

From this brief comparison alone, it ought to be evident beyond doubt that universalizability in Kant and Hare are two entirely different concepts. This is so even though Hare eventually moves to a position of trying to use universalizability in a way much like Kant's. I think he has not perceived the difference. And it turns out that there is in his use of the concept both deep confusion and self-contradiction. Let us see how.

Hare says, curiously, that "in the strict sense, legal judgements are not" universalizable.

The reason why they are not is that a statement of law always contains an implicit reference to a particular jurisdiction; 'It is illegal to marry one's own sister' means, implicitly, 'It is illegal in (e.g.) England to marry one's own sister.' But 'England' is here a singular term, which prevents the whole proposition being universal; nor is it universalizable, in the sense of committing the speaker to the view that such a marriage would be illegal in any country that was otherwise like England . . . (*FR*, p. 36).

But, first, on the grounds that have been given for judging a judgment universalizable, legal judgments are as universalizable as any, for they too have descriptive meaning. The example given, for example, surely means that it is illegal for *anyone* in England, not just some singular, specific, or particular individual. Second, on the basis of what was said by Hare on the example "This is red," the judgment that "It is illegal in England to marry one's own sister" surely commits the speaker to holding that it would likewise be illegal to marry one's own sister in any country that is "like [England] in the relevant respects" (*Ibid.*, p. 11), or, in other words, in any country "just like England" (for any country that allowed marriage with one's sister would not be "just like England"); and if the process does not work here it does not in the case of simple so-called judgments such as "This is red."

Hare says, moreover, and he has said this several times, that

> when a singular term is governed by the word 'like' or its equivalent, it has the property of being turnable into a universal term by substituting for 'like this' a term which describes the respects in which the thing in question is being said to be like this. If no suitable word exists, it is always possible to invent one . . . (*FR*, p. 11).

But, aside from the fact that this sounds like a recipe for transforming every singular term into a universal one and thus obliterating the distinction altogether, on this basis the legal judgment, even if it refers to England by containing the singular term "England", is actually universal (or at least universalizable) in referring to any country like England in the relevant respect. Hence the contradiction.

Of course it is true that Hare says the legal judgment is not "universalizable in the sense of committing the speaker to the view that such a marriage would be illegal in any country that was *otherwise like England*" (*FR*, p. 36, italics added). And it is also true that containing such a legal prohibition is hardly a significant point of similarity between countries, as these things are ordinarily estimated. Hitler's Germany may well have contained a law forbidding marriage between siblings, yet this would not be any sane or sensible ground for concluding that Hitler's Germany was "just like England". Nonetheless, if it did contain such a law, it was just like England in "the relevant respect", that is, the respect specified.

Thus the confusion. The definition Hare gives of universalizability leads to triviality. His intuition for how the term should be used, if it is to be used significantly, leads him to move from his theoretical account of its basis — in descriptive meaning rules — to otherwise sensible judgments inconsistent with the original account.[7]

Let us pursue this point a little further. Hare insists that all 'ought'-judgments are universal (*FR*, pp. 35, 36), presumably because they have descriptive meaning. But he also insists that decisions, orders, desires, and interests are not universalizable (*FR*, pp. 56, 36, 71, 157). Yet these also have descriptive meaning, they contain words subject to "descriptive meaning-rules" (*FR*, p. 13). Hare says, sensibly, that "To want to have something does not commit the wanter to wanting other people, in the same circumstances, to have it" (*FR*, p. 156). But, on the hypothesis presented, it does commit the wanter to wanting anything exactly like it in the same circumstances. If "This is red" is universalizable then so is "This is wanted." And if one feels that there is something wrong here, that is because there is something wrong with *this* concept of universalizability.

It is a further feature of Hare's conception of universalizability that universalizability is a merely logical thesis. "Offences against the thesis of universalizability are logical, not moral," he says; they amount to "abusing the word 'ought' ".

But the logical offence . . . lies in the *conjunction* of two moral judgements, not in either one of them by itself. . . . And . . . no moral judgements or principle of substance follows from the thesis alone. . . . What the thesis does forbid us to do is make different moral judgements about actions which we admit to be exactly or relevantly similar. The thesis tells us that this is to make two logically inconsistent judgements (*FR*, 32–3).

It is true, and it is an important point, that Hare tries later to show that "the thesis . . . is capable of very powerful employment in moral argument when combined with other premises" (*Ibid.*, p. 35). Nonetheless, the idea that the "thesis" of universalizability is "not a substantial moral principle but a logical one" is a standing one in Hare's writings. And the force of this standing idea escapes me. If moral conclusions can be derived from the application of the principle of universalizability, then it has moral implications, hence is not merely logical. Furthermore, if the judgments in question are "logically inconsistent" (p. 33), not both can be true, valid, sound, correct – one must be true and the other false. So the thesis presupposes that moral judgments can have truth-value. And one who makes a complex judgment of the kind here stigmatized is not merely "abusing the word 'ought' "; such a one is making a (complex) moral judgment that is unsound, and to act on a judgment that one knows to be morally unsound is morally wrong.

Hare makes essentially the same point further on, in a way that is especially illuminating for our purposes. "It is part of the meanings of the moral words", he says, "that we are logically prohibited from making different moral judgements about two cases, when we cannot adduce any difference between the two cases which is the ground for the difference in moral judgements" (*FR*, p. 216). This is much closer to what I regard as the truth of the matter, except for the barbarism "logically prohibited". Surely a person is not *prevented* from making such judgments, by logic or anything else. To say that it is logically prohibited is only a disguised way of advancing a moral conclusion. Logic as such strictly speaking prohibits nothing. Yet if one has a view that this most fundamental of all principles of morality is itself actually empty of moral content, perhaps because one has been overcome by the thesis that no one proposition can be both a proposition of logic and of morality, one is likely to start distorting the language by speaking of "logically prohibited". What "logically prohibited" actually means here is that it is self-contradictory, so that even though one can make the judgments – in the sense of holding the opinions, issuing the pronouncements – only one of them can be correct, morally. And this is a principle of moral substance derived from a principle of logic.

III. INFERENTIAL JUDGMENTS AND IMPLICIT GENERALITY

What misleads Hare on this matter, I think, is his ignoring of the fact that 'ought'-judgments (so-called), and moral judgments generally, are inferential in character; they rest on and must rest on reasons, and apart from their reasons are not genuine moral judgments at all. Hare does allude to this phenomenon on occasion – as when he says "The relevant respects are those which formed the grounds of the original judgment" (pp. 139–40) – but it is clear that he does not grasp its significance. For it is his view, as we have seen, that all descriptive judgments are universalizable, on a basis that implies that all judgments (and, indeed, statements) containing descriptive terms are universalizable. And this leads, as we have also seen, not just to triviality but to absurdity. Far better to have stuck to his earlier insight in *The Language of Morals*, where he talked, not about universalizability, but about supervenience and "consequential properties" (*LM*, pp. 80–81, 145, 153). Redness or being red is not a supervenient, consequential (or toti-resultant) characteristic, but rather a paradigm of one that is not. Nothing is red because it is square, or round, or oblong, or flexible, or shapeless. What links with universalizability in any significant sense – instead of this over-generalized one that Hare is using – is rather this feature of supervenience, or of being a consequential characteristic.

Now in *Generalization* I developed an account of the matter – which I have since seen no reason to revise – on which moral judgments are "inferential" in character, and have the characteristic of implicit generality (pp.

37–46, 51 ff.). Such statements as "This is red" are not inferential, and are not implicitly or in any other way general; indeed, they are not even *judgments*. Where there is judgment there is inference. So the analogies I found most illuminating are with causal judgments, "because"-statements, and judgments of probability. The point is that a genuine moral judgment must rest on reasons and involves implicit reference to the reasons on which it is based (*GIE*, pp. 55–9). And I claimed that not all statements have this character (whether descriptive or not), and that in connection with moral judgments "the characteristic of implicit generality is far from trivial, owing to its connection with the procedures through which such judgments are substantiated" (*GIE*, p. 44). This feature is a characteristic not of all statements, but of those that require reasons to be intelligible and cannot be established apart from inference.

But rather than merely repeat here arguments already given there, I propose to look at the matter again in a slightly different light, by considering the doctrine of the Primacy of the Particular.

This has been expressed by a number of writers, but by none more emphatically than by E. F. Carritt, in *The Theory of Morals*,[8] where it is expressed in a number of places. For instance, in Ch. 13, on "Moral Rules", we find the following:

No number of moral rules will save us from exercising intuition; for a rule can only be general, but an act must be particular, so it will always be necessary to satisfy ourselves that an act comes under the rule, and for this no rule can be given. (p. 114) . . .

. . . upon the particular instance, in which . . . the validity of rules first and most clearly appears . . . the rules are abstracted from instances and have to be applied to instances . . . (p. 115).

. . . I rather think that I morally apprehend that I ought to do this act and then intellectually generalize rules (p. 116).

Consider the following statement (p. 106): ". . . They get called duties by an empirical generalization because generally, perhaps ninety-nine times out of a hundred, we have judged it our duty to keep our promise or to obey our parents or the law." The first example here is ill-chosen for the point it is meant to illustrate, for one may well ask whether, even if it is accepted that other rules are ascertained and generalized only from particulars, this could *even make sense* with respect to the rule to keep promises. Is it really possible to maintain that the rule that one ought to keep one's promises is a generalization from instances in which promises have been kept and in which promises have not been kept? How could one discover, through simple induction by enumeration of instances, that the promise has any moral relevance *without the prior belief or conviction that it does*? And is this not a matter of a rule?

Consider now the following sentence (p. 70), which we may take as neatly summing up the doctrine of the Primacy of the Particular:

> When we criticize a particular moral judgement as being inconsistent with a principle, it is ultimately with other particular judgements that our comparison must be made. For the principle may be an inaccurate generalization.

This sounds, to be sure, almost self-evident, and surely Carritt thought it was. But now compare it with its *inversion*:

> When we criticize a (general moral) principle as being inconsistent with a particular moral judgment, it is ultimately with other (general) principles that our comparison must be made. For the (particular) judgment may be an inaccurate particularization.

The truth seems to be rather that neither pole, neither the particular nor the general, is necessarily prior. Sometimes we have certainty at one end of the spectrum and not at the other, and other times the situation is reversed. I can be more certain that torture for the sake of torture is always wrong (general principle) than I can be that *in this case* that is what is going on, or that in this case what someone is doing is wrong. For in order to be certain of the latter I would need to be certain about certain facts that I may not be able to ascertain. On the other hand, there are instances in which I can be (more) certain that it is wrong to be cruel to *this child* – or that the way in which *this* person (parent, teacher, etc.) treated *this child* is wrong – than I can about many rules or generalizations about the treatment of children.

The general is already implicit in the particular, and the particular is actually already implicit in the general. For instance, I can be certain that the way in which *this* teacher treated *this* child is wrong *because* I am certain that the treatment is cruel *and* that *cruelty to children is wrong* – and this latter is general. Also, for the general principle even to be intelligible, I must be able to instantiate it – not find an actual case, but describe an instance – and the instance will necessarily be particular. But uncertainties about facts will more often trip up certainty in particularization (application to the particular) than in generalization. That *this* is an instance of *that* general principle can be doubted. It can also be doubted whether the principle *applies* to the particular. But it can also be doubted whether the particular *instantiates* the principle.

IV. THE GENERALIZATION PRINCIPLE AND THE PRINCIPLE OF GENERIC CONSISTENCY

We have now considered at some length — even though with still not the detail it requires — what has up to now been perhaps the most famous and certainly the most widely discussed moral philosophy of recent years to make explicit use of a principle of universalizability, that of R. M. Hare. A still more recent attempt to develop a principle like the generalization principle and to use some of the resources of generalization in ethics (or so I will argue) is that of Alan Gewirth, in a series of writings going back to 1964 and culminating in his *Reason and Morality*.[9] I turn now to consider the relationships between the generalization principle and Gewirth's principle of generic consistency: "Act in accord with the generic rights of your recipients as well as yourself"; in the light of what has gone before it should prove illuminating. (In what follows I follow Gewirth's own practice of referring to his principle by the abbreviation "PGC", and of using such other abbreviations as appear useful and obvious, even though the increasing encroaching of initialisation [as Gilbert Ryle dubbed it] strikes me as in general [though, obviously, not as universally] deplorable. If everyone engaged in the practice with the frequency exhibited by some . . . well, but let us move on.) I have in another place discussed Gewirth's principle in its own right, considering it as a candidate for the role of sole and supreme principle of morality;[10] I here restrict myself to considering solely its relations to the generalization principle and to universalizability.

Now in his argument for the PGC, Gewirth is beyond any doubt presupposing the generalization principle. The generalization principle plays an essential role in his deduction of the PGC, because it plays an essential role in what Gewirth calls "the transition from the prudential to the moral" (146) and because, as Gewirth observes, "the reason for which an agent claims his rights to freedom and well-being must be generalized to apply to other persons as well" (102). Yet Gewirth denies that in his deduction of the PGC any moral principles are appealed to, either as premises or as principles of inference, thinks it essential that his PGC be deduced from premises that are morally neutral (21, 15, 356–7). And this is essential, if not to what Gewirth has actually accomplished, at least to the way he thinks about it. For he insists that the PGC is the one supreme principle of morality and also that no moral questions are begged in its justification, and he seems to think that these requirements are absolutely necessary, a matter of definition and more. "Since," he says, "by definition, a supreme moral principle is an ultimate principle of practical justification, it cannot be justified by being derived from a superior practical principle, for there is none" (16). If the Supreme Moral Principle were justified by deduction from some other moral principle, he thinks, then by definition the latter would be the Supreme Moral Principle. Hence it seems to follow that the Supreme Principle of Morality cannot be deduced from any other moral or normative principle. Let us consider this.

The appropriate passage for examination is this:

Whatever the description under which or the sufficient reason for which it is claimed that a person has some right, the claimant must admit, on pain of contradiction, that this right also belongs to any other person to whom that description or sufficient reason applies. This necessity is an exemplification of the *formal principle of universalizability in its moral application*, which says that whatever is right for one person must be right for any similar person in similar circumstances. But this *formal moral principle*, in turn, derives from a more general *logical principle of universalizability*: if some predicate P belongs to some subject S because S has the property Q (where the 'because' is that of sufficient reason or condition), then P must also belong to all other subjects $S_1, S_2, \ldots,$ S_n that have Q. If one denies this implication in the case of some subject, such as S_1, that has Q, then one contradicts oneself. For in saying that P belongs to S because S has Q, one is saying that having Q is a sufficient condition of having P; but in denying this in the case of S_1, one is saying that having Q is not a sufficient condition of having P (105, italics added).

Before we go on, notice the following. Gewirth speaks of the "formal principle of universalizability in its moral application"; call this FPUMA, or simply PUMA. PUMA is a formal moral principle. It derives, he says, from "a more general *logical principle of universalizability*" — call this LPU. Now PUMA is the same as "the moral principle of universalizability" — call it MPU. Hence PUMA=MPU, and MPU (it is said) derives from LPU. (Indeed, this last must hold, for the Logical Principle of Universalizability (LPU) is a *generalization* of the Moral Principle of Universalizability (MPU) (=PUMA), and of whatever other similar principles of universalizability there might be, such as perhaps, "Whatever is prudent for one person must be prudent for any similar person in similar circumstances" — though I do not know that the latter has ever come in for discussion.)

Now Gewirth continues:

The principle of universalizability even in its moral application [PUMA] is not itself a *substantial normative moral principle*, not only because, depending on the criterion it uses for relevant similarities or for the property Q, it gives results that are morally quite diverse and even opposed to one another, but also because it simply explicates what is involved in the concept of 'because' as signifying a sufficient reason. Hence, in using the principle of universalizability to establish the supreme principle of morality I shall not be using a *substantial moral principle* (105, italics added).

This last claim is what we must examine.

How has it been shown that PUMA derives from LPU? It hasn't, so far, not completely. The deduction depends on the assumption that what is right for one person, A, is right for A in virtue of some other property that A has (or of the act in question); that, in other words, the predicate "right" (or rightness) is a supervenient characteristic or, as I have called it (see above and *GIE*, pp. 44–6), an inferential term, with the result that moral judgments are inferential judgments. Now this (as was argued in *GIE*, Ch. 3, Sec. 2, on "The Moral Relevance of the Generalization Principle") is not merely a fact of language or logic, which is morally neutral, but has moral implications. Hence it is not true that a moral principle has not been used to establish the PGC.

It is claimed that LPU "is given deontic or moral application by inter-preting the predicate P . . . as a deontic or moral predicate" (106). But (1) this is still inference, which is involved in all interpretation; and (2) it must be true of moral predicates that they fit this pattern; if it weren't the predicate *P* could not be so interpreted.

In any case, Gewirth claims PUMA "is not itself a substantial moral principle". Presumably this means that it is neither a substantial principle nor a moral principle, but in my judgment this is wrong on both counts.

The claim that it is not *substantial* is to a limited degree correct, in the sense that it is a procedural not a substantive principle; formal, therefore not "substantial" in the sense in which that implies substantive, or the opposite of "procedural". But a principle can be formal and still substantial, and formal without being *merely* formal. For "substantial" means not seem-ing or imaginary; real; true; not illusive or illusory; not unimportant or trivial but of real importance or value; and in all these senses it is false that the Generalization Principle is not a substantial principle.

But let it be agreed that the generalization principle is not a substantive but rather a formal principle. It is certainly abstract, and there is almost always a question about how it is to be applied. (Even though Gewirth then goes on to show us how it is to be applied in a substantial way.) Is it a *moral* principle?

First, it is not shown not to be by showing that it follows from the logical principle of universalizability (LPU). For (a) it can be argued — and has been — that what we have here is a principle that is at one and the same time a logical principle and a moral principle, that is, a principle of morality that is a truth of logic.[11] I take it for granted — and see no reason not to — that any principle that has moral relevance is a moral principle (and it is consistent with that classification for it to be at the same time a principle of some other kind). I have shown how it does have moral relevance in *GIE, loc. cit.*, and so, incidentally, has Gewirth by the marvelous use he has put it to. But also (b) Gewirth, in speaking of the principle *in its moral application*, is already implying and taking for granted that it has a moral application; since it has a moral application it has moral implications, and since it has moral implications it has moral relevance; it is, consequently, a moral principle.

Second, it is a moral principle on Gewirth's own two criteria for "moral" (*RM*, p. 1). For it both purports to "take precedence over all other modes of guiding" conduct — and *judgment*, and it is "categorically obligatory", not just hypothetically or prudentially; it is a requirement for action — and also for judgment reasoning and inference; it is addressed to every actual or prospective agent; and it relates to the interests of others besides the agent. This is almost tautological, for the generalization principle says that if some act *d* is right for A, then *d* is right for every similar person in similar circumstances. The requirements of the generalization principle "are categorically obligatory in that compliance with them is mandatory for the conduct [and I would add here: the thinking and judging] of every person to whom [it is] addressed regardless of whether he wants to accept them or their results . . ." (1).

But Gewirth says that "the logical criterion of avoiding self-contradiction takes precedence over all other justificatory criteria . . ." (194), which is in apparent conflict with the claim of the supremacy of morality (1). The conflict disappears, however, when we see that it is the same principle being appealed to, which (perhaps in different renderings) is both a principle of morality and a truth of logic. For a judgment that violates the generalization principle (=FPUMA=MPU) is a self-contradiction. Thus we must qualify Gewirth's remark that a moral requirement "may not be overridden by any nonmoral requirement" (1), for a moral requirement may be overridden by the requirement that one not contradict oneself, and if that is a nonmoral requirement Gewirth's dictum is false. But if not, and the no-contradiction requirement in its moral application is a moral requirement, then the dictum is preserved. Thus, if one interprets and considers the generalization principle as I had presented it, no such question — such as "Which is the most supreme?" — and no such conflict arises. And Gewirth, after all, is claiming of the PGC that it is both a moral and a logical requirement (pp. 183–7), analytic as well as substantial (pp. 171–4). Others may have trouble with such conjunctions, but not Gewirth. Hence there should, on Gewirth's premises, be no such problem with respect to the generalization principle.

Now I had maintained that the generalization principle is a fundamental essential and necessary principle of morality. But I did not maintain that it is *the supreme* principle of morality. For, though fundamental, it is not sufficient, and must be taken together with others. That is now further confirmed by Gewirth's taking it along with and as essential to the PGC.

In a passage of great importance, Gewirth says that "rationality is internal to morality, not external to it", for "moral judgments appeal to reasons and lay claim to justification", and he takes it that this shows that "morality is part of the whole vast area of rationality" (361). I think this is sound, and on this matter of course we are and have been in fundamental agreement — though I take it he would also agree that this statement is not true of just *anything* put forward as morality, or as *a* morality. But if rationality is internal to morality that is because the first principle of morality is also a first principle of rationality, and the principle I refer to here is the principle Gewirth refers to as the principle of universalizability and that I call the Generalization Principle. From this point of view, and given that PUMA (= GP) is essential to the establishment of the PGC, the former is more fundamental.

Consider how the generalization principle (or MPU=FPUMA) is established. It is established by the inferential character of moral terms, concepts, and judgments. They rest on and must rest on reasons. Gewirth takes note of this fact in a number of places. Thus:

A moral judgement is reflective: it does not consist merely in conforming . . . to some accepted practice; it also carries with it an implicit claim . . . that [one] has made it after due consideration . . . (14).

This may be a bit too strong, for it seems to entail that there is no such thing as a moral judgment not made after due consideration. Other statements of the point are a bit more moderate.

Every right-claim . . . is made . . . under a certain description or for a certain reason that is held to justify the claim . . . the person who upholds the right must at least have it implicitly in view as the justifying ground of his claim. Without such a reason, he would be making not a right-claim but only a peremptory demand akin to that voiced by a gunman (104). . . . If the agent does not even implicitly have and give a justificatory reason, then he makes not a right-claim but a peremptory demand (112).

Now this is both a descriptive *and* a normative claim, for it says that what claims to be a moral judgment is not really or genuinely a moral judgment if it does not rest on reasons — if it does not it is specious, counterfeit, spurious, fraudulent. As I argued in *GIE* (Ch. 3, pp. 55–6), if it does not, then it is merely a vehicle for expressing the speaker's emotions and desires. This is the same as the claim that moral judgments are supervenient. The point is supported beautifully in a brilliant essay by Sid Thomas which argues, in my judgment soundly, that the concept of correct (sound, valid, true) moral judgment is logically prior to that of moral judgment, that we cannot tell whether something is a moral judgment at all without it being possible to identify sound moral judgments. It is worth noting that Thomas argues this by analogy with something else he also shows, that the concept of *deductive argument* presupposes that of *valid deductive argument*. For, as Thomas says, "the idea of *claiming to be correct* is essential to the notion of *any* deductive argument, fallacious or non-fallacious".[12]

But Gewirth claims that "the moral principle of universalizability . . . violates the requirement of categoricalness for a supreme moral principle . . ." because it "allows complete variability with respect to content . . . in accordance with the variable inclinations or ideas of agents" (106). He adds that "the universalizability principle sets no limits on the criteria of relevant similarity or the sufficient reasons for having the right to perform various actions, so that agents . . . can tailor these criteria or reasons to suit their own variable desires or prejudices". There is some truth in this, but not much, and what there is is not harmful. The element of truth is that the Generalization Principle is a formal and procedural principle and is compatible with a number of different theories of what is right and the grounds of rightness (as well as with different theories of value). But the examples and claims put forward to support this claim of *complete* variability and arbitrariness do not work – and are all of the same sort refuted in *GIE*, Chs. 2 and 3. It is true that the reasons set forth there have been subject to a number of quibbles and misunderstandings that have not yet been set completely right (though Thomas's paper, which has generally been ignored, is a good beginning). That is a task that I have undertaken here, though only tangentially and in a partial way (and which I am reserving on a larger scale for my general reconsideration of the subject). I shall deal here with just one or two points of most importance.

Consider the idea that someone can "claim the right to inflict various harms on other persons on the ground that he possesses qualities that are had only by himself or by some group he favors; or, alternatively, on the ground that his recipient possesses qualities quite different from his own" (106). This shows nothing, for, first, the relevance of the specified qualities to the infliction of harm remains to be shown (note that this presupposes, what is morally obvious, that to do anything that would inflict harm on someone is to do something that needs justification), and second, since *everyone* "possesses qualities that are had only by himself", if anyone can claim a right to inflict harm on that "ground", everyone can claim (and would have) the same right on that same ground [by application of the generalization principle]. In particular that would-be agent's recipients would have the same right to inflict harm on the agent, and the agent would have no right to complain (on any ground that did not give everyone the same right to complain). Notice that it is essential to the original claim that it be an exceptional one and that the act one is claiming a right to do be an exception to a general rule. But as was pointed out several times (though the point seems to have been generally overlooked by captious critics), what is important is not the specific and specified details of one's particular situation but the principle on which the specification is made [*GIE*, pp. 23, 89]. It follows that such a claim cannot show how one case differs from another. Similarly for the idea that one "may claim that he has the rights in question because ... he is white or male or American or highly intelligent ... or because he is named Wordsworth Donisthorpe or because he was born on such and such a date at such and such a place ..." (107). If such specifications of details were taken as specifying a relevant difference between the claimant and others, then on the same general grounds everyone would always and in every situation be relevantly different from everyone else. The point is that the principle on which the alleged distinction is made does not and cannot distinguish one case from another. *Everyone* differs from others on such grounds and in such ways as these, and that is just why the supposed "grounds" given are not *relevant* and could not be relevant to justifying "inflicting harms" on others. If any such claim could show that anyone has such a right as is being claimed, then it could show that that person has the right to do whatever he or she pleases, and, indeed, that everyone whatever has the right to do whatever he or she pleases – and both these statements are self-contradictory. They are self-contradictory because they involve the claim to have a right, and it is essential to the notion of a right that there is a difference between having a right to do something and wanting to do it. Hence it is impossible for everyone – and anyone – to have the right to do whatever he wants. Gewirth has himself based a good deal of his argument on the fact that a claim to have a right must be based on a reason, and it is an implication of the generalization principle (recognizable when the principle is correctly understood) that it must be based on a *genuine* reason – one that is genuinely generalizable – and not spurious ones of the sort just examined. The generalization principle specifies what restrictions there are on what can count as, what can be, a genuine reason. Something to be a genuine reason must be distinct — genuinely distinct not spuriously distinct — from "only a peremptory demand akin to that voiced by a gunman" (104).

Gewirth in his example speaks of Wordsworth Donisthorpe where I spoke of John Jones, John Smith, Ignatz McGillicuddy, and Stan Spatz III. Surely no one can think that this makes any difference. And "the principle on which the distinction is made" is not in the least obscure. In this case, it is to claim to be an exception to some rule — to have rights that others don't have — on the ground that one's name is what it is.

In an essay on the Generalization Principle of 1964 (and in a series of later essays prior to his book) Gewirth made the above and other criticisms of what I had said about the principle, and some other things I said, in *Generalization.*[13] I am reserving my replies to these various and sundry claims for my general reconsideration, mentioned before, of generalization in ethics. I will here notice only some of these points that have carried over into his book, with no modification, as canonical. Thus, he says:

> It has been suggested . . . that which qualities of persons or acts are relevant to justice or to moral rightness is to be determined by the specific purposes of the positions, rules, or institutions for which the qualities are to be selected. The trouble with this suggestion is that the purposes in question may themselves be unjust or otherwise immoral, so that to distinguish between qualities of persons or acts on the basis of these purposes would promote injustice rather than justice (108).

The reference to the present writer is unmistakable, and if the point so stated had been so stated in the work referred to [*GIE*, pp. 20ff.] the critical point so quickly made would be correct. But as an interpretation of what was actually said in the place referred to this is gross error, and I regret the negligence (as it now turns out to be) on my part which has enabled Gewirth to go on asserting it in essay after essay even unto this book, without correction or contradiction or rebuttal.

For in the passages alluded to (*GIE*, pp. 25–8, 29–30), what was attempted and all that was attempted was an account of how the generalization principle explained how there could be legitimate reasons for excluding someone from a certain class (kind) of employment. There was no reference whatever to "specific purposes" (the general heading under which Gewirth is attempting to relegate and thus dispose of the view to which he is thus alluding) nor was there any reference to "rules or institutions". These latter are Gewirth's own emendations. An excluding reason would not be legitimate simply by being applied beyond the individual specified to a (so-called) "class" just like that one. And it will not do to bring in just any purposes selected arbitrarily and particularly by someone in de facto authority, which could then be tailored to suit that party's prejudices. The purposes alluded to are no more something arbitrary than the context in which they would operate. The purposes would have to be the purposes in the sense of the function of the general position – something presumably generally and publicly ascertainable and ascertainable independently of the predilections and prejudices of the boss at the time or the people the boss works for. Any further restrictions would then need justification. A restriction to whites – like a restriction to blacks, blues or greens – could be justified in some cases, but then the justification would have to be set out and could not rest solely on whim or prejudice – in accordance with the considerations and restrictions just outlined above.

The point being argued here is actually set out nicely by Gewirth himself:

The criterion of relevant similarities, which gives content to formal justice, is the same as the sufficient reason for which, or the description under which, a person is held to have a certain right. Hence, for other persons to fulfill this sufficient reason is for them to be similar to the first person in respect of having the descriptive characteristics that were held to justify his having the right (106).

This was one main lesson of generalization in ethics, and it is to me surprising that it has been so easily overlooked. But it was not the only one, and it obviously needs restating, in the light of the misapprehensions it has generated. I hope that these brief remarks, compact as they are, have at least suggested the reasons why the Generalization Principle is not a *mere* principle of "formal justice" or of "simple consistency" (Gewirth, pp. 164ff.), empty of content and available to be filled in by anyone's whim or fancy. On the contrary, when properly understood and interpreted the Generalization Principle illuminates the concept of a genuine moral reason and what can genuinely count as one and what cannot, and shows that it is not open to anyone to invoke its form in justification of what is unjustifiable.

And I hope additionally that it is now somewhat clearer than it was before why I continue to prefer to speak of the generalization principle rather than the principle or thesis of universalizability.

V. "WHATEVER ONE PLEASES"

We need to consider just a bit further the point made above (p. 67) that the idea that one (or everyone) could have the right to do whatever one pleases is self-contradictory. For it has been disputed and, quite clearly, misunderstood by some others, in particular H-N. Castañeda. We need to see why and how and what has gone wrong.

Castañeda quotes a passage from *Generalization* which he thinks betrays, characteristically, a deep "ambivalence on the universality of (relevant) reason". The passage runs this way:

> Nor can the attempt to justify oneself by reference to a "rule" that refers to oneself by name (and which of course would not be a general rule at all) work any better. If John Smith can say "Everyone whose name is John Smith has the right to act in such and such a way," Stan Spatz III can say "Everyone whose name is Stan Spatz III has the right to act in such and such a way," and everyone else can invoke a similar "rule".... It would follow that everyone else has the right to act in whatever way he pleases. Now this is not just false − it is self-contradictory.[14]

Castañeda's comment is that

> the issue is whether Stan Spatz III is appealing to exactly the *same* relevant reason that Smith is appealing to in his statement. The answer is "yes" and "no", depending on what Smith's reason is. On the one hand, if Smith's reason is that whoever has the property of having a name has a right to do, say, A, then Stan Spatz's statement appeals to the same reason. But if Smith's reason is that whoever has the property of being named "John Smith" has a right to do A, and this is what Singer construes him as saying [No, this is not so, though the point can easily be amended to cover the case − MGS], then Stan Spatz III is not appealing to the same reason ... [Castañeda, pp. 292−3].

But this is not so. If *this* is what John Smith is appealing to, some general rule or principle that "everyone who has the name 'John Smith' has the right to do *A*" (and it is worth adding that if such a "rule" holds at all it would hold whatever *A* is), then John Smith has the obligation to explain how being named "John Smith" and not something else has any relevance to, can provide any ground for, doing the thing John Smith wants to do. I took it for granted in the passage quoted (and proceeded to explain it a bit further down the page) that merely having a certain name, whether John Smith or Stan Spatz III, or even Sam Sesame or Nincompoop Gewangaheela (indeed, even the name "Whatsisname", which for all I know someone might have − people are referred to often enough by it), is by and large and in general and by a nearly though not quite conclusive presumption altogether irrelevant to and incapable of grounding a claim to have a right. It could have such relevance, but only in the most extraordinary circumstances, and even there only when the circumstances form part of a well-understood class of such circumstances. (If John Smith is named as legatee in a will, then John Smith has the right to inherit and to such rights as that imports under that specific will, provided he is the right John Smith – the one named and intended by the testator. Here just having a certain name is certainly relevant, but it is just as certainly not enough, because, obviously, someone else could have the same name. And in this sort of case, what is intended is not anyone named John Smith, but one specific person with that name. In the case of the alleged "rule" about anyone named John Smith, John Smith, or anyone who claims the "right" under the "rule", must recognize that it would apply to *anyone* named John Smith.)

Now in the paragraph just after the one Castañeda has chosen to illuminate with his comments it was said, further, that:

The fact that one has a certain name or is a certain person may be relevant to the claim that one has the right to do something or is an exception to some rule. But the point is that one has to show how it is relevant. To do this is to show how one is genuinely different from others in the situation in question. It is to show that one is an exception on the basis of considerations that would not show everyone to be an exception. Though not everyone has the same name, everyone has some name, or can easily assume one. Thus it is not sufficient merely to specify the respects in which one differs from everyone else. For everyone else can do the same. What is important is the principle on which the circumstances are specified. . . . In practice this principle is not really so difficult to discover. . . . In [the case in question] the principle is the specification of one's name . . . (*GIE*, pp. 23–4).

So much for Castañeda's flat assertion that "what Singer construes [Smith] " as asserting is that "whoever has the property of being named 'John Smith' has a right to do *A*". Even if this assertion were not obviously absurd on the face of it, it could have been confuted simply by reading a little bit past page 23.

Castañeda picks up where I left him before by asking how "Singer [can] rule out Smith's reason", and suggesting that it can be done

Only by a principle analogous to Hare's thesis of universality, i.e., by barring proper names and other singular-referring expressions from the description of the circumstances which are regarded as relevant reasons. But the philosophically important thing to understand is that this requirement is simply an additional requirement over and above the other requirements constituting the meaning of 'reason'. . . .

Again no, not so. For reasons suggested above, I do not think the purely syntactical move by Hare (following Gellner [15]) works at all, and so I do not accept any such principle of universality as the one specified. Sometimes particulars are relevant and sufficient. What Castañeda has overlooked throughout is the (constant) reference to "the principle" on which the specification is made, on which the particular details are specified. If the principle is one that would give everyone the right — or simply to the effect that everyone has the right — to do what he pleases, then it is ruled out, not by some merely stipulated definition of "reason", as Castañeda suggests, but by the nature of a reason.

Castañeda goes on to claim that

"Everybody has the right to do as he pleases" is not self-contradictory. It may even be true: In a world in which everybody wishes to do what and only what he ought morally to do, or what he ought to do and what is consistent with it, everything a person of that world wishes to do is morally right (Castañeda, p. 293).

But this is false, flatly false, though I am glad the objection has been raised so that it can be squarely met. In such a world as Castañeda imagines he is imagining there could be no concept of having a right; and in any case *this* world is not that world. In this world we come to understand what having a right is by contrast with what one wants or wishes or even thinks would be in one's own interest. Hence Castañeda's point is quite irrelevant. And so, quite evidently, is the semantic mechanism of "possible worlds" in understanding moral discourse, moral thinking, and moral reasoning.

I must say that I appreciate Castañeda's appreciation of the book he was discussing and his kind words about its importance. He thinks the discussion he discusses is deep. I never thought it was deep, only obvious. It was, apparently, too deep, and not obvious.

Department of Philosophy
University of Wisconsin, Madison

NOTES

* Henri Poincare, *Science and Hypothesis* (1902), Ch. 9, in *The Foundations of Science* (Lancaster, Pa.: The Science Press, 1913), p. 128.

[1] There are some acute observations on the relations between the generalization principle and the Golden Rule, and on some confused things I had previously said about them, by M. J. Scott-Taggart, in "Recent Work on the Philosophy of Kant", *American Philosophical Quarterly,* 3 (July 1966), 171–209 at 198–200. The term "reversibility" was, I believe, first used by Kurt Baier, in *The Moral Point of View* (Ithaca: Cornell University Press, 1958), pp. 202–3. Baier's principle of reversibility was commented on by the present writer in "The Golden Rule", *Philosophy,* **XXXVIII**, (October 1963), 306–8.

[2] *Generalization in Ethics* (New York: Alfred A. Knopf, 1961); abbreviated henceforth as *GIE*.

[3] David Lyons, *Forms and Limits of Utilitarianism* (Oxford: Clarendon Press, 1965);

R. F. Harrod, "Utilitarianism Revised", *Mind,* **XLV** (April 1936), 137–56; J. Harrison, "Utilitarianism, Universalisation, and Our Duty to be Just", *Proceedings of the Aristotelian Society* (henceforth *PAS*), LIII (1952–53), pp. 105–34 (Cf. *GIE*, p. 346).

4 This has been well argued by Neil Dorman, *Generalization in Ethics* (1967), pp. 33ff., unpublished Ph.D. thesis on deposit at the University of Wisconsin Memorial Library, Madison; by John Atwell in "A Note on Decisions, Judgments, and Universalizability", *Ethics,* 77 (January 1967), 130–4; and by Norman Gillespie, "On Treating Like Cases Differently", *The Philosophical Quarterly,* 25 (April 1975), 151–8; also in an unpublished paper by Gillespie entitled "Exceptions to Universalizability", which has been circulated in several different versions – it is to be hoped that Gillespie will before too much longer settle on some one version or other so that it can be actually published and hence cited in a useful sense.

5 The works by Hare in which he has dealt with this matter are, chronologically: (1) "Universalisability", *PAS,* **LV** (1954–55), 295–312; (2) "Review of *Generalization in Ethics*," in *Philosophical Quarterly,* 12 (October 1962), pp. 351–6; (3) *Freedom and Reason* [abbreviated *FR*] (Oxford: Clarendon Press, 1963); (4) "Principles", *PAS,* **LXXIII** (1972–73), 1–18. (This last contains the latest and most explicit lecture.) Hare's *Language of Morals* (Oxford: Clarendon Press, 1952) will be referred to as *LM*.

6 G. C. Field, *Moral Theory* (London: Methuen 1921). Field's later essay is "Kant's First Moral Principle", *Mind,* **XLI** (January 1932), where "universalization" is spoken of on p. 19.

7 Some of the points made in this section were made – though in a different way and for a different purpose – in a perceptive and acute review of Hare's *Freedom and Reason* by Joseph Margolis, in *The Journal of Value Inquiry,* 5 (Winter 1970), 57–64, which I did not come across until just recently. I am pleased to acknowledge the priority and to have the independent confirmation.

8 E. F. Carritt, *The Theory of Morals* (London: Oxford University Press, 1928), page numbers cited in parentheses in this section.

9 Alan Gewirth, *Reason and Morality* (Chicago: University of Chicago Press, 1978), cited in parentheses and abbreviated as *RM*. The word "culminating" may need qualifying; Gewirth has continued to write on and develop further his ideas on this topic, largely though not solely in response to the large volume of critical literature that has already appeared.

10 "Gewirth's Ethical Monism", in *Gewirth's Ethical Rationalism*, ed. Edward Regis Jr. (Chicago: University of Chicago Press, 1984).

11 GIE, pp. 46–51. See also Sid B. Thomas Jr., "The Status of the Generalization Principle", *American Philosophical Quarterly,* 5 (July 1968), 176–8, 179–80.

12 Thomas, *op. cit.* note 11, pp. 180–2, 181.

13 Alan Gewirth, "The Generalization Principle", *The Philosophical Review,* **LXXIII** (April 1964), 229–42.

14 Hector-Neri Castañeda, "Imperatives, Oughts, and Moral Oughts", *Australasian Journal of Philosophy,* 44 (December 1966), 292, quoting *GIE,* p. 23 (in part), with the omission of the italics added by Castañeda while omitting the same internal sentences omitted by Castañeda.

15 E. A. Gellner, "Ethics and Logic", *PAS, LV* (1954–55), 157–78 at p. 163; cf. Hare, "Universalisability", *ibid,* pp. 295–6, 306–8.

WLODZIMIERZ RABINOWICZ

THE UNIVERSALIZABILITY DILEMMA

According to the Universalizability Principle, similar objects exhibit similar moral characteristics. This claim may be thought to be either trivial or unclear, depending on whether we interpret similarity as indiscernibility (cf. Leibniz's thesis about the identity of indiscernibles) or as identity in morally relevant respects (the notion of relevance seems to be essentially opaque). In Rabinowicz (1979), Part III, I have argued that there is a simple way out of this dilemma: we can construct a version of the Universalizability Principle which does not make any reference to the notion of relevance but which nevertheless avoids getting trivialized by Leibniz's thesis. Here follows a short and, hopefully, somewhat improved formulation of the same argument. For some of the improvements I am indebted to Sten Lindström and Sten Kaijser.

1. PRESENTATION OF THE DILEMMA

Assume that $W = \{w, v, u, z, \ldots\}$ is the set of possible situations (possible worlds), and let D and C be dyadic relations on W. D might be thought to obey the so-called seriality condition: for every w in W, there is some v in W such that wDv. We take C to be an equivalence relation (reflexive, symmetric and transitive).

If wDv then we shall say that v is a *deontic alternative* to w. Intuitively, v is a deontic alternative to w iff all obligations obtaining in w are discharged in v. Given this reading, the seriality condition on D becomes a consistency constraint: if some possible situation constitutes a deontic alternative to w, then it follows that all the obligations that obtain in w can be simultaneously discharged. Admittedly, this consistency constraint seems to be rather controversial. Therefore, I want to leave it open whether we should accept it or not.

C stands for the relation of 'copyhood'. Situations related by C are exactly similar to each other. That is, they are identical in all their 'non-individual', 'qualitative' aspects. To put it differently, if w and v are copies, then the only possible differences between them are of 'individual', 'numerical' nature. Thus, the individuals involved in w may be numerically distinct from those appearing in v. Or, to take another possibility, v may result from w by a

75

'permutation' of individuals, by moving individuals around from one position to another. Providing that such a permutation will not disturb any 'qualitative' aspects of the situation, w and v will be copies. To illustrate: Suppose that individuals a and b are involved in w. Imagine a situation, v, in which a and b reverse their roles, but which otherwise does not differ from w. Thus, b's circumstances in v, his behaviour, character, preferences, beliefs, etc. are exactly like those of a in w. And a in v is exactly like b in w. Then we shall say that w and v are copies. Generally speaking, two situations are copies of each other if, and only if, every individual existing in one of them has an exactly similar counterpart in the other situation.

In Rabinowicz (1979), Chapter 1, I have argued that the exact-similarity variant of the Universalizability Principle ('exactly similar situations involve exactly similar obligations') may be expressed by the following condition on C and D (here, as elsewhere, I omit universal quantifiers whenever possible):

(u) $wCv \,\&\, wDu \longrightarrow \exists z(vDz \,\&\, uCz)$.

Informally: If v is a copy of w, then every deontic alternative to w has a copy among the deontic alternatives to v. Since C is a symmetric relation, (u) also implies that every deontic alternative to a copy of w has a copy among deontic alternatives to w.

According to the standard semantics for deontic operators ('it is obligatory that', 'it is permitted that'), the set of deontic alternatives to a given situation determines the 'obligation-structure' of that situation. Thus, let X be any state of affairs, or, what here amounts to the same, any proposition. We shall think of propositions/states of affairs as subsets of W. Thus, we shall identify a proposition X with the set of possible situations that instantiate X. X is said to be *obligatory* in w iff every deontic alternative to w instantiates X. (Correspondingly, the proposition that X is obligatory coincides with the set of situations w such that all deontic alternatives to w instantiate X.) And X is *permitted* in w iff some deontic alternative to w instantiates X. (The set of such w constitutes the proposition that X is permitted. For details see, for instance, Føllesdal and Hilpinen, 1971.) Thus, if every deontic alternative to w has a copy among the deontic alternatives to v and vice versa, then we might conclude that w and v exhibit similar obligation-structures. Therefore, one way of reading (u) would be to say that exactly similar situations exhibit exactly similar obligation-structures. In consequence, (u) seems to be a fairly adequate formulation of the exact-similarity variant of the Universalizability Principle.

The same principle, when formulated in terms of 'relevant similarity', amounts to the claim that, as long as we permute or replace individuals, but keep everything else in the situation if not exactly identical then at least relevantly identical from the moral point of view, then the obligation-structure will not undergo any relevant changes. In order to express this idea in our framework, we must switch from C to a weaker relation R. If wRv, then the individuals appearing in w may be distinct from those in v, and, in addition, w and v may differ in some non-individual ('qualitative') respects, but *only* so far as these differences are morally irrelevant. Thus, two worlds are R-related to each other iff they share all morally relevant non-individual characteristics. R is thought to be an equivalence relation, just like C. However, while C entails R, the entailment does not go the other way round: R-similar situations need not be copies.

Consider now the R-variant of (u):

(ur) wRv & $wDu \rightarrow \exists z(vDz$ & $uRz)$.

Clearly, the relation between (ur) and the relevant-similarity version of the Universalizability Principle mirrors the relation between (u) and the exact-similarity version of the Principle.

The Universalizability Principle, as we have presented it, relies on the notion of similarity. It refers either to exactly similar, indiscernible cases or to relevantly similar ones. Now, it seems undisputable that no two individuals are exactly alike. And perhaps there is nothing contingent about that. According to Leibniz, indiscernibilities always amount to identities. In our framework, this standpoint may be formulated as follows:

Leibnizianism. If wCv, then $w = v$.

Thus, according to Leibnizianism, C is an identity relation and, therefore, condition (u) is trivially satisfied.

It does not help if we replace exact similarity by the relevant one. Because now we encounter another difficulty: the concept of relevant similarity is notoriously unclear. What does it *mean* to say that some feature of a situation is morally relevant? Sometimes it is claimed that the universalizability dilemma arises because we lack a workable *criterion* of relevance. But it seems to me that the problem is more serious than that. It is not just that we lack clear applicability criteria for the concept of relevance. What is missing in the first place is a satisfactory *definition* of the concept itself.

This dilemma can be avoided if we can find some non-standard formulation of the Universalizability Principle, a formulation which is *not* made trivial by Leibnizianism and which does *not* rely on the notion of relevance. We shall see below that such a formulation is, in fact, available but differs importantly from the usual versions of the Universalizability Principle. In particular, it does not rely on any notion of *similarity* at all. Instead of trying to replace **C** and **R** by some new kind of similarity relation, I shall introduce the concept of a *universal* (non-individual) aspect of a situation (Section 2). I shall suggest that this concept is already presupposed by our notions of **C** and **R**, so that it is not less clear than either of them. I shall then use this concept in constructing a new condition on **D** (Section 3). It will be seen that this condition, to which I shall refer as (uu), has the following properties: from the *anti*-Leibnizian point of view, (uu) is equivalent to (u); but, unlike the latter condition, (uu) is *not* trivialized by Leibnizianism. Finally, I shall discuss and criticize another triviality objection that may be raised against (uu) (Section 4).

2. UNIVERSAL ASPECTS

When we want to explain what it means to say that two objects are exactly similar to each other, we often employ the distinction between 'individual' ('numerical') and 'universal' ('qualitative', 'non-individual') features of an object. Thus, we have said above that two situations w and v are exactly similar iff they only differ in their 'individual' aspects. This explanation suggests that the distinction between universal and individual aspects is already presupposed by our notion of exact similarity (copyhood).

The distinction in question is equally crucial for our understanding of the relation **R**. Two situations are said to be **R**-related iff they exhibit the same morally relevant *universal* characteristics. That is, iff the differences between them are either irrelevant or purely 'individual'.

Here we shall take the concept of a universal aspect as a primitive notion, and we shall formulate a number of constraints that this concept should satisfy. We shall also assume that the concept in question is necessary in any satisfactory analysis of the relations **C** and **R**.

By an aspect of a situation we shall understand any proposition (state of affairs) that is instantiated by that situation. Thus, the distinction between universal and individual situation-aspects reduces to a distinction between two types of propositions. As we remember, propositions are in our framework represented as sets of possible situations (subsets of **W**).

We define individual propositions as non-universal ones:

D1. $X \in \mathbf{W}$ is individual =df X is not universal.

This definition amounts to the claim that the distinction between universal and individual propositions constitutes a partition: every proposition is either universal or individual and none is both.

As we already know, two situations are C-related iff they differ at most in their individual aspects. Thus, the definition of **C** is immediately forthcoming:

D2. $w\mathbf{C}v$ =df for every universal $X \subseteq \mathbf{W}$, $w \in X$ iff $v \in X$.

If the distinction between universal and individual propositions is to be of any interest at all, then the set of universal propositions must be neither empty nor all-inclusive:

Principle of Division. There are $X, Y \subseteq \mathbf{W}$ such that X is universal and Y is individual.

If there were no universal propositions at all, then D2 would have the absurd implication that any two possible situations are exactly similar to each other. On the other hand, it is equally implausible to assume that *all* propositions are universal. It seems, for instance, that any (consistent) proposition that entails the existence of some particular (contingent) individual must, *ipso facto*, be individual. (Note, however, that this is only a sufficient, but not a necessary condition of individuality. A proposition such as *Plato does not exist* seems to be individual even though it does not entail the existence of Plato. A more satisfactory, but still somewhat tentative, explication of the concepts of individuality and universality shall be given in Section 4.)

Here are some examples of individual propositions:

> Frege was a mathematician; Plato was an outstanding philosopher; John never repaid his debt to Mary.

On the other hand, the following propositions are universal:

> Some philosophers are mathematicians; The creator of the Theory of Ideas (whoever he was) was an outstanding philosopher; Some people never repay their debts.

What happens when we negate a universal proposition? Can we get an individual proposition as a result? It is difficult to see why we should allow for such a possibility. Therefore, I shall assume that the complements of universal propositions are themselves universal.

Principle of Complements. Universal propositions have universal complements.

I note without proof that the Principle of Complements allows us to simplify the definition of **C**

T1. $w\mathbf{C}v$ iff, for every universal X, if $w \in X$, then $v \in X$.

If we let $\mathbf{C}(w)$ be the set of all copies of w, then T1 amounts to the claim that $\mathbf{C}(w)$ is the product of the set of universal propositions instantiated by w.

The set of universal propositions is closed under complements. Is it also closed under products? Unfortunately, we cannot make this assumption. At least not as long as we want to make room for Leibnizianism.

T2. Leibnizianism $\Rightarrow$ The set of universal propositions is *not* closed under products.

In the presence of the Principle of Complements, closure under products and closure under unions are equivalent properties. (The union of a set is the complement of the product of the complements of its members. Correspondingly, the product of a set is the complement of the union of the complements of its members.) Thus, T2 has the following corollary:

Leibnizianism $\Rightarrow$ The set of universal propositions is not closed under unions.

Proof of T2. We shall say that $X \in \mathbf{W}$ is a *u-product* iff X is the product of a set of universal propositions. T1 guarantees that, for every w, $\mathbf{C}(w)$ is a u-product. Now, every proposition X can be represented as the union of a set of unit-sets: $X = \bigcup\{\{w\} : w \in X\}$. And, if Leibnizianism is true, then, for every w, w equals $\mathbf{C}(w)$. Thus, we get the following result:

Lemma 1. Leibnizianism $\Rightarrow$ Every proposition is the union of a set of u-products.

If the set of universal propositions were closed under products, then every u-product would be a universal proposition. What is more, every union of a set of u-products would be a universal proposition, since, as we already know, closure under products implies closure under unions (in the presence of the Principle of Complements). Thus, given Lemma 1, Leibnizianism would imply that *every* proposition is universal. But this is excluded by the Principle of Division. It follows, therefore, that the set of universal propositions cannot be closed under products. Q.E.D.

Lemma 1 above shows that, if Leibnizianism is true, then the distinction between universal and individual propositions is not a *radical* one. If Leibnizianism is true, then every individual proposition results from universal propositions by appropriate Boolean concatenations.

While Leibnizianism implies that individual propositions are Boolean concatenations of universal propositions, even Leibnizians may insist that *some* types of such concatenations never lead from universal propositions to individual ones. In particular, while they must reject unrestricted closure under products, they may well assume that the set of universal propositions is at least closed under *finite* products (and thereby also under *finite* unions.)

Principle of Finite Products: The product of a finite set of universal propositions is always universal.

It can be shown that such a restricted closure assumption is perfectly consistent with Leibnizianism.

Example 1 (due to Sten Lindström). Suppose that **W** is an infinite set. A subset X of **W** shall be said to be universal iff X is finite or its complement is finite. (In the latter case, we shall say that X is 'co-finite'.) Obviously, such a model satisfies the principles of Complements and Division. (The existence of individual propositions is guaranteed by the fact that an infinite set has infinite subsets with infinite complements.) And the Principle of Finite Products is satisfied as well. In order to prove that, it is sufficient to show that the product of any two universal propositions X and Y is universal.

Case 1. X or Y is finite. Then their product must be finite as well. And finitude implies universality.

Case 2. Both X and Y are co-finite. Then their complements are finite and thus the union of their complements is finite. But, in such a case, the complement of this union is co-finite, and it is easy to see that the complement in question equals the product of X and Y. Thus, again, the product of X and Y is universal.

Finally, it is clear that Leibnizianism holds in the model. For every w in **W**, there is a universal proposition, $\{w\}$, that contains nothing but w. Thus, no v distinct from w can be a copy a w.

We shall assume in what follows that the Principle of Finite Products holds. However, nothing much depends on this assumption. What we shall say below will still be acceptable to anyone who thinks that this principle need not be correct.

Definition D2 implies that every universal proposition is closed under **C**. That is, a universal proposition contains all the copies of its members. May we also assume the converse of this thesis and consider every proposition closed under **C** as *ipso facto* universal? Obviously, the Leibnizians would reject this assumption. According to them, *every* proposition, universal or not, is closed under **C**. But what about anti-Leibnizians? Cannot we simply identify anti-Leibnizianism with the claim that closure under **C** implies universality? In fact, this is what I propose to do.

Anti-Leibnizianism. Every proposition closed under **C** is universal.

How are we to motivate this proposal? It should be noted that anti-Leibnizianism, as I have defined it, is *not* a simple negation of Leibnizianism. The two standpoints are mutually exclusive (given the Principle of Division), but they are not exhaustive of all the possibilities there are.

Example 2 (due to Sten Kaijser). Let S be the circumference of a circle. It is possible to treat points that lie on S as sets, in such a way that,

(a) for any two distinct points a and b on S, a and b are disjoint sets;
(b) at least one point on S, call it a_1, contains at least two members.

(Thus, for instance, we may choose an arbitrary point on S, assign to it number 1, and then assign descending real numbers in the half-open interval $(1-0)$ to other points, as we move clockwise along S. Then, for any point a on S, if n is the number assigned to a, then we may identify a with the set consisting of n and of $-n$. Clearly, this construction satisfies conditions (a) and (b) above.)

Let us then look upon points on S in this way and let **W** be defined as the union of S. That is, **W** is the set of objects w such that, for some point a on S, w belongs to a. We shall say that a set P of points on S is normal iff P is a half-open 'slice' of S such that P is closed on its left and open on its right. In other words, the left-hand boundary of P belongs to P, while the right-hand boundary does not. (We think of left and right in terms of the clockwise movement along S.) It may be seen that the following holds:

(1) If P is normal, then the remaining part of S (the complement of P) is normal;
(2) The union of two normal point-sets is normal;
(3) *No* point on S is identical to the product of a *finite* set of normal point-sets.

A subset X of **W** shall be called *normal* iff X is the union of some normal point-set. And we shall say that X is *universal* iff X is the union of a finite set of normal subsets of **W**. Given (1)–(3) above, it is easy to show that the set of universal subsets of **W** satisfies the principles of Division, Complements, and Finite Products, but that it does not satisfy Leibnizianism: for any point a on S, the elements of a are copies of each other. And, according to our assumption (b), there is at least one point on S, a_1, that contains at least two distinct elements.

Nor does our model satisfy anti-Leibnizianism. Neither a_1, nor any other point on S, is normal. Therefore, a_1 cannot be universal. But a_1 is closed under **C**. That is, for every member w of **W** that is not an element of a_1, there is some universal $X \subseteq$ **W** that includes a_1 but does *not* contain w. We construct this X as follows: Let b be that point on S which contains w. Note that, by our assumption (a) above, there is only one such b. Note also that b is distinct from a_1. Let P be that half-open normal 'slice' of S which begins on its left with a_1 and which is bounded by b on its right. Note that a_1 belongs to P but b does not. We define X as the union of P. Since P is normal, X is normal. Therefore, X is universal. At the same time, X includes a_1 but it excludes b. In consequence, X does not contain w. This completes our argument.

We see, then, that positions intermediate between Leibnizianism and anti-Leibnizianism are possible. However, it seems to me that such positions lack plausibility. If you deny that **C** is an identity relation, then why should you settle for anything less than the outright identification of universality with closure under **C**? As we already know, if Leibnizianism is true, then the set of universal propositions is not closed under products, Clearly this is a rather uncomfortable feature of the Leibnizian approach. If we now look at Example 2, we note that this feature reappears in the 'intermediate' models. For instance, let a be any point on S and consider the set of all such $X \subseteq$ **W** that X is the union of some half-open normal 'slice' of S which begins on the left with a. Clearly, every such X is universal, but a, which constitutes their product, is *not* universal. In distinction from Leibnizian models, however, 'intermediate' models *also* contain some individual propositions that are not constructible from the universal ones by Boolean operations. (This applies, for instance, to all non-empty proper subsets of points on S.) Thus, such models are rather irregular and quite difficult to handle. One cannot but think that things would be much simpler for an opponent of Leibnizianism, if he assumed the existence of a *radical* division between universal and individual propositions. That is, if he assumed that *no* individual proposition can result from universal propositions by Boolean concatenations. Now, it turns out that the existence of such a radical division not only follows from but also entails our formulation of anti-Leibnizianism.

T3.   Anti-Leibnizianism $\Leftrightarrow$ The set of universal propositions constitutes a complete Boolean algebra (that is, this set is closed under complements and products).

Proof. From left to right: (i) by D2, if $X \subseteq W$ is universal, then X is closed under **C**. Since, by D2, **C** is symmetric, the closure of X under **C** implies that the complement of X is closed under **C**. But then by anti-Leibnizianism, the complement of X is universal. (ii) Consider any set of universal propositions. By D2, all members of that set are closed under **C**, so that its product must also be closed under **C**. But then anti-Leibnizianism implies that this product is universal.

From right to left: Suppose that $X \subseteq \dot{W}$ is closed under **C**. D2 implies that every equivalence class with respect to **C** is a u-product (i.e., the union of a set of universal propositions). Therefore, if X is closed under **C**, X must be the union of a set of u-products. By the right-hand side of T3, (1) every u-product is universal, and (2) every u-union (i.e., every union of a set of universal propositions) is universal. Thus it follows that X is a universal proposition.   Q.E.D.

It seems to me that T3 provides a strong reason for accepting my formulation of anti-Leibnizianism.

3. UNIVERSALITY AND UNIVERSALIZABILITY

Consider the following principle:

(uu)   If $X \subseteq W$ is universal, then the same applies to the proposition that X is obligatory.

As we remember, the proposition that X is obligatory is the set of all situations w such that every deontic alternative to w belongs to X.

Below we shall prove that, from an anti-Leibnizian point of view, (uu) is just another formulation of condition (u). But, unlike the latter condition, (uu) is not trivialized by Leibnizianism. Thus, (uu) seems to be a formulation of the Universalizability Principle which avoids both horns of the universalizability dilemma.

A remark before we start. Consider the following condition:

(uu′)   If $X \subseteq \mathbf{W}$ is universal, then the same applies to the proposition that X is permitted.

(The proposition that X is permitted consists of all situations w such that some deontic alternative to w belongs to X.)

We shall prove that (uu) and (uu′) are equivalent to each other:

T4   (uu) $\Longleftrightarrow$ (uu′).

Proof. The proposition that X is obligatory equals the complement of the proposition that the complement of X is permitted. And the proposition that X is permitted equals the complement of the proposition that the complement of X is obligatory. Therefore, by repeated applications of the Principle of Complements, it follows that the proposition that X is obligatory is universal whenever the proposition that X is permitted is universal. But then (uu) and (uu′) must entail each other.   Q.E.D.

We are now in a position to prove that, in the presence of anti-Leibnizianism, (uu) and (u) coincide.

T5.   Anti-Leibnizianism $\Rightarrow$ ((uu) $\Longleftrightarrow$ (u)).

Proof. Given T4, it will be sufficient to show that, for an anti-Leibnizian, (u) coincides with (uu′). Given anti-Leibnizianism, (uu′) becomes equivalent to the following condition:

(1)   If $X \subseteq \mathbf{W}$ is closed under $\mathbf{C}$, then the same applies to the proposition that X is permitted.

The following is a reformulation of (1):

(2)   If a deontic alternative u to w belongs to $X \subseteq \mathbf{W}$ and X is closed under $\mathbf{C}$, then, for every copy of w, some deontic alternative to that copy belongs to X.

Since $\mathbf{C}$ is reflexive and transitive, $\mathbf{C}(u)$, the set of all copies of u, must contain u and it must be closed under $\mathbf{C}$. And it is clear that any set X closed under **C** must include **C**(u) if it contains u. Therefore, (2) is equivalent to the following condition:

(3)   If u is a deontic alternative to w, then, for every copy of w, some deontic alternative to that copy belongs to **C**(u).

And (3) is just another formulation of (u).   Q.E.D.

In order to show that (uu), in contrast to (u), does *not* follow from Leibnizianism, we can use the same model that we have described in Example 1. Thus, we let **W** be an infinite set and we let $X \subseteq$ **W** be universal iff X is finite or co-finite. As we remember, this model is Leibnizian and it satisfies the principles of Division, Complements, and Finite Products, Now, let Y be any individual subset of **W**. (Thus, both Y and its complement are infinite.) And let w be an arbitrary member of Y. We define **D** as follows: For any v and u in **W**, if v belongs to Y, then v**D**u iff $u = w$; and if v does not belong to Y, then v**D**u iff $u = v$. It is obvious that, in such a model, (uu) does not hold: while $\{w\}$, being finite, is a universal proposition, the proposition that $\{w\}$ is obligatory coincides with Y. And Y was assumed to be individual.

4. UNIVERSALITY AND INTENSIONS

We have shown that (uu) is not made trivial by Leibnizianism. But is not (uu) trivial anyway? Isn't it perfectly obvious that, whenever X is a universal proposition, then the proposition that X is obligatory must be universal as well? In Rabinowicz, 1979, Part IV, I have argued that this appearance of triviality is misleading. Here I can only present a rough sketch of my argument.

When we talk about propositions we may mean (at least) two different things. On the one hand, we may treat propositions in an 'extensional' way, as sets of situations. This is what we have been doing up to now. But we may also look upon propositions as 'intensional' entities — as objects of propositional attitudes or as meanings of sentences. Such intensional propositions are true in some situations and false in others, but they are not reducible to sets of situations in which they are true. In fact, two distinct intensional propositions may be instantiated by exactly the same situations. This is the case, for instance, with the propositions such as

(a)   Some philosophers are mathematicians,

and

(b)   Some philosophers are mathematicians and either Frege is a
         philosopher or it is not the case that Frege is a philosopher.

(a) and (b) are distinct intensional propositions but they have the same
'extension': they are true in exactly the same situations. To put it differently, (a) and (b) correspond to the same extensional proposition (set of
situations).

Just as we distinguished between universal and individual extensional
propositions, it is possible to make an analogous distinction as far as intensional propositions are concerned. Roughly, an intensional proposition is
individual if it contains at least one particular (contingent) individual among
its 'constituents'. If no such individual constituent is present, then the intensional proposition is universal. Thus, proposition (b) above is individual since
it contains Frege among its constituents, while proposition (a) is universal.
(Essentially the same distinction is discussed in Kaplan, 1978. Kaplan refers
to individual and universal intensional propositions as, respectively, 'singular'
and 'general' ones.)

The universality-individuality distinction in the field of intensional propositions is analogous to the corresponding distinction among extensional
propositions. But the two distinctions do not coincide. In particular, it is not
true that the extension of an individual intensional proposition must always
be individual. Thus, in our example above, it seems that the extension of (b)
is universal, even though (b) itself is an individual (intensional) proposition.

Though the two distinctions do not coincide, it seems that the extensional
distinction is at least partially definable in terms of the intensional one. Thus,
let A and B be intensional propositions. We shall say that B is a *variant* of
A if B results from A by uniform replacement of all individuals occurring
in A by other individuals. Thus, for instance, the proposition that results
from (b) above by replacing Frege with Husserl constitutes a variant of (b).
Now, an intensional proposition A shall be said to be *essentially individual*
if, for some variant B of A, A and B have different extensions — there are
situations in which only one of them is true. (This definition of essential
individuality deviates somewhat from the one given in Rabinowicz, 1979,
Appendix to Part IV.) Intuitively speaking, an intensional proposition is
essentially individual if its extension *depends* on its individual constituents.

It is easy to see that our proposition (b), while being individual, is not
essentially individual. Replacing Frege with any other individual in (b)

does not lead to any change in extension. On the other hand, the following intensional proposition is essentially individual:

(c)   Frege is a philosopher.

Replacing Frege with Husserl changes the extension of (c). There are some possible situations in which Frege is a philosopher but Husserl is not and vice versa.

Let $X \subseteq W$ be the extension of some intensional proposition. We shall say that X is *individual* if X constitutes the extension of some essentially individual proposition; otherwise such an X shall be said to be *universal*.

Admittedly, this definition of universality/individuality distinction in the field of extensional propositions is only partial − nothing is said about those subsets of W which do not constitute extensions of any intensional propositions. (And if W is sufficiently large, then such subsets may well exist.) I think, however, that even such a partial definition may be of help. If our intuitions concerning the distinction in question can be fixed for a large class of extensional propositions, then, perhaps, it will give us some guidance as to how to deal with the remaining cases.

Just as we have distinguished between intensional and extension propositions, we may distinguish between intensional and extensional *propositional operations*. An n-adic intensional (extensional) propositional operation is a function that assigns an intensional (extensional) proposition to an n-membered sequence of intensional (extensional) propositions. Thus, for instance, the intensional conjunction is an operation that transforms any pair of intensional propositions A and B into their conjunction: *A and B*. The 'extensional conjunction', on the other hand, transforms any pair of extensional propositions X and Y into their product: $X \cap Y$. Another example: Define the *intensional Ought-operation* as the function that transforms any intensional proposition A into *It ought to be the case that A*. Correspondingly, the *extensional Ought-operation* transforms any extensional proposition X into the extensional proposition that X is obligatory (ought to be the case). Other examples are easily forthcoming. Thus, the intensional negation transforms any A into *It is not the case that A*; while the extensional negation transforms any X into its complement. In general, we may say that to intensional propositional operations correspond, as their extensions, certain operations on extensional propositions. If f is an n-adic intensional propositional operation, and g constitutes its extension, then the following holds: whenever f transforms intensional propositions $A_1, \ldots, A_n$ into an intensional proposition B, g transforms the extensions of $A_1, \ldots, A_n$ into the extension of B.

An intensional/extensional propositional operation shall be said to be *universal* iff it invariably yields universal values when applied to universal arguments. Otherwise, we shall say that such as operation is *individual*.

Thus, it is obvious that such intensional operations as negation and conjunction are universal. If neither A nor B contains any particular individuals among their constituents, then the same must apply to their conjunction and to their negations. On the other hand, consider for instance, the intensional operation that assigns to every A the intensional proposition *It is in John's interest that A*. Clearly, this operation is individual. The same applies to the extension of this intensional operation. Even if A is a universal proposition with universal extension, the proposition *It is in John's interest that A* is essentially individual, and therefore it has an individual extension. If X is the extension of A, then the set of all situations in which it is in John's interests that X holds is an individual extensional proposition. On the other hand, the extensions of intensional negation and conjunction are universal operations. This is guaranteed by, respectively, the Principle of Complements and the Principle of Finite Products.

Now, consider the following intensional variant of (uu):

(uu$_{int}$)   If an intensional proposition A is universal, then the same applies to the intensional proposition *It ought to be the case that A*.

(uu$_{int}$) says that the intensional Ought-operation is universal. It is easy to see that (uu$_{int}$) is trivially true. If A does not contain any particular individuals among its constituents then the same must obviously apply to the proposition *It ought to be the case that A*. This triviality of (uu$_{int}$) would be transferred to (uu), *if* (uu) were just a trivial consequence of (uu$_{int}$). But it is not. According to (uu), the *extensional* Ought-operation is universal: if X is universal, then the same applies to the extensional proposition that X ought to be the case. Now, this claim would follow trivially from (uu$_{int}$) only if the following principle were trivially true:

(P)   Universal intensional entities (such as propositions and propositional operations) always have universal extensions.

Given (P), the universality of the intensional Ought-operation would guarantee that the corresponding extensional operation is universal.

However, (P) is not a trivial principle. At least, it does not follow from our definition of the extensional universality/individuality distinction in terms of the corresponding intensional distinction. This definition does not entail that universal intensional propositions have universal extensions. Nor, *mutatis mutandis*, does it entail that the extensions of universal intensional propositional operations must be themselves universal.

In fact, I think that a person who rejects the Universalizability Principle would also reject principle (P). Thus, suppose that somebody, call him John, denies the Universalizability Principle, because he thinks that everybody under every possible circumstances, ought to act in such a way as to maximize the satisfaction of John's interests. To put it differently, it is John's opinion that the locutions *It ought to be the case that* and *It is in John's interest that* are extensionally equivalent. While these locutions admittedly stand for distinct intensional propositional operations, the operations in question have the same extension, according to John. As I have suggested above, the intensional operation that transforms every *A* into *It is in John's interest that A* has an individual extension. But if this operation is to have the same extension as the intensional Ought-operation, then it follows that the latter operation, while being universal, must have an individual extension. Thus, John's moral views are inconsistent with (P).

To conclude, (uu) is not trivial because (P) is not trivial. On the other hand, I am quite certain that (P) is universally valid. And this makes me certain that (uu) is universally valid as well.

Department of Philosophy
Uppsala University

REFERENCES

Føllesdal, Dagfinn and Hilpinen, Risto: 1971, 'Deontic Logic: an Introduction', in Hilpinen, Risto (ed.), *Deontic Logic: Introductory and Systematic Readings*, D. Reidel, Dordrecht, Holland, pp. 1–35.
Kaplan, David: 1978, 'Dthat', in Peter A. French, *et al.* (eds.), *Contemporary Perspectives in the Philosophy of Language*, University of Minnesota Press, Minneapolis, pp. 383–400.
Rabinowicz, Wlodzimierz: 1979, *Universalizability: A Study in Morals and Metaphysics*, D. Reidel, Dordrecht, Holland.

KAI NIELSEN

UNIVERSALIZABILITY AND THE COMMITMENT TO IMPARTIALITY

I

Let us assume here that we are willing to reason and act within the bounds of morality, that there is something that we recognize as the moral point of view which we are committed to and which in certain respects circumscribes our actions. Such a conception would also have a conception of justice as a proper part and it is at least plausible to believe that such a conception would have as an integral element a *principle of impartiality: a principle to the effect that all human beings have an equal right to the fulfillment of their interests.* What I want to inquire into is whether there is a statement of the *principle of universalizability* which is both *categorically prescriptive* and rationally undeniable which entails *the principle of impartiality.*[1] In fine, can we get *the principle of impartiality* from *the principle of universalizability*? I want to know whether it is the case that, if you start from *universalizability* and you are consistent, you will be required also to accept *the principle of impartiality*?

The received wisdom in ethical theory now (1982), in the aftermath of the extensive discussion of R. M. Hare's and Marcus Singer's accounts of universalizability and its placement in morality, is that no such acceptance is required.[2] I want to consider here whether the received or at least dominant view is also the right view or at least the most plausible view.

'Universalizability' is a term of art and there are a number of different readings of it. I want to start with something which is tolerably unproblematic and to move, only as far as necessary in the way of increasing precisification, to something which is so tied to the very concept of morality and moral judgment, that, if there are any conceptual truths at all, it cannot be denied that all moral judgments are in that sense universalizable. That is to say, I want to state a principle of universalizability which is unassailable and holds in virtue of what it is for something to be a moral or evaluative judgment.

II

To begin, then, at the beginning. *To say that a judgment of rightness or wrongness is universalizable is to say that whatever is right or wrong for*

91

Nelson Potter and Mark Timmons (eds.), Morality and Universality, 91–101.
© *1985 by D. Reidel Publishing Company.*

one person is right or wrong for every relevantly similar person in relevantly similar circumstances. More generally, and still hopefully uncontentiously, we might put it as J. L. Mackie puts it in the beginning of his discussion of universalizability: "Anyone who says, meaning it, that a certain action (or person, or state of affairs, etc.) is morally right or wrong, good or bad, ought or ought not to be done (or imitated, or pursued, etc.) is thereby committed to taking the same view about any other relevantly similar action (etc.)."[3] To claim universalizability for norms and evaluations is to claim that if *A* is a good pencil (teacher, comrade, institution) then anything exactly or precisely like *A* is also a good pencil (teacher, comrade, institution).[4] Intelligibly to assert that one pencil, teacher, comrade or institution is good and the other is not, there must be some difference between them in virtue of which this judgment can be made. The same thing holds for judgments of rightness or judgments concerning what ought to be done or what ought to be the case or what someone is morally justified in doing. If Axel is justified in doing *A* then anyone exactly like Axel is justified in doing anything exactly like *A* in exactly the same circumstances. Similarly, if *A* is the right thing to do for Mary or if *A* is something Mary ought to do, then anyone exactly like Mary and in the same circumstances ought to do *A* as well and the doing of *A* in such a circumstance is also the right thing for them to do.

It will, of course, be said that the people, objects, roles, institutions in question are never, and never can be, exactly alike, for they are at least numerically distinct. It is correct to respond to that that being merely numerically different doesn't count, but, that response not withstanding, it still remains the case that, numerical differences apart, there are also always differences between people, institutions, roles and the like.

To salvage universalizability from uselessness 'relevantly similar' must, in the above formulations, replace 'exactly alike' or 'exactly the same' and the like.

A perhaps more useable *principle of universalizability* will read: if an action or attitude is right, if something ought to be done or to be the case, of if something is good, then, anything relevantly similar to it is also right, ought to be done or ought to be the case or is good in relevantly similar circumstances and (where this is relevant) for relevantly similar persons.

The most obvious problem here is to specify acceptable criteria for what are to count as *relevant similarities*. It appears at least to be the case that nothing formal or definitional, except arbitrarily by way of stipulation, will establish criteria for relevant similarities. It appears at least to be the case that non-formal, and perhaps invariably contestable, evaluative or normative judgments must be made in coming to an agreement about what the criteria for relevant similarity are.

It does not appear at least to be the case that we can ascertain what the criteria are from simply becoming clear about the concept of morality or about what moral judgments are or what it is to take the moral point of view such that all informed people with such an understanding must agree on what the criteria for relevant similarities are.

It is also important to notice that the *principle of universalizability* does not tell us *what* is right or wrong, good or bad, or *what* ought or ought not to be done. It rather says that *if* one thing is right, good or ought to be done, then another thing relevantly similar to it is too.

The *principle of universalizability* so construed does not, note, take us to the *principle of impartiality*; namely, to a principle which asserts that *all human beings have an equal right to the fulfillment of their interests*. Only if we judge that there are no relevant differences in this respect between people could we conclude that all human beings have an equal right to the fulfillment of their interests on the ground that if A has a right to the fulfillment of his interests, then anyone else does too, because there are no relevant differences between A and other human beings. But that there are no relevant differences between A and any other human being will be challenged, e.g. the Son of Sam is not Malcolm X, Ronald Reagan is not Salvadore Allende. Moreover, the *principle of universalizability* will not itself determine that anyone, let alone everyone, has a right to the fulfillment of her/his interests. What it will tell us is that *if* Fran has a right to the fulfillment of her interests, anyone relevantly similar to Fran and in a relevantly similar situation will have an equal right to the fulfillment of her or his interests as well. It will not be right, in this respect, to treat Hans differently from Fran, unless there is a relevant difference between them or a relevant difference in their situations which justifies a difference in treatment. But the *principle of universalizability* or anything entailed by it will not tell us whether there is a relevant difference between them. It will not tell us that Fran has a right to have her interests fulfilled, let alone tell us – or legitimately give us to understand – that all of us have an equal right to the fulfillment of our interests.

Only on the assumption that we are sufficiently similar to be entitled to have our interests equally protected, to be equally free from the deliberate frustration of our interests, can we correctly claim that this is something the *principle of universalizability* supports. But without that assumption about human nature and entitlement, such an equal concern for the interests of all human beings is not established by the consistency requirements of *universalizability* alone. *Universalizability* by itself does not give us the rational foundations of justice.

These normatively substantive things the *principle of universalizability* cannot do. Yet, what seems at least unassailable about the *universalizability thesis* is this: on the one hand, if something is right, or if something ought to be done or if something is good, and, on the other hand, if another thing is not right, ought not to be done or is not good, then there must, simply as a matter of logic, be some difference between them which explains why one thing is right and the other not, why one thing ought to be done and the other not, why one thing is good and the other not. In spite of Don Locke's sharp criticism of the appeal to *universalizability* in ethics, this is something that he and R. M. Hare and Paul W. Taylor are all agreed upon.[5] This means that if something is the morally inappropriate thing to do in a certain circumstance, then there must be some reason why it is morally inappropriate; to say 'This is wrong' is to presuppose a moral principle – 'Whatever is like this in certain respects is also wrong.' If you want to talk that way, you can say that this means that the Principle of Sufficient Reason applies in ethics.

What is very often claimed by moral philosophers – philosophers I like to call ethical rationalists – who try to give some strategic deployment of universalizability in moral philosophy is the cluster of claims I shall make in the rest of this paragraph. When we reflect on what moral principles really are – what essentially their nature is – we will come to see that moral principles do not make exceptions of particular individuals just because they happen to be particular individuals. If a moral principle applies or does not apply to a particular person, it is not because he or she is that particular person, but because he or she possesses some feature or combination of features which could, at least in principle, be possessed by others.[6] It does not matter *who* you are – that is morally irrelevant; what counts is only general characteristics of you and your situation.

What is tempting to conclude from this, but what is now widely recognized to be a mistake, is that in seeing that moral principles are in the above senses universalizable, we can conclude that they are universal principles which apply to everyone alike and allow no exceptions, such that if I ought to do *Y*, you ought to do so as well. Bernard Mayo, for example, maintained in his *Ethics and the Moral Life* that a moral judgment "must be universalizable in the sense that it applies not only to me but to you; not only to you but to me; not only to us but to everybody. . . . "[7] But this *universalist* claim for *universalizability* plainly is not on. You can't get from *universalizability* to *universalism*. Some moral principles are meant to apply only to children or to old people or to soldiers or to doctors or to religious people or to Roman Catholic priests. The moral principle enjoining priests not to divulge what is told in the confessional, a doctor's Hippocratic oath, the duties of parents to children, the obligations of a psychoanalyst to his patients are very special and situational. The hat trick the *universalizability principle* does not pull off is that of grinding out universal substantive moral principles for us.

There is a sense in which all moral principles, indeed all principles *sans phrase*, are *universalizable*, but not in the sense that they are universal or that in general that they apply to everyone alike. A principle applies to everyone who falls within its scope, but that is a different matter. It is not even true that all moral principles apply to everyone irrespective of who he is. Some, as we have seen, apply only to priests, to doctors, to children, to parents, and, in some rare instances, only to a certain individual, e.g. to Jesus. "Moral Principles", as Don Locke has nicely put it, "may be universal in the sense of applying to everything of the particular sort . . . they are not universal in the sense of being applicable to everyone. . . . "[8]

It is true, of course, that they are in a sense generalizable even when applying, *in fact*, only to one individual. Thus, if Jesus should have accepted death on the cross to save humankind, it is true that anyone relevantly like Jesus and in a relevantly similar situation should do so as well. Even acts of supererogation are universalizable. If a person with relevantly similar commitments and other relevantly similar qualities and in a relevantly similar situation hove into sight, then he/she should also act as Jesus did. We cannot, of course, where the act is really an act of supererogation, insist that he must; 'must' is a stronger moral term than 'should': not all oughts are obligations. Typically very admirable acts, as heroic or saintly acts, are not required of us, though we, if we have considerable moral integrity, may require them of ourselves. If acts of supererogation were things society can rightly hold us to, as something we *must* do, then they would not, indeed could not, be acts of supererogation. But we still correctly, in the above circumstance, are to say that he should so act. We don't require it of him but we think his doing so is desirable. It is, to return to Jesus, an historical accident that only Jesus was in that situation. It is not a logical truth or any kind of conceptual truth, that no one else could be. Similarly, though parents have special obligations to their children, anyone who comes to be a parent has such obligations. This is what the universalizability thesis was trying to catch in claiming that moral principles applied to everyone alike. Still, in the sense specified above, moral judgments or principles do not all apply to everyone alike, and in that important straightforward sense, they are not all *universal*, though they are *universalizable*.

III

Can we, in the teeth of what I have argued above, derive the *principle of impartiality* ("All human beings have an equal right to the fulfillment of their interests") from the *principle of universalizability* in the way we have formulated it, either by immediate inference or in conjunction with some purely factual premises or from factual premises plus analytic premises?

My statement of the *principle of universalizability* was this: If an action or attitude is right, if something ought to be done or to be the case or if something is good, then anything relevantly similar to it is also right, ought to be done, or ought to be the case, or is good in relevantly similar circumstances, and for (where this is relevant) relevantly similar persons. But someone could plainly accept that and assert that we are so different that we do not all have an equal right to the fulfillment of our interests. Some of us are cruel, some kind, some lazy, some industrious, some avaricious, some generous, some without integrity, some with it, some concerned principally to feather their own nests, some with an intense concern for others, and most of us, in these and other respects, are at neither extreme of virtue or vice. I am not saying that the person who claimed that because of these manifest differences between us we do not all have an equal right to the fulfillment of our interests is justified in making that claim or that he should make that claim. What I am saying is that that claim is at least not self-contradictory or that there is anything *conceptually* incoherent or untoward about the assertion of it or that it violates the *principle of universalizability*. Something can be morally anathema yet conceptually in order, even perfectly intelligible, as a bit of moral discourse.

Yet such an assertion contradicts the *principle of impartiality* while remaining perfectly compatible with the *principle of universalizability*. Thus, the *principle of impartiality* cannot be derived from the *principle of universalizability*. An elitist or social Darwinian can believe that if something is right for him to do, it is also right for others to do who are relevantly similar to him and similarly placed — and thus accept universalizability — and still perfectly consistently deny that the great masses of people share a right to do what he and his elite peers have a right to do even when doing it would aid in the fulfillment of their interests, for he sincerely believes that such run-of-the-mill people are not relevantly similar to him. He accepts the *principle of universalizability*, but rejects the *principle of impartiality* (as we have defined it) and does this quite consistently. We may – I do, at any rate – wish to set ourselves in struggle against such elitists or social Darwinians, but we have no good grounds for thinking they are being inconsistent or have said anything conceptually untoward. Morally untoward, perhaps, but not conceptually untoward.

The same point can be made if we accept Don Locke's formulation of *universalizability*. Suppose we say that a person cannot sincerely and consistently make a moral judgment unless that person is prepared to accept "the same moral judgment in any relevantly similar situation, including those which affect you personally differently".[9] The elitist can say quite consistently, while accepting Locke's formulation, that he is so different and his relation to people is so different that he is not in a relevantly similar situation to that of the vast majority of other men. Since this is so, it would be wrong to claim that they had, compared to him and his peers, the same equal rights to fulfillment of their interests. There is no denial of universalizability in Nietzsche's doctrine of the *Übermenschen* and *Untermenschen*. But there is a rejection of the *principle of impartiality*. I deplore such a rejection of the egalitarian attitude. But I do not think that it is an inconsistent position.

IV

Paul W. Taylor, in an unfortunately neglected essay, "Universalizability and Justice", argues that universalizability logically compels an agent to assent to the following general principle: "If it is wrong for another to discriminate against him (the agent) on the ground of a difference he (the agent) does not acknowledge to be relevant, it must also be wrong for him (the agent) to discriminate against another on the ground of a difference the other does not accept as relevant." [10]

To probe this, consider the following rather desert-islandish case: Suppose the agent is a Jew living in an anti-Semitic society with strange religious beliefs that forbid innoculation for diseases including infectious diseases. He, in this anti-Semitic religious society, is not allowed to hold a professorship in any university on the grounds that he is a Jew. He rightly resents this and rightly enough does not acknowledge this as a relevant ground for discrimination, though it is all the same widely regarded in the society in which he lives as being a morally and legally acceptable relevant ground for such special treatment. Indeed it is part of the law of the land. He immigrates to a saner society. There there are no barriers, legal or otherwise, to his becoming a professor, but eventually the idea loses its allure and he becomes instead an immigration officer in his newly adopted land. A typically religious member of his former homeland wants to visit his new-found homeland, but refuses to get innoculations for a disease that he might quite likely be the carrier of or very well might contract and subsequently spread. He will not do so because it is against this putative tourist's religious principles to have such an innoculation. Indeed, as he sees things, to do so would be to act immorally. As an immigration official, our former professorial aspirant bars this person from entry into his country on the grounds that he has not had these inno-culations. (Let us suppose he has legal discretion to do so or not to do so.) He does so on the ground − indeed a not implausible ground (to understate the point) − that the aspiring tourist may spread a very dangerous infectious disease. But the aspiring tourist, let us assume, no more regards this dis-crimination against him as relevant than he, the immigration officer, regards his being barred from teaching in the universities of his former homeland on the ground that he is a Jew as relevant. Yet, it is very likely the case that his action in barring the would-be tourist was the morally correct decision to make. Surely it was not an unreasonable decision to make. Yet, if this is so, it violates Taylor's principle that he takes to be derivable from the *principle of universalizability*. A (the immigration officer) discriminates against B (the religious fanatic) on a ground that B does not acknowledge as relevant, but A regards his action as justified (morally right), but he insists that B is wrong to discriminate against him (A) on grounds that he (A) does not acknowledge as relevant. The symmetry of Taylor's principle is broken; there is no reciprocity here as Taylor's principle requires. The *principle of mutual acknowledgement*, a principle central to Taylor's argument, is the principle that a relevant difference, which would justify treating one person differently than another, must be such that it will be freely acknowledged by all whose interests are affected by such proposed differential treatment. Yet, it surely seems at least to be a principle which would be rightly rejected or at least overridden in such a context. Surely it is anything but evident that there must, in such circumstances, be the reciprocity of mutual acknowledgement that Taylor's principle requires for there to be a morally valid decision. It is not evident that morality requires it, let alone that not so acting is 'morally unintelligible', because it violates 'the logic of normative discourse'. Even if the moral situation were more anomalous than I believe it actually is, A's actions are still intelligible as moral actions. *If* they are incompatible with the *principle of universalizability*, then we should be suspicious of the claim that there can be no moral claims which are not universalizable. However, I think A's actions are plainly as compatible with universalizability as are actions in accordance with Taylor's principle of mutual acknowledgement. If this is so, Taylor has not shown that if we accept universalizability, we must accept his principle. A can (to show that it is so), as well as a person committed to the principle of mutual acknowledgement, believe that if X is right for A to do in situation Y, it is right for any relevantly similar person to do in a relevantly similar situation. The value replacing the variable X in Y could be 'prevent people not innoculated for diseases L, M and N entering his country at time T, whether or not they regard that discrimination as relevant'. He will quite consistently believe that B should also so act in situation Y, even if B does not see the situation in those terms. So, someone can quite consistently accept universalizability and still accept the negation of Taylor's principle, so it cannot be the case, as Taylor contends, that one is logically compelled to accept Taylor's principle if we accept universalizability. Taylor has not succeeded in showing that there is anything in the very nature or logic of moral discourse or normative discourse which compels us to reject criteria of relevant differences, not acceptable to all whose interests are affected by them. He has not shown how a clairvoyant understanding of the principle of universalizability must lead us to acknowledge that "criteria of relevant differences, not acceptable to all whose interests are affected by them, cannot be used as grounds for excluding anyone from having an equal right in deciding what criteria are to govern those social practices that affect his interests".[11] It is not clear that A and B, in my above example, have an equal right in deciding criteria of relevance for who can enter a country and who cannot. And even if I am somehow mistaken on this substantive moral point, I am not mistaken because I have said something which is incompatible with the *principle of universalizability*, while my interlocutor has consistently followed out its logic. What is morally mistaken or untoward need not be morally unintelligible or incoherent.

V

Getting substantive moral principles or maxims out of the *principle of universalizability* is like getting blood out of a turnip. There is a kind of ethical rationalism — often a strain of Kantianism, though, as John Rawls has shown, not the only Kantian strain — that seeks the rational foundations of justice and sometimes the whole of morality in an *a priori* or formal *principle of universalizability* which tries to establish itself as a principle which is rationally undeniable for anyone who can think clearly and has a firm understanding of moral discourse. I have not sought to show that the *principle of universalizability* can be rationally denied (that we could give conclusive or even rationally persuasive reasons for denying it), but I have sought to show that it is rationally deniable and indeed highly improbable that such a *principle of universalizability* is the 'rational foundation' of justice or of morality more generally. It is understandable that such a formalism and ethical rationalism should have such a strong hold on us. If it were true, logic alone, pure reason alone, would, at least in a general way, tell us how we ought to live. But such a rationalism is a myth. In moral philosophy it returns again and again like the repressed.[12] For moral philosophers on the quest for certainty, it, like the ontological argument for the existence of God, holds a persistent and powerful attraction, but both conceptions are thoroughly myth-eaten, revealing, once again, the irrational heart of philosophical rationalism.

Department of Philosophy
University of Calgary

NOTES

[1] D. H. Monro, *Empiricism and Ethics* (London, England: Cambridge University Press, 1977), Chapters 13–16.
[2] R. M. Hare, *The Language of Morals* (London, England: Oxford University Press, 1952); R. M. Hare, *Freedom and Reason* (London, England: Oxford University Press, 1963); and Marcus Singer, *Generalizaton in Ethics* (New York, NY: Alfred Knopf, 1961). The criticisms have been myriad and varied but some of the classic ones include: Don Locke, "The Trivializability of Universalizability", in *Readings in Ethical Theory*, eds. Wilfrid Sellars and John Hospers, 2nd edn. (New York, NY: Appleton-Century-Crofts, 1970), pp. 517–527; David Keyt, "Singer's Generalization Argument", *Philosophical Review* 72 (1963), pp. 466–476; George Naknikian, "Generalization in Ethics", *Review of Metaphysics* 17 (1964), pp. 436–461; Peter Winch, "The Universalizability of Moral Judgments", *Monist* 49 (1965), pp. 196–214; and Joseph Gilbert, "Neutrality and Universalizability", *Personalist.* 53 (1972), pp. 438–441.
[3] J. L. Mackie, *Ethics: Inventing Right and Wrong* (Harmondsworth, Middlesex, England: Penguin Books Ltd., 1977), p. 83.
[4] R. M. Hare characterizes universalizability as follows: the thesis of universalizability requires that if we make any moral judgment about a determinate situation, we must be prepared to make the same judgment about any precisely similar situation (p. 42). To say that moral judgments are universalizable is to say "that they entail identical judgments about all cases identical in their universal properties" (p. 108). Hare further remarks, " . . . if we make different moral judgments about situations which we admit to be identical in their universal descriptive properties, we contradict ourselves" (p. 21).

R. M. Hare, *Moral Thinking: Its Levels, Method and Point* (Oxford, England: Clarendon Press, 1981). The universalizability thesis, so stated, seems to me manifestly a correct conceptual thesis about moral discourse. The interesting question is whether it can generate any substantial moral norms or provide, as Hare believes, rational guidance in moral reasoning. My contention is that it does not. Where the universalizability thesis can be established simply by careful attention to the logic of moral discourse, it is trivial. Where it is given a richer reading it is not a thesis which is required by reason.

[5] Don Locke, "The Trivializability of Universalizability", p. 520; Paul Taylor, "Universalizability and Justice", in *Ethics and Social Justice*, eds. Howard E. Kiefer and Milton K. Munitz (Albany, NY: State University of New York Press, 1968), pp. 142–163; and Paul Taylor, "On Taking the Moral Point of View", *Midwest Studies in Philosophy* 3 (1978), pp. 35–61.

[6] Don Locke, "The Trivializability of Universalizability", p. 524.

[7] Bernard Mayo, *Ethics and the Moral Life* (New York, NY: Macmillan, 1958), p. 91.

[8] Don Locke, "The Trivializability of Universalizability", p. 527.

[9] Don Locke, "The Principle of Equal Interests", *The Philosophical Review* 90 (October 1981), p. 535.

[10] Paul Taylor, "Universalizability and Justice", p. 161.

[11] *Ibid.*, p. 167. R. M. Hare's latest book came into my hands too late to include a discussion of it in the body of my text. However, it does seem to me that his latest effort at achieving morally interesting results from universalizability runs afoul of the very same counter case I directed against Taylor. Moreover, it is absurd to claim, as Hare does, both that universalizability is a logical requirement for those who are going to reason morally and that it also "demands that we treat other people's prescriptions (i.e. their desires, likings, and, in general, preferences) as if they were our own" (p. 17). That latter claim is not on as a logical thesis. It would only gain plausibility if it had a different logical status and if we had made and justified the *substantive moral claim* that people are sufficiently alike to justify such similar treatment or that, alike or different, they are to be so similarly treated in these respects. But there are no conceptual guarantees for such claims which would require us to accept them on pain of logical error. R. M. Hare, *Moral Thinking*, p. 17. I should add here that the most uncompromising form of ethical rationalism is not in Hare's work, but in the work of Alan Gewirth. I have examined it in some detail in my "Against Ethical Rationalism", in *Gewirth's Ethical Rationalism*, ed. Edward Regis, Jr. (Chicago: The University of Chicago Press, 1984).

[12] I have, in various ways, tried to criticize such rationalism in my "On Needing a Moral Theory", *Metaphilosophy* (1982); "Grounding Rights and a Method of Reflective Equilibrium", *Inquiry* (9182); "Problems of Westermarck's Subjectivism", in *Edward Westermarck: Essays on His LIfe and Works*, ed. Timothy Stroup (*Acta Philosophica Fennica* 33, 1982); and "Baier on the Link Between Immorality and Irrationality", *Nous* March 1982).

FREDERICK A. OLAFSON

REFLECTIONS ON A PASSAGE IN MILL'S
UTILITARIANISM

There is a passage in John Stuart Mill's *Utilitarianism* that seems to me to have an important bearing on the topic of universalizability; but that has not, as far as I know, received much, if any, attention. It occurs in Chapter Three, "On the Ultimate Sanction of the Principle of Utility", and more precisely in the section in which Mill explains how the social feelings of mankind support the principle of utility. He speaks of these social feelings as "a desire to be in unity with our fellow-creatures";[1] and although he admits that this desire exists in very different degrees of development at different stages of civilization, he claims that it must be present in some degree in all human beings. "The social state", he declares, "is so actual, so necessary, and so habitual to man that except in some unusual circumstances, or by an effort of voluntary abstraction, he never conceives himself otherwise than as a member of a body. . . . "[2] It is at this point that the passage to which I wish to draw attention occurs; and it draws the conclusion to which the preceding observations point.

Any condition, therefore, which is essential to a state of society, becomes more and more an inseparable part of every person's conception of the state of things which he is born into, and which is the destiny of a human being. Now society between human beings, except in the relation of the master and the slave, is manifestly impossible on any other footing than that the interests of all are to be consulted. Society between equals can only exist on the understanding that the interests of all are to be regarded equally. And since, in all states of civilization, every person except an absolute monarch has equals, every one is obliged to live on these terms with somebody; and, in every age, some advance is made towards a state in which it will be impossible to live on other terms with anybody.[3]

This passage anticipates much of what Mill goes on to say about the role of social feelings in the Fifth Chapter in which he tries to show that the principle of utility can be reconciled with the principle of justice. In that discussion he argues that the special importance of the duties of justice is to be accounted for by the fact that "it is by a person's observance of them that his fitness to exist as one of the fellowship of human beings is tested and decided".[4] Mill then goes on to say that justice accordingly represents "certain moral requirements which regarded collectively stand higher in the

103

Nelson Potter and Mark Timmons (eds.), Morality and Universality, 103–114.
© 1985 *by D. Reidel Publishing Company.*

scale of social utility"; and he thus makes it clear that, in his view at least, a grounding of the principle of utility in the social nature of man as he has just described it remains consistent with utilitarian principles.[5] It is, however, by no means clear that this is really so. In Chapter Three Mill had argued that because man is a social being he must necessarily acknowledge the claim of moral equality somewhere in his life; and the suggestion seems to be that it is only through inconsistency that he avoids generalizing the principle of equal consideration to all contexts of human life. In any case, if someone did not accept the claim of equality *anywhere*, he would not be a social and therefore not a human being. But if the authority of the principle of justice is to rest on "its standing higher in the scale of utility", as Mill says in Chapter Five, a very different picture is suggested. In this picture the utility of observing the fundamental rules of justice is to be worked out as a preliminary to their being accepted, but it is not clear by whom. The choice lies between supposing that it is to be done by beings who are understood to embrace the principle of justice as a result of this calculation, and supposing that it is to be done by beings who are committed to that principle simply on the strength of their humanity even in advance of the calculation. In the former case the calculators would be in the position of entertaining the options of being just or not being just; and it is the calculation of the consequences of the one option and the other that is supposed to settle the question. In the latter case such options would never really be open to any *human* being since the necessarily social nature of human beings commits them, in Mill's view, to an acceptance of equality understood as a requirement of equal consideration of the interests of all. Any such equality is clearly so close to the principle of justice, as Mill characterizes it, that it would be impossible to be committed to the former and remain uncommitted to the latter.

It is not the purpose of this paper to belabor Mill yet again for the inconsistencies or fallacious inferences of which he may have been guilty in *Utilitarianism*. It does seem evident to me that in the passage I have quoted he has sketched a line of argument that is quite different from and perhaps not even reconcilable with the main argument about the relationship between justice and utility that he advances in Chapter Five. It also appears that Mill did not really see how very different the one line of argument is from the other. Instead of prosecuting him for these misapprehensions, however, I propose to explicate the line of thought that is sketched in the quoted passage because it seems to me to be a quite powerful and distinctive approach to ethical issues generally. In so doing I will not be trying to interpret Mill's text as much as I will be exploring the possibilities of a mode of argument which certainly springs from it but which I will develop in an idiom that owes much to contemporary ethical theory.

Before setting about this task it may be helpful to supply a little in the way of historical and philosophical context for the understanding of what is distinctive in the line of thought Mill develops in this passage. That line of thought clearly belongs to a long series of efforts that have been made by philosophers and others to give an account of the authority of ethical requirements as such and to do so in such a way as to supply a decisive rational motive for compliance with those requirements in spite of the continuing resistance with which they meet from instinct and impulse. These philosophical lines of argument differ conspicuously from one another, but most of them seek to establish that the appearance of sacrifice or loss on the part of the self that complies with ethical requirements is *merely* an appearance and that a deeper insight into the relationship between the self and the authentic requirements of morality assures us of an ideal compatibility between them. It can hardly be said, however, that the older, more rationalistic efforts to ground ethics in certain necessary truths of reason succeeded very conspicuously in overcoming the sense of externality and thus of arbitrariness in the relationship between these two terms. This was largely due to the fact that the interests whose long-run compatibility with ethical requirements was to be demonstrated were rarely allowed to speak for themselves but only through a kind of filter that in effect insured that the desired compatibility would be forthcoming. It is not surprising, therefore, that ethical theory gradually moved away from its original rationalistic and *a priori* mode toward an analysis of the conative and affective life itself in the hope of discovering there an ordering principle that might make an appeal to higher jurisdictions unnecessary. Utilitarianism is one theory of ethics that has emerged from this re-orientation of such inquiries, and social contract theory is another. In the case of utilitarianism an attempt is made to show that the intuitions we have as to what is right and wrong in human conduct are broadly the same as the conclusions that would be reached on the basis of a careful examination of the tendency of various types of actions to produce consequences of a painful or a pleasurable kind. Of course, the calculative principle that is appealed to here cannot by itself suffice to establish the relationship to one another of those who are to jointly employ it as their fundamental criterion for selecting common policies; and in the absence of some independent definition of that relationship, utilitarianism is vulnerable to criticism on the grounds that it may sanction actions that are intuitively unjust.

Social contract theory can be interpreted as an effort to supply this missing element in a utilitarian theory of ethics; and it does so by postulating one form or another of agreement among the members of a society as to the principles by reference to which the issues of policy they face are to be resolved. It thus secures a degree of equality based on reciprocity that is far likelier to satisfy our intuitive sense of justice than most forms of utilitarianism are. The difficulty for social contract theory, however, is to determine just how this agreement is to be conceived and, more specifically, whether in any interpretation that is not itself dictated by the very ethical principles that are to be established by the agreement itself, it can claim to be more than a contingent and perhaps not even especially likely phenomenon in human affairs. In that case, of course, its utility as a foundational principle in ethics would be quite drastically affected. But, whatever their weaknesses, there is also something sound in these attempts to found ethical distinctions on something that can plausibly be regarded as being so closely connected with the motivating grounds of human action that it cannot be consistently disavowed by the agents concerned. Indeed, I would argue that one reason why the sense of a radical duality as between the self and the ethical persists is that we still tend to conceive justification for ethical claims in terms of a simplistic, "external" model as though demanding that the world come furnished with ethical sign-posts to guide us on all the occasions of choice and then recoil in nihilistic disillusionment when it turns out that such sign-posts are not available. The remedy for the weaknesses in these "internal" modes of justification is surely to try to conceive the situation of the human agent who is expected to conform his conduct to ethical norms, in still more fundamental terms.

If this is the context in which the passage from *Utilitarianism* takes on the interest that I believe it can claim, that fact may be missed if we take its last clause as expressing its principal idea and thus conclude that what we have here is just another statement of an optimistic estimate of the prospects for social and moral progress that we no longer share. In fact, Mill *does* appear to be quite sanguine about these prospects; but what is really distinctive in this passage has to do rather with the connection that Mill makes between ethical obligation and the social nature of man and with the fact that in doing so he in effect bypasses the principle of utility which elsewhere in this essay he treats as the principle from which all ethical rules are capable of being derived. In other words, Mill's argument here appears to postulate a direct connection between our social natures and a relationship to at least some other human beings in which we acknowledge operative equivalence between their situation and our own. However optimistic he may be for the long-run, he is not, I take it, claiming that these social natures of ours entail any law of universal benevolence; and he was certainly quite well aware of the selective and restricted character of such ethically acceptable conduct as does in fact prevail. He is not even claiming that within the sphere of such acknowledged ethical relationships we are always in compliance with the requirements these entail, for that again would be an error of fact. What he would want to stress, at least as I read this passage, would rather be the fact that when we violate the presumptions that hold on both sides of such relationships we cannot consistently avoid a recognition that we have done something indefensible and indefensible precisely in terms of features of that situation that could not obtain without our implicit ratification. Again, the resources of human duplicity being what they are, we can and do repudiate the obligations entailed by even those forms of reciprocity on which we ourselves have most patently relied and we even declare ourselves to be justified in doing so and often with every outward sign of conviction on our part. But if the kind of view I am attributing to Mill is correct, as I think it is, then we cannot do this without the kind of inner duplicity that entails that, admit it or not, we *are* in the wrong or, alternatively, at the cost of a genuine dissociation within the life of the self which, just because it is not duplicitous, would constitute a threat to the integrity of our personality and thus, not too indirectly, to our status as social beings.

It may seem that this is a great deal to pack into such an innocent looking passage and that some less ambitious construal of Mill's words would be more consistent with his ethical theory as it is ordinarily understood. It is conceivable for example that Mill is saying simply that if no one were prepared to put anyone else's interest ahead of or on a par with his own, human society would be impossible. This is certainly true; and if it were doubted, we would only have to point to the fact that we all begin life as helpless infants and that somebody has to be willing to care for us if we, and thus human society, are to survive. But if this material dependency were all that the relationship between our social being and ethical requirements came to, it would be a good deal less interesting than I think it in fact is and we would not really get at the sense in which the point Mill is making supersedes the "agreement" or contractual model of ethics by taking it to a much deeper level of analysis. This can be shown by developing at much greater length than Mill does the implications of the fact that "everyone is obliged to live on . . . terms (of equality) with somebody". These implications are quite extensive and can, when more fully developed, cast a good deal of light on the whole issue of the universalizability of ethical judgments.

There is a long-standing dispute among philosophers as to whether reason — man's rational powers — suffices by itself to recommend as well as to motivate a course of action that satisfies the criteria of what intuitively seems to us to be moral conduct. The negative view of this matter is probably still the predominant one; and it typically bases itself on such considerations as those that have to do with the impassable logical gulf that is said to separate the "ought" from the "is". Against this view it has been persuasively argued that one of the most important features of human language and thought is precisely the capacity for validating a train of reasoning that reaches a judgment of obligation from certain kinds of factual premises such as, for example, the fact of having made a promise. A promise, however, is a form of agreement; and so an argument like this still seems to invite the response that if we were to make no such agreements, we would be subject to no obligations. But what would a life involving no such agreements really be like? Would it, for example, be a life in which anything like linguistic communication and the forms of social existence it mediates could still be said to occur? The reason for thinking that it might not is that in our present condition cooperation with other human beings in the various forms of social work and the even more fundamental fact of our *sharing* a world — a "doxastic environment" as it has been called — with other like beings appears to depend upon a prior acceptance on both sides of a set of conceptual instruments that function in a neutral manner as far as differences between persons and their points of view are concerned. In other words, although a particular object does not look quite the same to two persons — and perhaps in fact looks very different — they are able to agree that it is the same object. Similarly in practical situations we may have desires that conflict with one another and yet we are able to acknowledge when it is my turn and when it is yours to do the driving for our car pool. What is important for present purposes in such examples is not the substance of the common judgment that is reached on both sides, but rather the relationship between persons that they illustrate. This is a relationship in which an equivalence has been achieved between the positions occupied by two distinct and quite different human beings — an equivalence such that neither of the latter can claim to be inherently privileged in respect of the making of the kinds of determinations — of fact and of obligation — that were exemplified above. This absence of privilege means that something's looking such-and-such to me can count as a reason for concluding that it *is* a such and such only if a comparable experience by the other observer would count in the same way. It is true that we often distrust the observations of others and dismiss them in pretty summary fashion; but it is equally clear that virtually all our beliefs about the world rest on the assumed possibility of their being confirmed by an open class of observers and inquirers who occupy all the positions at which we are not able to be present ourselves. And in the light of this dependence it is hardly surprising that it should be a constitutive rule governing the pragmatics of communication that we are entitled to assume, in the absence of any indications to the contrary, that a statement by another human being represents his own genuine belief with respect to the matter in question and to censure him for lying if this proves not to be the case.

It should be noted that although the kind of intersubjective reciprocity I have been trying to describe underlies agreements of various kinds between different persons, it would not be plausible to view it as being itself in the nature of an agreement. It is proper to speak of "agreements", I think, only in cases in which we can equally well imagine the "agreement" not being made; and that is what I am· suggesting ·is not the case· for the principle of intersubjective reciprocity as such on which our dependency is of a quite different order. But it should be noted here that there is a misuse of this principle of equivalence that is all too common in ethical theory. This mistake consists in supposing, first, that it is the symmetrical character of the relationship of many inquirers to matters of empirical fact that is to serve as the model for our understanding of intersubjective reciprocity generally; and then, on the basis of this assumption, it is typically supposed that what we are looking for in the case of practical and evaluative determinations must be a feature of the situation in question that is somehow comparable in its "factuality" to the non-evaluative property that is being used as a model. That search invariably proves to be fruitless and it has the further disadvantage of narrowing our conception of intersubjective reciprocity in such a way as to make its extension to evaluative and ethical contexts dependent on just such dubious analogies as this. There are certainly important differences between the non-ethical or (at least in principle) "scientific" case and the ethical one and these undoubtedly have something to do with the ontological status of the "property" that is to be identified in the one case and in the other. But even in the scientific case the simplistic picture of properties that ultimately derives from perceptual experience and that represents them as just "there", waiting to be identified, has little to recommend it; and in any case it cannot serve as the vehicle for a conception of intersubjectivity that has, as K. O. Apel has put it, much more to do with the "subject–subject" relationship than it does with any particular type of "object" with which these "subjects" may concern themselves.[6]

All of this may of course seem to *assume* the truth of the very thesis I am supposed to be establishing, namely, that in the domain of practice and thus of ethics we are just as irreversibly committed to intersubjectivity as we are in the domain of "fact" and of science. Such a claim may well have a strange and implausible ring to it since if there is one tendency that seems inseparable from human nature as we know it, it is egocentricity; and if ethical properties are not somehow analogous to those upon which our most securely established cognitive apprehensions are directed, there seems to be nothing but the limits of our power to prevent such egocentricity from expanding to the limits of our world. By egocentricity here I mean an indifference in principle to intersubjective reciprocity and an implied refusal of the kind of equivalence among persons it carries with it. Not surprisingly, there is something very plausible about the claim that in the practical domain this kind of intersubjectivity is permanently *sub judice* and that it is to be acknowledged and espoused only for that range of cases in which it is judged to be in our egocentric interest to do so. There can be no doubt that the human race has in fact made heroic efforts to subordinate, in principle, the universal to the particular along these lines; and we have in the Melian dialogues as reported by Thucydides a remarkable statement of the logic of such a position as expounded to those who were being excluded from any significant relationship based on acknowledged equivalence. But, however fatally successful this egocentric attitude may be in practice, it is far from clear that it can achieve a coherent formulation of its own procedures. First of all, just how are we to understand the way in which such a person would alternatively step into and out of the circle of relationships that is governed by the principle of equivalence or non-uniqueness? After all, if he insists upon his freedom to decide when to regulate his conduct by reference to criteria that are intersubjective in the stipulated sense and when not to, doesn't this mean that even when he appears to stand within that circle of relationships the ultimate basis for his decisions remains egocentric? In the relevant sense there doesn't seem to be any way in which one can be *partly* egocentric. What *kind* of a reason, one may ask, could he give for such a policy of alternation and to whom, besides himself, could he give it? If he is asked why the same person to whom he has stood in a relationship characterized by intersubjective reciprocity is for other purposes to be treated in accordance with the logic of egocentricity, he cannot very well deny that that person is *capable* of functioning as a partner in the kind of relationship from which he is now to be excluded. The classic justification for a refusal of equivalence that cites the other's lack of the "rational" powers such a relationship would require is thus immediately called into question. But in that event the person who adopts an egocentric policy for certain life-contexts must also recognize in the "other", a being who is like himself in the relevant respects and who, therefore, consistently with the logic of their prior equivalence-governed relationship, must be addressing to him an implicit question as to the justification for this non-equivalent mode of treatment just *as he himself would do if the positions were reversed. Ex hypothesi*, there is no answer that he can give to this question since his decision has been taken outside the only framework of justification – the one based on the assumption of equivalence – within which an answer that would be congruent with the question could be given.

Am I saying then that it is impossible for such a person to remain on his egocentric course and that he will be compelled by the sheer logic of his situation to enter into a genuine ethical dialectic with the "other" who poses this implicit question to him? No, indeed, but I am saying that he will not be able to persist in this course of conduct without feeling the strain of contradiction within the policies by which that conduct is governed. One way of dealing with that sense of strain is to avoid an open acknowledgement that reciprocity has been abandoned and to give a reason for the conduct in which one is engaging vis-à-vis the excluded "other" – a reason that at least *seems* to be neutral and general as between the interests of the two persons who are involved, although what really recommends it is the fact that it licenses the piece of behavior that the agent is committed to, no matter what. This is the special form that hypocrisy takes when to refuse the request for justification altogether would expose one's policies and thus one's character more nakedly than one is willing to allow; and as Oscar Wilde pointed out, such hypocrisy is a covert acknowledgement of vice, i.e. of a violation of a norm that one recognizes as such. As I have already pointed out, we are sometimes able to avoid the necessity for this form of hypocrisy since by virtue of the way our society is arranged, we can disqualify large numbers of our fellow human beings altogether as possible sources of requests for justification on the grounds that they constitutionally lack some one or other of the capacities that are required for the role that is being denied them and are indeed better off in a position of non-equivalence. But this claim turns out to be equally hard to sustain in good faith since the societies in which it is most plausibly made are usually the ones that deny to those so disqualified the opportunities to demonstrate whether they have these capacities or not as well as those to acquire them by whatever form of education may be appropriate. The archetype of such societies is, of course, the slave-holding society; and there is no reason to think that such societies cannot achieve a high degree of stability under some conditions. But it is of very great interest to note that, in the recent historical literature dealing with slavery, evidence seems to be accumulating that suggests that a fully consistent enforcement of the thesis of non-equivalence is extremely difficult and that at many points the slaveholder finds himself acknowledging indirectly and reluctantly that his slaves have the same powers and preferences and even rights that he himself has. Short of the pure case of non-equivalence – extermination – which has the advantage of removing the beings who might be living testimony to the equivalence one refuses to grant them, there does not in fact seem to be any way in which a society that is based on non-equivalence can altogether avoid either relying on or in some other way acknowledging the very fact of intersubjective reciprocity among human beings that it is determined to deny.

The ethical situation, as I conceive it, is thus one in which we find ourselves placed willy-nilly and, one might even say, in spite of our best efforts to generalize the principle of egocentricity as a fully consistent rule of life. This means that the actual codes under which we live at one and the same time involve a reliance on intersubjective reciprocity and deny it anything like full expression. Indeed, I do not think it is really too much of a paradox to say that the ethical life is founded upon a contradiction or at least on such a loose and problematic relationship of particular to universal that it seems very much like one. The domain of ethics is constituted by the (for the most part) reluctant effort of mankind to acknowledge and respond to this peculiar situation; and it is as yet far from clear what the outcome of that effort will be or whether indeed it will prove continuous and vigorous enough so that one can justifiably speak of it as an "effort" in that sense of the term that would imply some substantial shared consciousness of the ethical as the central business of mankind. Nor is it just perversity or selfishness that make our ethical prospects so unclear. The fact is that we as individual human beings are principally formed within a social and moral order, whatever it may be, that inevitably incorporates major departures from the norm of reciprocity; and many of our quite legitimate interests in life are thus bound up in one way or another with this non-ideal ordering of social life. In these circumstances, any sudden demand that our practice be made conformable to a more adequate interpretation of the relationship of human beings to one another can raise grave uncertainties and entail real elements of risk for those who identify themselves with this demand. Even if I feel sure that our actual practices implicitly acknowledge a norm of coexistence which they fail to realize, it may be quite unclear in what sense it is *my* duty to take such a risk and in that discontinuity between levels of the moral life there is thus an element of quite genuine indeterminacy as regards the compatibility of legitimate self-interest with the demands of the ethical. (If there is any one feature that above all distinguishes the approach to ethical questions which I hope I am fairly representing here, I think it is a disposition to make that element of discontinuity (and resulting ambiguity) central in its analysis of the ethical situation instead of dealing with it under some such rubric as "supererogation" as though it were just a bit of frosting on a moral cake whose contours were already quite well defined.) In any case, perhaps the most remarkable fact about human beings is that they have occasionally the capacity to take that risk or perhaps not to perceive it as a risk at all since the interests that might have to be sacrificed are incommensurate with the ideal interest with which such persons identify themselves. The ultimate authority of the ethical is in my view derivative from the fact that it is at least possible to imagine a broader movement of mankind from where it is now toward the more perfect reconciliation of self-interest with community as exemplified by the lives of such persons as these; but it is not possible to imagine a movement in the opposite direction toward a fuller and more consistent egocentricity as anything in which we could collectively be said to have an interest.

It may of course be asked, and quite properly, what the more precise bearings of all this are on the philosophical issue about the universalizability of ethical judgments. What Mill's account does, at least in the interpretation of it I have offered, is to fill in the pragmatic context in which such judgments are made and to show how difficult it really would be to maintain a repudiation of the principle of universalizability in the circumstances of social life. It is these circumstances that tend to be forgotten or at least not given their full weight when the principle of universalizability is treated as a purely logical thesis and when the examples that are used as counter-instances are developed in a sovereign abstraction from any realistic acknowledgement of the conditions of reciprocity with other human beings under which we in fact must live and work. It is true that some of the strongest proponents of the principle of universalizability like Kant have also been rather sketchy in their treatment of the examples they have used. All such treatments of universalizability are either wholly monological in character or at best give scant acknowledgement to the fact that there is a real-world context for these arguments — a context of human beings to whom we stand in multiple relationships of cooperation and interdependence and who are themselves engaging (and are known to be engaging) in a consideration of their own of the form of reciprocity that is to obtain between them and their partners in this dialectic. Against all such theories, Mill's point must stand as a reminder that the true context of ethical reflection must always be that of an ethical community in which human beings stand to one another in determinate relationships that register the actual needs and circumstances and multiple forms of interdependency that in fact characterize our lives. In that context the requirement of universalizability is not simply an isolated logical thesis but widens out into an immensely intricate and powerful dialectic of actions and persons. This is not to say that when Mill's admonition is heeded and the artificiality of an abstractly logical treatment of such matters is avoided, serious and in certain cases intractable difficulties will not remain. Nevertheless, the point that Mill made in the passage I have quoted retains all its importance and a very considerable relevance to contemporary discussions in ethical theory.

Department of Philosophy
University of California

NOTES

[1] M. Cohen, Ed., *The Philosophy of John Stuart Mill: Ethical, Political, Religious* (Random House: New York, 1961), p. 358.
[2] Cohen, *op. cit.*, pp. 358–9.
[3] Cohen, *op. cit.*, p. 359.
[4] Cohen, *op. cit.*, p. 392.
[5] Cohen, *op. cit.*, p. 397.
[6] See especially his essay, "The A Priori of the Community of Communication as the Foundations of Ethics", in *Toward the Transformation of Philosophy* (Routledge and Kegan Paul: London, 1980).

MICHAEL GORR

REASON, IMPARTIALITY AND UTILITARIANISM

During the last thirty years R. M. Hare has developed and defended a meta-ethical view about the meaning of moral language which he calls "universal prescriptivism".[1] During this time Hare has also professed allegiance to a normative theory which constitutes a version of preference utilitarianism. What has never been made entirely clear, however, is his conception of the relationship between those two theories. In his earlier writings Hare maintained that:

Ethical theory ... provides only a clarification of the conceptual framework within which moral reasoning takes place; it is therefore, in the required sense, neutral as between different moral opinions ... On my view, there is absolutely no content for a moral prescription that is ruled out by logic or by the definition of terms (*FR*, pp. 89, 195).

The clear and uncontroversial implication of this is that a person's subscription to some particular set of substantive normative principles depends on factors in addition to his understanding of the fact that moral judgments are universal and prescriptive. Even in *FR*, however, Hare never seemed entirely comfortable with the claim that a rational and fully informed universal prescriber might choose non-utilitarian principles. For not only did he consistently use the perjorative epithet "fanatic" to designate such persons but, more importantly, he maintained that universal prescriptivism provided a "formal foundation" for the principle of utility (see, e.g., *FR*, pp. 122–23). Although he never clearly explicated his use of the term "formal" in this context, the clear suggestion was that there exists a special, non-contingent relationship between universal prescriptivism and utilitarianism that does not exist between universal prescriptivism and any other normative moral theory. But this, of course, is difficult to square with his thesis that universal prescriptivism is just a neutral analysis of moral language.[2]

Fortunately Hare's most recent writings shed considerable light on these issues. In his important paper, "Ethical Theory and Utilitarianism", and in his recent book, *Moral Thinking*, Hare appears to have modified his theory in at least one very important respect. He now holds that universal prescriptivism is not only not normatively neutral but in fact *entails* preference

115

Nelson Potter and Mark Timmons (eds.), Morality and Universality, 115–138.
© 1985 *by D. Reidel Publishing Company.*

utilitarianism. Consequently he has concluded that genuine fanaticism is no longer a difficulty or embarrassment for his position, because it can be shown to be a logical impossibility. However, a puzzling feature of the transition from the earlier to the later writings is that Hare nowhere indicates that he has, in fact, changed his beliefs in any fundamental respect. In *MT*, for example, he states that the account of fanaticism provided there "is not different in essentials from that given in *FR*" and concedes only that he has "seen some distinctions more clearly" (p. 170).

In this paper I shall argue, first, that the only way of making sense of Hare's earlier views concerning the normative neutrality of universal prescriptivism is to attribute to him an important thesis concerning what is involved in universalizing one's prescriptions, a thesis that is inconsistent with claims concerning the proper constraints on moral decision-making that he has defended to his most recent writings. Second, I shall attempt to show that his argument for utilitarianism is vitiated by its reliance upon an interpretation of the notion of impartiality that involves problems of coherence as well as plausibility. My criticisms here, if correct, have a significance that extends beyond Hare's theory since similar impartiality requirements figure prominently in the theories of a number of contemporary philosophers in both the Kantian and utilitarian traditions.[3] Finally, I shall suggest that Hare is mistaken in thinking that a requirement to be impartial in this sense is entailed by a mere specification of what is involved in adopting the moral point of view.

I

Let us begin by briefly reviewing the argument in *FR* for the thesis that universal prescriptivism is devoid of normative implications. To sincerely affirm a moral judgment is, on Hare's view, to prescribe acting in accordance with a universal moral principle from which, in conjunction with statements specifying one's beliefs concerning the relevant facts, the judgment can be derived. To in turn determine whether one can prescribe acting in accordance with a universal principle is to determine whether one would actually choose to perform that action if one knew that one would have to play, in a series of possible worlds otherwise identical to the actual world, the role of *each* person (including oneself) who would be affected. Moreover, it is not enough that one simply imagine oneself, with one's *own* interests, in the place of those other persons – rather, one must imagine oneself as being in their place while having, in turn, *their* interests and desires. This requirement, which I shall term the 'full reversibility test', is the very heart of universal prescriptivism. Hare would claim that to refuse to subject oneself to this test is just to refuse to adopt the moral point of view, for acting only on principles that would pass such a test is the requirement imposed by the formal rules of moral reasoning which correspond to the two fundamental formal properties of moral judgments, viz., universalizability and prescriptivity. On Hare's view, the deliberations and decisions of universal prescribers involve, therefore, a very strong and thoroughgoing kind of impartiality. As he notes in his well-known discussion of the debtor-creditor example:

All that is essential . . . is that [the creditor] should disregard the fact that he plays the particular role in the situation which he does, without disregarding the inclinations which people have in situations of this sort. In other words, he must be prepared to give weight to [the debtor's] inclinations and interests as if they were his own (*FR*, p. 94).

The question that I wish to address here concerns the kinds of choices that a sincere universal prescriber is capable of making. In *FR*, as I have already noted, Hare seems to have been of two minds on this issue. In places he maintains quite clearly that it is possible to sincerely and rationally prescribe *any* universal principle, regardless of how one's own interests (actual or hypothetical) will be affected. On the other hand, he suggests elsewhere the contrary view that only utilitarian principles could be prescribed, perhaps most clearly in the following passage:

But when I have been the round of all the affected parties, and come back, in my own person, to make an impartial moral judgment giving equal weight to the interests of all parties, what can I possibly do except advocate that course which will, taken all in all, least frustrate the desires which I have imagined myself having? But this (it is plausible to go on) is to maximize satisfactions (*FR*, p. 123).

Of course whether Hare is really claiming here that maximizing aggregate utility is the only rational choice depends on how we understand his use of the term "possibly". If what is meant is *logical* possibility then of course he would be making just this claim and the charge of inconsistency would seem to be sustained. But what else could Hare have meant? There are some passages (e.g., *FR*, pp. 110–111) which suggest that all Hare might have meant was that it would be *psychologically* impossible for the average person, given the sort of interests he is likely to have, to choose to do anything other than prescribe the maximization of overall desire satisfaction. But then the puzzle remains as to how Hare could have continued to assert that the relationship between universal prescriptivism and utilitarianism is "formal".

The conclusion I have been reluctantly forced to reach is that, when he wrote *FR*, Hare was just confused about this matter and that the source of his confusion was a failure to clearly distinguish between two different and incompatible interpretations of the *point of view* from which the full reversibility test is supposed to be applied. Recall that that test has force because it is supposed to be capable of demonstrating that a universalized moral principle (e.g., "All people who are unable to pay their creditors should be imprisoned") which underlies the *initial* prescription that I may make about a particular case (e.g., "Let Smith be put into prison if he cannot pay me what he owes me") may logically entail another prescription (e.g., "Let *me* be put into prison if I am unable to repay a creditor") that, as a matter of fact, I do not accept. Simple rationality, in other words, precludes a person from accepting a moral principle which entails a singular prescription which is inconsistent with another prescription to which he is committed. According to Hare the full reversibility test is capable of involving someone in a contradiction by showing that some set of moral beliefs (about both actual and hypothetical cases) that he *now* subscribes to is inconsistent. Thus he insists that when we ask someone to apply the full reversibility test it is crucial that

> when we are asking [him] to imagine himself in the position of his victim, we phrase our question, never in the form 'What *would* you say, or feel, or think, or how *would* you like it, if you were he?', but always in the form 'What do you say (*in propria persona*) about a hypothetical case in which you are in your victim's position?' (*FR*, p. 108).

On this view what someone (call him "Arthur") must do, if he is to adopt the moral point of view, is to test his initial judgments by (1) imagining himself playing, in turn, the role of each person (including himself) who would be affected by whatever action he proposes to perform on the basis of that initial judgment, and (2) determining whether *he*, Arthur, would consent, *in propria persona*, to having such an action performed if he knew he would actually undergo the relevant sequence of role reversals. Only if he would so consent could he claim that his initial judgment qualified as a *moral* one.

But what sorts of moral judgments are sincere and knowledgeable universal prescribers likely to make? In *FR* Hare concedes (at least most of the time) that a rational and sincere person might prescribe acting in accordance with non-utilitarian principles. These "fanatics" are persons so committed to an *ideal* (which, for Hare, seems roughly equivalent to a non-self-interested, non-utilitarian desire – see *FR* pp. 153, 159) that they are willing "to override all considerations of people's interests, even [their] own in actual or hypothetical cases" (*FR* p. 175). Exactly how commitment to such ideals could generate fanaticism is, however, never made entirely clear. Suppose Arthur is considering an action whose performance will affect Ben and Carla (and no one else). This is a situation in which Arthur is required to make his decision in accordance with the supposition that he will occupy, *seriatim*, the position of Ben and the position of Carla (as well as his own position) in a series of possible worlds otherwise identical to this one. Since occupying the position of another entails, on Hare's view, coming to have all of her desires, interests and inclinations in place of one's own, this suggests (as Hare himself has frequently pointed out; see, for example, *FR*, pp. 94–95) that universal prescriptivism is tantamount to a version of the "Ideal Observer" theory. Another way of putting the matter, then, is that Arthur is to proceed as if he were going to acquire all of the desires and interests of Ben and Carla in addition to retaining those he already has. In such a situation how would reason dictate that he act?

Although, so far as I know, Hare nowhere states this explicitly,[4] he seems to presuppose throughout his writings a Bayesian account of rational behavior according to which a rational agent always strives to maximize his own expected utility. It would seem, therefore, that if Arthur is willing to universalize his prescriptions (which, for Hare, is explicative of what is involved in adopting the moral point of view) then he has no alternative but to choose whatever action will maximize overall preference satisfaction (assuming, as Hare does, that utility *is* nothing more than preference satisfaction and that the familiar difficulties concerning the interpersonal commensurability of utilities can be surmounted). Since, as Hare points out, this is equivalent to (some version of) utilitarianism, it *does* appear inevitable that sincere, rational and informed universal prescribers will be utilitarians.

This in fact is precisely the conclusion Hare has drawn in his most recent writings. There he states quite explicitly that universal prescriptivism "leads to" (*ETU*, p. 117) or "generates" (*MT*, p. 111) the principle of utility; moreover he has in effect conceded that he no longer holds that universal prescriptivism is normatively neutral (*MT*, Ch. 12). But then what has happened to the notorious "problem of the fanatic" that so vexed Hare in *FR*? Was it not really a problem in the first place or have Hare's metaethical views changed since writing the earlier book? And if they have changed, how?

Perhaps the most direct way of approaching these questions is by a careful consideration of what Hare says about the possibility of fanaticism in *FR*:

If there are people so wedded to some fanatical ideal that they are able to imagine, in their full vividness, the sufferings of the persecuted, and who can still prescribe universally that this persecution should go on in the service of their ideals, even if it were they themselves who had to suffer thus, then they will remain unshaken by any argument that I have been able to discover. And it seems that there will always be such people . . . (*FR*, p. 184).

It is crucial to note here that Hare is not concerned with someone whose fanaticism is the result either of ignorance of some of the relevant facts or of an inability to fully and effectively appreciate the sufferings and feelings of others as required by the full reversibility test. These for Hare are not genuine fanatics (see *FR*, pp. 180–185 and *MT* pp. 170–176). Rather, genuine fanatics are those who, even after fully and knowledgeably subjecting themselves to the reversibility test, are willing "to override *all* considerations of people's interests, even [their] own in actual or hypothetical cases" (*FR*, p. 175, emphasis added).

Taken literally, however, this last statement is nonsense. Surely all decisions must be made on the basis of *some* set of desires or interests. And, as Hare himself acknowledges, to have an ideal is "*eo ipso* to have an interest in its fulfillment" (*FR*, p. 176). Consequently we must interpret Hare as claiming here only that the fanatic is so wedded to his ideal that he is willing to pursue it *despite* the fact that it will prejudicially affect the interests of *other* persons. The idealistic Nazi, presumably, is one who, although he has subjected himself to the full reversibility test and is therefore aware of the enormity of the suffering that his actions will impose upon others, is nevertheless prepared to act, as Hare puts it, "in disregard of" the interests of those others.

Unfortunately this way of putting the matter cannot be quite right either. After all, the whole point of the full reversibility test is to insure that one in fact give *close* regard to the desires and interests of other persons by requiring that one sympathetically imagine oneself *to be* those persons. So perhaps all Hare meant was that the fanatic is one who is prepared to disregard the interests of everyone else *after* he has "been the round of all the affected parties". The fanatical Nazi, that is, must be one who reasons as follows:

I admit that I would hate to be one of the Jews that I am proposing to kill. Still, I attach so much weight to my ideal of a pure Aryan world that I would be fully prepared to assent to the universal principle that all Jews be exterminated even if I knew that I would actually have to play the role of each Jew who would be victimized by such a policy.

What I shall now argue is that in the only two possible situations in which the Nazi might make such a claim either his proposed policy would be identical with that required of a utilitarian (at least of Hare's sort) or it would be ruled out by the canons of Bayesian rationality. If so, we would have to conclude that, contrary to what Hare (usually) claims in *FR*, but compatible with his more recent views, it is logically impossible for a person who is both rational and willing to take up the moral point of view (as understood by Hare) to be a genuine fanatic. Given Hare's definition of fanaticism, this is tantamount to claiming that anyone who is both rational and moral must be a utilitarian.

The first case is that in which the ideals of the Nazi are "so intensely pursued that the weight that has to be given to them, considered impartially, outbalances the combined weights of all the ideals, desires, likings, etc., that have to be frustrated in order to achieve them" (*ETU*, p. 121). But in this case preference utilitarianism would itself require that the Nazi's ideals ought to be realized. As Hare himself concedes (*ibid.*), the decision that the Nazi reaches is identical with the decision that any other rational and sincere person would reach in such a situation. Consequently it is incorrect to designate *this* Nazi a "fanatic". (Whether the fact that a theory has such a consequence is enough to condemn it is a question I shall not address here.)

In the second, more realistic, case, we may assume that the intensity of the Nazi's desires are rather less extraordinary and that their satisfaction would not outbalance the combined weight of all competing desires. In this case Bayesian rationality combined with the impartiality required by the full reversibility test would appear to rule out any non-utilitarian policy. The argument is as follows:

(1)   A rational person will always seek to maximize his expected utility (Bayesian principle).

(2)   Utility = preference satisfaction.

(3)   Adopting the moral point of view is equivalent to deciding how to act as if one had (or were going to come to have) all the preferences of all those who would be affected by one's action (full reversibility requirement).

(4)   Therefore, a rational person who adopts the moral point of view will always seek to maximize the total expected preference satisfaction of the group of all persons who would be affected by his action.

Why, then, did Hare fail to make such an argument explicit in *FR*? My hypothesis is that he was misled there by his insistence that, in order to satisfy the full reversibility test, a person is not to ask himself how he *would* feel about some proposed course of action if he were in the position of an affected party but, rather, how he *now* feels, *in propria persona*, about a hypothetical case in which he would be in that position. But to make a decision *in propria persona* is, presumably, to make it on the basis of one's knowledge of which desires, interests, and ideals one actually has. The genuine fanatic, then, must be someone who is willing to accord his actual interests precedence over his hypothesized interests (the interests he would have were he to assume the roles of other persons) simply because he realizes that the former *are* actual while the latter only hypothesized. Only in this way would it be *rational* for the fanatic to do what Hare accuses him of, viz., to pursue his ideal "in disregard of" the interests of others.

Of course allowing the fanatic such an option seems plainly inconsistent with the thoroughgoing impartiality involved in giving equal weight to equal interests. And in *ETU* Hare moved to seal off that escape route by introducing an important modification into the full reversibility test:

> ... I am not to take into account (when I ask what I wish should be done to me in a certain situation) my own present desires, likings, etc. There is one exception to this: I have said that one of the situations that I have to consider is my own present situation; I have to love my neighbor *as*, but *no more than* and *no less than*, myself, and likewise to do to others *as* I wish them to do to me. Therefore just as, when I am considering what I wish to be done to me were I in X's situation, where X is somebody else, I have to think of the situation as including *his* desires, likings, etc., and discount my own, so in the single case where X is myself, I have to take into account *my* desires, likings, etc. In other words, *qua* author of the moral decision I have to discount my own desires etc., and consider only the desires etc., of the affected party; but where (as normally) I am one of the affected parties, I have to consider my own desires etc., *qua* affected party, on equal terms with those of all the other affected parties.
>
> It will be asked: if we strip me, *qua* author of the moral decision, of all desires and likings, how is it determined what decision I shall come to? The answer is that it is determined by the desires and likings of those whom I take into account as affected parties (including, as I said, myself, but only *qua* affected party and not *qua* author) (*ETU*, p. 120. I have omitted some subscripts that do not affect the meaning of the passage).

This reformulation of the full reversibility test effectively jettisons the requirement that moral decisions be made *in propria persona*. Instead, Hare's present view seems to be that moral judgments, by their very nature *as* moral judgments, must be made from a completely impartial point of view rather than from the point of view of the agent himself. This additional requirement moves Hare even closer to a full-fledged Ideal Observer theory since he now holds not only that the moral deliberator must choose how to act on the supposition that he is going to acquire all the desires of all the persons who will be affected by what he is proposing to do but also that, in so choosing, he must disregard his knowledge of which of those persons he is.[5] Hare is certainly correct, therefore, in concluding that no genuine form of fanaticism could withstand exposure to such a complete and radical impartialism (the Nazi, for example, can no longer maintain that he is prepared to override the interests of others because of *his* commitment to a certain ideal). What remains to be considered is the plausibility of insisting that such impartialism is a constitutive element of the moral point of view.

II

Although each of the premises in the argument on p. 121 is open to question, I will be primarily concerned here only with the correctness of premise (3), i.e., the claim that a mere willingness to adopt the moral point of view by prescribing universally is tantamount to subjecting oneself to the full reversibility test. Recall exactly how that test is supposed to function. If Arthur claims he ought to perform a certain action even though he knows it will affect the interests of Ben and Carla, then he must be prepared to endorse some universal principle which would license such an action in such circumstances. To endorse such a principle, however, is to be prepared to assent to having the action performed even in situations where one's own interests would be jeopardized. Hare takes care to deny that this entails that Arthur is morally required to prescribe for all logically possible situations – rather, he insists only that, at the very least, Arthur must take into account those possible situations which are structurally like the actual situation but which differ insofar (and only insofar) as the parties involved exchange roles with one another.[6]

Suppose all of this to be correct. How does it follow that Arthur must choose as if he were going to assume, in a series of possible worlds, the role of *each* person who would be affected by his action? After all, even if he is denied knowledge of which person he will be, it can hardly be a formal requirement of morality that he also disregard his knowledge of the fact that he will play *one and only one* role in the situation in question. This criticism, however, is not as damaging as it might first appear. For I do not think that Hare is committed to the view that the impartiality definitive of the moral point of view requires that Arthur choose on the assumption that he will either simultaneously or serially assume the identity of all the other persons who will be affected by his action. Rather this is only a picturesque way of (in Hare's words[7]) "dramatizing" what the full reversibility test requires. In *MT* Hare suggests what he takes to be an alternative, though equivalent, way of putting the matter (a reformulation that has the effect of making his view essentially equivalent to that of John Harsanyi[8]): to determine whether he is willing to universalize his prescriptions the agent is to suppose that he has an *equal chance* of becoming any *one* of the persons (including himself) who will be affected by the action he is proposing to perform. It can be easily demonstrated that these two interpretations of the test are extensionally equivalent, yet the second does not involve the supposition that anyone will play the role of more than one person in any given situation.

There are, however, other objections to Hare's account of impartiality that cannot be gotten round quite so easily. In the remainder of this paper I shall argue for the following claims, each of which, if sustainable, would be sufficient to warrant rejection of that account:

(A) The contention that a person might be motivated by a *desire* to be fully impartial is incapable of a coherent, non-circular explication.

(B) Even if this incoherence could be eliminated, the claim that such impartiality is a mere formal requirement of morality is highly counterintuitive.

(C) The most defensible interpretation of Hare's metaethical theory does not by itself entail anything as strong as the full impartiality requirement.

III

The argument in support of the first of these claims (an argument which rests wholly on premises which Hare has explicitly endorsed) may be set out as follows.

1. A *moral judgment* $=_{def}$ a judgment made from the moral point of view.

2. A *judgment made from the moral point of view* $=_{def}$ a fully impartial judgment.

3. A *fully impartial judgment* $=_{def}$ a judgment made on the assumption that one has an equal chance of becoming fully identical with any of the persons − including oneself − who will be affected by how one acts.

4. *To become fully identical with a person* $=_{def}$ to acquire all of that person's properties (including all of his desires) and to lose all of one's own properties insofar as these are different.

5. Therefore, *a desire to make a fully impartial judgment* $=_{def}$ a desire to make a judgment on the assumption that one has a chance of acquiring all the properties (including desires) that one actually possesses that is equal to one's chance of acquiring all of the properties of any other person who will be affected by one's action.

6. Therefore, the definition of what a desire to make a fully impartial judgment consists in is viciously circular since it must *include* the fact that it is a desire to make one's judgment on the assumption that one has a chance of acquiring (among other things) a desire to make a fully impartial judgment.

Note that this argument does not demonstrate that there is anything incoherent in the concept of full impartiality itself. Nothing here entails that a person who lacked a desire to be fully impartial would be unable to *make* fully impartial judgments. What does follow, though, is that for such a person there would be no *practical* point to adopting the moral point of view since, *ex hypothesi*, he would not be concerned to *act* on the basis of the judgments he would thereby make. A moral philosopher, for example, concerned to understand and assess Hare's theory but lacking a desire *to be* fully impartial, would be able to make the required calculations but these would subserve a merely theoretical interest in determining the content of judgments made from the moral point of view. Hare, however, has insisted throughout his career that *assenting to* (as opposed to merely contemplating) a moral judgment has clear practical import. This he has explained by appeal to his theory that moral terms (at least in their most characteristic uses) are prescriptive and, therefore, that a person cannot sincerely assent to a moral principle without having a desire to act in accordance with that principle (see *LM*, Ch. 2, and *FR*, Ch. 5).

It must be conceded, of course, that a person could assent to a moral principle (in the sense just defined) for all sorts of reasons. Nothing Hare says, however, suggests that he would wish to call into question the Kantian claim that one's acts have moral worth only insofar as they are motivated by a desire to do what is morally right. But if the preceding argument is correct, this compels Hare to admit that *no* act can have moral worth in this sense since his theory entails that the moral motive is nothing more than a desire to be fully impartial, a desire which, I have argued, does not admit of a coherent explication.[9]

Hare could, of course, meet this objection if he could show that the desire to be fully impartial is properly definable in a way that does not involve a reference to itself. The simplest way of doing this, no doubt, would be to argue that a person, deliberating from the moral point of view, need consider only the possibility that he will come to acquire all of the desires that he actually has *except* the rather sophisticated, higher-order desire to be impartial. Of course such a response will appear *ad hoc* and therefore unconvincing unless a plausible reason can be supplied to justify making such an exclusion. Unfortunately considerations internal to Hare's theory suggest rather plainly that this is not possible. Hare has repeatedly insisted that the full reversibility test requires that one imagine oneself coming to acquire *all* the desires of *all* the persons who will be affected by how one is proposing to act. Moreover he admits to using the word "desire" in a wide sense "in which *any* felt disposition to action counts as a desire" (*FR*, p. 170). This means that when Arthur imagines himself to be Ben, he imagines himself coming to have all of the "pro-attitudes" that Ben has. The set of a person's pro-attitudes, however, will include everything from relatively simple, self-interested desires (e.g., desires for food or sex) to the more sophisticated desires Hare terms "ideals" (e.g., commitments to such goals as nuclear disarmament, the preservation of the snail darter or the extermination of non-Aryans).

And surely Hare is entirely correct here. What possible *formal* grounds could justify Arthur in excluding from consideration *any* of Ben's desires if Arthur's concern is merely to determine what he could universally prescribe. But if no such grounds exist, then nothing could justify Arthur in excluding from consideration any of his own desires when he imagines the situation in which he remains identical with himself. A disposition to be impartial, after all, may be one of Arthur's most distinguishing and important characteristics. For Arthur to imagine himself retaining all of his desires except that one would be for Arthur to imagine himself becoming fully identical not with himself but with (at best) some impoverished analogue of himself. (After all, absent his commitment to impartiality, Arthur might be an egoist rather than the generous and fair-minded person we all know and love.) It seems clear, therefore, the Hare could not license such an exclusion solely on the basis of an analysis of the concept of morality.

I know of no way of avoiding this difficulty which would not introduce significant modifications into Hare's theory. Still I would not wish to exclude the possibility that we may be able to construct a notion of impartiality that is both coherent and yet at least roughly congruent with the remaining features of Hare's theory. Suppose in fact that this can be done. Would there be anything to recommend our doing it? Hare of course, believes that there would be – viz., the fact that some such requirement is entailed by universal prescriptivism. I shall address that issue shortly. In the next section, though, I should like to concentrate on the intuitive plausibility of the full impartiality requirement as a constraint on the choice of fundamental moral principles *apart* from its connection to other elements in Hare's theory.

IV

I shall begin by considering David Gauthier's[10] interesting criticism of the impartiality requirement found in John Harsanyi's theory, a theory which, as I pointed out earlier, seems essentially equivalent to Hare's. Gauthier argues that Harsanyi's impartialism is an unsatisfactory foundation for a normative moral theory for two reasons. First, Gauthier maintains that there is a serious question (rather different from the one with which I have been concerned) as to the very intelligibility of requiring persons to deliberate on the basis of what Harsanyi terms the "equiprobability postulate", i.e., the assumption that a person has an equal chance of becoming any of the persons, herself included, who will be affected by what she does. Harsanyi's view (like Hare's) is that moral deliberation requires a moral agent: (1) to determine how and to what extent her action would affect the utility of each person involved; (2) to sum these utility increments (or decrements); and (3) to divide the result by the total number of persons involved (herself included). Hence "in choosing among prospects in ignorance of who one is, one maximizes expected utility by employing the average-utilitarian principle" (*op. cit*, p. 158). But Gauthier goes on to note that this is to treat moral judgments as a class of decisions made under uncertainty in which

the chooser does not know who he is, and so cannot express a single set of preferences, to be represented by a single utility function. Not only do the prospects among which he expresses preferences involve his coming to possess different personal characteristics; he is required to express each preference from the standpoint of the person with those characteristics. He does not have a single, unified standpoint from which to establish a preference ordering. The ordering that can be derived from calculating the average expected utility for each prospect is not the preference ordering of any individual chooser. The existence of a single interpersonal utility measure does not entail the existence of a single preference ordering (*ibid.*, p. 159)

Gauthier's charge here is a serious one. He is claiming that a knowledge of one's own utility function (which is tantamount to knowledge of a central aspect of one's identity as a person) is a requirement for making rational choices. He is therefore claiming that Harsanyi's theory is incoherent because it imposes a constraint on the making of rational moral decisions which has the effect of rendering any such decisions impossible.

I think this is a powerful criticism, but I am not convinced that it is as damaging as Gauthier thinks. No doubt if we assume that all choice-making depends (logically) on the existence of some set of preferences by which the choice can be motivated, and if we further assume that Harsanyi's theory requires that moral agents deliberate as if they had no preferences whatever, then Gauthier's criticisms would certainly be sustained. It seems to me, however, that Harsanyi could reply here in much the same way that Hare does (cf. *ETU*, p. 120). He could simply argue that it is rational for a person such as Arthur, deprived of the knowledge of his own utility function, to reason as if the utility of a given action to (say) Ben is identical with the utility *to himself* of *being* Ben in that situation. In other words, I see no reason why Harsanyi could not maintain that each moral agent is assumed to have (and assumed to know he has) one higher-order preference simply in virtue of knowing that he will turn out to be a *person*, viz., the desire to maximize the utility that is likely to accrue to whichever person he will actually turn out to be. There seems, at any rate, to be nothing in Gauthier's paper which would preclude Harsanyi from making such a response.

Perhaps anticipating the inconclusiveness of this first objection, Gauthier suggests another which he thinks will apply even if we suppose that individuals ignorant of their own identity would rationally choose on the basis of the average utilitarian principle:

Here we must draw an important distinction between an impartial bargain and an impartial choice. An impartial bargain reflects every point of view; its outcome is rational and fair for each fully informed bargainer. An impartial choice reflects no point of view; its outcome need be considered rational and fair by no chooser aware of his own identity. A rational bargain reconciles impartiality and individuality. An impartial choice secures its impartiality only by suppressing individuality, so that once individuality is reinstated, impartiality vanishes (*ibid.*, p. 160).

Whether Gauthier's theory is a more satisfactory account of impartiality than Harsanyi's is a matter than I am unable to discuss here. In the passage just quoted, however, Gauthier seems to suggest a criticism of Harsanyi's theory that does not rest solely upon a demonstration of the alleged superiority of Gauthier's (or any) bargaining model. That criticism is that Harsanyi's method of impartial choosing "suppresses" individuality since it "reflects no point of view". Unfortunately I think such a criticism is either open to the same sort of rejoinder made to Gauthier's first objection or is simply question-begging. After all Harsanyi could reply that his choice model *does* reflect a point of view, viz., the point of view of one who knows (1) that she is a utility maximizer, (2) that she has an equal chance of becoming any of the other persons involved in the choice situation, and (3) that, for each of these persons, the utility to her of becoming that person is equal to the utility that person himself would experience. Moreover Harsanyi — and even more so, Hare — would surely reject the charge that the "suppression" of individuality required by the equiprobability postulate is inappropriate as a constraint on the choice of moral principles. Indeed they would doubtless point out that a willingness to subject oneself to just such a thoroughgoing kind of impartiality is precisely what is involved in adopting the moral point of view. There is, after all, no good reason to believe that a serious commitment to moral concerns will be without correspondingly serious costs.

Although Gauthier's criticisms of Harsanyi are thus inconclusive, I think they at least point us along the right track. Let us consider again the example involving Arthur, Ben, and Carla. We are assuming that Arthur wishes to act in a morally permissible way in this situation. On Hare and Harsanyi's view this entails that he must choose in a fully impartial way, i.e., as if he had an equal chance of *being* Ben, Carla, or himself. Consider carefully what this means. It means that, for the purposes of determining the fundamental substantive principles of morality, the theory of Hare and Harsanyi requires a person to choose as if her concern with her own desires, interests, inclinations, ideals, and projects was no greater (though, of course, no less either) than her concern with the desires, interests, inclinations, ideals, and projects of anyone else. Starting with such an assumption, it is hardly surprising that Hare and Harsanyi end up with a strongly impartialist normative moral theory like utilitarianism, which bids us to take as our sole ultimate concern the maximization of aggregate preference satisfaction with no regard for the identity of those persons whose preferences are to be satisfied (except, of course, insofar as this information is needed to determine which course of action will in fact maximize aggregate preference satisfaction).

What I think gives Hare and Harsanyi's view its initial plausibility is the seemingly incontrovertible fact that *some* kind of impartiality is a central feature of the moral point of view.[11] Most of us believe, for example, that each person has the same set of fundamental natural rights even though we also believe that there are important natural differences between persons.[12] Most of us also believe that, from *some* morally relevant perspective, each person's life – indeed, each person – is of equal importance. Hence, since we expect our fundamental moral principles to reflect and give expression to this fact, we expect some sort of impartiality to be a requisite for any acceptable account of morality.

So far, I think, so good. My question is only whether this sort of impartiality is best interpreted as requiring that one be indifferent between all the goals and projects one actually has (except, of course, the desire to be impartial) and all those one would have if one were to become another person. Suppose Arthur wishes to become a novelist and Carla a surgeon. Is it really plausible to suppose that, in deciding upon the morally proper course of action, Arthur should choose as if it were the case that Carla's succeeding in her goal was as important *to him* as *his* succeeding in *his* goal (supposing, to avoid irrelevant objections, that the success of either person would be equally productive of utility)? Is it plausible to insist that this kind of impartialism is a *formal* condition of adequacy for moral judgments?

My own view – a view which I believe would be widely shared[13] – is that it is clearly not plausible to suppose this. I suspect, though, that Hare (and perhaps Harsanyi as well) would not be overly impressed with the claim (or even the *fact*) that their view is counterintuitive in this respect. For Hare, at least, is convinced that the full impartiality requirement is not just something that happens to be intuitively attractive but, rather, something that is *entailed* by a demonstrably correct thesis about moral language, viz., universal prescriptivism. Give Hare's well-known antipathy to moral intuitionism of any sort,[14] he would doubtless maintain that since his brand of impartialism can thus be argued for, any intuitions to the contrary carry little weight and ought to be disregarded.

Earlier (pp. 116–117) I gave a reconstruction of Hare's argument for the claim that, if someone sincerely assents to a singular moral prescription, he must be prepared to assent to some universalized moral principle regardless of which person he should turn out to be in that situation. Later on (p. 121) I suggested an argument that, from the assumption that one satisfies the formal requirements of morality by choosing on the basis of the equiprobability postulate, reaches the conclusion that all rational and informed moral agents will accept some form of utilitarianism. I shall not here call into question the soundness of either of these arguments. Rather, what I wish to investigate is the inference from the contention that a sincere moral agent must assent to some universalized moral principle (the conclusion of the first argument) to the claim concerning the equiprobability postulate (the central premise of the second[15]). It is the soundness of *that* inference that, I shall argue, is open to serious question.

V

Let us begin by considering how we are to analyze the assertion that a sincere universal prescriber must be prepared to assent to some universal moral principle regardless of which role he plays in the situation in question. Hare has argued, rightly I believe, that the general criterion of assent to a principle is a matter of how one is disposed to behave (see *LM*, p. 20). So what behavioral disposition must a sincere universal prescriber have? Suppose Arthur is contemplating the performance of some act *A* in the particular situation in which he presently finds himself. For dramatic purposes, suppose further that Arthur can insure that *A* occurs by pressing a button. It seems plausible to say that Arthur sincerely assents to the relevant universal principle in this situation only if he is prepared to press that button regardless of which person he imagines he will become.

In *FR*, it will be recalled, Hare maintained that Arthur's decision would have to be made *in propria persona*, i.e., on the basis of his knowledge of all of his own desires and inclinations. I have argued that in his later writings Hare gave up this view and now claims that Arthur's decision would have to be made from the standpoint of a wholly impartial observer. Nevertheless what is common to both formulations of the theory is the assumption that a necessary *and sufficient* condition for having sincerely assented to a universal principle is making one's decision as if one had a equal chance of becoming any of the other persons involved in the situation. It is that claim that I wish to challenge here.

To sincerely assent to a principle is, at the very least, to be disposed to act on the basis of that principle whenever and wherever it applies. If we suppose, with Hare, that complete role reversal is logically possible, then from the claim that

(A)   Arthur sincerely assents to universalized moral principle *P*,

we may validly infer that

(B)   Arthur would be prepared to act on the basis of *P* even if he
         believed he had an equal chance of becoming any one of the
         persons who might be affected by his acting on *P*.

Thus we may agree with Hare in maintaining that a willingness to reason on the basis of the equiprobability postulate is a necessary condition for adopting the moral point of view (at least if we ignore the coherence problems discussed in Section II). He is wrong, however, to hold that it is sufficient as well. For (A) also entails (among other things) the following:

(C)   Arthur would be prepared to act on the basis of P if, for any of the other persons who would be affected by his doing so, he believed that it was *certain* that he would become that person (and that it was certain that he would *not* become anyone else).

But, if I am correct, this will enable us to show that a sincere and rational universal prescriber need not be a utilitarian. We have already granted that, if doing A produces greater overall expected utility than failing to do A, Arthur would be irrational not to choose to do A if he were choosing on the basis of the equiprobability postulate. Furthermore, Arthur would be rationally required to do A even if he knew that one of the persons he might turn out to be − Ben, say, − would suffer a serious overall utility loss if A were performed so long as the average expected utility of doing A would exceed the average expected utility of not doing A. If, however, an additional requirement of Arthur's sincerely assenting to P is his willingness to press the button even if he knows for certain that he will definitely assume Ben's role (and no one else's), we may have to conclude that he does not assent to P since he may well not be prepared to press the button in *that* situation. The reason why he might hesitate is quite simple: he may be understandably unwilling to suffer the enormous utility loss that we are supposing would accrue to Ben just for the sake of adhering to P. Surely there is nothing irrational or inconceivable about such reluctance.

One implication of my interpretation of what it means to assent to a moral principle is that each role in a given situation carries with it the functional equivalent of a veto with respect to the performance of an act on the basis of that principle. In other words, in the case under discussion, we would be forced to conclude that Arthur could not assent to P so long as there was even *one* person such that Arthur would refrain from pushing the button if he knew he would become that person in some possible situation.

Hare has explicitly considered the possibility of so interpreting the requirements of universal prescriptivity. His response is as follows:

[A]lthough, considering some one distribution of the roles in isolation from the others, I may be disposed to reject the prescription because in that role I would be the victim, this does not commit me to rejecting it *simpliciter*. For it may be that the disadvantages to the person in that role are outweighed in sum by the advantages to the others. If this is the case, I may be willing to accept the disadvantages, were I in that role, as the price of the greater total advantages to the occupants of the other roles, any of which I might occupy.[16]

It is certainly true that, if we assume the existence of something like an interpersonal utility metric, there will be cases in which one person's disadvantages are outweighed by the sum of the advantages accruing to others. Unfortunately what is needed but not provided here is an argument for thinking that choosing on the basis of the equiprobability postulate is *sufficient* for satisfying the metaethical requirements of universal prescriptivism. In the absence of such an argument Hare's response simply begs the question.

It may be thought that, on my view, the criteria of assent to a moral principle are so stringent that it becomes very unlikely that anyone could ever be said to accept any substantive moral principle. After all, almost any moral principle is such that its implementation would generally result in at least some person's being worse off than he would be were some alternative principle enacted. (Only if acting on a principle were maximally productive of utility for *every* individual involved would this not be true.) Isn't the practical effect of my proposal, therefore, that virtually every principle proposed in virtually every situation is such that it will be vetoed by someone in that situation?

The flaw in this argument should be obvious. It wrongly assumes that I am claiming that a necessary condition of *my* assenting to a moral principle is that *everyone else* involved also assent to it. It may be readily conceded that there are very few principles indeed that would pass a test as stringent as that. But this is not my view. Rather, I am arguing only that a sincere universal prescriber must be willing to "press the button" in every case in which he knows that he will definitely *play the role of* another person. But the only assent required in such cases is the assent of the *universal prescriber* himself, not that of every person he is imagining he will become.

But how are we to determine what I would assent to if I knew I would definitely play the role of another person in a given situation? Here things get a bit sticky. On Hare's view, to imagine being another person is not simply to *imagine* coming to have all of his preferences but to *actually* come to have those preferences with respect to oneself in that situation:

If we are to make an informed moral judgment, we have to make it in full knowledge and awareness of the available facts; and the agent does not have this full knowledge and awareness of one of the available facts, namely the sufferings of his victim, unless he is aware of what it is like to be that person; and this he cannot be aware of unless he puts himself in thought in that person's position. But if he does this, he will be having the same desires as that person has. If he does not have them, he lacks the necessary awareness, because the desires are what he has to be aware of, and one can be aware of desires, in the required sense, only by having them. ... *Complete sympathy*, not mere empathy, is a requirement of moral thought.[17]

It is easy enough to see why Hare would be inclined to endorse what I shall call the "sympathy thesis". If moral deliberation requires that I literally come to *have* the desires of everyone concerned, and if I am rationally required to choose on the basis of Bayesian principles, then of course I will (necessarily) elect to maximize expected utility. But *why* does Hare think that *identifying* with other persons in this strong sense is required for the making of moral choices?[18] I suspect that the answer is connected with his belief that universal prescriptivism requires that moral agents choose *as if* they did not know their own preferences together with the conceptual truth that all choice-making requires the existence of *some* preferences to serve as motivation (see, e.g., *ETU*, p. 120). The function of sympathy would then be to *provide* those motivating preferences.

But even if this is Hare's argument, it is still a mistake to suppose that he has shown that a universal prescriptivist is *committed* to (something like) the sympathy thesis. This is because nowhere has Hare demonstrated that there is anything in universal prescriptivism which entails that, in deliberating, a moral agent *must* disregard his knowledge of which set of desires he has. As I argued in Section I, it was Hare's insistence in *FR* that moral decisions are made *in propria persona*, i.e., on the basis of a full awareness of one's own identity, that allowed for the possibility of fanaticism and thereby blocked the inference to utilitarianism. I also argued that it was Hare's later endorsement of the contrary view that moral decisions must be made from a wholly impartial viewpoint that both eliminated the problem of fanaticism and permitted the derivation of utilitarianism. But there seems to be nothing in the doctrine of universal prescriptivism that *requires* this change! To ask whether a person sincerely assents to a moral principle is to ask only whether *that* person, with *his* particular constellation of preferences, would assent to that principle. (In Arthur's case, it is to ask only whether Arthur, if rational and fully informed, would press the button.) But what permissible *formal* restrictions may be imposed on the making of such a choice? One certainly cannot maintain that a moral deliberator must disregard *all* of his preferences in deciding how to act. That, as Gauthier rightly points out, would be incoherent. But then how could an appeal confined to the universality and prescriptivity of moral language provide a warrant for Hare's view that a moral deliberator, *qua* moral, will disregard knowledge of any of his preferences *except* for his higher-order preferences for impartiality and utility maximization (i.e., those he has simply in virtue of being moral and rational)? Such a requirement would seem clearly to qualify as a *substantive*, not a merely formal, constraint on moral decision making.[19] As Harry Silverstein has pointed out, "any requirement that imposes restrictions on what may be regarded as a *basis* or *ground* for undertaking [a commitment to some moral principle] ... cannot be justified merely by reference to universality and prescriptivity".[20]

If what I have argued in this paper is correct, Hare's attempt to show that universal prescriptivism provides a "formal foundation" for utilitarianism must be judged a failure. This is because, even after the confusion and inconsistency found in his earliest writings on the subject have been eliminated, his derivation still depends on the following four theses, the first two of which are demonstrably false, the last two of which are at least implausible and in need of far more support than Hare provides: (1) sincerely assenting to a universal moral principle does not merely entail but is equivalent to affirming that principle in a situation in which one makes one's decision on the basis of the equiprobability postulate; (2) the desire to be fully impartial is a coherent one; (3) one's decision to affirm or reject a moral principle is to be made not *in propria persona* but from the standpoint of an Ideal Observer; and (4) one cannot imagine (in the sense relevant for morality) the feelings and desires of another person without coming to *have* those feelings and desires. Finally, I have also called into question the intuitive plausibility of full impartiality as a formal constraint on moral decision making. Although, as I conceded earlier, the latter criticism would carry little weight with Hare, it would certainly have to be taken seriously by anyone who holds that a condition of adequacy for a moral theory is some significant measure of congruence with our considered moral judgments.[21]

Department of Philosophy
Illinois State University

NOTES

[1] Among the more important of Hare's writings are the following: *The Language of Morals* (hereafter "*LM*") (Oxford: Clarendon Press, 1952); *Freedom and Reason*

(hereafter "*FR*") (Oxford: Clarendon Press, 1963); "Reply to R. S. Katz" in B. Y. Khanbai *et al.* (eds.), *Jowett Papers 1968–1969* (Oxford: Basil Blackwell, 1970), pp. 44–52; "Rawls' Theory of Justice" in Norman Daniels (ed.), *Reading Rawls* (New York: Basic Books, 1975), pp. 81–107; "Ethical Theory and Utilitarianism" (hereafter "*ETU*") in H. D. Lewis (ed.), *Contemporary British Philosophy*, Fourth Series (London: Allen and Unwin, 1976), pp. 113–131; "Relevance" in A. I. Goldman and J. Kim (eds.), *Values and Morals* (Dordrecht: D. Reidel, 1978), pp. 73–90; "What Makes Choices Rational," *The Review of Metaphysics,* **32** (1979), 623–637; and *Moral Thinking* (hereafter "*MT*") (Oxford: Clarendon Press, 1981).

2 Actually, as my colleague Mark Timmons has pointed out to me, the thesis that metaethics is normatively neutral is ambiguous. On the one hand, it could be understood to mean that an analysis of the meaning of moral language does not *require* or *presuppose* any substantive moral principles. So interpreted, the thesis is one that Hare has always endorsed and it is not called into question by anything he maintains in his later writings. On the other hand, the neutrality thesis could also be understood as a denial of the claim that *from* a correct analysis of moral language (together, perhaps, with other, non-moral, premises) we may *derive* substantive normative principles. The quotation on p. 115 suggests that Hare also accepted this second version of the thesis when he wrote *FR*. His present view, however, seems to be that this version is false and that the inference in question is a valid one (see, e.g., *ETU*, pp. 116–117, and *MT*, p. 111).

3 These include: Kurt Baier, *The Moral Point of View* (Ithaca: Cornell University press, 1958); John Harsanyi, "Morality and the Theory of Rational Behavior", *Social Research,* **44** (1977), 623–656; Thomas Nagel, *The Possibility of Altruism* (Oxford: Clarendon Press, 1970); John Rawls, *A Theory of Justice* (Cambridge, Mass.: Harvard University Press, 1971); and Peter Singer, *Practical Ethics* (Cambridge: Cambridge University Press, 1979).

4 In "Reply to R. S. Katz", however, he does state that it would be "logically impossible for a person to prescribe that he himself should have more rather than less suffering" (p. 51). There is also some question as to whether Hare regards rationality as independent of or as entailed by universalizability. A discussion of these matters is found in H. M. Robinson, "Is Hare a Naturalist?", *Philosophical Review,* **91** (1982), 76–77.

5 See, in this connection, Robert Fullinwider's instructive discussion of the similarities between Hare's appeal to the standpoint of the Ideal Observer and Rawls's use of the veil of ignorance ("Fanaticism and Hare's Moral Theory", *Ethics,* **87** (1977), 172–173).

6 This is because a requirement of assenting to a singular moral prescription of the form "*P* ought to do *A* in situation *S*" is that the agent at least be prepared to assent to a minimally universalized prescription of the form:

> Anyone who has a set of characteristics qualitatively identical to those *P* possesses ought to perform an action whose characteristics are qualitatively identical to those *A* possesses in any situation qualitatively identical to *S*.

I term this principle "minimally" universalized because it is the one universal prescription the agent *must* assent to if he assents to the original singular prescription (since it is *entailed* by any other more general universal principle to which he might appeal to justify his assenting to the original singular prescription).

7 "What Makes Choices Rational", p. 635.

8 Harsanyi has argued that a version of preference utilitarianism "is the only ethical theory consistent with both the modern theory of rational behavior and a full commitment

to an impartially sympathetic humanitarian morality" ("Morality and the Theory of Rational Behavior", pp. 654–655). The theory of rational behavior to which Harsanyi refers here is Bayesian. Moreover the commitment to an "impartially sympathetic humanitarian morality" is explicated in terms of what he calls the "equiprobability postulate", viz., "the fictitious assumption of having the same probability of occupying any possible social position" (*ibid.*, p. 632). To satisfy the demands imposed by that assumption, Harsanyi requires not only that we imagine ourselves being in the situation of the other persons involved but that we also imagine ourselves having their tastes, preferences and desires (*ibid.*, p. 638). Finally, utility is defined wholly in terms of the satisfaction of those tastes, preferences and desires (*ibid.*, p. 644). In all essential respects, therefore, Harsanyi's theory seems identical to Hare's.

[9] It should be noted that circularity also arises in cases where one of the persons ("*B*") that the moral deliberator ("*A*") is imagining he will become *also* has a desire to be fully impartial. For *A*'s desire to be fully impartial is a desire to choose how to act on the supposition that he has a chance of turning out to be *B*, a person who (we are supposing) also has a desire to be fully impartial. But any attempt to explicate in turn the content of *B*'s desire to be fully impartial will necessarily involve essential reference to *A*'s desire to be fully impartial (since *B*'s desire to be fully impartial must be cashed out as a desire to choose how to act on the supposition that he has a chance of turning out to be *A*).

[10] David Gauthier, "On the Refutation of Utilitarianism" in Harlan B. Miller and William H. Williams (eds.) *The Limits of Utilitarianism* (Minneapolis: University of Minnesota Press, 1982), pp. 144–163.

[11] See, for example, Paul Taylor, "On Taking the Moral Point of View", *Midwest Studies in Philosophy,* **III** (1978), 35–61.

[12] For an alternative account of impartiality that is developed along these lines, see Kai Nielsen, "Universalizability and the Commitment to Impartiality", this volume.

[13] Some recent critical discussions of the view that what I have termed "full impartiality" is a constitutive element of the moral point of view are Lawrence Blum. *Friendship, Altruism and Morality* (London: Routledge and Kegan Paul, 1980), Ch. 3; John Cottingham, "Ethics and Impartiality", *Philosophical Studies,* **43** (1983), 83–99; John Kekes, "Morality and Impartiality", *American Philosophical Quarterly,* **18** (1981), 295–303; and J. L. Mackie, *Ethics: Inventing Right and Wrong* (Hammondsworth: Penguin Books, 1977), Ch. 4.

[14] Most forcefully stated in "Rawls' Theory of Justice", *passim.*

[15] Although Hare *usually* writes as if this connection can be made, there is at least one passage in his writings where he expresses doubt: "My own theory secures impartiality by a combination of the requirement that moral judgments be universalizable and the requirement to prescribe for hypothetical reversed-role situations as if they were actual (I am not sure whether the second is an independent condition or not)" ("Rawls' Theory of Justice", p. 93).

[16] "What Makes Choices Rational", pp. 634–635.

[17] "Relevance", pp. 80–81.

[18] See the criticisms of the sympathy thesis in H. M. Robinson, "Imagination, Desire and Prescription", *Analysis,* **41** (1981), 55–59, and Ingmar Persson, "Hare on Universal Prescriptivism and Utilitarianism", *Analysis,* **43** (1983), 43–49.

[19] It should be noted that Rawls (rightly) regards the veil of ignorance (which is the

functional equivalent of Hare's impartiality requirement) as a *substantive* constraint on moral decision making. See, for example, *A Theory of Justice*, Section 40 and "Kantian Constructivism in Moral Theory", *The Journal of Philosophy*, 77 (1980), 515–72. A discussion of the rationale which underlies the veil of ignorance constraint may be found in my paper, "Rawls on Natural Inequality", *The Philosophical Quarterly*, 33 (1983), 1–18.

[20] Harry S. Silverstein, "Universality and Treating Persons as Persons", *The Journal of Philosophy*, 71 (1974), 60.

[21] An earlier version of this paper was read before a philosophy colloquium at Illinois State University. For helpful comments and criticism I am particularly grateful to Harry Deutsch and Mark Timmons.

WILLIAM G. LYCAN

ABORTION AND THE CIVIL RIGHTS OF MACHINES

Abortion poses a crucial and vexing social issue, squarely because it poses an even more crucial and vexing moral issue. In this paper I shall approach abortion as a moral question, letting social, political and legal thinkers draw their own conclusions as they may.

Some moral questions are reasonably easy to answer upon reflection. Others are less tractable. The latter often are so hard to settle mainly because of the difficulty of agreeing on all the relevant facts. (For example, a great deal of the disagreement over the Vietnam war was purely factual disagreement — whether such-and-such treaties were in force, whether the U.S. had a clear and feasible military objective, whether a Viet Cong victory would in fact be followed by a bloodbath, whether the war was a civil war or indeed the invasion of one nation by another, etc., etc. — and the issues were liberally thickened with deliberate distortions and lies.) What I shall argue here, in contrast, is that the wrenchingly difficult abortion question is difficult, not because of any unsettled factual matters, but because of an important indeterminacy in our moral consciousness. Specifically, I shall argue that a fetus is a being of a uniquely exceptional sort, about whose putative rights we simply have no clear moral intuitions (at least, we have no clear *and responsible* intuitions about them). No further fact-gathering — or even metaphysical proof — will help; we are in the position of simply having to develop our moral senses further in order to see what to do, or not to do, about fetuses.

1. I shall be arguing that sobering skeptical claim, and tentatively exploring a solution, by somewhat roundabout means. I want to consider the abortion issue in the light of a comparison between fetuses and some hypothetical machines of several different kinds. I shall begin by exhibiting a disanalogy between fetuses and machines of the first kind, and arguing my skeptical claim on the basis of that disanalogy. Then I shall contend that fetuses do *not* differ in any morally relevant way from machines of one of the other kinds, and that some of our reasonably clear moral feelings about the latter may be extended *via* universalizability to the former: my defense of this contention will be a very weak one, but if my earlier reasoning is correct, the universalizing argument is (alas) the strongest we are likely to get.

139

Nelson Potter and Mark Timmons (eds.), Morality and Universality, 139–156.
© 1985 *by D. Reidel Publishing Company.*

In order to carry out this strategy, I shall have to begin with a discussion of machines and their claims, such as they may be, to civil rights.[1]

One of the important consequences common to currently prevailing materialist theories of mind is the claim that human beings are nothing more than complex organisms of a very sophisticated kind, composed entirely of physical matter.[2] It seems to follow from this that it is possible (as they say) in principle to build our own androids, artificial humans, which would have at least as firm a claim to be called *persons* as we do. Given the progress that has been made in recent years by researchers in artificial intelligence (AI), on machine perception, problem-solving, sensorimotor function and the like, it seems quite conceivable (even if unlikely) that androids of the sort I am imagining *will* be constructed, say within the next five hundred years. Perhaps AI researchers will build an electronic computer whose inner logical states are isomorphic to psychologically relevant states of the human nervous system. However, there are indications[3] that no digital computer will ever successfully simulate human performance of any real complexity. We might have to build up an exact duplicate of a human body, cell by cell, or learn to synthesize DNA and grow our own. In any case, an android or robot-person thus constructed would be capable of having any known mental state or of undergoing any known mental event or process, if its maker desired to endow it with such a capacity.[4]

Suppose, now, that scientists or commercial firms see fit to turn out a substantial number of such androids, for whatever purposes. It would seem that these artificial humans, if they are indeed as clearly entitled to be called *persons* as we are, will have moral rights of exactly the same sort we have, whatever those rights may be. If so, and if you and I live up to our moral responsibilities, the androids will be admitted to full membership in the community of ends, and there will accrue to them all the various privileges that everyone else enjoys.

It is of course not uncontroversial that a manmade object could be sentient or conscious. The androids I am talking about will be made, by human engineers, entirely out of physical matter, and all their attributes will be physical attributes; many philosophers even in our scientistic time deny that any such object could ever be more than a "*mere* machine". Nonsentient physical objects are not persons and surely have no rights at all.

If I am ever to get to the main topic of this paper, I cannot take up this much-gnawed bone of contention; I shall merely state my reason (a simple one) for rejecting our hard-hearted human chauvinists' claim, and regard my later conclusions concerning abortion as conditional upon this rejection.

2. I reserve the right to suppose that a smart AI researcher, neuroanatomist or geneticist might build a robot that could *behave* in any way that a human could possibly behave. It is reasonable to hypothesize that one day we will be confronted with a much-improved version of Hal, the soft-spoken computer in Stanley Kubrick's *2001* (younger readers may substitute *Star Wars*' C3PO). Let us call this more versatile robot *Harry*. By hypothesis, Harry is humanoid in form (he is a miracle of miniaturization, and has lifelike plastic skin), and he can converse intelligently on all sorts of subjects, play golf, write passable poetry, control his occasional nervousness fairly well, make love, prove mathematical theorems (of course), show envy when outdone, throw gin bottles at annoying children, etc., etc. We may suppose he fools people into thinking he is human. Now the question is, is Harry actually conscious? Is he a person, or is he just a mindless walking hardware store whose movements are astoundingly like those of a person?

Plainly his acquaintances would tend from the first to see him as a person, even if they were aware of his dubious antecedents. I think it is a plain psychological fact, if nothing more, that we could not help treating him as a person, unless we resolutely made up our minds, on principle, not to give him the time of day. But how could we really tell that he is conscious? Well, how do we really tell that *any* humanoid body is conscious? Surely we tell, and decisively, on the basis of our standard behavioral criteria for mental states.[5] And by hypothesis, Harry fulfills all our criteria with a vengeance; moreover he does so *in the right way* — the processing that comprises his behavior's etiology is just like ours. It follows that we are justified in believing him to be conscious.

This justification is less than deductive, of course, behaviorism being false. For that matter, it provides practical certainty only so long as the situation is not palpably extraordinary or bizarre. The human chauvinist thinks precisely that Harry is as bizarre as they come. But what is (relevantly) bizarre about him? There are quite a few human-chauvinist answers to this, each of which singles out some feature or alleged feature of Harry and protests that nothing with that feature could be conscious or have a mental life. Such objections have been replied to amply in the literature, and I believe it is relatively easy to show that none of the extant complaints is sound. Instead of rehearsing the moves here,[6] I want to discuss a contrasting methodological view of the *dialectics* of machine consciousness, for it is the dialectical issue that bears on the abortion controversy.

3. None of the brute facts about Harry *compels* us deductively to call Harry

a person (or not to call him one). In light of this, some philosophers have maintained that our language does not contain rules that specifically and determinately govern talk about the minds of nonhumans; no lexical entry or law of logic says either that talented artifacts are conscious or that they are not. Hilary Putnam has written (1964, p. 690) that " . . . the question: are robots conscious? calls for a decision on our part, to treat robots as fellow members of our linguistic community, or not to so treat them" – not for any more factual discoveries. Raziel Abelson (1966, p. 308) imagines a case in which Earth is visited by a Martian spaceship which, upon landing disgorges creatures that are android-*like* and plainly nonhuman.

Would we automatically admit this creature [the first one we observed] into the Kantian society of rational beings? No doubt some of us would; but others, more stubbornly skeptical, would suspect it to be a product of Martian engineering, able to simulate psychologically motivated behavior although cold and empty 'inside', lacking the 'internal' states of feeling and emotion that real persons have. Would there be any rational ground for denying such skeptics a logical right to be skeptical? I can think of no logical or semantical rule they might be accused of violating. In other words, we simply do not have established criteria for deciding whether *creatures other than human beings* are to be considered as persons subject to psychological description.

This suggests that there is no fact of the matter, that the "decision" as to whether or not the Martian, or Harry, is conscious is really arbitrary and/or governed only by local convenience.

I think this view is squarely wrong. Even if no logical or semantical rule legislates pro or con, we have perfectly sound epistemic procedures, already in play, that legislate pro. (One such might be formulated as, "When a humanoid organism is visibly damaged, moving its limbs, rubbing the damaged part, grimacing and groaning, then (other things being equal) we believe that that organism is feeling pain.") As I have said, Harry satisfies all the antecedent conditions of such rules. In what ways are other things not equal? When it comes right down to it, the only differences between Harry and you or me are his *origin* (a laboratory is not a proper mother, in the words of the song), and the *chemical composition of his anatomy*, if his maker has, e.g., used silicon instead of carbon. To exclude him from our community for either or both of these reasons seems to me to be a clear case of race prejudice (literally) and nothing more.

Further, to say that we shall "just have to make a decision" is to suggest that our choice will be purely verbal, a matter of arbitrary stipulation concerning how a certain English word is to be used; shall we extend our use of 'person' to cover such-and-such unusual cases, or not? Since there is no factual right or wrong about an answer to this question, no important or substantive issue can hang on it. But an important issue does hang on the question of whether robots are persons, viz., that with which we began, that of robots' natural and civil rights. If flawless human simulators like Harry have moral rights, and if we fail to respect those rights, say by enslaving Harry or murdering him for fun, then moral wrong will have been done, and that is no arbitrary matter, but a very serious one.

4. Let us turn (finally) to the case of abortion.[7] Some philosophers and laymen have felt that the abortion issue is not primarily a moral issue at all, but a difficult factual or metaphysical one. Is a fetus a *person* or is it not? Once we have answered this tough question of fact, it is thought, the current moral debate will be easily settled. For a *person*, we all agree, has the right not to be killed merely for the sake of someone else's convenience, while an organism that is clearly not a person has no such right. The difficulty, then, lies in ascertaining the facts.

I disagree entirely with this reconstruction of the problem. It seems to me that the question, "Is a fetus a person or not?" *is* a purely verbal one, calling for an arbitrary, stipulative decision as an answer. For there are no further (relevant) facts for us to learn about fetuses. We know, more or less, which properties fetuses share with full-grown humans and which they do not. In this sense, all the facts are in.[8] The only possible answer to the question, "Is a fetus a person?" is, "Well, yes and no; it's a borderline case − a fetus is like a clear case of a person in respects *A*, *B*, and *C*, but unlike a clear case in respects *D*, *E*, and *F*, and it also has properties *G* and *H*." Whether you want to call such a being a 'person' or not is up to you; the implicit lexical rules of English (that we already have) are not detailed enough to give a verdict one way or the other. If this is right, the moral issue returns in full force: is it wrong to kill a being having this particular set of properties? The question of whether or not such beings are to be *called* 'persons' is trivial and irrelevant.

Notice that this conclusion defuses at one and the same time both the most popular anti-abortion argument and the most popular pro-abortion argument to be found in letters to the editor. The anti-abortion argument is, "A fetus is a person, and it is always wrong to kill a person merely for convenience; therefore, abortion is immoral." The pro-abortion argument is, "A fetus is not a person, but a mere appendage, a growth like a wart, 'protoplasmic rubbish'; therefore it has no intrinsic right not to be killed for convenience, and if no actual person has any objection to its disposal, it may be aborted with impunity." Both these arguments, one from each side of the issue, assume that the fetus is a clear case with respect to personhood. But this is precisely what a fetus is not. Our moral question is that of whether a fetus is *enough like* a clear case of a person to be covered by the moral prohibition against killing persons for convenience, or, on the other hand, enough like a mere wart or growth to be morally neglected. Our popular anti-abortion "argument" simply assumes the former, while our popular pro-abortion "argument" simply assumes the latter. Thus, each *begins* by taking an unsupported stand on the very question at issue.[9]

My view is, then, that so far there is no clearly right intuitive answer to the question, "Does a thing *like that* (having those undisputed descriptive properties) have the right not to be killed for convenience?"

5. Now are robots in the same sort of situation? The view of Putnam and Abelson suggests that they are, but I think they are not. The difference is this: In the case of the fetus, as I have said, all the morally relevant facts are in; there is no further scientific or metaphysical research that needs to be done. But in the case of Harry, the human chauvinist and I do *not* agree on all the morally relevant facts. One factual question, that of whether Harry really has thoughts, desires, feelings and so on, is just what is at issue. It is precisely these properties (the mental ones) that make the moral difference in our dispute; people's moral attitudes toward conscious beings differ vastly from their attitudes toward inanimate ones. If I am right in rejecting Putnam and Abelson's "arbitrary decision" thesis, this constitutes a crucial difference between Harry and a fetus. What, then, of our analogy between fetuses and machines?

There is a good deal more to the matter of machine consciousness. We have considered cases of just two kinds: "mere" machines, such as refrigerators, which invite no inclination at all to believe that they are conscious, and extremely gifted machines like Harry, whom (I have argued) we do and should want to call persons. But it is reasonable to think that not all future machines will fall into one or other other of these two groups. For AI researchers may well build machines which will appear to have some mental capacities but not others. The most obvious example is that of a sensor or perception, which picks up information from its immediate environment, records, it, and stores it in memory for future printout. (We already have at least crude machines of this kind. When they become versatile and sophisticated enough, it will be quite natural to say that they see or hear and that they remember.) But the possibility of "specialist" machines of this kind raises an unforeseen contingency and thereby a Sorites paradox. As I have said, we have clear cases of two types: flawless human simulators such as Harry, and current unsophisticated machines which obviously do not qualify as persons but which may behave in a goal-directed way. Examples of this second type are refrigerators, radars that track flying objects, and record-changers that "think" there is still a record to be dropped onto the turntable whenever I have left the changer-arm locked in the "up" position. In fact, we have many current machines that can naturally be said to "think" or "want" or "intend" this or that, but always in the sneer-quoted sense. As is common in philosophy, we can construct a many-dimensional spectrum of possible situations connecting the two types of clear case. And we are at a loss as to where the cutoff point or "personhood" line should be drawn between them, even though we feel there is considerable sense to the question of just where on this spectrum we are allowed to drop the sneer quotes. How complex, eclectic, and impressive must a machine be, in order to be rightly judged conscious?

I cannot believe that there is any precise point or line (Putnam and Abelson are surely right at least to that extent). Moreover, if we accept any prevailing account of how the words of a natural language fit the world, there is no reason why there ought to be any antecedently given cutoff, especially since very few of the indefinitely large number of intermediate cases has ever been actualized. So, in many of these cases that fall midway between record-changers etc. and the egregiously capable Harry, it looks as if we really just will have to make a decision. (Notice, it does not follow from this that our views about *Harry*, the clear case, must likewise rest on a "decision".) What this result seems to come to is that the term 'person' is intrinsically vague and may express what is only a family-resemblance concept. In this respect, the concept of a person is not unlike that of baldness or that of a game, only much more convolute due to the much greater variety of possible intermediate cases.

Philosophers of a Cartesian bent will find this claim repugnant to their common sense. Consciousness, they will say, is consciousness; either a thing is conscious or it is not. How could there be a borderline case of consciousness? (Descartes himself willfully ruled one borderline case out of court when he judged *a priori* that *animals* were mindless machines.) But there is a good reason why people should have thought until now that the concepts of consciousness, personhood and so on are "closed", viz., the brute fact that, so far as we know, there never has been a nonhuman person. To infer that there never could be one, however, would be simply fallacious.

Let us see what we can now say about the moral rights of machines. So far as our two clear cases go, matters are pretty straightforward. Machines in the definitely nonsentient group have, in themselves, no rights at all. (I think we may safely make this claim of any definitely nonsentient being, or at least – to avoid prejudging the abortion issue – of any being that by itself has not even the faintest potential or capacity for being conscious, be it inorganic, dead, or living. There may be plentiful aesthetic reasons against, say, destroying plants. There may even be moral reasons against doing that; but these moral reasons (so far as I can see) inevitably involve the feelings or desires of conscious beings – of humans, extraterrestrials, or God. None of the reasons against destroying plants issues from any natural right intrinsically possessed by the plants themselves.)

Our other clear case, that of Harry and his comrades, is equally trouble-free. If Harry is as much a person as you or I, then, other things being equal, he is entitled to whatever moral consideration we are. To deny him any standard human right (consistently with the Universalizability Principle), we would have to point to some morally relevant difference between Harry and the rest of us. But there are (as I remarked above) only two noticeable differences: Harry is an artifact, and he may be made of hardware instead of soft stuff or silicon instead of carbon. The moral relevance of these differences is no greater than their psychological relevance. If we object to race discrimination in our present society, we should object to discrimination against Harry on the basis of his birthplace. Location and mode of origin are not morally relevant characteristics of beings – or at least, some positive moral argument would have to be provided if anyone wanted to maintain that they were relevant in this or any case. Nor does Harry's physical composition seem germane. We do not discriminate against a person who has a wooden leg, or a mechanical kidney, or a nuclear heart regulator. Of course I cannot prove that there is no moral difference between merely having a prosthesis of some currently available kind and being made entirely of laboratory parts, but I am at a loss to *see* any moral difference – again, some strong moral argument would be required of anyone who proposed to deny Harry his moral rights or civil liberties.

But what, now, about all the many possible intermediate cases of robot-persons, those which have some human capacities but not others? Here the moral issue becomes difficult, especially since it is hard for us now to imagine what such various sorts of beings will be like. But it is an issue that must be settled, because we shall soon be faced with the intermediate robots themselves, much sooner than we might ever be faced with perfect simulators like Harry. One obvious reason for this is that the intermediate robots will be much easier to design and construct. Another reason, much more significant morally, is that we will be designing machines, as we always have, mainly as *labor-saving devices*, as servants who will work for free; and servants of this kind are (literally) made to be exploited. The exploitation of beings whom we are at all inclined to describe as conscious is always suspect at the outset.

Some hypothetical machines, then, are borderline cases of personhood, mentally *and* morally speaking. There are others. For moral purposes, animals are borderline. (Some tenderhearted people think that even plants are borderline.) A more trenchant case is that of a brain-damaged human being in irreversible coma. And it is easy to imagine alien beings who are like clear cases of persons in some respects but like trivial mechanical devices in other respects.

It is to such intermediate cases that I believe fetuses should be compared *ab initio*. A fetus is comparable, not to the formidable Harry, but to a *medium-grade* machine, one which has some distinctively human attributes or analogues of them, but which completely lacks other important humanoid features.

We have at least one practical way of treating beings as morally borderline: we award them some rights but not others. Thus, an animal has the right not to be gratuitously tortured — at least, we would do moral wrong to torture it — but it may be "enslaved" and used to bear burdens. Is there a way of saying, responsibly, what rights (if any) a fetus has in common with mature human beings and what rights it does not have?

6. In order to make such a distinction we must inquire in more detail just *what sort* of borderline case of personhood a fetus is, i.e., what kinds of properties it shares with mature humans and what kinds it shares with warts. To catalogue these two groups of properties would be a big job. On the one hand, obviously, a fetus is made of the same biochemical matter as we; its anatomy is a crude version of ours; it has a unique human genetic code; etc. On the other hand, it does not think, reason, or use a language; it has no desires or wants; it has no moral sense; it has no concept of its own future or of its own welfare, nor any wish to go on living; it has no emotions or memories. These two lists could be extended indefinitely, but one thing is clear: the properties on the first list, species-distinctive biological properties, do not carry nearly the moral weight that those on the second list do. As Harry's case shows, biochemical constiution is all but irrelevant; Harry could be made out of anything, and have any genetic makeup, and still have all

the moral rights we do. It is his ability to reason, to feel, to have needs and desires and so on, that makes him worthy of moral consideration. Therefore it is tempting to conclude, as some people do, that the properties the fetus shares with mature humans are morally negligible, while those human attributes it lacks are precisely the ones which confer moral status, and so the fetus does not have any moral rights at all.

To conclude this would be to overlook the one striking factor that distinguishes fetuses *from other* borderline cases of personhood, viz., the poignant habit they have of *normally developing into* mature people. Fetuses are potential persons, over and above being marginal ones. And surely it is this fact that gives rise to most of the ongoing moral controversy over abortion.[10] It is also this fact, I think, that explains the uncertainty of our moral feelings about abortion and the consequent intractability of the moral problem: The difficulty is that a fetus is the *only* sort of object in our experience that has this property. In this respect it is completely unique. There is nothing that a fetus is *like*, nothing about which we have any clearer moral intuitions and to which the fetus may usefully be compared.[11]

My thesis, more generally put, is that fetuses occupy, or perhaps constitute, a gap in moral space. To see this, let us run the abortion issue briefly by each of the major types of ethical theory and note the resulting indeterminacies.

6.1. *Utilitarianism.* A notable virtue of good old Benthamian Act-Utilitarianism is its ready applicability, or so I enjoy telling my introductory ethics students: given any complete set of facts about a proposed act, Bentham's theory immediately yields an unequivocal decision. The act of having an abortion seems to be an exception, however, since the issue concerns, not what numbers to fill in on our utility chart or what weighting function to use in determining our overall ratings, but what "affected parties" to list in our left-hand column in the first place. The anti-abortion partisan wants, of course, to list the fetus as a recipient of massive disutility, while the defender of abortion typically does not.[12] (A complication here is that "disutility" cannot mean unpleasant *feelings*, since an aborted fetus has no experiences at all. But this is a general problem for utilitarian theory; we want to say that a painless murder whose victim is taken totally by surprise is in some sense disutile for the victim, but not because it causes unpleasant experiences.)

A move to Rule-Utilitarianism avails naught, for the same reason: the abortion issue is over *whose* utilities and disutilities to figure into our totals, and this question precedes the application of any utilitarian formula. And likewise for the proponent of "utilitarian generalization" who asks "What would happen if everyone did that?"

6.2. *Ideal contractarianism.* John Rawls' method of rational agreement behind a "veil of ignorance" (1971) is an equally nice illustration of our indeterminacy. Crudely (I suppress all subtle details of Rawls' own procedure), I ask myself whether I, as a rational egoist ignorant of the "place" I was to occupy in society, would agree to choose a set of social principles that sanctioned abortion. My answer would have to be, "That depends on whether some of the 'places' available for occupancy are those of aborted fetuses." In Rawls' "original position" one tries to minimize one's chances of drawing an unacceptable career or station in life from fortune's lottery-jar; but the prior question for us is that of whether an aborted fetus can be said to have a "career" or to constitute a "life" in the first place. So Rawls' method seems ineffectual against the abortion controversy.

Similar remarks would apply, I should think, both to purer forms of contractarianism and to purer forms of "ideal observer" theory.

6.3. *Universalizability and the Golden Rule.* Let us test abortion against the form of moral argument made famous by R. M. Hare (1963). Hare's characteristic pattern of reasoning would run as follows:

I want to abort fetus F because F's continued existence is inconvenient for me. By universalization on this reason, I obtain the general principle that whenever the continued existence of a fetus is inconvenient for person P (and other relevant features of the situation are the same), P should short that fetus. Suppose I were a fetus and were inconvenient for someone. Do I (having my present, actual inclinations) accept the prescription 'Let me in that case be aborted forthwith', which follows from the foregoing principle by the prescriptivity of moral judgments? If not, I am inconsistent, and may not justifiably utter or act on the prescription 'Let me abort F.'

The problem, as will be foreseen, is with the hypothesis "Suppose I were a fetus. . . . " If we think of fetuses as little people, the former supposition makes fairly good sense; but if we think of fetuses as warts or protoplasmic eruptions only, the supposition makes no more sense than "Suppose I were a wart." And that, as before is the very issue that divides our disputants.

In a paper (1975) specifically directed toward the abortion controversy, Hare himself departs slightly from his customary format and offers a more traditional Golden-Rule argument against abortion. He begins by suggesting that the traditional formulation of the Rule admits of "logical extension": Do unto others as you are *glad was* done to you (a change of mood and tense alone seems morally negligible). If like most people I am glad that my parents did not abort me,[13] since I am glad to be alive, then by Hare's extended rule I should not abort anyone else.

The difficulty here is pretty plain, and simply echoes earlier ones: How are we antecedently to determine whether a fetus counts as any*one* else, as an "other" unto whom we may or may not do things? Hare simply assumes *personal* continuity obtaining between my present self and the fetus that during 1945 gradually developed into the human that I am: I can be glad that *I* was not aborted in, say, January of that year only if *I*, a person, *existed* in January of that year, and that is just what is at issue. As it stands, then, Hare's argument begs the question (though it does at least nudge our intuitions by reminding us that we do say things like "If my parents had aborted *me*"). The dubiousness of appeal to the Golden Rule here can be brought out more clearly by a return to the traditional formulation: "How would you like it if you were a fetus and someone aborted you?" This query is at least intelligible if we are thinking of fetuses as little people, but is senseless if we are thinking of them as warts.[14]

I do not contend that universalizability is a useless tool with which to approach the abortion controversy, *tout court*. I shall make a different sort of appeal to it in the next section.

6.4. *Claims and respect for persons.* Here is perhaps our clearest case. A theorist who thinks of morality in terms of the inviolability of persons, natural rights, and claims grounded simply in the kind of being one is, will be stymied from the outset. For our uncertainty over the moral status of the fetus can be expressed precisely as uncertainty over which if any of the fetus' attributes are claim-creating attributes. The anti-abortionist says "Humanity", the abortion defender says "None", and both tend to agree that the answer is obvious. No further, deeper potential source of rights lies beneath.

I have blamed our impasse on the uniqueness of the fetus as a life-form. But here is where universalizability may yet help us out, since we universalize over merely possible as well as over actual beings. In what remains I shall develop an analogy that I think has the best chance — though a very poor chance — of helping to distill our cloudy moral feelings on this topic.

7. A virtue of my families of hypothetical machines is that they may be dreamed up at will. So it is possible to construct a mechanical analogue of a fetus, about which we may have clearer intuitions, and then argue that no morally relevant feature distinguishes the analogue from the real thing. As

a first attempt, let us suppose that a technician is in the process of *building* a full-fledged human-simulating robot like Harry. Let us further suppose that the technician has reached only a certain early stage of construction, and that, although it is made of the right materials, is of a highly individual basic design (which determines the personality it will have when it is finished), and so on, the proto-machine does not yet have any of the higher functions underlying the cognitive and conative capacities that we deem morally significant. Let us now ask whether the technician has the right to destroy the proto-machine for reasons of convenience. It seems clear enough that he does have this right; it is hard to imagine anyone taking him to task for deliberately dismantling the project.

But our analogy is far from perfect at this point. For one thing, the machine progresses toward personhood only under the steady impetus of the technician's skilled activity; the machine would not grow of its own accord if left to itself. By contrast, the fetus grows into a full-fledged person in the normal course of events, barring medical mishap. And this active potentiality, as opposed to the proto-machine's merely passive potentiality, inclines us to worry more about the moral rights of the fetus.

To recognize this distinction is to court all the nasty metaphysical and methodological difficulties that attend claims or requirements involving "the normal course of events". (One such difficulty that looms large here is that "the normal course of events" can be traced backwards in time as well as forwards. Most of us would not want to prohibit ordinary contraception on the grounds that in the normal course of events a sperm cell will make its way into the female's womb and perform its nefarious job.) But we may sidestep these problems by just complicating our imaginary situation a bit in order to simulate this feature of fetal status. Let us suppose that the technician's proto-machine is plugged into a much larger machine whose job it is to build robots. (The larger machine is a professional mother. We need not suppose that it is itself a person – it *might* be a "mere" machine but in pursuit of our analogy we might also suppose that the larger machine *is* a person and has a desire not to build any more robot offspring.) The technician sets the mother-robot going, provides it with raw materials, and *leaves*. Now it is true to say that, given the normal course of events (barring material shortages, power failures, etc.), the mother-robot will continue construction and eventually complete the protomachine, turning it into a full-fledged human simulator.

Let us ask whether it would be wrong for the technician to interrupt the mother-robot's activity at an early stage (with its concurrence if it is a person), unplug the proto-machine from the mother, take it off the work-bench, and dismantle it?

I cannot feel any moral disapproval upon considering this case, though quite possibly it is underdescribed. If I am right in judging that it would not be morally wrong, and if my analogy is unobjectionable, then we ought to conclude by universalizability that abortion of the fetus is not wrong either. But there is (at least) one final adjustment that perhaps our analogy needs and that might have the effect of reversing this intuition. A remaining difference between our present proto-machine and a human fetus is that the machine is being constructed from the outside, so to speak, while the fetus grows from the (its) inside even though it is *nourished* from the outside. (A human mother does not collect a lot of parts of the right sort and then put them together.) This fact gives the fetus a kind of positive integrity and autonomy that the proto-machine lacks. So let us now suppose that the technician or the mother-robot has begun by constructing a small set of pre-programmed growth cells, which then begin on their own (according to their own predetermined "genetic" plans) to multiply and eventually to form whole organ systems, being supplied from time to time with new raw materials as growth proceeds. Our original set of cells thus grows "from the inside" first into a mere proto-machine and then eventually into a full-fledged robot-person. The technician and the mother-robot only provide nourish-ment on a regular basis. The proto-machine will now have the same sort of developmental integrity or autonomy that a human fetus has.

Does this supposition change our (my) original intuition about the per-missibility of interrupting and halting the growth process? I do not find that it does in my own case. Perhaps this new scenario is less clear than its predecessor, but I still cannot see or feel anything wrong with splitting up and discarding the lattice of growth cells, so long as no very significant degree of growth has already taken place. So my own tentative conclusion remains the same: that it is not immoral to abort a pre-viable fetus.

Why should our intuitions about the proto-machine now be any more reliable, even if they are clearer, than our original intuitions (if any) about fetuses? That is, it may be wondered, what is the force of the analogy? The analogy serves two purposes for me: (1) It forces us to disregard biochemical constitution, which I have argued on independent grounds is morally negli-gible. The *biological* humanity of a fetus undoubtedly sways intuition toward opposition to abortion, but it should not; warts, fingernails and hair are genetically human too, while Harry, God, and intelligent Venusians are not. (2) The analogy reminds us, if we need reminding, that human beings are organisms, parts of nature, and that consequently fetuses are not tiny spiritual sparks destined to burst into immaterial flame. This is not to deny that mature humans have uniquely complex and intelligent minds, or that they are created and watched over by God, or even (if the reader insists) that they have immaterial souls. For *apropos* the abortion issue, even these fundamental matters are insignificant. That a mature human, or Harry for that matter, has an immaterial soul that is watched over by God entails nothing about the ensoulment of fetuses, and short of divine revelation any fact of such a matter is inaccessible to us (though I think the frequency of spontaneous abortion counts against the thesis of divine ensoulment at conception). Notice that my claim about the *special* intractability of the abortion issue is not impugned by the possibility that God could suddenly reveal the moral truth, for God could suddenly reveal the truth about anything. The mere existence of a correct answer to the abortion question does not even faintly suggest a direction in which to seek its natural or metaphysical ground.

8. Several possible sources of disquiet remain. First, obviously, I have no way of proving that my analogy *is* adequate to support the transfer of a moral conclusion from my hypothetical machine to an actual fetus. Someone might yet find a morally relevant difference between the two beings even though none occurs to me so far.

Second, my tentative conclusion may be extended to fetuses at later stages of development. I have leaned heavily on characteristic properties of mature persons such as reasoning, desire, and a concept of one's own welfare. The trouble (cf. Tooley (1972)) is that *infants* possess these things only in the most minimal sort of way, and still most of us regard infants as being fully protected, morally speaking, from killing for convenience:[15] so the properties I have cited cannot be the only relevant ones in virtue of which we forbid the killing of human beings. Therefore I still bear the onus of showing why my mechanical analogy should not be extended to authorize the killing of more mature organisms whose right to live we want to respect.

My own moral feelings against killing the unborn increase rather sharply as the fetus quickens and begins closely to resemble an infant, and this fact needs further accounting for in terms of analogies and disanalogies. I cannot pursue these matters further here, but I shall close with one comforting thought for those who find no moral objection to the aborting of a three-week embryo but who strongly object to that of an eight-and-a-half month near-neonate, and who are wondering how they are possibly to draw a justified line between those cases.

A fact oddly neglected by moral philosophers is that immorality comes in degrees.[16] Given two actions both of which are morally wrong, it still may be the case that one is morally worse than the other. So I offer the following model for assessing the moral status of abortion generally: As the fetus gradually develops from conception and implantation through quickening and viability toward birth, so the aborting of it becomes first touchy, then questionable, then dubious, then morally undesirable, then unmistakably wrong, then very wrong, and finally a moral crime or atrocity. The gradual spectrum of fetal development is neatly (if *ad hoc*) matched by an equally gradual spectrum of increasing moral disapproval. The exact matching I would not like to try to specify. But the upshot, if my earlier tentative conclusion was right, is that abortion is permissible so long as it is performed *early*.

Perhaps increasingly subtle further thought along these lines will be able to make this judgment precise and provide it with full justification. But perhaps not. My argument is an analogical argument, and as such it has the characteristic defect of analogical arguments: the stronger the analogy, the weaker the argument! If we continue to refine the case of our proto-machine until we have captured every single feature of the human fetus that *might* legitimately affect our moral feelings about fetuses, we will probably find that our originally clear intuition concerning the proto-machine has clouded over; the closer we make the machine to a real fetus, the more doubts we will begin to have about aborting the machine.[17] So my strategy may in the end come to nothing. Unfortunately, if my earlier meta-arguments are correct, my analogical strategy yields the strongest form of argument we are ever going to get. The moral may be, depressingly, that we are simply *stuck*.[18]

Department of Philosophy
University of North Carolina, Chapel Hill

NOTES

[1] I have discussed this issue more fully in a longer ms. (1972) from which parts of the present paper are drawn. Earlier treatments appear in Putnam (1964) and Simak (1957); cf. also Lem (1974).

[2] For my own theory in detail, see Lycan (1981).

[3] See Dreyfus (1979).

[4] One must go a bit cautiously here, since some human mental attributes are specifically tied to human biology. It is doubtful that a robot made of hardware could ever *feel physically tired*, for example (metal fatigue is not fatigue), or suffer hangnail pain.

[5] This is not to say, of course, that to be in a mental state *is* just to behave in certain

ways. On the failure of the "Turing test" as a metaphysical criterion, see Block (1981); cf. also Lycan (1979).

[6] See Turing (1950), Scriven (1960), and my (1972).

[7] In order to keep discussion manageable I shall consider just the relatively narrow question of whether it is wrong for a mother to abort a pre-viable fetus solely for reasons of convenience, or more specifically, whether *the fetus* is wronged thereby (I shall disregard considerations of weakening the general respect for life, etc.).

[8] Similar points are made by Wertheimer (1971) and by Hare (1975).

[9] I do not mean to imply here that no one has tried to support these conflicting assumptions with more fundamental arguments. I construe these supporting arguments as respective attempts to build up the two conflicting analogies by pointing out more properties that the fetus has in common with a mature human being on the one hand and with a mere anatomical curiosity on the other.

There is a second reason, incidentally, why our two popular arguments beg the question. It is that, for many people at least, the possession of moral rights is part of the concept of "personhood", part of what the very word 'person' means. At least for such people, therefore, to assume that "a fetus is a person" is simply to assume that it is wrong to kill a fetus for convenience, and to assume that "a fetus is no person but merely a growth inside its mother" is simply to assume that a fetus has no right to life.

[10] A few philosophers, such as Tooley (1972) and Werner (1974), pooh-pooh the relevance of potentiality and offer counterexamples to some possible "potentiality principles". I am unconvinced by their arguments, and find it hard to dismiss the potentiality intuition. For an explicit defense of it, see Pluhar (1977).

[11] Some recent authors have experimented with comparisons to sundry imaginary beings. This is a feeble strategy, for reasons I shall state below, but it is the one I shall be pursuing also.

[12] I say "typically" here because it is possible (though difficult) to defend abortion while admitting for the sake of argument that fetuses are full-fledged persons with full panoplies of rights; see Thomson (1971). I shall ignore this qualification in what follows.

[13] I *think* most people are glad that my parents did not abort me.

[14] Hare responds, in effect, to the objection I am making here, by contending that it is possible to harm a being even before that being exists. (See also Pluhar (1977, p. 167).) I concede that that is possible, *if* the being goes on to exist, since 'harm' can be given a timeless use; but I can make no sense of the suggestion that a "being" who never exists in the actual world at all can be harmed in the actual world (I think only David Lewis could make sense of that). Anticipating this, Hare complains that it is "too easy a way of avoiding crime".

[15] An exception is Mary Anne Warren (1973). I wonder how many people might agree with her.

[16] But see Pluhar (1977, pp. 165–166).

[17] I think Judith Thomson's argument about people-seeds (1971) succumbs in this way; see Werner (1974, p. 71).

[18] An earlier version of this paper has been presented in colloquia at the University of Michigan, Victoria University of Wellington, the University of Adelaide, Hampshire College, Amherst College, Kalamazoo College, the Ohio State University, the University of Dayton, and Franklin and Marshall College. I am grateful to all those audiences for their vigorous and uncommonly illuminating discussion.

BIBLIOGRAPHY

Abelson, R.: 1966, 'Persons, P-Predicates, and Robots', *American Philosophical Quarterly* 3.

Block, N. J.: 1981, 'Psychologism and Behaviorism', *Philosophical Review* 90.

Dreyfus, H. L.: 1979, *What Computers Can't Do* (Revised Edition), Harper Colophon Books, New York.

Hare, R. M.: 1963, *Freedom and Reason*, Oxford University Press, London.

Hare, R. M.: 1975, 'Abortion and the Golden Rule', *Philosophy and Public Affairs* 4.

Lem, S.: 1974, 'The Seventh Sally, or How Trurl's Own Perfection Led to No Good', in *The Cyberiad* (tr. Michael Kandel), Seabury Press, New York.

Lycan, W. G.: 1972, 'The Civil Rights of Robots', public lecture presented at Kansas State University.

Lycan, W. G.: 1979, 'A New Lilliputian Argument Against Machine Functionalism', *Philosophical Studies* 35.

Lycan, W. G.: 1981, 'Form, Function, and Feel', *Journal of Philosophy* 78.

Pluhar, W. S.: 1977, 'Abortion and Simple Consciousness', *Journal of Philosophy* 74.

Putnam, H.: 1964, 'Robots: Machines or Artificially Created Life?' *Journal of Philosophy* 61.

Rawls, J.: 1971, *A Theory of Justice*, Harvard University Press, Cambridge.

Scriven, M.: 1960, 'The Compleat Robot: A Prolegomena to Androidology', in S. Hook (ed.), *Dimensions of Mind*, Collier Books, New York.

Simak, C.: 1957, 'How-2', in T. E. Dikty (ed.), *Five Tales from Tomorrow*, Fawcett Crest Books, New York.

Thomson, J. J.: 1971, 'A Defense of Abortion', *Philosophy and Public Affairs* 1.

Tooley, M.: 1972, 'Abortion and Infanticide', *Philosophy and Public Affairs* 2.

Turing, A. M.: 1950, 'Computing Machinery and Intelligence', *Mind* 59.

Warren, M. A.: 1973, 'On the Moral and Legal Status of Abortion', *Monist* 57.

Werner, R.: 1974, 'Abortion: The Ontological and Moral Status of the Unborn', *Social Theory and Practice* 3.

Wertheimer, R.: 1971, 'Understanding the Abortion Argument', *Philosophy and Public Affairs* 1.

PART III

KANTIAN UNIVERSALIZABILITY

ONORA O'NEILL

CONSISTENCY IN ACTION

1. UNIVERSALITY TESTS IN AUTONOMOUS AND IN HETERONOMOUS ETHICS

Many recent discussions of universality tests, particularly those in English, are concerned either with what everybody wants done or with what somebody (usually the agent: sometimes an anonymous moral spectator) wants done either by or to everybody. This is true of the universality tests proposed in Singer's Generalization Argument, in Hare's Universal Prescriptivism and generally of various formulations of Golden Rules as well as of Rule Utilitarianism. Since universality tests of these sorts all make moral acceptability in some way contingent upon what is *wanted* (or, more circumspectly expressed, upon what is preferred or found acceptable or promises the maximal utility) they all form part of moral theories which are *heteronomous*, in Kant's sense of that term. Such theories construe moral acceptability as contingent upon the natural phenomena of desire and inclination, rather than on any intrinsic or formal features of the agent or his intentions. If we rely on any of these proposed criteria of moral acceptability, there will be no types of act which would not be rendered morally acceptable by some change or changes in human desires.

By contrast Kant's proposed universality test, the Categorical Imperative, contains no reference either to what everybody wants done or to what somebody wants done either by or to everybody. Kant's first formulation of the Categorical Imperative, the so-called Formula of Universal Law, runs

> Act only on that maxim through which you can at the same time will that it should become a universal law.[1]

We are invited here to consider that we *can* will or intend, what it is *possible* or *consistent* for us to 'will as a universal law' (not what we *would* will or *would* find acceptable or *would want* as a universal law). Since the principle contains no reference to what everybody or anybody wants, nor to anything which lies beyond the agent's own capacity to will, it is part of a moral theory for agents who, in Kant's sense of the term, act *autonomously*. The principle asserts that such agents need only to impose a certain sort of consistency on

159

Nelson Potter and Mark Timmons (eds.), Morality and Universality, 159–186.
© 1985 *by D. Reidel Publishing Company.*

their actions if they are to avoid doing what is morally unacceptable. It proposes an uncompromisingly rationalist foundation for ethics.

Nevertheless, Kant interpretation, particularly in English, is rich in heteronomous readings of the Formula of Universal Law and in allegations that (despite claims to the contrary) it is impossible to derive non-trivial, action-guiding applications of the Categorical Imperative without introducing heteronomous considerations.[2] Textual objections apart (and they would be overwhelming objections), such heteronomous readings of Kant's ethics discard what is most distinctive and challenging in his ethical theory. These are the features of his theory on which I intend to concentrate. I want to challenge the view that Kantian ethics, and non-heteronomous ethical theories in general, must be seen as either trivially empty or relying covertly on heteronomous considerations in order to derive substantive conclusions. To do so I shall try to articulate what seem to me to be the more important features of a universality test for agents who, in a certain sense of the term, act autonomously, that is without being determined solely by their natural desires and inclinations.[3]

I shall take Kant's Formula of Universal Law as the canonical case of such a universality test, and shall argue that it is neither trivially formalistic nor requires supplementing with heteronomous considerations if it is to be action guiding. However, my main concern here is not to explicate Kant's discussion of his universality test, nor to assess the difficulty or adequacy of his various moves.[4] I shall say nothing about his vindication of the Categorical Imperative, nor about his powerful critique of heteronomy in ethics, nor about his conception of human freedom. By setting aside these and other more strictly textual preoccupations I hope to open the way for a discussion of some features of universality tests for autonomous agents which have an interest which goes far beyond a concern with reading Kant accurately. I hope to show that Kant's formula, taken in conjunction with a plausible set of requirements for rational intending, yields strong and interesting ethical conclusions which do not depend on what either everybody or anybody wants, and so that reason can indeed be practical.

Over the last twenty years considerable light has been shed on the underlying structure of heteronomous ethical theories (as well as on other, particularly economic and political, decisions) by drawing on studies of the formal aspects of decision making under various conditions which have been articulated in various models of rational choice. In such discussions it is generally taken for granted that rational choosing is in some way or other contingent upon a set of desires or preferences.[5] I shall suggest that a similar concentration on certain requirements of rationality which are not contingent upon desires or preferences can help to provide a clearer picture of the underlying structure and strength of an ethical theory for autonomous beings.

The sequence of argument is straightforward. Section 2 provides an explication of Kant's Formula of Universal Law and of some of the ways in which this affects the character of an ethic for autonomous beings. Section 3 discusses some ways in which intentional action can fall into inconsistency even when the question of universalizing is not raised. Sections 4, 5 and 6 show how requirements for rational intending can be conjoined with Kant's universality test to yield determinate ethical conclusions.

2. MAXIMS AND MORAL CATEGORIES

The test which Kant's Formula of Universal Law proposes for the moral acceptability of acts can be divided into two aspects. In the first place it enjoins us to *act on a maxim*; secondly it restricts us to action on those maxims *through which we can will at the same time that it should be a universal law*. It is only the latter clause which introduces a universality test. However, for an understanding of the nature of this test it is essential in the first place to understand what Kant means by 'acting on a maxim'. For, contrary to appearances, this is not a trivial part of his criterion of morally acceptable action. Because a universality test for autonomous beings does not look at what is wanted, nor at the results of action, but merely demands that certain standards of consistency be observed in autonomously chosen action, it has to work with a conception of action which has the sort of formal structure which can meet (or fail to meet) standards of consistency. It is only those acts which embody or express syntactically structured principles or descriptions which can be thought of as candidates either for consistency or for inconsistency. Mere reflexes or reactions, for example, cannot be thought of as consistent or inconsistent: nor can acts be considered merely instrumentally as means for producing certain outcomes. In requiring action on a maxim Kant is already insisting that whatever is morally assessable should have a certain formal structure.

A maxim, Kant tells us, is "a subjective principle of action"; it is "the principle on which the subject acts".[6] A maxim is therefore the principle of action of a particular agent at a particular time; but it need not be 'subjective' in the sense that it seeks to fulfill that particular agent's desires. In speaking of maxims as subjective principles Kant is not adopting any sort of heteronomous standard, but means to propose a standard against which the principles agents propose to act on, of whatever sort, may be tested. The Categorical Imperative provides a way of testing the moral acceptability of what we autonomously propose to do. It does not aim to generate plans of action for those who have none.

While maxims are the principles of action of particular agents at particular times, one and the same principle might be adopted as a maxim by many agents at various times or by a given agent on numerous occasions. It is a corollary of Kant's conception of human freedom that we can adopt or discard maxims, including those maxims which refer to our desires.

On the other hand acting on a maxim does not require explicit or conscious or complete formulation of that maxim. Even routine or thoughtless or indecisive action is action on *some* maxim. However, not all of the principles of action that a particular agent might exemplify at a given time would count as the agent's maxim. For principles of action need only incorporate *some* true description of an agent and *some* true description of his act and situation, whether these descriptions are vacuous and vague or brimming with detail. But an agent's maxim in a given act must incorporate just those descriptions of the agent, the act and the situation upon which the doing of the act depends.

An agent's maxim in a given act cannot, then, be equated simply with his intentions. For an agent's intentions in doing a given act may refer to incidental aspects of the particular act and situation. For example, in making a new visitor feel welcome I may offer and make him or her some coffee. In doing so there will be innumerable aspects of my action which are intentional – the choice of mug, the addition of milk, the stirring; and there will also be numerous aspects of action which are 'below the level of intention' – the gesture with which I hand the cup, the precise number of stirs and so on. But the various specific intentions with which I orchestrate the offer and preparation of coffee are all ancillary to an underlying intention. *Maxims are those underlying intentions by which we guide and control our more specific intentions*. In this particular example, had I lacked coffee I could have made my visitor welcome in other ways: the specific intention of offering and making coffee was subordinate to the maxim of making a visitor welcome. Had I had a quite different maxim – perhaps to make my visitor unwelcome – I would not in that context have acted on just those specific intentions. In another context, e.g. in a society where an offer of coffee would be understood as we would understand an offer of hemlock, the same or similar specific intentions might have implemented a maxim of making unwelcome.

The fact that maxims are underlying or fundamental intentions has important implications.[7] It means in the first place that it may not be easy to tell on which maxim a given act was done. For example, a person who helps somebody else in a public place may have the underlying intention of being helpful — or alternatively the underlying intention of fostering a certain sort of good reputation. Since the helpful act might equally well be done in futherance of either underlying intention, there may be some doubt as to the agent's maxim. Merely asking an agent what his underlying maxim is in such a situation may not settle the issue. The agent might himself be unsure. Both he and others can work out that if he would have done the action even if nobody had come to know of it, then his underlying intention would not have been to seek a certain sort of reputation. But he may after all be genuinely uncertain what his act would have been had he been faced with the possibility of helping, isolated from any effects on his reputation. Isolation tests can settle such issues[8] — if we know their outcome; but since most such tests refer to counterfactual situations we often don't know that outcome with any great certainty. Further, isolation tests provide only a *negative* test of what an agent's maxim is not. Even the person who has used such a test to show that his maxim is not to acquire a reputation may still be unsure whether his maxim was just to be helpful. He may perhaps wonder whether his underlying intention was not to preserve a certain sort of self image or to bolster his own sense of worth. Kant remarks on the opacity of the human heart and the difficulty of self-knowledge; he laments that for all we know there never has been a truly loyal friend.[9] And he does not view these as dispellable difficulties. Rather these limits to human self-knowledge constitute the fundamental context of human action. Kant holds that we can know what it would be to try to act on a maxim of a certain sort, but can never be sure that what we do does not reflect further maxims which we disavow. However, the underlying intentions which guide our more specific intentions are not in principle undiscoverable. Even when not consciously formulated they can often be inferred with some assurance, if not certainty, as the principles and policies which our more specific intentions express and implement.

On a certain view of the purpose of a universality test the fact that the maxim of a given action is neither observable nor always reliably inferable would be a most serious objection. For it would appear to render the outcome of any application of a universality test of dubious moral importance — since we might mistakenly have applied the test to a principle other than the agent's maxim. Further, even if the maxim had been correctly formulated, whether by the agent or by others, the maxim itself might reflect mistaken beliefs or self-deception in the agent, or the agent's act might fail to live up to his maxim. How then could any test applied to the agent's maxim be expected to classify acts into moral categories such as the right and the forbidden? For these categories apply to the outward and observable aspects of action. It is after all common enough for us to think of acts which are at least outwardly right (perhaps even obligatory) as nevertheless reflecting dubious intentions (I aim to kill an innocent, but mistakenly incapacitate the tiger who is about to maul him), and of acts whose intentions are impeccable as issuing tragically in wrong action (I aim for the tiger but despatch the innocent).

The answer Kant gives to this problem is plain. It is that rightness and wrongness and the other 'categories of right' standardly used in appraisal of outward features of action are *not* the fundamental forms of moral acceptability and unacceptability which he takes the Categorical Imperative to be able to discriminate.[10] Since the locus of application of Kant's universality test (and perhaps of any non-heteronomous universality test) is agents' fundamental intentions, the moral disinction which it can draw is in the first place an intentional moral distinction, namely that between acts which have and those which lack moral worth. In an application of the Categorical Imperative to an agent's maxim we ask whether the underlying intention with which the agent acts or proposes to act — the intention which guides and controls his other more specific intentions — is consistently universalizable; if it is, according to Kant, we at least know that the action will not be morally unworthy, and will not be a violation of duty.

The fact that Kant is primarily concerned with judgments of moral worth is easily forgotten, perhaps because he speaks of the Categorical Imperative as a test of *duty*, while we often tend to think of duty as confined to the *outward* aspects of action. It is quite usual for us to think of principled action as combining both duty and moral worthiness, which we regard as separate matters (e.g. showing scrupulous respect for others) or alternatively as revealing a moral worthiness which goes beyond all duty (e.g. gratuitous kindness which we think of as supererogatory). Correspondingly it is quite usual for us to think of unprincipled action as in any case morally unworthy but still, in some cases, within the bounds of duty (e.g. the case of a would-be poisoner who mistakenly administers a life-saving drug). This is quite foreign to Kant's way of thinking, which sees the *central* case of duty as that of action which has moral worth, and regards as *derivative* that which accords merely in external respects with morally worthy action. On Kant's view the would-be poisoner who inadvertently saves life has violated a duty by acting in a morally unworthy way.

By taking an agent's fundamental or underlying intention as the point of application of his universality test Kant avoids one of the difficulties most frequently raised about universality tests, namely that it seems easy enough to formulate *some* principle of action for any act, indeed possibly one that incorporates one of the agent's intentions, which can meet the criterion of any universality test, whatever the act. Notoriously some Nazi war criminals claimed that they were only 'doing their job' or only 'obeying orders' — which are after all not apparently morally unworthy activities. The disingenuousness of the claim that such acts were not morally unworthy lies in the fact that these Nazis were not only doing this, and indeed that in many cases their specific intentions were ancillary to more fundamental intentions which might indeed have revealed moral unworthiness in the agent. (Such fundamental intentions might range from 'I'll do whatever I'm told to so long as it doesn't endanger me' to a fundamental maxim of genocide.) The fact that we can formulate *some* universalizable surface intention for any action by selecting among the agent's various surface intentions is no embarrassment to a universality test which is intended to apply to agents' maxims, and offers a solution to the problem of relevant descriptions.

It is equally irrelevant to a universality test that applies to maxims that we may be able to find some non-universalizable intentions among the more specific intentions with which an agent implements and fills out any maxim. If in welcoming my visitor with a cup of coffee I intentionally select a particular cup, my specific intention clearly cannot be universally acted on. The very particularity of the world means that there will always be aspects of action, including intentional aspects, which could not be universally adopted or intended. Kant's universality test, however, as we shall see, construes moral worth as contingent not on the universalizability or otherwise of an agent's specific intentions but on the universalizability of an agent's fundamental or underlying intention.[11]

For Kant, then, the Categorical Imperative provides a criterion in the first place for duties to act on underlying intentions which are morally worthy. It is only as a second and derivative part of his ethical theory that he proposes that the Categorical Imperative also provides a test of the outward wrongness and rightness of acts of specific sorts. He proposes in the *Groundwork* that acts which accord in outward respects with acts done on morally worthy maxims of action should be seen as being 'in conformity with' or 'in accord with' duty. The claim that we can provide a *general* account of which specific actions conform to the outward expressions of morally worthy maxims is highly controversial. We have already noted that there are many ways in which ancillary intentions may be devised in undertaking action on a given maxim, and there may be no single specific intention which is indispensable in all circumstances for action on a given maxim. Hence it is not generally clear what outward conformity conforms to. Kant appears to accept that the notion of outward conformity to duty is empty in many cases of duties of virtue, which are not sufficiently determinate for any particular more specific intentions to be singled out as required. He speaks of such duties as being 'of wide requirement'. But he also speaks of duties of narrow or strict require-ment, and includes among these duties of justice and certain duties of respect to ourselves and to others.[12] Hence he takes it that there could in principle be a merely outward conformity to these strict or 'perfect' duties. Whether this claim is justified depends on the success of his demonstration that the underlying maxims of justice and respect have determinate specific implica-tions for all possible human conditions. If they do not, then there will be no wholly general account of the requirements of justice and respect for all possible situations. It is then at any rate not obvious that we can derive a standard for the outward rightness of acts from a standard for the moral worth of underlying intentions. This is a major problem which I intend to set on one side in order to explore the implications of a universality test which applies to underlying intentions and so aims, at least primarily, at a test of the moral worth rather than the outward rightness of actions.

The fact that Kant's universality test focuses on maxims, and so on the moral worth of action, implies that it is a test which agents must seek to apply to their own proposals for action. This is not, however, because an agent is in a wholly privileged epistemological position with respect to his own underlying intentions. No doubt others may often have some difficulty even in discerning all of an agent's surface intentions, and may be quite unsure about his underlying intention. But Kant does not regard the agent's vantage point as affording infallible insight into his own intentions – self-consciousness is not transparent – and would not deny that on occasion others might arrive at a more accurate appreciation of an agent's underlying intention than the agent could himself reach.

The reason why a universality test in an autonomous ethical theory is primarily one for the use of agents rather than of moral spectators is rather that it is only an agent who can adopt, modify or discard maxims. While a test of the outward moral status of acts might be of most use and importance to third parties (legislators, judges, educators – those of us who pass judgment on others), because it may be possible or indeed necessary to prevent or deter or praise or punish in order to elicit or foster outward action of a certain sort, it is difficult if not impossible for outward regulation or pressure to change an agent's underlying intention. Surface conformity can be exacted; intentional conformity is more elusive.[13] Precisely because we are considering what a universality test for autonomous beings must be like, we must recognize that the test is one which we can propose to but not impose upon moral agents.

3. INCONSISTENCY WITHOUT UNIVERSALIZING

This account of acting on a maxim shows at least how action can be construed in a way which makes consistency and inconsistency possible, and provides some grounds for thinking that a focus on maxims may avoid some of the difficulties which have arisen in attempts to apply universality tests unrestrictedly to principles of action of all sorts. This opens the way for showing how action on a non-universalizable maxim is inconsistent and for considering whether such inconsistency constitutes a criterion of moral unworthiness. Before dealing with these topics it will be useful to run over some of the many ways in which action on a maxim may reveal inconsistency even when universalizing is not brought into the picture.

It is, of course, true that any act which is done is possible, taken in itself. But it does not follow that the intentions which are enacted are mutually consistent. There are two sorts of possibilities here: in the first place there may be an internal inconsistency within an agent's maxim; in the second place there may be contradictions between the various specific intentions an agent adopts in pursuit of his maxim, or between some of these specific intentions and the agent's maxim. These two sorts of contradiction correspond closely to the two types of contradiction which Kant thinks may arise when attempts to universalize maxims fail, and which he characterizes as involving respectively 'contradictions in conception' and 'contradictions in the will'.[14] Since I am also interested in charting the inconsistencies which can arise independently of attempts to universalize, as well as in those which arise when universalizing fails, I shall use the rather similar labels 'conceptual inconsistency' and 'volitional inconsistency' to distinguish these two types of incoherence in action. A consideration of the different types of incoherence which maxims may display even when the question of universalizability is not raised provides a useful guide to the types of incoherence which non-universalizable maxims display.

A maxim of action may in the first place be incoherent simply because it expresses an impossible aspiration. An agent's maxim might be said to involve a conceptual inconsistency if his underlying intention was, for example, both to be successful and to be unworldly, or alternatively to be both popular and reclusive, or both to care for others and always to put his own advantage first, or both to be open and frank with everybody and to be a loyal friend or associate, or both to keep his distance from others and to have intimate personal relationships. Agents whose underlying maxims incorporate such conceptual inconsistencies do not, of course, succeed in doing impossible acts; rather then pattern of their action appears to pull in opposite directions and to be in various ways self-defeating. At its extreme we may regard such underlying incoherence in a person's maxim, and consequent fragmentation of his action, as tragic or pathological (and perhaps both), since there is no way in which he or she can successfully enact the underlying intention. In other cases we may think of the pattern of action which results from underlying conceptual incoherence as showing no more than ambivalence or presenting conflicting signals to others, who are consequently at a loss as to what they should expect or do, finding themselves in a 'double bind'.

However, not all cases of disjointed action constitute evidence of an internally inconsistent maxim. For it may well be that somebody adopts some accommodation of the potentially inconsistent aspects of his underlying intention. For example, somebody may adopt the maxim of being competitive and successful in public and professional life but disregarding such considerations in private life; or of being obedient and deferential to superiors but overbearing and exacting with all others. Provided such persons can keep the two spheres of action separated, their underlying intention can be internally consistent. Hence one cannot infer an inconsistency in someone's underlying intentions merely from the fact that he or she exhibits tendencies in opposing directions. For these tendencies may reflect a coherent underlying intention to respond or act differently in different types of context or with different groups of people. A non-universalized maxim embodies a conceptual contradiction only if it *aims* at achieving mutually incompatible objectives and so cannot under any circumstances be acted on with success.

A focus on maxims which embody contradictions in conception pays no attention to the fact that maxims are not merely principles which we can conceive (or entertain, or even wish) but principles which we *will* or intend, that is to say principles which we adopt as *principles of action*. Conceptual contradictions can be identified even in principles of action which are never adopted or acted upon. But a second and rather different type of incoherence is exhibited in some attempts to will maxims whose realization can be quite coherently envisaged. Willing, after all, is not just a matter of wishing that something were the case, but involves committing oneself to doing something to bring that situation about when opportunity is there and recognized. Kant expressed this point by insisting that rationality requires that whoever wills some end wills the necessary means in so far as these are available.

Who wills the end wills (so far as reason has decisive influence on his actions) also the means which are indispensably necessary and in his power. So far as willing is concerned, this proposition is analytic: for in my willing of an object as an effect there is already conceived the causality of myself as a working cause – that is, the use of means; and from the concept of willing an end the imperative merely extracts the concept of actions necessary to this end.[15]

This amounts to saying that to will some end without willing whatever means are indispensable for that end, insofar as they are available, is, even when the end itself involves no conceptual inconsistency, to involve oneself in a volitional inconsistency. It is to embrace at least one specific intention which, far from being guided by the underlying intention, is inconsistent with that intention.

Kant, however, explicitly formulates only *one* of the principles which must be observed by an agent who is not to fall into volitional inconsistency. The 'Principle of Hypothetical Imperatives', as expressed in the passage just quoted, requires that agents intend any indispensable means for whatever they fundamentally intend. Conformity with this requirement of coherent intending would be quite compatible with intending no means to whatever is fundamentally intended whenever there is no specific act which is indispensable for action on the underlying intention. Further reflection on the idea of intending the means suggests that there is a *family* of Principles of Rational Intending, of which the Principle of Hypothetical Imperatives is just one, though perhaps the most important one. The following list of further Principles of Rational Intending which coherent intending (as opposed to mere wishing or contemplating) apparently requires agents to observe may not be complete, but is sufficient to generate a variety of interesting conclusions.

First, it is a requirement of rationality to intend not merely all *indispensable* or *necessary* means to that which is fundamentally intended but also to intend some *sufficient* means to what is fundamentally intended. If it were not, I could coherently intend to eat an adequate diet, yet not intend to eat food of any specific sort on the grounds that no specific sort of food is indispensable in an adequate diet.

Secondly, it is a requirement of rationality not merely to intend all necessary and some sufficient means to what is fundamentally intended, but to seek to make such means available when they are not. If it were not, I could coherently claim to intend to help bring about a social revolution but do absolutely nothing, on the grounds that there is no revolutionary situation at present, so settling for rhetoric and gesture rather than politics. But if I do this, I at most wish for, and do not intend to help to bring about, a social revolution.

Thirdly, it is a requirement of rationality to intend not merely all necesary and some sufficient means to whatever is fundamentally intended but to intend all necessary and some sufficient *components* of whatever is fundamentally intended. If it were not, I could coherently claim to intend to be kind to someone to whom, despite opportunity, I show no kindness in word, gesture or deed, merely because acting kindly is not the sort of thing which requires us to take means to an end but the sort of thing which requires that we act in some of the ways that are *constitutive* of kindness.[16]

Fourthly, it is a requirement of rationality that the various specific intentions we actually adopt in acting on a given maxim in a certain context be mutually consistent. If it were not, I could coherently claim to be generous to all my friends by giving to each the exclusive use of all my possessions.

Fifthly, it is a requirement of rationality that the foreseeable results of the specific intentions adopted in acting on a given underlying intention be consistent with the underlying intention. If it were not, I could coherently claim to be concerned for the well-being of a child for whom I refuse an evidently life-saving operation, on the grounds that my specific intention – perhaps to shield the child from the hurt and trauma of the operation – is itself aimed at the child's well being. But where such shielding foreseeably has the further consequence of endangering the child's life, it is clearly an intention which undercuts the very maxim which supposedly guides it.

There may well be yet further principles which fully coherent sets of intentions must observe, and possibly some of the principles listed above need elaboration or qualification. The point, however, is to reveal that once we see action as issuing from a complex web of intentions, many of which are guided by and ancillary to certain more fundamental intentions under particular conditions, intending coherently and avoiding volitional inconsistency becomes a demanding and complex affair.

Reflection on the various Principles of Rational Intending reveals a great deal about the connections between surface and underlying intentions to which a rational being must aspire. Underlying intentions to a considerable extent express the larger and longer term goals, policies and aspirations of a life. But if these goals, policies and aspirations are willed (and not merely wished for) they must be connected with some set of surface intentions which express commitment to acts that, in the actual context in which the agent finds himself, provide either the means to or some components of the underlying intention, or at least take the agent in the direction of being able to form such intentions, without at any point committing the agent to acts whose performance would undercut his underlying intention. Wherever such coherence is absent we find an example of intending which, despite the conceptual coherence of the agent's maxim, is volitionally incoherent. In some cases we may think the deficiency cognitive – the agent fails despite available information to appreciate what he needs to do if he is indeed to act on his maxim (he may be stupid or thoughtless or calculate poorly). In other cases we might think of the deficiency as primarily volitional: the agent fails to intend what is needed if he is to will his maxim and not merely to wish for it to be realized. Each of these types of failure in rationality subdivides into many different sorts of cases. It follows that there are very many different ways in which an agent whose intentions are not to be volitionally inconsistent may have to consider his intentions.

Perhaps the most difficult of the various requirements of coherent willing is the last, the demand that the agent not adopt specific intentions which in a given context may undercut his own maxim. There are many cases in which agents can reach relatively clear specific intentions about how they will implement or instance their maxim, yet the act selected, though indeed selected as a means to or component of their underlying intention, backfires. It is fairly common for agents to adopt surface intentions which, when enacted, foreseeably will produce results which defeat the agent's own deeper intentions. Defensive measures generate counterattack; attempts to do something particularly well result in botched performances; decisive success in battle is revealed as Pyrrhic victory. It is perhaps unclear how long a view of the likely results of his own action an agent must take for us not to think action which leads to results which are not compatible with his underlying intention is irrational. But at the least the standard and foreseeable results of his action should not undercut the underlying intention if we are to think of an agent as acting rationally. Somebody who claims to intend no harm to others, and specifically merely intends to share a friendly evening's drinking and to drive others home afterwards, but who then decides on serious drinking and so cannot safely drive, cannot plausibly claim to intend merely the exuberant drinking and bonhomie and not the foreseeable drunkenness and inability to drive safely. Given standard information, such a set of intentions is volitionally incoherent. For it is a normal and foreseeable result of exuberant drinking that the drinker is incapable of driving safely. One who intends the drinking also (given normal intelligence and experience) intends the drunkenness; hence cannot coherently also intend to drive others home if his underlying intention is to harm nobody.[17]

This brief consideration of various ways in which agents' intentions may fail to be consistent shows that achieving consistency in action is a difficult matter even if we do not introduce any universality test. Intentions may be either conceptually or volitionally incoherent. The demand that the acts we do reflect conceptually and volitionally coherent sets of intentions therefore constitutes a powerful constraint on all practical reasoning. This provides some reason for thinking that when these demands for consistency are extended in the way in which the second aspect of Kant's Formula of Universal Law requires we should expect to see patterns of reasoning which, far from being ineffective or trivial, generate powerful and interesting results.

4. INCONSISTENCY IN UNIVERSALIZING

The intuitive idea behind the thought that a universality test can provide a criterion of moral acceptability may be expressed quite simply as the thought that if we are to act as morally worthy beings we should not single ourselves out for special consideration or treatment. Hence whatever we propose for ourselves should be possible (note: not desired or wanted – but at least *possible*) for all others. Kant expresses this commonplace thought (it is, of course, not his argument for the Categorical Imperative) by suggesting that what goes wrong when we adopt a non-universalizable maxim is that we treat ourselves as special:

... whenever we transgress a duty, we find that we in fact do not will that our maxim should become a universal law – since this is impossible for us – but rather that its opposite should remain a law universally: we only take the liberty of making an *exception* to it for ourselves (or even just for this once) . . .[18]

It is evident from this understanding of the Formula of Universal Law that the notion of a community of other autonomous agents is already implicit in the Formula of Universal Law. It is not the case that Kant only introduces that notion into his ethics with the Formula of the Kingdom of Ends, which would imply that the various formulations of the Categorical Imperative could not be in any way equivalent. To universalize is from the start to consider whether what one proposes for oneself *could* be done by others. This seems to many too meagre a foundation for ethics but not in itself an implausible constraint on any adequate ethical theory.

Clearly enough whatever cannot be consistently intended even for oneself also cannot be consistently intended for all others. The types of cases shown conceptually or volitionally inconsistent by the methods discussed in the previous section are *a fortiori* non-universalizable. This raises the interesting question of whether one should think of certain types of cognitive and volitional failure as themselves morally unworthy. However, I shall leave this question aside in order to focus on the types of failure in consistent intending which are *peculiar* to the adoption of non-universalizable intentions.

I shall therefore assume from now on that we are considering cases of maxims which are in themselves not conceptually incoherent, and of sets of underlying and surface intentions which are not themselves volitionally inconsistent. The task is to pinpoint the ways in which inconsistency emerges in some attempts to universalize such internally consistent intentions. The second part of Kant's Formula of Universal Law enjoins action only on maxims which the agent can at the same time will as a universal law. He suggests that we can imagine this hypothetical willing by working out what it would be like "if the maxim of your action were to become through your will a universal law of nature".[19] To universalize his maxim an agent must satisfy himself that he can both adopt the maxim and simultaneously will that others do so. In determining whether he can do so he may find that he is defeated by either of the two types of contradiction which, as we have already seen, can afflict action even when universalizing is not under consideration. Kant's own account of these two types of incoherence, either of which defeats universalizability, is as follows:

We must *be able to will* that a maxim of our action should become a universal law – that is the general canon for all moral judgement of action. Some actions are so constituted that their maxim cannot even be *conceived* as a universal law of nature without contradiction, let alone be *willed* as what *ought* to become one. In the case of others we do not find this inner impossibility, but it is still impossible to *will* that their maxim should be raised to the universality of a law of nature, because such a will would contradict itself.[20]

Kant also asserts that those maxims which when universalized lead to conceptual contradiction are the ones which strict or perfect duty requires us to avoid, while those which when universalized are conceptually coherent but not coherently willable are opposed only to wider or imperfect duties.[21] Since we probably lack both rigorous criteria and firm intuitions of the boundaries between perfect and imperfect duties it is hard to evaluate this claim. However it is remarkably easy to display contradictions which arise in attempts to universalize maxims which we might think of as clear cases of violations of duties of justice and self-respect which Kant groups together as perfect duties; and it is also easy to show how contradictions emerge in attempts to universalize maxims which appear to exemplify clear violations of duties of beneficence and self development, which Kant groups together as imperfect duties. By running through a largish number of such examples I hope to show how groundless is the belief that universality tests need supplementing with heteronomous considerations if they are to be action guiding.

5. CONTRADICTIONS IN CONCEPTION

Maxims which may lead to contradictions in conception when we attempt to universalize them often do not contain any conceptual contradiction if we merely adopt the maxim. For example, there is no contradiction involved in adopting the maxim of becoming a slave. But this maxim has as its universalized counterpart − the maxim we must attempt to 'will as a universal law' − the maxim of everybody becoming a slave.[22] But if everybody became a slave there would be nobody with property rights, hence no slave holders, hence nobody could become a slave.[23] Consider alternatively a maxim of becoming a slave holder. Its universalized counterpart would be the maxim that everybody become a slave holder. But if everybody became a slave holder then everybody would have some property rights, hence nobody could be a slave, hence there could be no slave holders. Action on either of the non-universalizable maxims of becoming a slave or becoming a slave-holder would reveal moral unworthiness: it could be undertaken only by one who makes of himself a special case.

Contradictions in conception can also be shown to arise in attempts to universalize maxims of deception and coercion. The maxim of coercing whoever will not comply with my will has as its universalized counterpart the maxim that everybody will coerce others when they do not comply with his will: but this requires that each party coerce others, including those who are coercing him, hence that each party both complies with others' will (being coerced) and simultaneously does not comply with others but rather (as coercer) exacts their compliance. A maxim of coercion cannot coherently be universalized and reveals moral unworthiness. By contrast, a maxim of autonomous coordination can be consistently universalized. A maxim of deceiving others as convenient has as its universalized counterpart the maxim that everyone will deceive others as convenient. But if everyone were to deceive others as convenient then there would be no such thing as trust or reliance on others' acts of communication, hence nobody could be deceived, hence nobody could deceive others as convenient.

An argument of the same type can be applied to the maxim which is perhaps the most fundamental for a universality test for autonomous action, namely the maxim of abrogating autonomy. One whose maxim it is to defer to the judgment and decisions of others – to choose heteronomy [24] – adopts a maxim whose universalized counterpart is that everyone defer to the judgments and decisions of others. But if everyone defers to the judgments and decisions of others, then there are no autonomous decisions to provide the starting point for deferring in judgment, hence it cannot be the case that everybody defers in judgment. Decisions can never be reached when everyone merely affirms 'I agree'. A maxim of 'elective heteronomy' cannot consistently be universalized.

Interpreters of Kant have traditionally made heavier weather of the contradiction in conception test than these short arguments suggest is necessary. There have perhaps been two reasons for this. One is clearly that Kant's own examples of applications of the Categorical Imperative are more complex and convoluted than these short arguments suggest.[25] But while detailed analysis of these examples is necessary for an evaluation of Kant's theory, it is clarifying to see whether a contradiction in conception test works when liberated from the need to accommodate Kant's particular discussion of examples.

But a second reason why the contradiction in conception test has seemed problematic to many of Kant's commentators is perhaps of greater importance for present concerns. It is that while many would grant that we can detect contradictions in attempts to universalize maxims simply of slave-holding or coercing or deceiving or deference, they would point out that no contradiction emerges if we seek to universalize more circumspect maxims such as 'I will hold slaves if I am in a position of sufficient power' or 'I will deceive when it suits me and I can probably get away with it' or 'I will defer in judgment to those I either admire or fear.' Still less do contradictions emerge when we aim to universalize highly specific intentions of deception or deference such as 'I will steal from Woolworths when I can get away with it' or 'I will do whatever my Parish Priest tells me to do.'

However the force of this objection to the claim that the contradiction in conception test can have significant moral implications is undercut when we remember that this is a test which applies to agents' maxims, that is to their underlying or fundamental intentions and that as a corollary it is a test of moral worth. For what will be decisive is what an agent's fundamental intention in doing a given act really is. What counts is whether the expression of falsehood expresses a fundamental attempt to deceive, or whether agreement with another (in itself innocent enough) expresses a fundamental refusal to judge or think for oneself. For an agent cannot truthfully claim that his underlying intent was of a very specific sort unless the organization of his other, less fundamental, intentions reveals that his intention really was subject to those restrictions. Precisely because the Categorical Imperative formulates a universality test which applies to *maxims*, and not just to any intention, it is not rebutted by the fact that relatively specific intentions often can be universalized without conceptual contradiction. Conversely, further evidence for the interpretation of the notion of a maxim presented in Section 2 is that it leads to an account of the Categorical Imperative which is neither powerless nor counterintuitive. However, for the same reason (that it applies to maxims and not to intentions of all sorts) the Categorical Imperative can most plausibly be construed as a test of moral worth rather than of outward rightness, and must always be applied with awareness that we lack certainty about what an agent's maxim is in a given case. This is a relatively slight difficulty when we are assessing our own proposed maxims of action, since we at least can do no better than to probe and test the maxim on which we propose to act (but even here we have no guarantee against self-deception). And it means that we will always remain to some extent unsure about our assessment of others' acts. Kant after all insists that we do not even know whether there *ever* has been a truly morally worthy act. But that is something we do not need to know in order to try to do such acts. Self-deception may cloud our knowledge of our own maxims; but we are not powerless in self-guidance.

6. CONTRADICTIONS IN THE WILL

Just as there are maxims which display no conceptual incoherence until attempts are made to universalize them, so there are maxims which exhibit no conceptual incoherence even when universalized, but which are shown to be volitionally inconsistent when attempts are made to universalize them. Such maxims cannot be 'willed as a universal law'; attempts to do so fail in one way or another to meet the standards of rationality specified by the group of principles which I have termed Principles of Rational Intending. For to will a maxim is, after all, not just to conceive the realization of an underlying intention; that requires no more than speculation or wishing. Willing requires also the adoption of more specific intentions which are guided by and chosen (in the light of the agent's beliefs) to realize the underlying intention, or, if that is impossible, as appropriate moves towards a situation in which such specific intentions might be adopted. Whoever wills a maxim also adopts more specific intentions as means to or constituents of realizing his underlying intention, and is also committed to the foreseeable results of acting on these more specific intentions. Since intending a maxim commits the agent to such a variety of other intentions there are various different patterns of argument which reveal that certain maxims cannot be willed as a universal law without contradiction.

Clearly the most comprehensive way in which a maxim may fail to be willable as a universal law is if its universal counterpart is inconsistent with the specific intentions which would be necessary for its own realization. Universalizing such a maxim would violate the Principle of Hypothetical Imperatives. The point is well illustrated by a Kantian example.[26] If I seek to will a maxim of non-beneficence as a universal law, my underlying intention is to help others when they need it and its universalized counterpart is that nobody help no others when they need it. But if everybody denies help to others when they need it, then those who need help will not be helped, and in particular I will not myself be helped when I need it. But if I am committed to the standards of rational willing which comprise the various Principles of Rational Intending, then I am committed to willing some means to any end to which I am committed, and this must include willing that if I am in need of help and therefore not able to achieve my ends without help I be given some appropriate help. In trying to universalize a maxim of non-beneficence I find myself committed simultaneously to willing that I not be helped when I need it and that I be helped when I need it. This contradiction, however, differs from the conceptual contradictions which emerge in attempts to universalize maxims such as those considered in the last section. A world of non-benevolent persons is conceivable without contradiction. Arguments which reveal contradictions in the will depend crucially upon the role of the various Principles of Rational Intending – in this case on the Principle of Hypothetical Imperatives – in constraining the choice of specific intentions to a set which will implement all underlying intentions. It is only because *intending* a maxim of non-benevolence as a universal law requires commitment to that very absence of help when needed, to which all rational intending requires assent, that non-benevolence cannot coherently be universalized.

A second Kantian example,[27] which provides an argument to volitional incoherence, is a maxim of neglecting to develop any talents. A world of beings who develop no talents contains no conceptual incoherence. The maxim of an individual who decides to develop no talents, while imprudent, reveals no volitional inconsistency. For it is always *possible* that he finds that others fend for him and so that there will be means available for at least some autonomous action on his part. (It is not a fundamental requirement of practical reason that there should be means available to any project he adopts, but only that he should not have ruled out all autonomous action.) However, an attempt to universalize a maxim of neglecting talents commits one to a world in which no talents have been developed, and so to a situation in which necessary means are lacking not just for some but for any sort of autonomous action. Any autonomous agent who fails to will the development, in himself or others, of whatever minimal range of talents is required and sufficient for *some* autonomous action is committed to internally inconsistent sets of intentions. He intends both that autonomous action be possible and that it be undercut by neglect to develop even a minimal range of talents which would leave some possibility of autonomous action. This argument shows nothing about the development of talents which may be required or sufficient for any *specific* projects, but only points to the inconsistency of failing to foster such talents as are needed and sufficient for autonomous action of some sort or other. It is an argument which invokes not only the Principle of Hypothetical Imperatives but the requirement that rational beings intend some set of means sufficient for the realization of their underlying intention.

These two examples of arguments which reveal volitional inconsistencies show only that it is morally unworthy to adopt maxims either of systematic non-benevolence or of systematic neglect of talents. The duties which they ground are relatively indeterminate duties of virtue. The first of these arguments does not specify whom it is morally worthy to help, to what extent, in what ways or at what cost, but only that it would be morally unworthy to adopt an underlying intention of non-benevolence. Similarly the second argument does not establish which talents it would be morally worthy to develop, in whom, to what extent or at what cost, but only that it would be morally unworthy to adopt an underlying intention of making no effort to develop any talents. The person who adopts a maxim either of non-benevolence or of non-development of talents cannot coherently universalize his maxim. He or she must either make an exception of himself, and intend, unworthily, to be a free-rider on others' benevolence and talents, or will be committed to some specific intentions which are inconsistent with those required for action on his own maxim.

Another example of a maxim which cannot consistently be willed as a universal law is the maxim of refusing to accept help when it is needed. The universalized counterpart of this underlying intention would be the intention that everyone refuse to accept help when it is need. But autonomous beings cannot consistently commit themselves to intending that everyone forgo a means which, if ever they are in need of help, will be indispensable for them to act autonomously at all.

A further example of a non-universalizable maxim is provided by a maxim of ingratitude, whose universalized counterpart is that nobody show or express gratitude for favours received. In a world of autonomous but non-self-sufficient beings a universal maxim of ingratitude would require the systematic neglect of an important means for ensuring that help is forthcoming for those who need help if they are to realize their intentions. Hence in such a world nobody could coherently claim to will that those in need of help be helped. Yet we have already seen that failure to will that those in need of help be helped is volitionally inconsistent. Hence, willing a maxim of ingratitude also involves a commitment to a set of intentions not all of which can be consistently universalized. The volitional inconsistency which overtakes would-be universalizers of this maxim arises in two stages: the trouble with ingratitude is that, practised universally, it undercuts benevolence; the trouble with non-benevolence is that it cannot be universally practised by beings who (being autonomous) have at least some underlying maxims, yet (lacking self-sufficiency) cannot guarantee that their own resources will provide means sufficient for at least some autonomous project.

The hinge of all these arguments is that human beings (since they are autonomous adopters of maxims) have at least some maxims or projects, which (since they are not self-sufficient) they cannot always realize unaided, and so must (since they are rational) intend to draw on the assistance of others, and so must (if they universalize) intend to develop and foster a world which will lend to all the support of others' benevolence and talents. Such arguments can reveal the volitional inconsistencies involved in trying to universalize maxims of entirely neglecting the social virtues — benevolence, beneficence, solidarity, gratitude, sociability and the like — for beings who are autonomous yet not always able to achieve what they intend unaided. It follows from this that the social virtues are very differently construed in autonomous and in heteronomous ethics. An ethical theory for autonomous agents sees the social virtues as morally required, not because they are desired or liked but because they are necessary requirements for autonomous action in a being who is not self-sufficient. The content of the social virtues in an autonomous framework cannot be spelt out in terms of the provision of determinate goods or service or the meeting of certain set needs or the satisfaction of a determinate set of desires. Rather the content of these virtues will always depend on the various underlying maxims and projects, both individual and collaborative, to which autonomous agents commit themselves. What will constitute beneficence or kindness or care for others will depend in great part on how others intend to express their autonomy, and to collaborate in exercising their autonomy, in a given context.

7. CONTRADICTIONS IN THE WILL AND FURTHER RESULTS

The patterns of argument which can be used to show underlying anti-social intentions morally worthy make use of various Principles of Rational Intending in addition to the Principle of Hypothetical Imperatives. In particular they draw on the requirements that rational agents intend not merely necessary but sufficient means to or components of their underlying intentions, and that they also intend whatever means are indirectly required and sufficient to make possible the adoption of such specific intentions. However, the particular features of the fifth Principle of Rational Intending – the Principle of Intending the Further Results – have not yet been displayed. Attempts to evade this Principle of Rational Intending lead to a peculiar sort of volitional inconsistency.

Good examples of arguments which rely on this principle can be developed by considering cases of maxims which, when universalized, produce what are frequently referred to as 'unintended consequences'. For example, I can adopt the underlying intention of improving my economic well-being, and the specific intention of doing so by competing effectively with others. The maxim of my action can be consistently universalized: there is no conceptual contradiction in intending everyone's economic position to improve. The specific intention of adopting competitive strategies is not inconsistent with the maxim to which it is ancillary; nor is universal action on competitive strategies inconsistent with universal economic advance (that indeed is what the invisible hand is often presumed to achieve). But if an agent intends his own economic advance to be achieved solely by competitive strategies, this nexus of intentions cannot consistently be willed as universal law, because the further results of universal competitive activity, by itself, are inconsistent with universal economic advance. If everyone seeks to advance by these (and no other) methods, the result will not put everybody ahead economically. A maxim of economic progress combined with the specific intention of achieving progress merely by competitive strategies cannot be universalized, any more than the intention of looking over the heads of a crowd can be universally achieved by everyone in the crowd standing on tiptoes.[28] On the other hand, a maxim of seeking economic advance by means of increased production can be consistently universalized. It is merely the particular specific intention of advancing economically by competitive strategies alone that leads to volitional inconsistency when universalized. Competitive means are inherently effective only for some: competitions must have losers as well as winners. Hence, while it can be consistent to seek individual economic advance solely by competitive methods, this strategy cannot consistently be universalized. Once we consider what it would be to intend the consequences of universal competition – the usually *unintended* consequences – we can see that there is an inconsistency not between universal competitive activity and universal economic progress, but between the *further results of intending only universal competitive activity and universal economic progress*. Economic progress and competitive activity might each of them consistently be universal; indeed it is possible for them to coexist within a certain society. (Capitalist economies do experience periods of general economic growth.) Nevertheless there is a volitional inconsistency in seeking to achieve universal economic growth *solely by way of* universal adoption of competitive strategies.

This argument does not show that either the intention to advance economically or the intention to act competitively cannot be universalized, but only that the composite intention of pursuing economic advance solely by competitive tactics cannot be universalized. It does not suggest that either competition or economic progress is morally unworthy, but only that an attempt to achieve economic progress solely by competitive methods and without aiming at any productive contribution is not universalizable and so morally unworthy.

Similarly there is no inconsistency in an intention to engage in competitive activities of other sorts (e.g. games and sports). But if such competition is ancillary to an underlying intention to win, then the overall intention is not universalizable. Competitive games must have losers. If winning is not the overriding aim in such activities, if they are played for their own sake, the activity is consistently universalizable. But to play competitively with the fundamental intention of winning is to adopt an intention which makes of one's own case a necessary exception.

8. CONCLUSIONS

The interest of an autonomous universality test is that it aims to ground an ethical theory on notions of consistency and rationality rather than upon considerations of desire and preference. Kant's universality test meets many of the conditions which any such universality test must meet. In particular it focuses on features of action which are appropriate candidates for assessments of coherence and incoherence, namely the maxims or fundamental intentions which autonomous agents may adopt and the web of more specific ancillary intentions which they must adopt in a given context if their commitment to a maxim is genuine. While Kant alludes specifically to conceptual inconsistencies and to those volitional inconsistencies which are attributable to non-observance of the Principle of Hypothetical Imperatives in attempts to universalize intentions, there is in addition a larger variety of types of volitional inconsistency which agents who seek to subject their maxims to a universality test (and so not to make an 'exception of their own case) must avoid. A universality test applied to autonomously chosen maxims and their ancillary, more specific, intentions can be action-guiding in many ways without invoking any heteronomous considerations.

However, precisely because it applies to autonomously chosen intentions, a universality test of this sort cannot generally provide a test of the rightness or wrongness of the specific outward aspects of action. It is, at least primarily, and perhaps solely, a test of the inner moral worth of acts. It tells us what we ought to avoid if we are not to use our autonomy in ways which we can know are in principle not possible for all others. Such a test is primarily of use to agents in guiding their own moral deliberations, and can only be used most tentatively in assessing the moral worth of others' action, where we are often sure only about specific outward aspects of action and not about the maxim. This point will not be of great importance if we do not think it important whether an ethical theory enables us to pass judgment on the moral worth of others' acts. But specific outward aspects of others' action are unavoidably of public concern. The considerations discussed here do not reveal whether or not these can be judged right or wrong by Kant's theory. Kant no doubt thought that it was possible to derive specific principles of justice from the Formula of Universal Law; but the success of this derivation and of his grounding of *Rechtslehre* is beyond the scope of this inquiry.

The universality test discussed here is, above all, a test of the mutual consistency of (sets of) intentions and universalized intentions. It operates by showing some sets of proposed intentions mutually inconsistent. It does not thereby generally single out action on any one set of specific intentions as morally required. On the contrary, the ways in which maxims can be enacted or realized by means of acts done on specific intentions must vary with situation, tradition and culture. The specific acts by which we can show or fail to show loyalty to a friend or respect to another or autonomy in our dealings with the world will always reflect specific ways of living and thinking and particular situations and relationships. What reason can provide is a way of discovering whether we are choosing to act in ways (however culturally specific) which we do not in principle preclude for others. The 'formal' character of the Categorical Imperative does not entail either that it has no substantive ethical implications or that it can select a unique code of conduct as morally worthy for all times and places. Rather than presenting a dismal choice between triviality and implausible rigorism, a universality test for autonomous action can provide a rational foundation for ethics and maintain a serious respect for the diversity of content of distinct ethical practices and traditions.

Philosophy Department
University of Essex

NOTES

[1] I. Kant, *Grundlegung zur Metaphysik der Sitten*, tr. H. J. Paton as *The Moral Law*, Hutchinson, London, 1953 (hereafter *Grundlegung*), p. 421 (Prussian Academy pagination).

[2] Heteronomous readings of Kant's ethics include Schopenhauer's in *On the Basis of Morality*, tr. E. F. J. Payne, Bobbs Merrill, Indianapolis, 1965, Section 7, but are most common in introductory works in ethics. Recent examples include William K. Frankena, *Ethics*, Prentice Hall, New Jersey, 1963, p. 25; Gilbert Harman, *The Nature of Morality*, Oxford University Press, New York, 1977, p. 73 and D. D. Raphael, *Moral Philosophy*, Oxford University Press, Oxford, 1981, p. 76. Allegations that Kant, despite his intentions, must invoke heteronomous considerations if he is to reach substantive ethical considerations can notoriously be found in J. S. Mill, 'Utilitarianism', in *Utilitarianism, Liberty and Representative Government*, J. M. Dent & Sons, London, 1968, p. 4, but are now more common in the secondary literature on Kantian ethics. Examples include C. D. Broad, *Five Types of Ethical Theory*, Littlefield Adams and Co., New Jersey, 1965, p. 130 and (with respect to imperfect duties) M. Singer, *Generalization in Ethics*, Alfred Knopf, New York, 1961, p. 262.

[3] In Kant's terminology such action is *spontaneous* (not determined by alien causes, negatively free) and it is a further claim that it is also *Kantianly autonomous* (determined by pure practical reason). The argument here will not hinge on this strong and distinctive conception of human autonomy, but only on the weaker and more common

conception of autonomy as independence from determination by outside forces including desires.

4 I have done so in O. O'Neill (O. Nell), *Acting on Principle*, Columbia University Press, New York, 1975. The account I offer here reflects some changes in my understanding of Kant's notion of a maxim. For this I am particularly indebted to Otfried Höffe, 'Kants kategorischer Imperativ als Kriterium des Sittlichen', *Zeitschrift für Philosopische Forschung*, 31, 1977, pp. 354—84.

5 Even a very wide-ranging and reflective recent discussion of rational choice theory such as Jon Elster's in *Ulysses and the Sirens*, Cambridge University Press, Cambridge, 1979, does not discuss any non-heteronomous conceptions of rational choosing.

6 *Grundlegung*, p. 421, n.; see also p. 401, n. 1; as well as I. Kant, *The Metaphysics of Morals*, of which Part II, the *Tugendlehre* appears as *The Doctrine of Virtue*, tr. M. J. Gregor, Harper and Row, New York, 1964 (hereafter *Metaphysic of Morals*), p. 225 (Prussian Academy pagination).

7 However, the claim that maxims are underlying or fundamental intentions should not be collapsed into the claim, which Kant makes in the *Religion*, that for any agent at a given time there is one fundamental maxim which underlies all his other maxims. I shall not here consider whether there are fundamental maxims in this sense. But see I. Kant, *Religion within the Limits of Reason Alone*, tr. T. Greene and H. Hudson, Harper and Row, New York, 1960, p. 16ff.

8 This is presumably why Kant often argues from isolation tests. E.g. *Grundlegung*, pp. 398—9 and 407.

9 See, for example, *Metaphysics of Morals*, pp. 440 and 445—6; *Grundlegung*, pp. 407—8 and *Religion*, p. 16.

10 See *Grundlegung*, 397—8 (" . . . the concept of *duty*, which includes that of a good will"). The persistence of the view that Kant is primarily concerned with a criterion of right action perhaps reflects a modern conception that duty *must* be a matter of externals more than it reflects the Kantian texts. See also *Acting on Principle*, Ch. 4 and O. O'Neill, 'Kant After Virtue', *Inquiry*, 26, 1983, pp. 387—406.

11 The points mentioned in this and in the preceeding paragraph suggest why a focus on maxims may make it possible to bypass a variety of problems which are said to plague universality tests when applied to principles which are 'too general' or 'too specific'; these problems include those of invertibility, reiterability, moral indeterminacy, and those of the generation either of no results or of trivial or of counter intuitive results.

12 Kant then does not see all acts which are specific, strict requirements of duty as matters of justice. There are also strict or perfect requirements for some duties of virtue, such as refraining from suicide, mockery or detraction which he views as indispensable means to the rather indeterminate maxims that we act on when we act on a maxim of virtue. See *Metaphysic of Morals*, pp. 421ff. and 463ff. and *Acting on Principle*, pp. 52—8.

13 Cf. *Metaphysic of Morals*, pp. 380—81.

14 *Grundlegung*, p. 424 and cf. Sections 5 and 6 below.

15 *Grundlegung*, p. 417.

16 Kant's discussions of duties of virtue suggest that he would in any case count the necessary constituents or components of some end — and not merely the instrumentally necessary means to that end — as among the means to that end.

17 The fifth requirement of Rational Intending clearly deals with the very nexus of

intentions on which discussions of the Doctrine of Double Effect focus. That doctrine claims that agents are not responsible for harm which foreseeably results from action undertaken with morally worthy intentions, provided that the harm is not disproportionate, is regretted and would have been avoided had there been a less harm producing set of specific intentions which would have served the same maxim in that situation. (The surgeon foresees but regrets the pain unavoidably inflicted during life-saving procedures, and so is not to be held responsible for inflicting this pain.) While the Doctrine of Double Effect holds that agents are not to be held responsible for such results, it allows that agents do, if 'obliquely' rather than 'directly', intend the results. It is therefore quite compatible with the Doctrine of Double Effect to insist that an agent whose oblique intention foreseeably undercuts the fundamental intention for the sake of which what is directly intended is done acts irrationally. For where the fundamental intention is undercut the forseeable results of specific intentions were not proportionate; rather they defeat the very intention to which they are supposedly ancillary.

[18] *Grundlegung*, p. 424.

[19] This is the so-called Formula of the Law of Nature, cf. *Grundlegung*, p. 421, as well as p. 436, 'Maxims must be chosen as if they had to hold as universal laws of nature' and *Metaphysic of Morals*, p. 225, 'Act according to a maxim which can at the same time be valid as a universal law.' In this discussion I shall leave aside all consideration of the relationships between different formulations of the Categorical Imperative and in particular of the differences between versions which are formulated quite generally 'for rational beings as such' and those versions which are restricted to the human condition ('typics'). These topics have been extensively discussed in the secondary literature including in H. J. Paton, *op. cit.*; John Kemp, *The Philosophy of Kant*, Oxford University; R. P. Wolff, *The Autonomy of Reason*, Harper and Row, New York, 1973, Ch. 2; Bruce Aune, *Kant's Theory of Morals*, Princeton University Press, Princeton, New Jersey, Chs. II to IV.

[20] *Grundlegung*, p. 424.

[21] *Ibid.*, as well as *Metaphysic of Morals*, Introduction, esp. p. 389.

[22] For further discussion of the notion of the universalized counterpart of a maxim cf. *Acting on Principle*, pp. 61–3.

[23] For an application of the Formula of Universal Law to the example of slavery see also Leslie Mulholland, 'Kant: On Willing Maxims to Become Laws of Nature', *Dialogue*, 17, 1978.

[24] To see why Kant thinks that the abrogation of autonomy would be the most fundamental of moral failings see I. Kant, 'An Answer to the Question "What is Enlightenment?"', tr. H. B. Nisbet, in Hans Reiss, ed., *Kant's Political Writings*, Cambridge University Press, Cambridge, 1970 as well as Barry Clarke's discussion of 'elective heteronomy' in 'Beyond the Banality of Evil', *British Journal of Political Science*, 10, 1980, pp. 17–39.

[25] Cf. the various works of commentary listed under note 17 above as well as Jonathan Harrison, 'Kant's Examples of the First Formulation of the Categorical Imperative' and J. Kemp, 'Kant's Examples of the Categorical Imperative', both in R. P. Wolff, ed., *Kant: Foundations of the Metaphysics of Morals*, Bobbs Merrill, Indianapolis, 1969.

[26] Cf. *Metaphysic of Morals*, pp. 447–64 for Kant's discussion of the various virtues of love and sociability.

[27] Cf. *Metaphysics of Morals*, pp. 443–7 for Kant's discussion of the duty to seek to

develop talents (duty to seek one's own perfection). It is important to remember that 'talents' here are not to be understood as any particularly unusual human accomplishments, but rather as any human powers which (unlike natural gifts) we may choose either to cultivate or to neglect. The morally significant talents are powers such as those of self-mastery and self-knowledge.

[28] Cf. F. Hirsch, *Social Limits to Growth*, Harvard University Press, Cambridge, Mass., 1976.

GEORGE NAKHNIKIAN

KANTIAN UNIVERSALIZABILITY AND THE OBJECTIVITY OF MORAL JUDGMENTS

In the *Grundlegung zur Methaphysik der Sitten*, Kant derives five conclusions that are among the fundamental fixtures of his moral philosophy. Kant concludes that (1) there is but one "supreme principle of morality". In the penultimate paragraph of the *Preface* Kant states that "[t] he sole aim of the present groundwork is to seek out and establish *the supreme principle of morality* " (Kant's italics). Kant believes that we can understand more easily what that principle is, if we consider it under three different formulations, which, he thinks, are equivalent for two reasons. The first reason is that each formulation selects the same actions as being either morally obligatory, morally forbidden, or morally permitted, in complete agreement with the sound natural understanding of man. The second reason is that each formulation emphasizes an essential aspect of morality that is conceptually distinguishable, but inseparable from the other two. The first of these aspects is that the moral worth of an action depends entirely upon whether or not reason can sanction everybody's doing it. This is the aspect of *universality*. The second aspect is that rational nature is an *absolute end*. The third is that autonomous agent-legislators are *peers*. In the process of understanding each one of these aspects, we come to understand the others and see their necessary interconnections. We also see that all three are grounded upon the same foundations. These are that man is a species of rational being. His reason is of such a nature as to make him an autonomous agent, namely, an agent who is capable of generating, and acting in accordance with, moral principles that are binding on all rational beings who are capable of moral transgression. Because of his autonomy, man is not merely an object of convenience, either to himself or to others. Therefore, (2) under no circumstances is it justified to treat a human being as an object of convenience only. Kant further views the world in which man exercises his agency as being a cosmos of mutually harmonizable purposes. Therefore, (3) treating humanity, be it in oneself or others, as an end and never as a means only requires that each human being conduct himself in such a way as to actualize (contribute to the actualization of) the possible harmony of the purposes of autonomous agents. Therefore, (4) morality as a distinctive domain of actions, thoughts, and injunctions is defined by the principles and conditions

187

Nelson Potter and Mark Timmons (eds.), Morality and Universality, 187–233.
© 1985 *by D. Reidel Publishing Company.*

that direct the realization of this possible harmony. "Thus morality consists in the relation of all action to the making of laws whereby alone a kingdom of ends is possible" (Kant, 434).[1] The supreme principle of morality selects the principles that define morality as a domain. Because moral principles determine absolute ends of action, moral requirements reign supreme over those of all other domains, such as religion, art, law, science, politics, education, custom, and the like. Moreover, in the world of mutually harmonizable ends, each man's autonomy makes each man an equal among equals with respect to being in a position to discern moral principles that are valid for all rational beings. But being valid for all rational beings, (5) moral principles must be universal, necessary, and, therefore, *a priori*. They are deliverances of pure practical reason. Reason's being the same in all men, and the world in which man's agency is exercised being a system of mutually compatible purposes seem to be the viewpoint from which it appears evident to Kant that moral principles must be universally valid, hence, necessary and *a priori*.

The aspect of *universality* is emphasized in the formulation, K_1, of the fundamental principle of morality: Act only on that maxim which you can will to become a universal law of nature. The universality of moral principles is attested to by their being universalizable. Imbedded in K_1 is the idea that he who is doing the willing is any autonomous legislator-agent, in short, any self-conscious rational agent (whose will is not holy) (Kant, 414) who, as such, is an absolute, never a merely subsidiary, end. Consequently, rational beings "must serve for every maxim as a condition limiting all merely relative and arbitrary ends" (Kant, 436). K_2 explicitly delimits the *absolute end*: So act as to treat humanity, whether in your own person or in that of any other, in every case as an end withal, never as a means only. K_2 is implicit in K_1. Stating it explicitly helps us understand that K_1 morally forbids an action, if the end for the sake of which it is done or the circumstances in which it is done imply treating at least one rational being as a means only. K_3 emphasizes the *peer status* of moral agent-legislators: Act according to the maxims of a member of a merely possible kingdom of ends legislating in it universally. The peer status of moral agent-legislators is implicit in both K_1 and K_2. Moral autonomy is identical in every man; hence, every man is an equal among equals as a moral agent-legislator. K_1 and K_2 emanate from, and address themselves to, any self-conscious rational agent whose will is less than holy. This is what K_3 makes explicit.

Kant's important and abiding contribution to normative ethics is in K_2 and K_3. His defense of these formulas is not convincing, but there are, as I hope to show, good reasons for accepting them, provided that the notions of treating someone as an absolute end and of moral peerdom are cut loose from their Kantian moorings. Even after that is done, however, K_2 and K_3 are not on an equal footing. Properly understood, K_2 has no objectionable implications. But while there is an element of truth in K_3, K_3 has two objectionable implications. The element of truth is that all moral agents are equals among equals. The first of the objectionable implications of K_3 is that in assessing the moral worth of an action, it is irrelevant to take account of how others do, or may be expected to, act. K_3 morally requires moral agents to act in the actual world as they would were they members of an ideal community of moral agents each of whom obeys the moral law. According to this requirement, a moral agent is morally obligated to act in exactly the same way whether he is the only decent person in an assembly of cut throats or a member of a community of decent people. Such an implication is contrary to good sense. The second objectionable implication of K_3 is that any one moral agent's moral legislations are valid for all his peers. As I propose to show later in this essay, it does not follow from the peerdom of moral agents that all moral principles are universally valid. The gist of my argument is that Kant misconstrues the nature of moral peerdom. He thinks that all moral agent-legislators are peers because the pure reason of each discloses to him the very same principles of right conduct as it discloses the same principles of logic, i.e., of right thinking. More exactly, Kant's idea is that reason discloses a single *fundamental* principle of morality from which the very same principles of right conduct are elicited by any rational being. This is a mistake. As a family of purely intellectual powers, reason is the same in all rational agents, but the basic assumptions upholding a particular rational agent's view of the world need not be the same for all. Moral agents are peers because each must live by what he believes, yet fully rational beings can see the world from fundamentally divergent perspectives, where the differences are so basic as to preclude the possibility of anyone's being in a position to refute someone else's discordant basic assumptions. These unarguable assumptions can generate incompatible moral policies. Thus, the universality of reason does not entail that all of the moral principles of any rational agent are universally valid for all. Kant was wrong to think otherwise.

Therefore, even as buttressed by K_2 and K_3, K_1 is indefensible. I shall show that K_1 does not work. K_2 and K_3 stand on the idea of moral autonomy and the idea of a kingdom of ends, but these do not provide solid enough foundations for either K_1, K_2, or K_3. Moreover, I shall argue that K_1 cannot work. The reason is that universalizability is in principle a mistaken criterion. Patching up Kant's metaphysics cannot save K_1.

Kant's insight into the absolute worth of self-conscious rational beings, such as we are, is a decided advance over certain earlier moral theories, Plato's and Aristotle's for example. Plato's moral psychology and moral epistemology are, in my judgment, incompatible with K_2 or with the element of truth in K_3. Perhaps Aristotle can accommodate the element of truth in K_3, but he cannot accommodate K_2. Kant himself, however, provides no credible foundations for K_2 and K_3. In defense of K_2, Kant must establish that there are absolute ends, that as rational beings, human beings are absolute ends, and he must explain what treating someone as an end means. I shall argue that Kant's defense of the proposition that there are absolute ends is shaky. The same is true of his argument that rational nature is an absolute end. And Kant's explanation of what it means to treat someone as an end assumes, falsely, as I shall show, that the purposes of autonomous agents comprise a mutually harmonious set. I shall end this essay by endeavoring to show why Kant is right, notwithstanding the weakness of his foundations, that human beings are absolute ends of morally justified action, and that they are, as moral agent-legislators, equals among equals, although no one of them can, *pace* Kant, legislate universally for all.

K_1 DOES NOT WORK

Two key concepts in the formulation of K_1 are that of a maxim and that of contradiction in the will. For Kant a maxim formulates a personal policy, and is of the form: Whenever I am in circumstances C, I shall (am resolved to, will to) do A, so as to achieve an end E. As I read Kant, every maxim involves what I shall call 'a practical situation'. A practical situation is a complex made up of an action of a certain kind, a set of circumstances within which it is done, and the purpose for the sake of which it is done. As I understand Kant, a kind of action is a constituent of many different practical situations, and the moral worth of an action can be judged only if the action is viewed as being a constituent of a practical situation. The same action may be permissible in one practical situation and impermissible in another.

K_1 speaks of willing a maxim to be a universal law of nature. Strictly speaking this cannot be. A maxim is neither a description nor a prediction. It is a policy resolution. Besides, although there is a degree of universality in a maxim, it is not sufficiently universal to qualify as a law of nature. Kant's theory needs to refer to a maxim, the fully universal counterpart of a maxim, e.g., let whoever is in circumstances C be resolved to do A so as to realize E, and the universal law of nature counterpart of the fully universal counterpart, e.g., whoever is in circumstance C does A so as to realize E. These distinctions are useful for understanding Kant's theory that some kind of universality is a necessary condition for being a valid moral principle. Kant takes it for granted that for each practical situation there is, in principle, a corresponding maxim. Kant's explanation of why this should be so is rather opaque. Kant asks:

Where can [the moral worth of a practical situation] be found if we are not to find it in the will's relation to the effect hoped for from the action? It can be found nowhere but *in the principle of the will*, irrespective of the ends which can be brought about by such an action; for between its *a priori* principle, which is formal, and its *a posteriori* motive, which is material, the will stands, so to speak, at the parting of the ways; and since it must be determined by some principle, it will have to be determined by the formal principle of volition when an action is done from duty, where, as we have seen, every material principle is taken away from it (Kant, 400).

There is a more direct and more easily understandable explanation why moral deliberation requires invoking universal principles. If while in C my doing A so as to achieve E has a certain moral quality — it is obligatory, forbidden, permitted, indifferent, or optional —, then whenever I am in C, my doing A so as to achieve E must have the same moral quality. There is a general principle behind this. Whatever action (in its practical situation) is morally (say) permitted to some agent, is morally permitted to any agent in a relevantly similar practical situation. Kant does not explicitly formulate this principle, but it is hard to imagine that he could reject it and still be consistent with his insistence on universalizability as a necessary and sufficient condition for the validity of moral principles. With the general principle in mind, it is easy to see that if my doing A in C here and now so as to achieve E is (say) morally permitted, then my doing A so as to achieve E whenever I am in C is also morally permitted. The consequent is equivalent to the proposition that my maxim, "I am resolved to do A whenever I am in C so as to achieve E", is morally legitimate. But if whenever I am in C I am morally permitted to do A so as to achieve E, then, by the above general principle, anyone who is in C is morally permitted to do A so as to achieve E. The proposition that anyone who is in C is morally permitted to do A so as to achieve E is equivalent to the proposition that it is morally legitimate that everybody be resolved to do A in C so as to achieve E. Note that the moral legitimacy of everybody's being resolved to do A in C so as to achieve E is the same as the moral legitimacy of the fully universal counterpart of the maxim. So far we have a view according to which the fully universal counterpart of the maxim is morally legitimate if, and only if, the maxim is morally legitimate, and the maxim is morally legitimate if, and only if, the action mentioned in the corresponding practical situation is morally permitted. Thus far we have some Kantian terminology but no theoretical claims that anyone can find objectionable if he accepts what I have referred to as being the general principle behind all this.

The distinctive part of Kant's theory of universalizability as a test of moral legitimacy comes just beyond this point. According to K_1, the completely universal counterpart of the maxim is morally legitimate if, and only if, the universal law of nature counterpart of the fully universal counterpart of the maxim can be willed to become a universal law of nature. If K_1 works, we have (but for perhaps some minor emendations) a necessary and sufficient condition for determining the moral quality of an action as a constituent of a practical situation.

In order to grasp the meaning and implications of the K_1 test of moral appraisal, it is necessary to remind ourselves of what Kant thinks a law of nature is. For Kant a law of nature is an actual invariant universal correlation. The law that the volume of a gas is directly proportional to its temperature is a correlation of efficient causality. Kant believes that the laws of nature include teleological laws as well. "It is ... seen at once", says Kant, "that a system of nature by whose law the very same feeling [self-love] whose function is to stimulate the furtherance of life should actually destroy life would contradict itself" (Kant, 422). Kant is here expressing his conviction that "the function of self-love is to stimulate the furtherance of life" is a law of nature. Self-love, in other words, is an efficient cause whereby nature accomplishes the end of furthering, and, by implication, preserving life. Kant views the (phenomenal) world as being constituted by a system of actual laws of nature. The existence and content of this system of laws is independent of human volition. There is, in other words, prior to any human volition and action, a world that has a determinate causal and teleological structure. Kant believes that efficient causality is strictly deterministic. He may or may not be right about this and about the purposiveness of nature. But there is no gainsaying his assumption that morally appraisable conduct presupposes that the world in which actions occur must have a determinate structure independently of human volition and action.

Some universal generalizations may have the *form* of a law of nature and not *be* one. Among these, some are possible laws of nature because they are compatible with the system of laws constituting nature. There are also universal statements of the requisite form that are not possible laws of nature because conjoining them to the system of constitutive laws yields an inconsistent set of laws. For instance, "Everyone who commits suicide is motivated by self-love" is not, for Kant, a possible law of nature because "self-love is a mechanism for self-preservation" is a member of the system of the constitutive laws. When, therefore, in K_1 Kant speaks of being able to will a maxim to be a universal law of nature, part of what he means is that the law of nature counterpart of the maxim's fully universal counterpart can be conjoined to the constitutive laws of nature without generating a self-contradictory set of laws. Accordingly, being able to will a maxim to be a universal law of nature implies that the universal law of nature counterpart of the (fully universalized) maxim is a possible law of nature. (Note that in order to be able to apply K_1 one needs to know, ideally, the system of the constitutive laws of nature, and, practically, a good many of its constituents. Thus, for Kant, a human moral agent-legislator needs to know a great many empirical laws.)

What, now, is the conceptual connection between being a possible law of nature and contradiction in the will? The question is focal, because contradiction in the will is Kant's ultimate criterion for an action to be morally impermissible in its practice situation. K_1 says so. Unfortunately, Kant's own explanation of contradiction in the will is confused. Witness the manner in which Kant uses suicide from self-love to illustrate contradiction in the will. He sets out to explain how K_1 shows that suicide from self-love is morally impermissible. It is morally impermissible, Kant argues, because "anyone whose life threatens more evil than it promises pleasure commits suicide from self-love" is not a possible law of nature. For, self-love is a mechanism for preserving life (Kant, 422). Self-love is also a motive for seeking personal advantage (Kant, 422). From considerations of personal advantage, one might wish to commit suicide. But this motive is *at the same time* a natural mechanism for self-preservation. Therefore, whenever anyone is acting from a motive to secure personal advantage, he is, *a fortiori*, acting from a motive to preserve his life. Hence, the system of laws constituting nature is incompatible with the proposition that anyone who faces more evil than good in continuing to stay alive commits suicide from a motive of securing personal advantage.

If this argument proves anything, it proves that suicide from self-love is physically impossible. Here physically impossible means that even a single agent's performing the "action" is incompatible with the laws that constitute nature. I say "action" because a physically impossible doing is not a morally appraisable action. This remark is implied by the conjunction of two principles, both of which Kant accepts – the libertarian principle that an agent can do an action if, and only if, he can refrain from doing it, and the principle that "ought" implies "can". A morally appraisable action must, therefore, be minimally, a consistently thinkable doing. More than that it must be physically possible, that is, the laws of nature must allow that a single agent can do it. Given Kant's assumption that self-love is a mechanism for self-preservation, suicide from self-love is physically impossible. The correct conclusion for Kant would have been that suicide from self-love is not an action at all, hence, it is not a thing to which deontic concepts apply. Instead of saying this, Kant concludes that suicide from self-love is morally impermissible. But if suicide from self-love is morally impermissible, then refraining from committing suicide from self-love is morally obligatory. But if refraining is morally obligatory, then by the "ought" implies "can" principle, refraining is physically possible. But if refraining is physically possible, then committing the act is also physically possible. But given Kant's assumptions about the function of self-love, no one can commit suicide from self-love, hence, no one can refrain from committing suicide from self-love; therefore, for Kant to conclude that suicide from self-love is morally impermissible is incoherent because that conclusion is incompatible with the conjunction of the principle that "ought" implies "can", the principle that an agent can do something if, and only if, he can refrain from doing it, and the conclusion that suicide from self-love is physically impossible. The conclusion follows from Kant's assumptions, and the two principles are essential components of his normative ethics.

In order to have a clear view of the practical situations that are candidates for moral appraisal, it is necessary to make finer and more accurate discriminations than Kant makes. He writes as if contradiction in the will exists whenever willing the universal law counterpart of a maxim to be a universal law of nature is impossible, either because it is impossible that everyone does the action in that maxim's practical situation, or because everyone's doing the action in that practical situation implies that something happens which the agent-legislator would not want to happen. Suicide from self-love and lying promises for self-interested ends are offered as examples of the first (Kant, 423). Neglecting to develop one's talents and not helping others who need help are offered as examples of the second (Kant, 423). Kant states explicitly that these are the two exclusive and exhaustive ways in which contradiction in the will arises:

These are some of the many actual duties – or at least of what we take to be such –

whose derivation from the simple principle cited above [K_1] leaps to the eye. We must *be able to will* that a maxim of our action should become a universal law − this is the general canon for all moral judgment of action. Some actions are so constituted that their maxim cannot even be *conceived* as a universal law of nature without contradiction, let alone be *willed* as what *ought* to become one. In the case of others we do not find this inner impossibility, but it is still impossible to *will* that their maxim should be raised to the universality of a law of nature, because such a will would contradict itself (Kant, 423–24).

Clearly, finer discriminations are needed under each one of these two ways of producing contradiction in the will, if we are to avoid the confusions lurking in Kant's suicide example. We need an exhaustive classification of practical situations with respect to their feasibility. For, the fundamental criterion for moral permissibility can apply only to feasible doings. Let us begin the classification with a list of practical situations that are intrinsically unfeasible, i.e., that are not consistently thinkable. It is illuminating to include these intrinsically unfeasible cases in a systematic classification, because they bring out important contrasts between what is impossible independently of the laws constituting nature, and what is physically impossible.

A. *Intrinsically Impossible Practical Situations*

(a) The description of the action is self-contradictory. Examples are: squaring the circle, destroying the indestructible, killing the immortal. No matter what the objective and the circumstances of the action are thought to be, because the action itself is logically impossible, it is logically impossible to reach the objective through the action in those circumstances.

(b) The objective of the action is self-contradictory, e.g., pulling the trigger so as to kill the immortal; using compass, paper, and pencil so as to square the circle.

(c) Both the action and the objective are logically impossible, e.g., squaring the circle so as to do the logically impossible; being unaware of the pain I feel so as to be aware that I have a sensation which I do not have.

(d) The action and the objective generate a contradiction, as in moving a finger so as to keep it motionless.

(e) The action and the circumstances generate a contradiction, as in drinking water where there is none.

(f) The circumstances and the objective generate a contradiction, as when someone intends to dream while he remains fully awake.

Any one of the intrinsically impossible cases would produce some sort of contradiction in the will because willing[2] (as against wishing) something to happen in the world implies believing that it can happen. But no intrinsically impossible practical situation is possible in any sense of 'possible'. Willing an intrinsically impossible practical situation is like believing a self-contradictory proposition. Kant never mentions the intrinsically impossible cases presumably because he is concerned only with actions in the sense of consistently thinkable doings. Intrinsically impossible practical situations are not proper objects for moral appraisal. Kant gives no indication of thinking otherwise.

B. *Physically Impossible Practical Situations*

For Kant, an example of this ought to be suicide from self-love. I have already explained why. Not even a single act of suicide from self-love is possible, given (what Kant thinks are) some of the laws constituting nature. Physically impossible practical situations are, also, not proper objects for moral appraisal. The fact that a physically impossible practical situation cannot be universally practised (in Kant's terms, the maxim of the action cannot be conceived as a universal law of nature) cannot be a reason why it is morally impermissible for anyone to do it. Its being physically impossible rules it out of moral consideration.

C. *Physically Possible Practical Situations that Cannot Be Universal Practice*

(a) Although some instances of the practical situation can occur, not everybody can do the action in that practical situation, i.e., the practical situation cannot be universal practice, because from the mere description of the action and its objective, even apart from the laws of nature and contingent facts, it follows that not everybody can do it. There is no example of this in the *Grundlegung*. There is a good one in the *Metaphysical Elements of Ethics*, VIII, (2) (a), pp. 304–14, in T. K. Abbott's *Kant's Theory of Ethics* (Kant, VI, 393). If everyone sacrifices the whole of his happiness, no one can be happy. So the action of sacrificing the whole of one's happiness to make someone else happy cannot be *conceived* as universal practice because, regardless of circumstances, the objective of the action becomes unrealizable, if the action is universally done. This is so apart from any assumptions about how people would react (as in the case of lying promises), and apart from whether or not nature is a teleological system (as in the suicide example). Everybody can sacrifice the whole of his own happiness, and some people can sacrifice the whole of their happiness to make someone else happy, but no one can secure anyone's happiness in a world in which everyone sacrifices the whole of his own happiness. This case should not be confused with any of the intrinsically impossible cases. The action of an intrinsically impossible practical situation is impossible for everyone to do for the same reason that it is impossible for even a single individual to do. The reason why not everybody can sacrifice the whole of his own happiness in order to make someone else happy does not imply that a single occurrence of the action is not possible. In willing it to be a universal law of nature that everyone sacrifices the whole of his own happiness to make someone else happy, there would be a contradiction in the will in that a state of affairs that cannot be *conceived* to be a universal practice is assumed to be a possible universal practice. For, that assumption is a presupposition of the willing. So far I see nothing objectionable. But K_1 implies that because of this contradiction in the will no one has the moral right to sacrifice the whole of his own happiness to make someone else happy. The moral judgment is correct, but Kant's justification for it is questionable, as we shall see.

(b) Although the practical situation can have some instances, a constitutive teleological law makes it impossible for the maxim of the action to have a corresponding law of nature. An example of this is implicit in Kant's theory. According to Kant there are instances of actions caused by heteronomy. But that every act of a human moral agent is done from heteronomy is *inconceivable* as a law of nature, because, Kant argues (Kant, 394–96), the purpose of reason in human moral agents is to cause them to act autonomously. A premise for that conclusion is that "[in] the natural constitution of an organic being – that is, of one contrived for the purpose of life – ... no organ is to be found for any end unless it is also the most appropriate to that end and the best suited for it" (Kant, 395). It is inconsistent with this assumption to suppose that reason never succeeds in accomplishing the end for which it is the most appropriate and best suited organ. There would be a contradiction in willing it to be a universal law of nature that every act of a human moral agent is caused by heteronomy because we would be willing to be a universal law of nature a generalization which is inconsistent with a constitutive law of (human) nature.

(c) People being people, some instances of the action can occur, but not everybody can do the action of the maxim. The lying promise is a case in point. Kant's argument is of questionable soundness, but deductively valid. If everybody does it, then nobody can do it. If nobody can, then nobody does. If nobody does, then not everybody does. Therefore, if everybody does, then not everybody does. Therefore, not everybody does. In other words, lying promises are not, and cannot be, universal practice. The contradiction in the will consists in the fact that the purpose of the lying promise in unrealizable, if the lie that is to realize that purpose is universal practice. In willing that everyone make a lying promise to extricate himself from trouble, I am willing the impossibility of realizing the very purpose that I wish to realize through the maxim of my action. The reason for this impossibility is that "everyone makes a lying promise to extricate himself from a difficulty" is not a possible law of nature.

D. *Physically Possible Practical Situations that Can Be Universal Practice*

Examples are (1) being in a position to help someone who needs help and helping him so as to contribute to his well-being and, also, (2) being in a position to help someone who needs help and not helping him so as to avoid inconvenience for oneself.

(i) Can be willed to be universal practice, e.g., (1).
(ii) Cannot be willed to be universal practice, e.g., (2).

(α) Because if everybody did do it, something could happen to everybody that nobody wants to happen to him. Kant's example is the impossibility of willing the universal practice of no one contributing anything to the well-being of anyone else. "For a will which decided in this way would be in conflict with itself, since many a situation might arise in which the man needed love and sympathy from others and in which by such a law of nature sprung from his own will, he would rob himself of all hope of the help he wants for himself" (Kant, 423). It is possible, says Kant, for there to be a universal law of nature that no one who is not in distress gives help to anyone who needs help. But no one can will this state of affairs, for, everyone, including those who are well-off, would want to get help, if they needed it. The contradiction in the will consists in this: in willing that no one who needs no help ever helps anyone in need of help, I imply that I would be willing to get no help were I to need help; but in fact I *would want* such help. The counter-factual conditional is false.

(β) Because no one (who is rational) can will the doing of the action to be a universal practice, for, "a rational being necessarily wills" that the action not be done. Kant's example is the maxim of neglecting to cultivate talents the cultivation of which would make us useful for all sorts of purposes. The basic idea behind this example is Kant's theory that nature has purposes for us, that the development of our talents is one such purpose, and that it is contrary to reason to refrain from doing whatever is necessary for realizing the purposes of nature for us (see pp. 212–219, below).

The Kantian position on contradiction in the will can now be stated clearly. We begin by observing that intrinsically impossible and physically impossible practical situations cannot be constituents of maxims. This condition is implied by the conjunction of two principles – that "ought" implies "can", and that an agent can do an action if, and only if, he can refrain from doing it. Kant subscribes to both principles. An action, according to Kant, is to be morally appraised by testing its maxim. But intrinsically impossible and physically impossible doings are not morally appraisable actions. Therefore, they cannot be constituents of maxims. All and only physically possible actions can be morally appraised. Kant should be understood as proposing that with respect to physically possible actions there are two criteria for discerning contradiction in the will. The first, illustrated by (C), (a)–(c), asks: Can the maxim of the practical situation have a conceivable law of nature corresponding to it? The answer is "no", if the practical situation cannot be universal practice, for reasons that differ in different types of cases. The second criterion for discerning contradiction in the will, illustrated by D, (ii), (α) and (β), asks: Can the action that *can* be universally practised, be *willed* to be universally practised? The answer is "no", if, as a necessary consequence of everyone's doing it, something would happen that nobody wants to happen, or something would happen that a rational being would necessarily not want to happen.

Contradiction in the will is Kant's fundamental criterion for a maxim's being morally unacceptable. But how, according to Kant, does this carry over to the assessment of the moral worth of singular acts of particular agents? Recall K_1: Act only on that maxim which you can will to become a universal law of nature without contradiction in the will. Is K_1 saying that a certain agent's making a lying promise is morally wrong, if the lie cannot be a constituent of *any* practical situation that can be willed to be a universal law of nature, i.e., that the lie conforms to *no* maxim which is universalizable? Or, is K_1 saying that the lying promise is morally wrong in the practical situation of which the lie is a constituent, if that particular practical situation cannot be willed to be a universal law of nature, i.e., that the maxim of *that* lie is not universalizable? It is clear that in accordance with the idea that the moral worth of a kind of action is assessible only by viewing the action as a constituent of a practical situation, these questions do not imply that K_1 is ambiguous. They rather help us see that K_1 is presupposing that there are in principle actions that are impermissible in *any* practical situation, and actions that are impermissible in some practical situations, but not impermissible in others. K_1 can test the moral worth of a kind of action in the context of its practical situation. If, when in need of borrowing money making a lying promise to repay so as to secure the loan, cannot be, or cannot be willed to be, a universal law of nature, then, according to Kant's theory, it is categorically forbidden to make a lying promise in such circumstances and for such a purpose. This does not establish that making lying promises to repay a loan is categorically forbidden *per se*. That would require proof that *no* practical situation in which making such a promise is a constituent is universalizable. As the number of possible practical situations for an action is inexhaustible, a case by case review could not provide conclusive proof that an action of a certain kind is categorically forbidden *per se*. Kant's theory, however, implies that there are other ways of knowing that a kind of action is categorically forbidden *per se*. For example, there is no circumstance within which, and no purpose for which, it is morally permissible to treat a human being as a mere object of convenience. This is explicit in K_2, and implicit in K_1 and K_3. Rather than being an epistemologically useful test for assessing the moral worth of actions *per se*, K_1 is intended to determine the moral worth of an action as a constituent of a practical situation.

In addition to the category of actions that are morally permissible and morally forbidden, there is a third class of actions, those that are morally indifferent. Kant does not list this as a distinct category, yet his universalizability criterion requires that this be recognized as a distinct category. Presumably, no one can consistently will to live in a world in which there is an adequate number of farmers who are farmers because they want to be, and everyone in that world who has yet to choose a vocation chooses to be a farmer because he wants to be one. And no one can consistently will that in that same world, no one who has yet to choose a vocation chooses to be a farmer for reasons of personal preference. If every novice chose to be a farmer, the consequences would be disastrous. If none made that choice, again the consequences would be highly undesirable because there would be no adequate replacement for the existing farmers who died or retired. By applying K_1, we could infer that for any novice to choose to be a farmer would be morally wrong, and to choose not to be a farmer would also be morally wrong. Consequently, one and the same agent would have a moral obligation both to choose to be a farmer and to choose not to be a farmer. This is not only counter-intuitive, but it is also inconsistent with Kant's principle that "ought" implies "can". Thus, unless Kant made an appropriate adjustment to take account of the problem posed by the farmer example, K_1 would not conform to the sound judgment of the ordinary man (to paraphrase Kant), and the theory would be inconsistent to boot.

In his book, *Generalization in Ethics* (N.Y., Knopf, 1961), Marcus Singer deals with the problem illustrated by the farmer example by distinguishing between actions that are morally indifferent because they are "invertible", from actions that are morally obligatory and morally forbidden. Singer believes that a necessary condition for the valid application of a universalizability criterion is that the following two statements cannot both be true: (1) the consequences of every member of class K's doing A would be undesirable on the whole, and (2) the consequences of no member of class K's doing A would be undesirable on the whole. If (1) and (2) are true, then the action is "invertible", and, if it is invertible, then it is morally indifferent. That is to say, not everybody who is morally permitted to do it must have a special reason why he may, and not everybody who is morally permitted not to do it must have a special reason why he may refrain. Transposed into Kant's theory, the above two conditions would be: (3) every K's doing A cannot be consistently willed, and (4) every K's refraining from doing A cannot be consistently willed. If (3) and (4) are true, then the action is morally indifferent on account of its invertibility. Note that there are also actions that are strictly optional. One example is entering a room with the left foot first. Presumably, actions that are strictly optional are of no concern whatever to morality.

The existence of invertibility suggests an emendation for K_1: Act only on that maxim which you can consistently will to be a universal law of nature, unless the action of the maxim is invertible. This amounts to saying that if the action of a maxim is not invertible and the maxim of the action can be willed to become a universal law of nature, then one may act on the maxim. This provision bars the unwanted result that if we apply K_1 to the farmer example, we obtain a counter-intuitive moral judgment and also find an inconsistency in Kant's theory. Further restrictions may be necessary to secure K_1 from certain other types of counter-examples. However, we need not concern ourselves with what they might be. As we are about to see, the basic difficulty with K_1 is the universalizability requirement. No matter how many restrictions we put on it, the trouble remains.

Clearly, then, contradiction in the will is Kant's fundamental criterion for distinguishing morally wrong actions from actions that have some other moral property. If an action is morally wrong, then it is morally obligatory to refrain from doing it. Thus, contradiction in the will is also the criterion for distinguishing actions that are morally obligatory from those that are not. It is clear that the criterion applies only if actions are considered as universally practised. Two questions need an answer from Kant. The first question is: Why must an action be a *possible* universal practice in order to be morally obligatory? The second question is: Why is contradiction in willing such a universal practice the mark of the morally impermissible?

Kant provides three answers in the *Grundlegung* to the first question. The first is the contention that K_1 selects actions as being morally obligatory or morally forbidden in complete agreement with the sound natural understanding of man, "the common reason of mankind" (Kant, 405), "ordinary intelligence", "the judgment of ordinary reason" (Kant, 404). Kant's examples of the lying promise, not cultivating one's talents, suicide, and not helping those in need are intended to fortify this hypothesis.

Kant's first answer to the first question is refuted by counter-examples. Consider the following maxim:

M_1:   Whenever I conceive a hitherto unknown invention that will benefit mankind, I shall be the first to patent it so as to make a fortune and benefit mankind at the same time.

In order for the universal law of nature counterpart of M_1 to be possible, there must be exactly one person who conceives the hitherto unknown invention. According to K_1, therefore, if more than one person conceives the invention, none of them is morally permitted to be the first to patent it. It is clear that the permissibility of being the first to patent the invention should not depend entirely on the number of people who happen to conceive it. Therefore, measured by ordinary moral intuition, K_1 is too narrow.

Take another example.

M_2:   Whenever I believe that a friend is sick in the hospital, I shall visit him so as to comfort him.

My belief that my sick friend is in the hospital may be false, in which case it is not possible for me to visit him there. But surely I am not morally in the wrong for going to the hospital with the intention of visiting my sick friend. M_2 does not seem to be a morally objectionable policy; yet, according to K_1, the mere fact that I believe falsely that my friend is in the hospital is sufficient to make M_2 morally unacceptable. Once again, measured by ordinary moral intuition, K_1 is too narrow.

Another example of exactly the same sort is the maxim:

M_3: In order to create an eccentric precedent and enhance my reputation as being a whimsical person, whenever I am appointed editor of a journal of Icelandic jokes, I shall publish Icelandic jokes, but only by those who have been published already in a journal of Icelandic jokes.

If, unknown to me, mine is the only journal of Icelandic jokes in existence, neither I nor anyone else can publish a single Icelandic joke under M_3. The policy cannot be universally practised. Yet, bizarre, eccentric, even crazy as it might be, the policy is clearly not morally wrong.

The preceding counter-examples show that K_1 is too narrow a criterion. It classifies as morally impermissible actions that plain moral intuition does not find to be so. Here is a counter-example to show that K_1 is too broad as well. It validates actions that are clearly wrong. Consider:

M_4: Whenever I can extricate myself from grave difficulty only by making a lying promise, I shall (am resolved to) make a lying promise, provided that the circumstances are such as to preclude anyone else's ever finding out that I am lying.

This is clearly a morally objectionable policy. But it is not clear that K_1 rules it out. Such lying promises can be universally practised, and the universal practice would not in time undermine the possibility of making promises. Such lies would be very rare because it is very seldom that nobody will ever find out that I have lied. In real life more lies are told without destroying the practice of promising than would be told under M_4. Moreover, the lie can, without contradiction in the will, be willed to be universal practice. Weighing my desire to extricate myself from grave difficulty against my desire not to be duped, I may decide that I would rather live in a world in which, on rare occasions, I get out of trouble by lying, and am lied to in a similar way, than to live in a world in which I can never extricate myself from difficulty by lying, and, in turn, I am never duped. At any rate, if we appeal to unsophisticated moral intuition, this preference seems to have nothing irrational about it. (We shall shortly see, when we buttress K_1 with K_2 and K_3, that Kant has more to say on the subject, but it will be seen to be insufficient to defend his theory.) It seems to contain no contradiction in the will, yet the action is intuitively objectionable. A self-serving lie told with no chance of exposure seems to be more unpalatable than one that can be detected.

These counter-examples should suffice to refute Kant's contention that the sound judgment of the plain man requires that in order to be morally obligatory an action (in a practical situation) must be such that "everyone does it" is a possible law of nature.

Kant's second answer to the question: why must an action be a *possible* universal practice in order to be morally obligatory is an argument on pp. 399–400 of the *Grundlegung*. This is where Kant is trying to establish that "an action done from duty has its moral worth *not in the purpose* to be attained by it, but in the maxim in accordance with which it is decided upon". The point Kant is trying to make is that the moral worth of an action does not derive from the purpose it seeks to realize. It derives from the *principle of volition* by which the action occurs without regard to any object of desire. Kant's reasoning for this conclusion is that when we are faced with a decision to act we face only two things; blind psychological drives that push us toward an action or pull us away from it, and the *a priori* principle of the will which has nothing psychological about it because it emanates from pure reason. Psychological drives are not self-justifying. A choice as to what to do can be justified, only if it is a reasoned choice. Reasoned choice includes choice resulting from deliberation about means to contingent ends. Such reasoning, however, is not the whole of reasoned choice. Nor is it properly speaking moral choice. The principle of categorical imperatives in its three presumably equivalent formulations, K_1, K_2, and K_3, is, according to Kant, the ultimate rational criterion that can be a causal determinant of morally justified volition, which, in turn, can be causal determinant of morally justified conduct.

The reasoning in Kant's second answer is incomplete. The inference is premised upon the assumption that but for the presence of respect for an *a priori* principle of pure practical reason, moral motivation cannot spring from reason. That assumption is not self-evidently true, and Kant provides no support for it. As a rational being, a moral agent desires to conform his actions to justified true beliefs about their moral worth. An action motivated by that desire is motivated by a desire of reason, hence, it is motivated by a rational motive. Kant's argument does not show that a motive is rational and moral, only if it consists of a desire to act in conformity with an *a priori* principle, which, because it is *a priori*, implies universality. For practical principles, universality consists of universalizability, and that presupposes that the action of a practical principle is a *possible* universal practice, if it is morally permissible. This requirement that the action be a possible universal practice, is embedded in K_1. It should come as no surprise, for we have known all along that the *a priori* principle of the will to which Kant alludes is ultimately the K_1 formulation of the alleged fundamental principle of practical reason. But K_1 cannot be a representation of the fundamental principle. The counter-examples to the universalizability requirement are sufficient to settle that issue.

Kant's third answer to the first question is in the following intriguing and obscure passage:

Inexperienced in the course of world affairs and incapable of being prepared for all the chances that happen in it, I ask myself only 'Can you also will your maxim should become a universal law?' Where you cannot, it is to be rejected, and that not because of a prospective loss to you or even to others, but because it cannot fit as a principle into a possible enactment of universal law (Kant, 403).

The normative principle which is a fully universal prescription corresponding to the maxim is the principle Kant means to single out. A rational being cannot legislate such a prescription, if willing it to be acted on by everyone involves a contradiction in the will. For, if it does, then the principle "cannot fit as a principle into a possible enactment of universal law". I take this to mean that it cannot be a member of the class of valid moral principles. And why not? Because a practical situation that involves contradiction in the will cannot generate a universal law of nature, and it must generate a universal law of nature, if it is to be the practical situation of a valid maxim. How might Kant have come to this conclusion? Kant repeatedly insists that a valid moral judgment is universally valid for all rational beings. This implies that (1) an action has a given moral value (permitted, forbidden, obligatory, indifferent) when someone does it if, and only if, it has that same moral value when anyone else does it. So Kant is implicitly committed to (1). Kant further assumes that (2) "ought" implies "can", and also that (3) applied to a particular human moral agent "can" means that the action is physically possible for that agent. These principles support the premises of the following hypothetical syllogism:

If some particular person ought to do A, then everyone ought to do A (understood as A in its practical situation).

If everyone ought to do A, then everyone can do A.

If everyone can do A, then it is physically possible that everyone does A.

∴ If some particular person ought to do A, then it is physically possible that everyone does A.

But that it is physically possible that everyone does A is equivalent to the proposition that everyone's doing A is a possible law
of nature.

∴ If some particular person ought to do A, then it is a possible law
of nature that everyone does A.

This, I think, is the tacit reasoning behind Kant's requirement that a morally
obligatory action must be a possible universal practice, and a morally impossible action must be such that refraining from doing it is a possible universal
practice.

The reasoning has some coherence. If, in order to be morally obligatory,
an action must be a possible universal practice, then not doing it must be a
possible universal practice, if doing it is morally wrong. For, an action is
morally wrong if, and only if, not doing it is morally obligatory.

Furthermore, the theory is complete. In addition to enabling us to determine the morally forbidden and the morally obligatory, it enables us to
determine the morally indifferent and the morally permissible. Actions that
are "invertible" are morally indifferent, and invertibility uses universalizability
as a criterion. The morally permissible is that which is not morally wrong,
and an action is not morally wrong, if it is not invertible and its maxim is
universalizable.

The imputation to Kant of the (tacit) hypothetical syllogism gains in
credibility because it accords with K_1's requirement that a moral agent test
the maxim of his action by seeing if he can consistently will its practical
situation to be a universal law of nature. As we saw earlier, the impossibility
of conceiving a certain (physically possible) practical situation as being a
universal practice is sufficient for its action to be morally impermissible
(in that practical situation). Accordingly, letting P stand for a practical
situation and Ap for its action-constituent, from K_1 it follows that:

(1)   If it is not a possible law of nature that everyone does Ap, then
          let me refrain from doing Ap.

From (1) we infer:

(2)   If it is not a possible law of nature that everyone does Ap, then
          there is someone who ought to refrain from doing Ap.

Now (2) has two contrapositions, because its consequent has two contraries
that are not equivalent:

(a)   There is someone who ought to do Ap.
        and
(b)   There is someone who is permitted to do Ap, but it is not the case that he ought to do Ap.

One of the contrapositions is:

(3)   If there is someone who ought to do Ap, then it is a possible law of nature that everyone does Ap.

(3) is identical with the conclusion of the hypothetical syllogism that I imputed to Kant.

The second contraposition is:

(4)   If there is someone who is permitted, but not obligated, to do Ap, then it is a possible law of nature that everyone does Ap.

(4) is false. Whoever among the invited guests arrives at the party first is permitted, but not obligated, to be the first to arrive; but it is not a possible law of nature that everyone is the first to arrive. Kant seems to be unaware of the fact that (4) is false. He must accept (4) because he accepts K_1. K_1 is saying that Ap is permitted if, and only if, Ap is universalizable, and (4) is a component of this biconditional. Because the truth-value of (4) is independent of the truth-value of (3), Kant could have rejected (4) while defending (3) on the supposition that universalizability reflects a fundamental feature of moral reasoning. But if Kant had rejected (4), he would not have a criterion (in the form of a sufficient condition) for moral wrongness. The falsity of (4) shows that Kant's criterion (if not universalizable, then morally impermissible) does not work. I shall challenge (3) as well, by arguing below that universalizability cannot be a basic criterion in moral reasoning.

Where does Kant go wrong in these reasonings that I am imputing to him? I suggest that the confusion in Kant's thinking may be over the proposition, "everyone can do A". "Everyone can do A" is ambiguous. If it is equated with (i) "Anyone is such that *he* can do A", it says one thing. Equated with (ii) "Everybody's A-ing is feasible", it says something quite different: (i) can be true, while (ii) is false. For example, any one of the invited guests is such that he could be the first to arrive, while every invited guest's being the first to arrive is not feasible. But (ii) cannot be true and (i) be false. (Note the analogy with the pair of propositional functions, "Everyone stands in the relation R to someone or other" and "There is someone who stands in the relation R to everyone.") Moreover, (i) is equivalent to (iii) Everyone is such that it is physically possible for him to do A, and (ii) is equivalent to (iv) It is physically possible that everyone does A. Now the fact that everyone is such that it is physically possible for him to do A can be, for Kant, at most a necessary condition for A's being *morally appraisable*. It is evident that it cannot be the fundamental criterion for being *morally permissible*, because many an action that satisfies (iii) is morally impermissible. Kant's fundamental criterion for the moral appraisal itself (as expressed in K_1) implies that an action is morally permissible only if (v) it is a possible law of nature that everyone does it. And, because obligation implies permissibility, it follows that one ought to do A only if everyone's doing A is a possible law of nature. This locates the irreparable defect in Kant's ultimate criterion. That criterion yields the absurd conclusion that it is morally impermissible for a guest to be the first to arrive. Kant cannot defend his criterion by appealing to invertibility. An action can be tested for invertibility only if it is possible that everyone does it. The irreparable mistake in Kant's K_1 criterion for moral permissibility is so blatant as to cause wonderment that a philosopher of Kant's acuteness should have made it. The only explanation that I can give of this amazing error is that Kant equated "Everyone can do A" with (iv) Everybody's A-ing is physically possible which, indeed, is equivalent to (v) It is a possible law of nature that everyone does A. But (iv) is the wrong reading of "Everybody can do A". Being the first to arrive at the party is a morally appraisable action because (iii) is true of it. (iv) is not true of it, and that implies that (iv) is neither necessary nor sufficient for the moral appraisability of some human actions.

Furthermore, (v) is not a necessary condition for someone to be morally permitted to do A. The guest example (iv) proves that fact. Corresponding to (iii) Everyone is such that it is physically possible for him to do A is (vi) Everyone is such that he is permitted to do A, and corresponding to (iv) It is physically possible that everyone does A is (vii) It is permitted that everyone do A. (vi) is true of the invited guests. (vii) is false of them because everyone's being the first to arrive is inconceivable, and, therefore, it is not a morally appraisable collective action − it is not the sort of thing that can be morally permissible or morally impermissible. (Note, again, that "It is permitted that everyone do A" is to "There is someone who is R to everyone" as 'Everyone is such that he is permitted to do A" is to "Everyone is R to someone or other.") A necessary condition for it to be true that everyone is such that he is permitted to do A is that everyone is such that it is physically possible for him to do A. "It is physically possible for everyone to do A" (=It is a possible law of nature that everyone does A) is not a necessary

condition for it to be true that everyone is such that he is permitted to do
A. "It is physically possible for everyone to do A" is a necessary condition
for it to be true that it is permissible for everyone to do A. But not all
permissibility statements are of the form "It is permissible that everyone do
A." Some are of the form "Everyone is permitted to do A." Kant's K_1
incorporates the erroneous presupposition that all universal permissibility
statements are of the form "It is permissible that everyone do A."

As a statement of *the* fundamental principle of morality, therefore, K_1 is
irreparably defective. It does not, and cannot, provide *the* ultimate standard
for moral permissibility because some judgments about moral permissibility
are beyond its scope. The reasons that imply this conclusion also explain why
some of the counter-examples to K_1 are in principle decisive. Furthermore,
even those permissibility judgments that are within the scope of K_1 are not
adequately accounted for by K_1. The grounds for this assessment will become
clear as we turn to a consideration of Kant's answer to the second question:
Why is contradiction in the will the mark of the morally impermissible?

Kant's answer to this question is an amplification of his third answer to
the first question (why must a practical situation be a *possible* universal
practice in order to be morally permissible or morally obligatory?). We must
now turn to reporting and evaluating Kant's answer to the second question.

It is generally agreed that morally obligatory action should be physically
possible.[3] How can an individual have a moral obligation to do that which
is impossible in the world in which the action is to be done? After all, one of
the necessary conditions for being a moral agent is to be capable of acting
intentionally, and acting intentionally not only implies believing in the
existence of specific causal connections, but it also implies that causal connections actually obtain. Action is a causally possible doing. It is a species
of causation. Moral agency is, thus, possible only in a universe that is causally
ordered independently of, and antecedent to, an agent's actions. Furthermore,
according to Kant's third answer to the first question, morally obligatory
action has to be a possible universal practice.

Because action is a species of causation, the possibility of a universal
practice must be causal. And, more than that, it must be teleological. That
this must be so is evident in Kant s theory. Kant sees the world in which
human beings function as moral agents as a teleologically ordered universe.
That such a universe should also be causally ordered is a trivial consequence
of the axiom, which Kant accepts, that causal mechanisms are necessary
for implementing puposes. Teleology and efficient causality do not exclude
each other. On the countrary, the former presupposes the latter.

In Kant's teleologically ordered nature (with its underlying causal mechanisms) rational beings, hence, human beings, are the "ends":

Thus a kingdom of ends is possible only on the analogy of a kingdom of nature; yet the kingdom of ends is possible only through maxims − that is, self-imposed rules − while nature is possible only through laws concerned with causes whose action is necessitated from without. In spite of this difference, we give to nature as a whole, even although it is regarded as a machine, the name of 'a kingdom of nature' so far as − and for the reason that − it stands in relation to rational beings as its ends. Now a kingdom of ends would actually come into existence through maxims which the categorical imperative prescribes as a rule for all rational beings, *if these maxims were universally followed*. Yet even if a rational being were himself to follow such a maxim strictly, he cannot count on everybody else being faithful to it on this ground, nor can he be confident that the kingdom of nature and its purposive order will work in harmony with him, as a fitting member, towards a kingdom of ends made possible by himself . . . (Kant, 438).

Kant is assuming that the generation and maintenance of beings who are ends in themselves, who occupy the apex of a hierarchy of beings, is nature's purpose. A kingdom of ends, namely, a law-governed community of rational beings, is a possible ideal to which nature aspires. This aspiration can be realized, but only if "maxims which the categorical imperative prescribes . . . *were universally followed*". If they were "the kingdom of nature and its purposive order [would] work in harmony" with any member of the kingdom, i.e., the intent of every man of good will to satisfy his wants and needs *lawfully* would result in the mutually harmonious realization of everyone's legitimate needs and wants. If we add to all this Kant's assumption that morally acceptable maxims must be universalizable, it follows immediately that the only valid maxims are those which enjoin actions conforming to nature's purposes. This is precisely the condition that the test of contradiction in the will nails down. For, as we have seen, even when a practical situation can be conceived to be universal practice, willing it to be so involves contradiction in the will, if such willing is incompatible with nature's ideal but realizable purposes, or with the causal mechanisms that exist as necessary conditions for implementing them.

But invoking nature's purposes and the causal mechanisms underlying them does not show what K_1 says to be true. K_1 says that a practical situation is morally permissible if, and only if, it is universalizable. Yet, we have seen that there are, independent of teleology and efficient causality, grounds for denying Kant's crucial contention that a practical situation is morally permissible, only if it is a *possible* universal practice. So far, then, Kant is on extremely shaky ground when he requires, through K_1, that a morally permissible action be a possible universal practice.

K_1 fares no better with respect to the second way in which Kant says that there can be contradiction in the will. This way covers the class of actions that are possible universal practice, but cannot be willed to be actual universal practice because a necessary consequence of that practice is that something would happen which nobody wants to happen, or something would happen that necessarily no rational being would want to happen. Typically, in these cases two objectives of the same agent become irreconcilable when the action of the maxim is universal practice. But how does it follow from that that the action of the maxim is morally wrong? For one thing, if the conflict as such is the ground for ascribing moral wrongness, then we can abolish the wrongness either by giving up the action of the maxim together with its objective, or by giving up the conflicting objective that is external to the maxim. Thus, in the example of the maxim, "I shall give no aid to anyone who is in distress and needs my help", the conflict of objectives can be avoided by giving up either the objective of not disturbing one's comfort, or by giving up the desire to be helped when one is in need of help. Now Kant may say that giving up the desire to be helped is not an option because it is necessarily had by any rational being who could need help. If, however, giving up the desire is too much to ask, then subduing it is surely possible. Kant must grant this, for he insists that the desire to be happy is universal and necessarily implicated in rational natures, but that the sense of duty can subdue it. Indeed, he goes so far as to say that duty may require the sacrifice of the whole of one's happiness. Surely a universal and necessary desire may be subdued in the light of considerations other than requirements of duty. Why, then, not consider subduing the desire to be helped, and thereby avoid the conflict between it and the desire not to experience discomfort for somebody else's sake? When faced with a conflict between two objectives (intentions, purposes, desiderata, ends-in-view, goals, etc; choose your own favorite term) what dictates that we abjure the maxim (with its objective) that is being tested? In short, on what basis do we choose which of the two incompatible objectives to forego? So far, Kant's K_1 offers no clue to the answer to that question.

If Kant should appeal, as he does in the suicide example, to the purposes that nature has implanted in man, and suggest that the objective to eliminate is the one that is incompatible with nature's own purposes, we would face an ambiguity. Is nature here conceived to contain actual purposes built into the very nature of things in the world or is nature a set of realizable ideal purposes? Kant must confront this question because he, in fact, refers to three classes of purposes. One class includes the purposes that nature implants in human beings. Examples are the pursuit of happiness and self-preservation. A second class consists of purposes that nature has for us. An example is the end of developing the talents that exist in a moral agent (see p. 219, below). The third class of purposes consists of the purposes that nature itself has. An example of this is the emergence and maintenance of autonomous beings. The first and third class of purposes are *de facto*. They actually exist in nature itself or in the things that nature contains. The second class of purposes are realizable ideals. Now we can ask Kant. If nature is a system of actual purposes, why should they be taken as providing norms? Consider self-love. If it is an actual purposive mechanism for self-preservation, and K_1 is sufficient to show that its frustration is immoral, then there should be but one maxim of suicide, *the* maxim of suicide. But there is no such thing as *the* maxim of suicide. Here is another. Whenever I have the moral certainty that my life promises to be a series of unrelieved degradations, sufferings, and deprivations, with no hope of respite, I will kill myself out of concern for the dignity of my life. Given this maxim, suicide cannot be classified as being immoral by K_1 in conjunction with the assumption that in man the purpose of self-love is self-preservation. As one concerned with the dignity of his life, a rational agent may decide to end it. As one endowed by nature with a mechanism of self-preservation, he is disposed to preserve it. K_1 is powerless to decide which of these is the morally obligatory choice.

If, on the other hand, nature is conceived as being not only constituted by a system of actual causal and teleological laws, but also as being a system of ideal but realizable purposes (and Kant assumes that it is precisely that), then there should be no possible clash among ideal purposes. A system of ideal purposes requires that the purposes be compatible. Unfortunately for us the living and for Kant's theory, a clash among ideal purposes is possible. Surely included in ideal purposes are the *desiderata* of reason itself. A clear examplar of a rational end, i.e., an end that reason judges to be worthwhile, is the preservation of the moral sanity of a person, what Kant would call his good will. Moral sanity has the same worth regardless of where it is found. From reason's point of view John's moral sanity has exactly the same worth as Robert's. The desirable state of affairs is one in which both are preserved. But suppose that accidentally, and through no fault of his, John is falling toward Robert in such a way that upon impact, and without harm to John, Robert's brain will be so damaged as to turn him into a moral simpleton. Suppose that the only way Robert can avoid that outcome is to jump out of the way with the result that upon impact with the ground, John's brain will suffer exactly the damage that Robert's would have, if Robert had not jumped out of the way. It is clear that reason would like to see both moral sanities preserved. It is also clear that under the circumstances this is not possible. Thus, in our world it is possible to face a situation in which the components of a universally shared rational objective are not in harmony. Kant is simply mistaken that:

since laws determine ends as regards their universal validity, we shall be able – if we abstract from personal differences between rational beings, and also from all the content of their private ends – to conceive a whole of all ends in systematic conjunction (a whole both of rational beings as ends in themselves and also of the personal [lawful] ends which each may set before himself); that is, we shall be able to conceive a kingdom of ends which is possible in accordance with the above principles (Kant, 433).

That nature is teleological is, to say the least, dubious. That nature is, furthermore, a system so constituted that in it there is no conflict of rational desiderata, is false, and that is enough to undermine Kant's contention that nature as a teleological system of ideal but realizable worthwhile ends sets the objectives for morally justified conduct.

Without the assumption that nature is a system of compatible realizable ideals, the test of contradiction in the will is seriously undermined. Applied to one class of cases, the test decides against actions that, if universally practised in their specific practical situations, would make it impossible to achieve some lawful purpose of the agent who has willed the universal practise. This would be sufficient to show the moral wrongness of the practice, if morally good conduct consisted of acting in such a way as to contribute to the actualization of the possible harmony of the rationally sanctioned purposes of moral agents. But morally good conduct cannot be so defined because the rationally sanctioned purposes of moral agents can conflict.

That K_1 is not a criterion for the morally impermissible is further supported by the fact that its application can yield incompatible moral judgments. Is it morally permitted that (I refuse to help someone who needs my help? Consider the maxim's universal law of nature counterpart: No one helps anyone in need of help. But since I wish to be helped when I need help, I cannot consistently with this will that nobody help anybody. Therefore, it is immoral not to render needed help. This is Kant's argument. But by exact parity of reasoning, we can prove the opposite. Is it morally permitted to render needed help? Consider the universal law of nature that corresponds to this maxim: Whenever anyone is in need of help, he gets it from anyone who is in a position to help. But since I also wish not to be inconvenienced, I cannot consistently with that wish will that whenever anyone is in need of help he gets it. Therefore, it is immoral to render help where help is needed. What in Kant's theory allows the first inference and rules out the second? Certainly not K_1. Note that the conclusion of the first inference is incompatible with that of the second.

So far we have found no support for Kant's contention that K_1 is a formulation of the fundamental principle of morality. Could it be that instead of being the rock-bottom principle of practical reason, K_1 is derivable from synthetic *a priori* principles that are more evident than it? In raising this question, we are going beyond Kant's theory. Nevertheless, if such a derivation is possible, K_1 can be reinstated as a derived principle that may all the same be deeply illuminating.

In *Generalization in Ethics* Marcus Singer deduces the principle of the generalization argument (PGA), a principle that is closely analogous to K_1. Singer believes that (PGA) is the fundamental principle of morality.

Here is the derivation:

(C_1):   If the consequences of x's doing A are undesirable on the whole, [and the consequences of x's not doing A are not undesirable on the whole], then x (morally) ought not to do A.

∴ (GC_1): If the (collective) consequences of everyone's doing A would be undesirable on the whole, while the (collective) consequences of no one's doing A would not be undesirable on the whole, then it ought morally to be that at least one person refrains from doing A.

(GP):   If it ought morally to be that at least one person does not do A, then no one is (morally) permitted to do A, unless there is a special reason why he may.

∴ (PGA): If the (collective) consequences of everyone's doing A would be undesirable on the whole, while the (collective) consequences of no one's doing A would not be undesirable on the whole, then no one is (morally) permitted to do A, unless he has a special reason that exempts him.

The connection with Kant is close. Consider Kant's lying example.

(KGC$_1$): As the collective consequences of everyone's making a lying promise in order to extricate himself from difficulty are undesirable on the whole in that the universal lying would in time destroy the practice of making promises, while the collective consequences of no one making such promises would not be undesirable on the whole, then it (morally) ought to be that at least one person does not make a lying promise.

(KGP): As it morally ought to be that at least one person does not make such promises, then no one is morally permitted to make such promises, unless he has a special reason.

∴ (KPGA): As the (collective) consequences of everyone's making such promises are undersirable on the whole, while the (collective) consequences of no one's making such promises are not, no one is (morally) permitted to make such promises, unless he has a special reason why he may.

(KPGA) is not equivalent to K$_1$. Contradiction in the will is not involved in (KPGA). Furthermore, while K$_1$ is supposed to be *the* fundamental principle of morality, (KPGA) is derived. Nevertheless, the two principles have significant affinities. Both are judgments about the moral worth of actions, but only as actions are viewed as *possible* for everyone to do. K$_1$ does not mention exempting reasons. (KPGA) does. Kant need not find this unacceptable. If there are actions that are morally impermissible in any practical situation, then there are no exempting reasons and no one is morally permitted to do them under any circumstances. For actions such that in some practical situations they are morally permissible, the circumstances or the intention will be the exemptive reasons. (KPGA) looks to be sufficiently close to Kant's K$_1$ to qualify as a vindication of K$_1$, provided that the premises for (PGA) are true, and Singer's theory includes a clear and non-circular criterion for being a reason that exempts (a respect that makes for morally relevant similarity). I have argued elsewhere that Singer's theory fails on both counts.[4] Toward the end of this essay I shall argue that no universalizability criterion can succeed.

Up to this point, we have been unable to support Kant's contention that K$_1$ is a formulation of the fundamental principle of morality. Nor have we found justification for the hypothesis that K$_1$ is derivable from synthetic *a priori* principles of pure practical reason that are more evident than it. We have yet to scrutinize Kant's conviction that K$_1$, K$_2$, and K$_3$ cannot be understood and applied separately. We have yet to see if combining the idea of contradiction in the will and the universalizability it presupposes, (K_1), the idea of rational agents being ends in themselves, (K_2), and the idea of the peer status of autonomous agent-legislators, (K_3), can neutralize alleged counter-examples and solve the problem of eliciting a criterion for deciding, when there is contradiction in the will involving conflict among ends, which of the incompatible objectives is worth retaining. Remember that this variety of contradiction exists just in case a *possible* universal practice would, if actualized, inevitably lead to consequences that nobody would want, or which no rational being could want.

The formula K_2 makes it a categorical imperative to treat rational nature, be it in oneself or others, as an end and never as a means only. Kant must establish that there are absolute ends, that as rational beings, human beings are absolute ends, and he must explain what treating someone as an end means.

Kant's argument that there must be absolute ends is as follows:

(1)   [I]f all value were conditioned − that is, contingent − then no supreme [practical] principle could be found for reason at all.

(2)   "If then there is to be a supreme practical principle and − so far as the human will is concerned − a categorical imperative, it must be such that from the idea of something which is necessarily an end for every one because it is an *end in itself* it forms an *objective* principle of the will and consequently, it can serve as a practical law" (Kant, 428−29).

In Chapter 3 of the *Grundlegung* Kant states clearly that freedom of the will, which is the ground of the possibility of categorical imperatives, cannot be *proved*, but that every moral agent *assumes* that he, himself is free, that his will is an efficient cause of a very special and unique kind. What Kant seems to be saying is that every moral agent must affirm the reality of a supreme practical principle because the only firm belief consistent with the indelible conviction of one's own freedom is that there are categorical imperatives. So, the tentative sounding premise (2) may be read, in view of what is to come, as asserting that there is a supreme practical principle such that from the idea of something which is necessarily an end for everyone it forms an objective principle of the will. Consequently, every moral agent must infer from (1) and the assertive version of (2) that there are values that are not conditioned, not contingent, not relative to contingently existing personal wants, wishes, needs, or purposes; that there are, in fact, values that are absolute, that "can provide ... universal principles, ... principles valid and necessary for all rational beings and also for every volition – that is, . . . practical laws" (Kant, 427).

That as rational beings, human beings are absolute ends, and the only absolute ends in nature (in the arena of morally criticizable human conduct), Kant tries to prove as follows:

(1) Everything man-made has conditional value only.
(2) All non-rational beings "whose existence depends, not on our will, but on nature" have "only a relative value as means and are consequently called *things*".
(3) "Rational beings, on the other hand, are called *persons* because their nature already marks them out as ends in themselves – that is, as something which ought not to be used merely as a means" (Kant, 428).

Premises (1) and (2) are debatable. Indeed, if premise (2) is conjoined to the assumption that non-human animals are non-rational, as Kant seems to think, then it follows that non-human animals are just *things* that we can do with as we please. I find this to be a strenuously objectionable view. However, although the proper treatment of animals is by no means a negligible ethical issue, it is peripheral to the problem at hand. The most important contention is (3), and we need to examine Kant's reasons for it. We noted earlier that in Kant's teleologically ordered universe rational beings are the "ends". Kant seems to be implying that the generation and maintenance of rational beings who are moral agents is nature's purpose. Nature intends them to occupy the apex in a hierarchy of beings. Kant also says that "the will of a rational being must always be regarded as *making universal law*, because otherwise he could not be conceived as *an end in himself*" (Kant, 434). "Making universal law" is involved in autonomy. So, Kant seems to be implying that nature's end is to produce autonomous beings who, because of their autonomy, occupy the apex of the hierarchy.

Persons, therefore, are not merely subjective ends whose existence as an object of our actions has a value *for us*: they are *objective ends* – that is, things whose existence is in itself an end, and indeed an end such that in its place we can put no other end to which they should serve *simply* as means; for unless this is so, nothing at all of *absolute* value would be found anywhere (Kant, 428).

Rational beings are *objective ends* because their production and maintenance is the end that nature seeks. It is because of that that a rational being is, *for every rational being*, an end in the sense that whereas anything non-rational can lawfully be used as a *means only*, rational nature is "such that in its place we can put no other end to which [it] should serve *simply* as a means".

If this is Kant's argument for (3), it comes to nothing. Why should we believe that nature's ultimate and final end is to produce autonomous beings, even assuming (what I shall later deny) that autonomous beings in Kant's sense exist at all? Plato, for one, believes that guided by the Form of the Good, the best among us, if given the chance, can mould people, institutions, and artifacts to imitate ideal archetypes, and that this type of activity is what reason as *eros* aims at when reason is operating at its highest reaches. Plato believes that the best activity is creativity at that level, and the best things in the world are the products of such activity. This, too, is a teleological view, but the place of honor in Plato's teleological cosmos is occupied by activities and entities different from Kant's. If Kant is to persuade us that he is right and views like Plato's are wrong, he owes us a convincing argument. He offers no such thing. Instead, he seems to be elevating anthropocentrism into a supposititious philosophical axiom.

Inasmuch as the Kantian basis for rational beings being *objective ends* for all rational beings is the *obiter dictum* that the end of nature is to produce beings who are autonomous by nature, we have so far no reason at all for believing that rational beings are, indeed, *objective ends*.

Assessing Kant's views is all the more difficult because objective ends are to be treated as ends, and never as means only, and the latter notion needs clearer statement than it receives in Kant. In the illustrations from duties to others immediately following K_2, the formula of ends in themselves, Kant says some unhelpful things about what it is to treat someone as a means only, and not at the same time as an end (see Kant, 429–30).

Can suicide "be compatible with the idea of humanity *as an end in itself*"? No, says Kant, because in killing, maiming, or spoiling a human being for a certain end, one is treating rational nature merely as a means. The culpable end is to do away with an intolerable life. But why is this a culpable objective? Kant does not say. He simply says that acting with that intention implies that the suicide is using his own person merely as a *means* to maintain a tolerable state of affairs to the end of his life and this, he implies, amounts to using himself *merely* as a means. Not so, if Kant means to imply that the suicide acts with no consideration, respect, or appreciation for his humanity. We noted earlier that a person can put an end to a life of unrelieved degradation and indignity precisely because he believes that no human being should allow himself to be so treated.

"Secondly, . . . the man who has a mind to make a false promise to others will see at once that he is intending to make use of another man *merely as a means* to an end he does not share. For the man whom I seek to use for my own purposes by such a promise *cannot possibly agree with my way of behaving toward him, and so cannot himself share the end of the action"* (Kant, 429). The key is in the phrase I have just emphasized. Interesting as this sounds, it will not do. There are obvious counter-examples to it. So long as a thief adheres to his objective of stealing, he *cannot possible* agree to my turning him over to the police in order to prevent the crime. He, himself, cannot share the end of my proposed action. But surely the thief cannot complain that I am doing him wrong. So by this criterion, there is nothing necessarily wrong with treating someone as a means only. Therefore, the criterion fails as an explanation of treating someone as a means only.

"Thirdly, in regard to contingent (meritorious) duty to oneself, it is not enough that an action should refrain from conflicting with humanity in our own person as an end in itself: it must also *harmonize with this end*" (Kant, 430). An essential part of Kant's argument is what he goes on to say, namely that nature has purposes for humanity that can be realized only by human choice and action (*the purposes* or *ends of nature* for humanity), as distinct from *natural purposes or ends*, such as happiness, which all men seek. Inclination can cause failure to act so as to realize the purposes of nature, but inclination cannot cause failure to act in the hope of realizing a natural purpose.(See also Paton's translation of the *Grundlegung*, the translator's note on p. 139 to the text, p. 69 and the reference to *Critique of Judgment*, § 67.)

There is no immediately obvious connection between treating oneself as an end in itself and striving to realize the purposes of nature for humanity. Presumably for Kant a person "promotes" humanity in his own person as an end in itself only if he strives to realize the purposes of nature for humanity. But why is this "promoting" necessary for treating oneself as an end in itself? How does it "harmonize" with the end of treating humanity as an end in itself?

I believe that the answers to these questions are implicit in Kant's unsupported but supportable proposition that,

[t]here is . . . *one* end that can be presupposed as actual in all rational beings (so far as they are dependent beings to whom imperatives apply); and thus there is one purpose which they not only *can* have, but which we can assume with certainty that they *do* have by a natural necessity – the purpose, namely of *happiness*. . . . a purpose which we can presuppose *a priori* and with certainty to be present in every man because it belongs to his very being (Kant, 415).

And again, "the natural end which all men seek is their own happiness" (Kant, 430). I take Kant to be asserting that seeking one's own happiness is entailed by being a finite moral agent. Kant does not explain why "we can presuppose *a priori*" that all imperfectly rational (and self-conscious) agents seek (by way of consciously aiming at) their own happiness as a matter of "natural necessity". What Kant is asserting, however, is justifiable and true. The necessity in question is *a priori*; it is based on conceptual connections, not on particular causal laws. The reference to imperfectly rational beings to whom imperatives apply is significant. The reference makes it clear that the subjects of discussion are moral agents. An imperfectly rational being is, for Kant, a rational being whose volitions can be determined by influences other than reason. The sum total of such extra-rational influences Kant collects under the rubric of "inclinations". Thus, the reference is to rational beings who have inclinations and will to act. They are imperfectly rational agents. When Kant asserts that an imperfectly rational being seeks his own happiness because to seek it "belongs to his very being", he implies that it is not possible to be a finite moral agent and not to prefer the enjoyments of satisfied inclinations to the frustrations of thwarted inclinations. For, as Kant conceives it, happiness is a sum total of satisfied inclinations and a concurrent sense of contentment. As a self-conscious creature capable of suffering and enjoyment, a human moral agent must necessarily prefer enjoyment to suffering. According to Kant, the happiness that every finite moral agent seeks as a necessity of his nature, insofar as he is a creature necessarily endowed with inclinations, is happiness *per se*, not happiness achieved under the rule of pure practical reason. Happiness achieved under the rule of pure practical reason is an objective not of inclination but of pure practical reason itself. This rational objective is as much a necessity of a human moral agent's nature as is the "pathological" objective to secure his own happiness *per se*. The conflict between duty and happiness exists in human moral agents because the animal part of their nature (as moral agents) is necessarily seeking the agent's own happiness *per se*, while the rational aspect of that nature forbids the satisfaction of any inclination that involves dereliction of duty. With regard to natural purposes, then, such as happiness, that all human moral agents have, a human moral agent would be treating himself as an end, and not merely as a means, only if he acknowledged, and acted on the conviction, that securing his own happiness, but only in morally permissible ways, is a necessity of his nature as a finite moral agent. Otherwise his thinking and actions would thwart rather than "promote" humanity (in the guise of finite moral agent) in his own person. In short, this way of treating oneself as a means only involves negligence about natural purposes that one has as a human moral agent. Such conduct would not "harmonize" with the end of treating humanity as an end in itself because it would be a violation of the person by way of negligence about needs that reason requires to be met.

The foregoing account is a proposal as to what Kant could have said on the subject of what it would mean for someone to treat himself as an end, and not as a means only, relative to actions that are intended to realize a "natural purpose", such as securing one's own happiness. We are now in a position to provide a plausible answer to the original question: Why is promoting "the purposes of nature for humanity" (of which an example is developing one's talents) "necessary for treating oneself as more than a means only". And how does "promoting" such purposes "harmonize" with the purpose of treating humanity in oneself as more that a means only? We have noted that for Kant securing one's own happiness is a purpose or end that every human moral agent has necessarily insofar as he is a creature of inclinations, and, insofar as he is rational, securing his own happiness in morally permissible ways only is an end that overrides the objective of achieving happiness no matter how. As a rational being a human moral agent can come to see that a necessary condition for securing his own happiness is that he be effective and not powerless. He can also come to see that developing one's talents is a necessary condition for being effective. To neglect developing talents in such a way as to make the agent effective is, therefore, to make oneself less effective than one might be in promoting the natural purpose of achieving one's own happiness, and such neglect can be seen clearly as not "harmonizing" with the natural purpose of achieving happiness lawfully.

In the immediately preceding paragraphs I have proposed a way of explaining Kant's doctrine as to how we can treat ourselves as ends, and not as means only, in connection, first, with "the natural purposes" we have as human, hence, finite, moral agents, and, second, with "the purposes that nature has for us", as finite moral agents. I have not tried, because I do not know how, to produce a plausible explanation of Kant's assumption that one of nature's own ends is to produce and maintain autonomous beings, and that, therefore, autonomous beings are absolute ends in themselves.

The fourth example (Kant, 430) sets out the following criterion: x treats y as an end, and not as a means if, and only if, so far as in him lies, x furthers the ends of y. "For the ends of a subject who is an end in himself must, if this conception is to have its *full* effect on me, be also, so far as possible, my ends." Again, this cannot be Kant's most considered idea because there are counter-examples. I suppose in some way it is possible for me to make the thief's end my end also. Suppose I work up a great deal of sympathy for him, I dwell on his enormous handicaps, I talk myself into believing that the rich victim will not suffer any inconvenience at all. He may not even miss the stolen goods, I say to myself. So, I decide to help the thief. At least two things go wrong here. In the first place, I am treating the rich victim as a means only. And it is by no means clear that I am treating the thief as an end in himself in any way that would be deemed commendable.

The ease with which most of these criteria for treating someone as an end and not as a means only are refuted, suggests that Kant's point may be something more general and fundamental. We should be faithful to the text and fair to Kant, if we noted that the foundations for K_3, the kingdom of ends formula, are identical with the foundations for K_2, the end in itself formula. The starting point is Kant's assumption that nature is a teleological system of mutually harmonious, i.e., mutually realizable, worthy ends, and that nature so conceived sets the objectives for morally justified conduct. If the maxims that a member of the possible kingdom of ends would legislate were universally followed, says Kant, the intent of every person of good will to satisfy his wants and needs *lawfully* would result in the mutually harmonious realization of everyone's legitimate purposes (see p. 210 above). This suggests that to treat a rational being as an end, and never as a means only, is to act in such a way that one's actions never interfere with the mutually harmonious realization of everyone's legitimate purposes; that, indeed, whenever feasible, they promote that harmony.

According to this criterion of treating a person as an end and not as a means only, the fact that while standing firm on his resolve to steal, the thief cannot possibly agree to my proposing to turn him over to the police so as to prevent the burglary, is no embarrassment to Kant. Nor is the fact that I am unable to make his ends mine, and, thereby, to help him achieve it. The objective of the thief cannot be a member of a set of mutually harmoniously realizable ends. Consequently, it fails of legitimacy.

If we combine the force of K_2 and K_3 with K_1, the requirement of universality (or universalizability) may look stronger. For now only those maxims survive the test of moral legitimacy that legislate in favor of actions that promote the realization only of those objectives of an agent which every agent would find to be realizable with his own.

Is K_1 thus buttressed by K_2 and K_3 able to evade the four counter-examples, $M_1 - M_4$, to K_1 standing by itself (see pp. 202–3, above)? Kant might try to dismiss the counter-examples by suggesting that they should not appear to be genuine to anyone who, having thought about K_2 and K_3, has come to a correct understanding of morality in terms of legislation that promotes the realization of universal harmony. This defense is not promising. Let us recall that in order that there be a universal law of nature associated with M_1, there has to be exactly one person who conceives the invention.

If more than one person conceives the invention, K_1 implies that none of them is morally permitted to be the first to patent it. This is counter-intuitive and remains so, even if K_2 and K_3 are brought to bear on the case. I see no way of formulating a maxim which will pass the test of K_1 for allowing someone to be the first to patent the invention regardless of the number of people who conceive the invention. Similarly, ten people are about to compete in the one hundred yard dash. Each of them is resolved to be the winner. Only one can be. Is universal harmony impeded by that person's victory? Again, is universal harmony impeded when only one of five men who are madly in love with the same woman can marry her, and one of them does marry her? If Kant were to say that winning the race and marrying the woman are, indeed, instances of impeding universal harmony, and that, therefore, it is morally wrong for anyone to win a race or to marry a woman some other man also wants to marry, his position would be contrary to sound judgment. But if such actions as these are not instances of impeding universal harmony, and are, therefore, morally permissible, then why does K_1 rule that they are morally impermissible?

M_2 and M_3 are not universalizable, but for a reason different from why M_1 is not. The promulgator of the maxim has false beliefs about the circumstances, and the truth about the circumstances implies that the action cannot be done. Kant might suggest that a person who believes falsely that he can act on a certain maxim cannot legislate the practical situation of that maxim into a universal law of nature. Hence, he cannot legislate a law of nature the existence of which either does not impede or positively promotes universal harmony. Assuming Kant's theory that either not impeding or positively promoting such harmony is necessary for being a morally permitted action, it follows that any intuition must be morally unreliable, if it finds that the practical situations depicted in M_2 and M_3 are morally permissible, the facts being what they are. Thus, Kant might say, strong as they may have seemed, M_2 and M_3 are not decisive counter-examples to K_1. But we have seen that universal harmony of all rational ends is not possible. Therefore, Kant's theory that either not impeding or promoting such harmony is necessary for being a morally permissible action cannot diminish the force of M_2 and M_3 as being counter-examples to K_1.

A Kantian rebuttal of M_4 is not easy. In the *Grundlegung* Kant argues that a self-serving lie is morally impermissible because it is not a conceivable universal practice (Kant, 403) and because to tell such lies is to use another merely as a means (Kant, 429–30). I have given reasons for believing that these arguments are inconclusive. Twelve years after the appearance of the

Grundlegung, Kant published an essay, "On a Supposed Right to Lie from Benevolent Motives".[5] In it Kant defends the proposition that whenever one cannot avoid answering "yes" or "no", one has an unconditional duty to speak honestly, i.e., to say what one believes to be the truth. Otherwise "I commit a wrong against duty generally in a most essential point. That is, so far as in me lies I cause that declarations should in general find no credence, and hence that all rights based on contracts should be void and lose their force, and this is a wrong done to mankind generally" (Beck, p. 347). This is the old argument, the one in the *Grundlegung*, that by speaking dishonestly I contribute my mite toward causing the breakdown of trust, which, in turn, undermines the practices that are necessary for realizing universal harmony.

Kant's reasoning fails for two reasons. The first is that not impeding universal harmony cannot be a necessary condition for an action to be morally permissible. The second reason is that Kant's conclusion cannot be right that moral agents have an unconditional duty to speak honestly. For, it is possible to declare honestly two propositions the second of which implies the contradictory of the first. By Kant's principle, we would have an unconditional duty to declare a proposition that happens to be self-contradictory. But its being self-contradictory is a reason why we ought not to declare it. Hence, it cannot be that we have an unconditional duty to speak honestly. We have only a *prima facie* duty to speak honestly. If this is correct, then in K_2 and K_3 Kant has no new weapon for disposing of M_4 as an example to show that K_1 is too broad.

K_1 CANNOT WORK

The foregoing considerations show that even buttressed by K_2 and K_3, K_1 does not work. Now I want to show that K_1 cannot work. The universalizability requirement must be extirpated. It cannot be a necessary condition for being a morally legitimate practice.

K_1 cannot work for two reasons. One is the existence of possible conflict among rationally sanctioned objectives. The other is the possibility that rational beings, including human moral agents, may consistently see some aspects of the world in fundamentally different ways. Such fundamental metaphysical differences may yield different moral principles, and therefore, not all moral principles are necessarily universally valid for all moral agents. Kant says that "[a] rational being must always regard himself as making laws in a kingdom of ends" (Kant, 434). He also says that "a rational being must always be regarded as *making universal law* . . ." (Kant, 434). From these remarks there follows a characteristically Kantian dogma: that a rational being must always regard himself as making moral laws that are necessarily valid for any other rational being as they are for him. I shall show that this dogma is false. The truth is that a rational being would, if adequately critical, believe the contradictory of Kant's dogma.

K_1 cannot work *as buttressed by K_2 and K_3*, because the Kantian foundations for K_2 and K_3 are false. This we saw earlier, in the illustration of a conflict of rational ends as in the case of John and Robert. K_1 cannot work even apart from the shaky foundations Kant provides for it. No universalizability criterion for moral legitimacy, Kantian or not, can work. Not all of the Buddha's moral principles can agree with those of St. Paul, although neither one of them is necessarily irrational or unqualified to be a moral agent. Some moral principles are universally valid; others are not. Rational beings who are *bona fide* moral agents can live by incompatible moral principles that are valid, but not universally shared.

Let me illustrate with the principle of self-defense. Under our English-American laws it is legitimate to defend oneself or a third party against physical assault. The law sanctions killing in self-defense or in defense of another person. The law requires that the victim save himself by running away, if he can. But it is a legitimate defense to argue in court that running away was impossible, and that it was necessary to kill in order to defend oneself or someone else.

Now one may question the morality of the law. There are people who believe that the principle of self-defense is morally legitimate. The Jains of India, however, would certainly refuse to recognize our laws on self-defense as being morally legitimate for them. If a Jain came to live in the United States and faced a situation in which he had to kill or be killed, he would not kill, if he acted on his principles. The Jains believe that all evil is a form of violence. They also believe in reincarnation and karma. As rational beings concerned with the quality of their lives, they avoid scrupulously all forms of violence in their own conduct because they believe that if they acted violently, their karma would take them away from the path of salvation. They would be condemned to wander from one body to another and suffer instead of coming to rest in Nirvana.

Belief in reincarnation and karma are metaphysical beliefs. Within the framework of Indian metaphysics, they are premised upon the assumption that the destiny of the human soul is not in the hands of a divine providence, which contradicts the theistic belief that the destiny of the human soul is in God's power. The two contradictory positions are conflicting *basic* meta-physical beliefs. Each one circumscribes a metaphysical framework that identifies a particular community of agreement, that is, a community of individuals who view the world from the same metaphysical framework, People may be born into a community, absorb its metaphysics, and never question it. Or, an individual may conceive a new metaphysical framework. as religious prophets do. The Apostle Paul experiences the world as being the work of God. Buddhist monks sometimes report that in meditation they experience the truth of reincarnation and karma. "Tough-minded" positivists experience the world as being nothing more than what well-grounded scientific thinking encompasses. These are instances of basic metaphysical beliefs, provided that they satisfy the following definition: a proposition, p, is metaphysically basic for x if, and only if, (1) x believes that p, and the belief is independent of x's deriving, or being able to derive, p from a proposition more evident to x than p; (2) there are no scientific or formal procedures or criteria for determining whether p is true or not; (3) p conflicts with no established scientific proposition; (4) p is not self-contradictory, and there is no proposition accepted by x that in conjunction with p implies a contradiction.

A metaphysical proposition that is basic can be believed by more than one person. Together they constitute a community of agreement. The belief is objective for the members of the community but not quite in the way that scientific beliefs are objective. In science there are standard procedures for reaching intersubjective agreement. A necessary condition for the effectiveness of these procedures is the contingent fact that there is universal intersubjective agreement about sense-perceptions. Abnormalities are explained. Scientific objectivity depends upon the possibility of testing scientific hypotheses by appeal, from time to time, to universally intersubjective sense-perceptions. There is no possibility of comparable tests where basic metaphysical pro-positions are concerned. Such propositions are objective for the members of the community of agreement in virtue simply of that agreement. Moreover, a basic metaphysical proposition cannot be refuted by anyone outside the community of agreement, nor can anyone in the community prove it to anyone outside. And no one in the community needs proof in order to believe. Two incompatible basic metaphysical beliefs present two possible views of the world, not both of which can be true, and no one can ever be in a position to prove which, if either one, is true. The situation which I have described is what I identify as the metaphysico-centric predicament. Any fully rational person may be in that predicament.[6] The fact that basic metaphysical beliefs are not supported by evidence is not a reason for thinking that they are arbitrary or irrational. Being grounded in evidence cannot be a necessary condition for rational belief, for, if it were, no belief could be rational. The demand would generate a vicious infinite regress.

Two points deserve emphasis. The first is that fully rational beings can have incompatible basic metaphysical beliefs. The second is that these basic beliefs imply moral principles, and incompatible basic beliefs can imply incompatible moral principles. Being incompatible, the basic beliefs cannot all be true. Being beyond the possibility of cogent refutation from a framework alien to their own, basic metaphysical beliefs are articles of faith. Those who believe them sincerely must proclaim them as their cherished convictions. They must, at the same time, insofar as they think under reason's rule, admit that *basic* commitments are not knowledge. Nobody knows, and nobody can know, which among the rival basic beliefs in true. Thus, the metaphysico-centric predicament underlies the ethico-centric predicament.

Not all moral principles, therefore, need be universally valid for all rational beings. We must admit the theoretical possibility of moral principles that are valid within a particular community of agreement only. These are the moral principles that the members of that community may not reject, if they are to be consistent with their basic metaphysical commitments. A Jain will reject the principle of self-defense that much of Judeo-Christian morality sanctions. The Jain's uncompromising pacifism is valid for him; it is valid relative to his basic convictions about reality. The same is true of some of us who are not uncompromising pacifists. Some of us who believe in the legitimacy of self-defense need not share the Judeo-Christian basic assumptions. Incompatible basic metaphysical assumptions may imply incompatible moral principles, but they need not. The fact, however, that they may, and that they do, is not to be ignored.

All this has immediate relevance to Kant's K_2 and K_3. Universalizability as a criterion for the morally legitimate is in principle mistaken. K_2 and K_3, however, are defensible once they are released from their Kantian moorings.

K_3 emphasized the peer status of moral agents. This is correct. Kant is simply mistaken in his way of explaining what this peer status is. He thinks of it as consisting of the universality of reason's moral principles. But, if my argument is correct, there is no such universality. Reason is universal, but the particular moral principles that reason sanctions are not necessarily universally valid for all rational beings. Reason, as I conceive it, is a family of purely intellectual powers, but nothing about these powers enables us to determine what specific metaphysical articles of faith a rational being is bound to adopt.

Hume said: "Nothing so like as eggs". He could just as well have said: "Nothing so like as two human brains". But we all know how inexhaustibly many mind-bogglingly different views of reality emerge from the workings of the human brain.

The correct account of the peer status of moral agents, I suggest, is that all moral agents are in the same ethico-centric predicament. Not a single one of them can *know* if his conception of the world is true or not, because the basic metaphysical assumptions on which the conception rests are articles of faith. All moral agents are, thus, alike in being fully rational, in forming moral principles in the same way, and in not knowing, yet having to proclaim with serious conviction, articles of faith that shape their view of the world and much of their view of how they are to conduct themselves in it. Thus many moral principles are, in theory, framework-dependent, and are valid only for those who share the basic assumptions of a metaphysical framework. Inasmuch as two fully rational beings can adopt incompatible frameworks, their moral principles may differ. Thus, not all moral principles are valid absolutely. Many are valid only relative to framework. They are valid not because they are knowable, but because they are the only principles that can be reaffirmed consistently with one's basic assumptions.[7] Each moral agent, then, can see that like every other moral agent he is compelled to adopt principles and to act on them without being able to prove that the assumptions about how things are in reality, from which his principles follow, are necessarily and universally true. This is the respect in which all moral agents are peers. Nobody has an inside line on which system of principles is valid absolutely. Every moral agent is in the ethico-centric predicament because every moral agent is in the metaphysico-centric predicament.

Now we come to K_2. Rational and self-conscious agents are ends in themselves, but not in the Kantian way of being necessitated by reason to legislate principles that direct the realization of the possible satisfaction of all rationally desirable ends. They are ends in themselves because they are all fully rational, and also because by exercising their powers of pure reason they can come to see that they are all in the ethico-centric predicament. The awareness that every moral agent is in this predicament must, as far as reason is concerned, create tolerance and respect, and respect precisely of the sort that is a core dispositional component of rational love. We can love people who belong to a particular community of agreement, different from our own, if we become aware that their basic metaphysical differences from us are not owing to blindness or perversity on their part; that like us, they are operating beyond the bounds of universal intersubjectivity and are being honest about the experiences that place them in a particular community of agreement, and for that we can love them no less (and no more) than we love ourselves for doing the very same sort of thing. From reason's point of view, each moral agent is an end in himself in that no one of them is justified in treating another as having less title to his own conscientious convictions.

Rational and self-conscious agents are ends in themselves and not mere things to be manipulated at will for another reason. Normal adults provide a clear example. Normal adults can become righteously indignant. This is possible because they have a concept of fair play. It is axiomatic for them that what is right, wrong, permitted, optional or whatever, for one person is likewise for any relevantly similar other. This axiom does not enable anyone to determine that a certain way of acting is right, permitted, etc. Moreover, it provides no way of deciding if two agents are relevantly similar. It is, nonetheless, not otiose. If two moral agents happen to agree that in a given situation they are relevantly similar, then one of them cannot justifiably claim a right in that situation that he withholds from the other. Power relationships aside, the person who is being unfair knows that the other person knows it too, and both know that the person who is being treated unfairly is justified in being righteously indignant. Nothing like this can go on between a moral agent and a filing cabinet. A moral agent simply cannot view either himself or another moral agent as a thing lacking the capacity for indignation. Moral agents are absolute ends and not mere objects of convenience to themselves and to other moral agents because they can justifiably claim rights, privileges, immunities, and the like that derive from commonly shared axioms and commonly perceived situations, independently of contracts, agreements, understandings, contingent desires, customs, conventions, religious convictions, etc.[8]

Commonly shared axioms and perceptions can be the basis of concord, friendship, and community among those who are sufficiently principled and fairminded to act on them. But even here the harmony is not perfect. Personal wants and desires clash. Not everybody can have everything he wants. Nevertheless, a realistic acceptance of the conditions of human existence, which implies an acceptance of the inevitable frustrations even in the best practical situations, is possible for those who are rationally loving.

Where there is no awareness of commonly shared axioms or where there is divergence in basic metaphysical assumptions about realities behind appearances, there can be conflict, enmity, and division to the point of murderous violence. It may be necessary to defend by violent means a way of life, or even life itself. But anyone who grasps the nature and implications of the ethico-centric predicament can put up the required defense without having to hate. For, the more a moral agent understands the human condition, the closer he is to loving rationally. And he who loves rationally does not hate, not even those whom he may need to kill in order not to be killed.

Although not all moral principles are universally valid for all (finite) moral agents regardless of their membership in a community of agreement, some moral principles are universally valid. All moral agents exercise the same powers of pure reason. Anyone who exercises their powers can, on reflection, come to see that every moral agent is in the metaphysico-centric, hence, in the ethico-centric predicament. Anyone who acknowledges the reality of these predicaments must admit that no moral agent has a moral right to treat another agent disrespectfully. The availability to human moral consciousness of this universally valid moral judgment is consistent with the fact that all (finite) moral agents are in the metaphysico-centric and ethico-centric predicaments. Indeed, this particular moral judgment is implied by the existence of the predicaments. There is, thus, no inconsistency in thinking that while some moral principles are universally valid for all (finite) moral agents, some are valid not universally but only for members of a community of agreement. As a member of a community of agreement different from yours, I may hold that everyone ought morally to do A, while you hold that everyone ought morally to refrain from doing A. From my moral perspective I can judge that you ought *morally* to do A, yet I can consistently add that inasmuch as your moral principle concerning A is the opposite of mine, you ought *everything considered* to refrain from doing A. One of the factors to be considered is the inviolability of your integrity as a rational agent caught, like every other (finite) rational agent, in the metaphysico-centric predicament. The *moral ought* and the *everything considered ought* are not the same. Kant was wrong to equate them. He equated them because he views moral judgments as being overriding, and he views them as overriding because he conceives of morality as having to do with realizing the lawful purposes of beings that are *absolute* ends. I have recited my reasons for rejecting his conception of what it is to be an absolute end. Kant ties the concept of being an absolute end to the concept of being autonomous. I have argued that no one is autonomous in Kant's sense. The dignity of the moral agent derives from his rationality, but not in the way that Kant thinks.

The ethico-centric predicament implies that all moral principles cannot be necessarily valid for all moral agents. If all moral agents happened to see reality from a backdrop of identical basic assumptions, their moral principles might be identical, but this would be a contingent matter. The possibility of difference exists in the metaphysico-centric, hence ethico-centric predicament. Pure reason as a family of purely intellectual powers does not provide any clues as to what a human being who exercises them is bound to believe about the structure and meaning of reality. Beyond reason's formal requirement of consistency, a requirement that is constitutive of its powers, and the further requirement to respect universally intersubjective evidence, there is no theoretical limit to the different basic metaphysical assumptions that can shape a rational being's views about reality. Now the moral principles to which a moral agent finds himself conscientiously committed must at least be consistent with his beliefs about the structure and meaning of reality. Inasmuch as these beliefs may be different in different moral agents, some of their moral principles may be different. And because the basic metaphysical assumptions that shape these beliefs are articles of faith, all moral agents are in the ethico-centric predicament. This is why any universalizability criterion for moral validity, be it Kantian or not in detail, is in principle an egregious error.[9]

Department of Philosophy
Indiana University, Bloomington

NOTES

[1] All references to Kant are from his *Groundwork of the Metaphysics of Morals*, translated and analysed by H. J. Paton, Harper & Row, 1964. (Originally published by Hutchinson, London, under the title *The Moral Law*. Quotations used here are by permission of Hutchinson.) The page numbers are from the pagination of this work in Volume IV of *Kants Werke* published by *Preussischen Akademie der Wissenschaften* of Berlin, 1902–42. Paton gives these pages in the margin of his translation.

[2] Note that willing to do *A* is different from willing that *A* be universal practice. In the first instance the agent is set to do *A*. He is in a state such that unless he is prevented from doing *A*, he does *A*, if he has an opportunity to do *A*. Willing that a kind of action be universal practice is not a state of that description. It is, rather, very much like legislating that a state of affairs be actual (Let it be the case that everyone does *A*) and, at the same time implying that as actual the state of affairs would be acceptable to the one doing the legislating.

[3] The validity of the principle that "ought" implies "can" has been questioned because of alleged counter-examples. For instance, Jones borrows a book, and thereby incurs an obligation to return it. If he burns the book, he makes it impossible for himself to

discharge that obligation. Does this show that the "ought" implies "can" principle is false? I think not. Burning the book does not cancel the obligation to return it. But that fact can no longer be apprehended by thinking that Jones ought to return the book that he borrowed. The fact is that, other things being equal, Jones ought not wilfully to have made it impossible for himself to discharge the obligation to return the book. He is culpable and, therefore, he ought to make amends. These judgments presuppose that Jones could have refrained from burning the book and that he can make amends. The "ought" implies "can" principle is one of the conceptual truths that together define "ought" as a modal operator on actions construed as possible doings. Note that "It would not be morally bad (undesirable, unacceptable) if everyone did A" and "Everyone is morally permitted to do A" are equivalent. K_1 presupposes this equivalence. To be able to will everyone's doing A is to find, according to K_1, that it is not morally bad for everyone to do A, and that is equivalent to the proposition that everyone is morally permitted to do A.

4 See my "Generalization in Ethics", *The Review of Metaphysics*, **XVII**, No. 3 (March 1964), pp. 437–61.

5 Reprinted in Lewis White Beck, ed. and tr., *Immanuel Kant, Critique of Practical Reason and Other Essays in Moral Philosophy*, University of Chicago Press, 1949.

6 See also Alvin Plantinga's two papers, "Is Belief in God Rational?", in *Rationality and Religious Belief*, ed. C. Delaney, University of Notre Dame Press (1979), pp. 7–27, and "Is Belief in God Properly Basic?", *Nous*, **XV**, No. 1 (March 1981), pp. 45–51. William L. Rowe's unpublished paper, "The Rationality of Religious Belief", is a provocative rejoinder.

7 Kant himself supplies a good example. He assumes that every moral agent is convinced that he, himself, is free to act. Kant implies that consistently with that indelible and undemonstrable conviction a moral agent can only believe that there are (universally valid) laws that prescribe conduct. The conviction of freedom is an example of a basic framework assumption. It is equivalent to the conviction that pure reason exercises a special and unique efficient causality. The conviction is based on no evidence. It springs from experiencing ourselves as free. "From the presupposition of this Idea [of freedom] there springs . . . consciousness of a law of action, the law that subjective principles of action − that is, maxims − must always be adopted in such a way that they can also hold as principles objectively − that is, universally − and can therefore serve for our own enactment of universal law" (Kant, 449). In the next paragraph Kant adds: "It looks as if, in our Idea of freedom, we have in fact merely taken the moral law for granted − that is, the very principle of the autonomy of the will − and have been unable to give an independent proof of its reality and objective necessity. In that case we should still have made considerable gain inasmuch as we should at least have formulated the genuine principle more precisely than has been done before. As regards its validity, however, and the practical necessity of subjecting ourselves to it we should have gone no further. Why must the validity of our maxim as a universal law be a condition limiting our action? On what do we base the worth we attach to this way of acting − a worth supposed to be so great that there cannot be any interest which is higher? And how does it come about that in this alone man believes himself to feel his own personal worth, in comparison with which that of a pleasurable or painful state is to count as nothing? To these questions we should have been unable to give any sufficient answer" (Kant, 449–50).

[8] An agent is a moral agent because he is rational, self-conscious, and capable of action, not because he has properties that belong to him only, either necessarily or contingently. A moral agent has rights, privileges, obligations, immunities, and the like because he is a moral agent, not because as an individual he is uniquely distinguished from everyone else. A moral agent's necessary identity with himself, for instance, which belongs to him only, cannot, therefore, be a morally relevant difference that gives him privileges and the like to be denied to others. A moral agent is an absolute end because he is a moral agent, and for no other reason.

[9] While writing this essay I have benefited from discussions with colleagues, especially Hector-Neri Castañeda and Paul Eisenberg. I am particularly grateful to Eisenberg for reading an earlier draft and commenting on it incisively.

PART IV

CONSEQUENTIALIST UNIVERSALIZABILITY

JONATHAN HARRISON

UTILITARIANISM, UNIVERSALIZATION,
HETERONOMY AND NECESSITY
or
UNKANTIAN ETHICS

My main object in this paper will be to try to show that there is a large area of agreement between a Kantian ethical theory and the teleological ethical theories which, primarily in the *Fundamental Principles of the Metaphysics of Morals*, he so strongly opposed. The manner in which I shall do this is by showing that Kant's criticism of teleological theories in general does not apply to utilitarianism, the most influential teleological ethical theory. The reason for proceeding in this way is that Kant himself seldom if ever says anything about utilitarianism. It may be that he was not familiar with a sufficiently evolved form of utilitarianism for him clearly to have considered it.

The objections which Kant thought made teleological ethical theories unsatisfactory are considered in the following pages one by one.

TELEOLOGICAL ETHICAL THEORIES AND THE PURITY OF ETHICS

Kant thought that any teleological ethical theory must undermine the purity of morals. He believed this partly because he thought: (1) that it must make its appeal directly to inclination for the end which it said ought to be realised; but (2) he also thought that any teleological ethical theory had to be empirical, and that no empirical theory could do anything other than appeal to inclination.

(1) Kant was wrong in thinking that a teleological ethical theory could appeal only to inclination. Utilitarianism, for example, tells us that it is our *duty* to bring into existence the maximum amount of good, whether this be for ourselves or for others. But there is no very obvious reason why we should want the good of others. Hence there is no reason why we should not seek the good of others purely from a sense of duty or from respect for the moral law which imposes seeking others' good upon us. Since utilitarianism does not make our duty to seek good dependent on our wanting it, it is not open to Kant's charge that it is impossible to derive from the varying objects of desire any rule which applies equally to everyone. In any case, the statement that we ought to seek for everyone what he finds good is in no way impugned

Nelson Potter and Mark Timmons (eds.), Morality and Universality, 237–265.
© 1985 *by D. Reidel Publishing Company.*

or made 'relative' or 'subjective' or — as we shall see later — contingent by the fact that what is good for one person is not necessarily good for another.

(2) Kant seems to think that if any appeal to ends is made in supporting a moral principle, then it can be known only empirically. (Hence Kant — who did not have the benefit of reading Kripke — concluded that it cannot be necessary, and he believed, as we shall see, that a contingent principle would weaken the stringency of duty.) I think this is a mistake. We can, of course, know only empirically what actions will produce any given end, but the statement that, *if* an action does produce an end, then we ought to perform it, can be as *a priori* as any other propositions expressed by means of the word 'ought', for example, the non-teleological proposition that we ought to be just, regardless of the consequences.

TELEOLOGICAL ETHICAL THEORIES AND THE STRINGENCY OF DUTY

Kant thought that no teleological ethical theory could give a satisfactory account of the stringency of duty; that is to say, he thought that our duties were stringent, whereas a teleological ethical theory must lead to the conclusion that they were not. He thought this because he thought that, if our duties were stringent, propositions about duty would have to be necessary. Teleological ethical theories, however, would imply that such propositions were contingent.

The following questions arise: (1) Are statements about duty necessarily true? (2) If propositions about duty are not necessarily true, does it follow from this that our duties are not stringent? (3) Would a teleological ethical theory lead to the conclusion that propositions about duty are not necessarily true? (4) Are our duties stringent?

(1) My own view is that Kant was right in thinking that statements about the principles of duty are, if true, necessarily true. That they are necessarily true follows from the fact that one can be fully justified in making such statements only after one has established all the matters of fact which are relevant to them. Since there are no further relevant matters of fact on which we can base our decision that something is a duty, that it is a duty must be something we claim to know *a priori*. From this I believe it follows that that it is a duty is, if true, necessarily true.

(2) It seems to me that Kant was mistaken in thinking that, if statements about duty are not necessarily true, this implies that our duties are not stringent. He thought this because, if statements about duty are contingent, it follows that they may be false. Hence if it is only a contingent statement

that I ought to keep my promises, it follows that it might be the case that it is not my duty to keep my promises. To say that it might not be the case that it is my duty to keep a promise looks lax.

It does not follow, however, from the statement that it might be the case that it is not my duty to keep my promises that it might be that I do not have to do my duty. There is a great deal of difference between saying that something, which is a duty, might not be a duty, and saying that it might be that I do not have to do my duty. If something, which is a duty, were not a duty, then I may omit it with impunity, but this is not at all to say that I may omit doing my duty with impunity; though I may omit that which is a duty with impunity, this is only because, when I may omit it, it is not a duty. The statement that duties may be omitted is ambiguous between (i) those actions which are in fact duties might not be duties, in which case they may be omitted, and (ii) those actions which are in fact duties may be omitted, even while they remain duties. If moral judgements are contingent, this implies the first of these two statements, but not the second. Only the second, however, weakens the stringency of duty.

In holding that moral judgements have to be necessarily true, since otherwise this weakens the stringency of duty, Kant may also have been overlooking a distinction between two senses of the word 'must'. There is the sense of 'must' in which we say that an action must be done, which is sometimes a colloquial way of saying that it is a duty. There is also the sense of 'must' in which we say of a proposition that it must be true. From the fact that a proposition is contingent it follows that it is not true of it that it must be true. It does not follow, however, that it does not truely say that something is necessary, for example that an action must be done.

Kant may also be overlooking a distinction (which empiricist philosophers since the time of Hume have also overlooked) between necessity-stating and necessity-bearing propositions. The proposition that a white tie must be worn with tails is necessity-stating (for it says that something, the wearing of white ties, is necessary) but not necessity-bearing, because there are circumstances (e.g., circumstances where the rules governing such matters are changed) in which we would not have to wear a white tie with tails. Therefore the statement about this proposition, that it must be true, is not true. It does not follow from the fact that propositions such as that promises must be kept are not necessity-bearing that they are not necessity-stating, nor that they cannot make *true* statements about necessity.

An important example of a proposition which is necessity-stating without being necessity-bearing is the proposition that if you drop a piece of china on a hard surface it must break. Philosophers who think that it follows from the fact that it is not necessarily true that it must break, that it is false that it must break are confusing these two kinds of necessity. It can be true that the china must break, even though it is not a necessary truth that it must break. There is no reason, incidentally, why a proposition (e.g., that two and two *must* be four) should not be both necessity-stating and necessity-bearing. Some propositions (e.g., that two and two *are* four) are necessity-bearing without being necessity-stating. Most propositions, e.g., that the cat is on the mat, are neither.

Though I speak of two senses of 'must', it is not clear to me that this word is ambiguous. The fundamental idea in the notion of 'necessity' is that of there being no alternative to something. From the fact that there is an alternative to the truth of the proposition that a piece of china must break, it does not follow that there is an alternative to its breaking. From the fact that there is an alternative to its being true that a white tie must be worn with tails it does not follow that there is a (sociably acceptable) alternative to a white tie's being worn with tails. From the fact that there is an alternative to the truth of a proposition about duty, it does not follow that there is a (morally permissible) alternative to doing that action which is a duty.

(3) I also believe that Kant is mistaken in thinking that, if a teleological ethical theory is true, moral judgements cannot be necessary. Kant thinks that, since it is just a contingent fact that man desires the things he does, it follows that any ethical theory which derives duty from the fact that certain things, e.g., happiness, are good must make moral judgements contingent. But it may not follow, from the fact that something is desired, that it is good (for we may desire things that are bad). Hence, from the fact that it is a contingent fact that what is desired, is desired, it does not follow that it is a contingent fact that what is good, is good. What does follow is that it is not a necessary truth that we desire what is good.

Kant also thinks that, because it is just a contingent fact that an action produces results that are good, it would, if we made duty dependent upon the goodness or badness of the consequences of our actions, just be a contingent fact that we had a duty to do an action which had good consequences. For if, as is perfectly possible, it did not produce these good consequences, it would not be our duty to do it. It does not follow from this, however, that the principle of utilitarianism, that we ought to perform actions which have the best possible consequences, is contingent. For what this principle asserts is the hypothetical truth that *if* an action produces the best possible consequences, *then* it ought to be performed. It does not follow from the fact that the *antecedent* of this hypothetical proposition is contingent that the *proposition as a whole* is. 'Intuitionists' – I am not saying that Kant was one – can do no better, for all they are committed to is such propositions as that if we have made a promise, we ought to keep it, or that if we have incurred a debt, we ought to pay it, and the antecedent of these hypothetical propositions are just as contingent as is the antecedent of the principle of utilitarianism. Any ultimate moral principle, indeed, and not just utilitarianism, must be hypothetical, and none is prevented from being necessarily true by the fact that the question whether or not its antecedent is fulfilled is one about a contingent matter of fact. There is no reason, therefore, why utilitarianism should not apply to all rational beings, and not just to men.

(4) Not only does a teleological ethical theory like utilitarianism not lead to the conclusion that duty is not necessarily stringent; since our duties are *not* necessarily stringent, it would not be an objection to them if they did lead to this conclusion.

Anyone holding that duty is absolutely stringent may be asserting the propositions that we ought always to do what we ought to do, or that we ought always to do our duty. The first looks as if it is a tautology. It should not be forgotten, however, that the statement that we ought to do all the things we ought to do may mean either that we ought to do them all collectively or that we ought to do them all individually. The former is less obviously true than the latter.

Let us suppose, for the sake of argument, that if something is our duty, then we ought to do it. It may be that this proposition, too, is a tautology. It does not follow from it, however, that our duties are absolutely stringent, and that we ought to do our duty, however badly we want not to. We have a large number of duties which are such that, if we wanted not to do them more badly than we do, or if doing them caused us more inconvenience than it does, we would not have a duty to do them. For example, it may be that it is my duty to keep a certain minor promise, which I do not greatly object to keeping, and which it does not cause me a large amount of inconvenience to keep. It does not follow from the fact that we ought always to do our duty that to keep such minor promises would still be a duty, even if keeping them caused us more inconvenience than it does. Perhaps, if it would take up a large amount of time to keep them, or make us ill, or miss an important dinner date, it would not be the case that we have a duty to keep them. To take another example, from the fact that it is my duty not to make a false recantation, and from the fact that I ought always to do my duty or what I ought to do, it does not follow that it would be the case that I ought not to make this recantation, however severely I was tortured for not making it.

One must distinguish between torture causing one not to do one's duty, and torture causing an action, which would otherwise be a duty, not to be a duty. One must further distinguish: (1) the proposition that given that something is my duty, it *is* my duty, however, badly I want not to do it; and (2) the proposition that something, which is my duty, *would* still be my duty, however badly I wanted not to do it. The first is of the form $p \supset q$, asserted quite properly on the grounds of q. The second is an unfulfilled conditional, and so is in no way entailed by the truth of q. Philosophers have too often confused the statement that circumstances might arise in which members of some class of actions would not be a duty, with the statement that circumstances might arise in which I would not have to do my duty. Either might be meant by saying that rules about duty admit of exceptions. Kant himself says that *imperfect* duties (e.g., our duty to help others and to develop our talents) may have exceptions in the interest of inclination, but he may have meant not that they might be overridden by inclination, but that since they were unspecific, they allowed latitude to inclination.

Some people might wish to maintain that, when duty is modified by inclination, it is not a case of something which would otherwise be my duty being caused not to be a duty by inconvenience or contrary inclination, but a case of something which would otherwise be a duty being caused not to be a duty by its conflicting with another duty, in this case, a duty to oneself. The existence of this latter duty implies that one *ought* not to cause oneself an excessive amount of inconvenience, override one's inclinations to more than a certain extent, or to allow oneself to be subjected to more than a given amount of pain. I am sure that this is sometimes a correct account of the matter. But that this account is not always right is shown by that fact that sometimes, when my duty is overridden by contrary inclination or inconvenience, I would not be blamed if I did my duty, in spite of this inclination and inconvenience. Indeed, I might even be praised for doing something – not divulging the names of my comrades, for example – which, because it is overridden, is not a duty. If the correct view was that my duty was overridden not by contrary inclination or inconvenience, but by a duty to myself, one would be blamed for performing that action which would have, had it not been overriden, been one's duty. We do not, however, always blame people for ignoring interest or inclination contrary to duty.

Up to now I have been talking about factors which justify me in not doing my duty, i.e., which justify me in doing an action which otherwise would be a duty. Duties also vary in stringency in that it is easier to find an acceptable excuse for omitting some duties than others. To discuss excuses, however, would take me too far from my present topic. One would expect a utilitarian to say that the stringency of duties varied roughly with the harm done by omitting them.

TELEOLOGICAL ETHICAL THEORIES AND KANT'S THREE PROPOSITIONS ABOUT DUTY

Kant made or implied the following three assertions about duty, the first of which is a matter of conjecture, as he himself does not state what it is: (1) 'a good will is not good because of what it effects or accomplishes . . . : It is good through its willing alone − that is, good in itself' (Kant, 1785, Ak. IV, 394); (2) 'An action done from duty has its moral worth, *not in the purpose* to be attained by it, but in the maxim in accordance with which it is decided upon; it depends therefore, not on the realization of the object of the action, but solely on the *principle of volition* in accordance with which, irrespective of all objects of the faculty of desire, the action has been performed' (Kant, 1785, Ak. IV, 399–400); (3) 'Duty is the necessity to act out of reverence for the law' (Ibid.).

The *first* of these three propositions is obviously not incompatible with utilitarianism. It is incompatible with hedonistic utilitarianism, because if you think that pleasure is the only good, you cannot consistently think that anything else, for example a disposition to do one's duty, is good. (A hedonistic utilitarian can and does think that this disposition is good as a means to pleasure as, indeed, it is.) A non-hedonistic (agathistic) utilitarian, who thinks that things other than pleasure can be good as an end, has no difficulty, however, in allowing that the disposition to do one's duty for its own sake is good.

The *third* proposition is also fairly obviously compatible with utilitarianism. It tells us that duty is the necessity of acting from reverence for the law, but since it does not tell us what the law is for which we must have reverence, it is open to a utilitarian to give his own account of it. The utilitarian can say that (roughly) the law upon which it is our duty to act is that we should at all times and at all places, irrespective of our own personal inclinations, seek the greatest good of the greatest number. If the Kantian argues that producing the greatest good cannot be our only duty, for it ignores the fact that we must do our duty with *reverence* for the law which demands this, the following may be said in reply. One's *only* duty cannot be to act out of reverence for the law; there must be some law, other than the law which says that we must act from reverence for the law, in accordance with which it is our duty to act. Given that there must be such a law, there is no reason why a utilitarian should not claim to have given an account of it. The non-hedonistic utilitarian can hold as much as anyone else that we have a duty not just to bring about the greatest good, but to bring this about in the proper spirit, i.e., out of reverence for the law, because our doing so is one good among others. If there is any difficulty with this view, it is the difficulty of reconciling the statement that we ought to try to produce the greatest good with the statement that we ought not just do this, but to do it from a sense of duty. But the difficulties in holding this view have nothing specifically to do with utilitarianism. Whatever account we give of what makes an action a duty, whether it is a utilitarian account or not, we will have difficulty in maintaining that we both have a duty to do something, and a duty to do it from a sense of duty. Either one can reconcile utilitarianism with the view that we ought to act with respect for the moral law, in which case there is no difficulty, or one cannot, in which case, since every moral theory must be faced with the same problem, we cannot have a duty to act with respect for the moral law. (This does not imply that it is not a very good thing when we do act with such respect.)

Kant's *second* proposition is more difficult to reconcile with utilitarianism. It can be divided into two parts, the proposition that an action done from duty does *not* derive its moral worth from the purpose to be attained by it, and the proposition that it *does* derive its moral worth from the maxim in accordance with which it is done. (Kant thought that the second proposition followed from the first, because he thought that there were no alternatives other than an action's moral worth being derived from its purpose and its being derived from its maxim.)

I suspect, however, that there were two propositions that Kant confused. The first is that an action is *right* or *wrong*, a duty or not a *duty*, according as to whether it does or does not produce the greatest good of the greatest number. The second is that it derives its *moral worth* from whether or not it is successful in producing the greatest good of the greatest number. Though every utilitarian is committed to the first — and there are alternative utilitarian views — he is not committed to the second, and the second does not follow from the first.

When Kant suggests that, if the purpose of someone performing an action is that of trying to produce a given result, his action will have value only so long as it actually produces that result, he is guilty of another confusion. There is an important sense in which the purpose of a utilitarian need not be that of producing the greatest good. Let us imagine a Kantian utilitarian, whose object is to do his duty, but who believes that what his duty is is to produce the greatest good. Then the actions he thinks he ought to perform will each have two features, the feature of producing the greatest good, and the feature of being his duty. His primary purpose will be to do his duty, and to produce the greatest good will only incidentally be his purpose. He produces the greatest good because this is the only way in which he can achieve his object of doing his duty. Hence his purpose has not been defeated if his action does not produce the greatest good.

There is still the difficulty that, not only has he not produced the greatest good, he has also, if that is his only duty, not done his duty. But this is a difficulty that any moral theory must face. Whatever my duty is, even if it is a duty to be just though the heavens fall, I may fail to do it, through no fault of my own, because I am mistaken about the facts of the situation in which I am placed. I can try to escape by maintaining that my duty is to *try* to do some action or other, so that I have done my duty so long as I have tried to be just, even though I have not succeeded. But then a utilitarian can maintain that my duty is not to produce the greatest good, but to *try* to produce the greatest good, and that I have done my duty so long as I have tried, whether my action results in the greatest good being produced or not. Hence it does not follow from the fact, which the utilitarian certainly must maintain, that it is my duty to bring into existence a certain kind of result, that my action has value only so long as it actually brings into existence the result in question.

TELEOLOGICAL ETHICAL THEORIES AND HYPOTHETICAL IMPERATIVES

It may be that Kant thought that teleological ethical theories had to be stated in hypothetical imperatives, and that only non-teleological ethical theories (e.g., his own, if he thought that there could be any non-teleological ethical theories other than his own) could give rise to categorical imperatives. If he did think this, then he was mistaken. Utilitarianism maintains that it is the duty of every man to act in such a manner as to produce the greatest good. It maintains that every man *ought* to act in this way, whether he *wants* to act in this way or not. Maintaining utilitarianism is quite different from maintaining such things as that, if one wants to produce the greatest good, and keeping promises produces the greatest good, then we ought to keep our promises. Utilitarianism does not assert that, if promise-keeping produces the greatest good, we ought to keep our promises if we *want* to produce the greatest good; it asserts that we then ought to keep our promises, whether we want the greatest good or not.

The difference between 'If you want the greatest good, you ought to keep your promises' and 'You ought to keep your promises, if this leads to the greatest good' is (a) that the antecedent of the former is, though the antecedent of the latter is not, about the wants of the person contemplating performing the action in question, and (b) that one can, without doing too much violence to its meaning, substitute 'it is your duty to' for 'you ought to' in the second, although one certainly can not do this in the first. It follows from this that Kant has misconceived the nature of the difference between a 'categorical' and a 'hypothetical' imperative (though he is, of course, quite right in thinking that there are imperatives of these two different kinds). There is no reason why so-called categorical imperatives should not in fact be hypothetical, nor any reason why so-called hypothetical imperatives should not in fact be categorical. 'If you want to know the time, you ought to ask a policeman' is a 'hypothetical' imperative, but then so is the non-hypothetical 'You ought to ask a policeman' (which follows logically from the former, together with the assertion of the former's antecedent, that the person addressed does in fact want to know the time). 'If you have made a promise, you ought (i.e., it is your duty) to keep it' is a perfectly good 'categorical' imperative, though in fact in form it is hypothetical.

TELEOLOGICAL ETHICAL THEORIES AND
THE TWO KINDS OF GOODNESS

Kant quite properly distinguishes between two kinds of goodness. There is first of all that kind of goodness which is possessed by those things which are the objects of desire, and by people to the extent that they acquire or possess such objects. There is secondly that kind of goodness which is possessed by actions which are done from duty, and by people insofar as they perform such actions. The second is moral goodness. The first is non-moral goodness. In the *Critique of Practical Reason* Kant points out that the German language, unlike Latin, has different words — "das Gute" and "das Wohl" for the two kinds of goodness.

Kant — though he does not, so far as I know, himself draw the analogy — may have thought that he had accomplished something like a Copernican revolution in ethics as well as in speculative philosophy. All previous ethical theories, he supposed, had tried to derive the rightness and wrongness of actions from their resulting in good or bad consequences, or from the weal or woe of their effects. According to such theories, one must find out which actions produce goodness, in order to find out which actions are right. Kant's own theory, on the other hand, does the exact opposite of this, and makes goodness dependent upon the doing of what is right. One must first find out what actions are right in order to know what people and what actions are good. Hence it would be putting the cart before the horse to try to derive the rightness of an action from its producing goodness. Utilitarianism would be just one ethical theory among others which made this fundamental mistake. I liken this to a Copenican revolution because, just as, in his critique of speculative reason, Kant argued that nature conformed to our cognitive capacities rather than our cognitive capacities conforming to nature, so, where practical reason is concerned, Kant argued that goodness was derived from the doing of our duty rather than duty derived from the production of goodness. He drew from this the conclusion that all teleological ethical theories were false, since they derived rightness from goodness, instead of the other way round.

It is not at all obvious, however, that the two views of duty are incompatible. Why should you not first say with utilitarianism that actions are right (or duties) if they produce consequences that are good (in that sense of 'good' which appertains to consequences), and also say that, when a man performs an action which for this reason is right or a duty, and furthermore does it from a sense of duty, he and his actions are good (in that sense of 'good' which appertains to the doing of duty and to the people who do it)?

Kant appears to have thought that if the goodness of a man depends upon his performing actions which were right for the reason that they produce good consequences, it would follow that, if his actions did not produce these consequences, he and his actions would not be good. This is a mistake, however (a mistake not made by Hume). What would be good in a man would be the *disposition* to perform actions which were duties, from a sense that they were duties, and the disposition would exist, and be good, even when (perhaps because the man who possessed it was in prison or because luck was against him) he did not get a chance to manifest his goodness in actions which actually produced good consequences, or even if the actions he did perform all, through no fault of his own, went awry.

It may well be that Kant made a further mistake in *exaggerating* the goodness of the good will (the disposition to do one's duty for duty's sake) as compared with the goodness of consequences. It may have been his view (as it was Newman's) that the former kind of goodness was so excellent that the smallest amount of it exceeded in value the largest possible amount of the latter kind of goodness. In that case, a world which contained some moral goodness, and much goodness of the other kind, would be infinitely worse (if these two words make sense) than a world in which everyone was extremely miserable, but in which, in addition to the amount of virtue contained in the first world, someone had not committed some minor act of wrongdoing. If we could choose which of these two worlds to produce, we ought to produce the former rather than the latter. No amount of freedom from pain can compensate for a single venial sin.

If this view was Kant's, it is too extreme. Virtue is good, but it is not *that* good. Both moral and non-moral goodness are subject to a law of diminishing value. Decreasing increments of moral goodness are of progressively declining value, because they will be manifested in my doing less and less important duties, starting with refraining from killing people and ending with keeping trivial promises to people who do not much care whether I keep them or not. Successive increments of non-moral goodness are of progressively declining value because one starts with avoiding abject poverty and disease and internecine strife, and ends with caviar and brandy and more than one lover.

Though the earlier increments of moral goodness may have more value than the earlier increments of non-moral goodness, it is fairly obvious to any sensible person that a time comes when increments of non-moral goodness are preferable to more and more increments of moral goodness. If a woman were choosing virtues for her children, she *might* start with wanting them to have moral goodness but, if she did, I am sure that, rather than choosing them to go on being morally better and better, she would prefer, probably quite quickly, to have a certain amount of intelligence, health, good looks and physical strength. A man with these qualities in abundance, but totally lacking in moral goodness, would be a monster; but then a man whose moral goodness was raised to the last degree (whatever that may be) but who was cretinous, ugly, weak and ill, would also be worthy of pity rather than admiration.

If there are these two kinds of goodness, however, it would seem absurd to hold, as a hedonistic utilitarian must, that whether an action is right or not can depend only upon whether or not it produces non-moral goodness. For surely we might be faced with a choice whether to perform actions which have among their consequences both non-moral and moral goodness, in various proportions, and then it would seem absurd to maintain that one should consider only the non-moral goodness, and not at all the moral goodness, which these alternative actions produce.

It is not, however, as absurd as all that. For one thing, this is because the moral goodness that my action will have, if I perform it from a sense of duty, logically cannot be taken into consideration in determining whether what I am contemplating doing is or is not right. It must be right for some other reason than that its performance would be morally good, before my doing it *can* be morally good. For another thing, it may be argued that though moral goodness is distinct from non-moral goodness, if what is right consists in producing what is non-morally good, then producing moral and non-moral goodness can never conflict with one another, for those actions which possess moral goodness are just those actions the *consequences* of which possess non-moral goodness; hence it is logically impossible that there ever should be a conflict. It has even been argued that moral goodness cannot be among the consequences of our actions, because noone can make anyone else morally good. One can influence his behaviour only by inducements or threats, and these can produce action from inclination, never action from duty.

Since only the first of these three arguments is satisfactory, there *can* be a conflict between producing moral and non-moral goodness. One reason for this is that not everybody thinks that it is their only duty to produce non-moral goodness, but even those people who have views about what their duty is which according to a teleological ethical theory are erroneous can perform actions, which, though wrong, possess moral goodness because their agents wrongly believe them to be right, and do them for this reason. If I can prevent such a man performing an action which does not produce non-moral goodness, because he thinks it is his duty to do it in spite of this fact, then perhaps I have produced non-moral goodness – by preventing him from performing a harmful action which he supposes to be his duty – at the expense of producing moral badness – by causing him to perform an action which he considers to be wrong. I may, for example, corrupt a gaoler in order that he shall release his innocent prisoners. And it seems very unlikely that punishment and reward do not sometimes produce moral reformation, as well as offering worldly inducement to outward conformity. There is nothing like the fear of being found out to increase the sensitivity of one's conscience.

The fact that we can be faced with a choice between producing non-moral and moral goodness is fatal to the hedonistic utilitarian view that our only duty is to bring into existence non-moral goodness. It is not, however, fatal to the non-hedonistic utilitarian view that our only duty is to bring into existence goodness of some kind or other. Hence, though the distinction that Kant has drawn between moral and non-moral goodness is a just and important one, its existence is not fatal to all teleological ethical theories, but only to those which, like hedonistic utilitarianism, do not consider moral goodness to be a form of intrinsic goodness, but as good only as a means to something else.

UTILITARIANISM AND TREATING PEOPLE AS A MEANS

It may be that Kant thought that teleological ethical theories were wrong because they entailed that it was right to treat people merely as a means. What it is to treat someone as a means, which Kant did not think was always wrong, and what is the difference between this and treating him merely as a 'means, which he did think always wrong, is obscure. If there were just I and a large number of inanimate objects alone on a desert island, I would be able to treat the latter in any way I pleased. I could treat them entirely as means to my own ends, and their existence would impose no moral limits upon the kinds of action that it was permissible for me to perform. Their being there need in no way stop me from doing just what I wanted to do. If, however, I were marooned on an island with some other people, then the existence of these people *would* impose some limit on the things that it was morally permissible for me to do. The fact that they existed and had ends (and – though Kant omits to mention this – were susceptible to pleasure and pain) imposes a moral limit on the ends which I myself may legitimately adopt.

It is very difficult, however, to evolve a formula which clearly distinguishes between the ways in which one may treat others, and the ways in which one may not treat them, or between treating them as means and treating them *merely* as means. The hunchback of Notre Dame was being treated as a means, since men used his back as a table, but it was not in Kant's view necessarily impermissible to use him in this way because he did it voluntarily and was paid for his service. Had he been compelled to lend his back, and had not been paid, then, presumably he would have been treated merely as a means. But the difference is obscure. The principle that one should (a) consent and (b) 'share in the end of the very same action' (be paid?) would legitimise prostitution and keeping a brothel. J. S. Mill, however would have thought such things permissible – though he presumably thought that epithets of condemnation other than 'wrong' then applied to them (see *Utilitarianism*, Chapter 5).

There are obviously cases when the claims of some people have to be totally ignored, as when the interests, and indeed the lives, of other people cannot be preserved except at the expense of theirs. It is customary then to say that the difference here between treating these people as a means and treating them merely as a means is that in the first case though the claims of these people have been *overridden*, they have at least been *considered*. If a man is left to drown so that the lives of other passengers will not be jeopardised, the captain did at least consider his claim to be rescued before deciding not to try to save him (a thought which must have been a great consolation to him). It is a disturbing consequence of this view that there may be no *overt* difference between treating someone as a means and treating him merely as a means.

However, the statement that one is acting rightly so long as one considers everyone's claims (though they may be overridden when they conflict with those of others) is not even remotely satisfactory as the formulation of the supreme principle of morality that Kant intended the formula we are discussing to be. For a supreme principle of morality should enable one to decide (given adequate knowledge of the circumstances to which it is being applied) whether absolutely every action that you are contemplating performing is right or whether it is wrong. This principle will not enable you to do this, because the statement that, in the event of a conflict between the claims of two people, both should be considered, does not give you any guidance for deciding which claims should override the other. Whichever claim you admit, you have at least considered them both. Utilitarianism, however, does this, for it tells you that you should prefer the claim of one person to those of others if and only if you maximise, or think you can maximise, or probably will maximise, pleasure or good as a result. I am not saying that this view is correct. Indeed, I think it is not. But it does at least do something that Kant's Formula of the End in Itself cannot do, which is to provide us with a feature which all and only right actions are supposed to possess.

The statement that we ought never to treat other people as a means is obviously incompatible with utilitarianism, but then it is not true. The statement that we should never treat them merely as a means may be true, but it is not incompatible with utilitarianism. For a utilitarian not only may, but must *consider* the claim of the people whose interests are overridden in the sense that he would demand that they be satisfied, if it were not for the claims of others. (Kant himself can do no better. It is fairly obvious that a utilitarian can give a tolerable account of what it is to perform actions which harmonize with human beings' ends.)

TELEOLOGICAL ETHICAL THEORIES AND THE KINGDOM
OF ENDS

Kant asked us to act always in such a manner that we can regard ourselves
as law-making members of a Kingdom of Ends. I find it difficult to decide
what he meant by this. If he meant that we always ought to act as if we were
a member of a group of people who were, like ourselves, *subject* to the moral
law, it is difficult to see why he said 'as if'. We *are* a member of a group of
such people. On the other hand, if he meant to say that we should always
act as if we were a member of a group of people who *acted* on the moral
law, then this is patently false. We would in that case never have a right to
sue anyone for damages, because in a society in which everyone acted on
the moral law, we would never be damaged. It could never be right to punish
anyone, because in such a society noone would be punished (because noone
would do any wrong). It could never be wrong to leave the door of one's
car unlocked, because in such a society there would be no risk of anybody
taking it.

It is difficult to see, too, how Kant could have hoped to deduce any
material principle about our actual duties from this formulation of the
categorical imperative. It is possible that he did not intend any such deduction to be made. On the other hand, he thought it equivalent to other formulations of the categorical imperative from which he did think such deductions
could be made.

In so far as the formula of the Kingdom of Ends simply tells us to act
as if we were a member of a group of rational beings who *had* duties, then
it seems compatible with all moral theories, utilitarianism included. However,
if it means that we ought to act as if we were a member of a community of
people who actually *did* their duty, then it would be incompatible with
utilitarianism (and also with any other known moral theory). For utilitarianism would demand that we should sometimes punish people, on some
such grounds as that this deterred others from committing similar offences,
whereas, as we have seen, this interpretation of the Formula of the Kingdom
of Ends would imply that we ought not to. For we ought to behave as it
would be that we ought to behave in a society in which everyone obeyed the
moral law, and in such a society it would not be right to punish anybody.

It may be that at the back of Kant's mind is some such idea as that we
ought to act in a manner that would be right, if we were ruled by a law
prohibiting all and only those actions that were immoral. For if the sovereign
in the Kindgom of Ends prohibits things, which he would do, then it looks as

if a case could be made for saying that what he would prohibit would be everything that was morally wrong. Similarly, he would *compel* everything the *omission* of which was wrong. (To say that there is such a being is, of course, to go beyond the evidence; the most one can do is act as if there were one.) In this case, the Kingdom of Ends would not be just people (or rational beings) but people bound together by the fact that they were all subject to a common set of positive laws.

There is a sense in which a utilitarian (and, I would add, any other sensible person) could not sanction acting as if there were a set of laws which prohibited all and only those things which are immoral when, in actual fact, there are laws which (quite rightly) do not prohibit everything that is immoral, which (also quite rightly) prohibit many things which are not immoral, which are often incomplete and inconsistent, and which allocate conflicting duties to members of different groups of people, e.g., nations. It can scarcely be our duty to ignore these actually existing laws in determining what it is we ought to do. It can hardly be that we should ignore the fact that there is a law prohibiting our bringing various mixtures of water and alcohol across the stretch of water known as the English Channel without informing a man in uniform on the grounds that such behaviour is not wrong antecedently to its being prohibited. It can scarcely be our duty to ignore the fact that there is a law prohibiting killing, whereas there is not a law prohibiting ordinary promise-breaking. It can scarcely be our duty to ignore a law making conscription compulsory, on the grounds that fighting for one's country is immoral; the fact that there is such a law may give rise to a *prima facie* duty to fight, even though this may be overridden by the greater consideration that killing other men is wrong. Given that everyone belongs to a country with different laws, which often demand that a man who is a member of one country does something (e.g., raid a city or sink a battleship) which the laws of another country demand that he prevent, it is scarcely creditable that we should behave just as if we were all citizens of a world state (less still citizens of a universe-wide state consisting of rational beings on other planets) united by one set of laws prohibiting all and only those things that are immoral, legislated over by a sovereign whose sphere of jurisdiction includes all the rational beings there are. A utilitarian could quite properly condemn those forms of behaviour mentioned above on the grounds that it would be harmful to behave in all these ways. One must enforce driving on the left (or the right) hand side of the road, for example, even though there is nothing antecedently immoral about driving on either. It would be extremely harmful to behave as if there were laws enforcing certain immoral acts when in fact there are none, and extremely harmful to behave as if there were not laws enforcing certain acts which are, antecedently to being enjoined, not immoral. It would be extremely harmful for a citizen of one country to behave just as if he were a citizen of another, on the grounds that they are both citizens of the world, and members of the kingdom of ends. A utilitarian demands that we act in such a manner as to produce the greatest good, and in order to do this we need to take full account of the complexities, divergencies, irrationalities, inadequacies and immoralities of existing legislation. It is not the only factor we have to take account of, but it is one of the most, if not the most, weighty of them.

It does not follow from this, however, that there is not a set of moral laws which apply equally to all men everywhere. Given that the positive law exists, the moral law, if it is complete (which logically it must be) must tell you how to act in relation to it. But this function of the moral law is one of which a utilitarian can give a perfectly good account, an account which is implicit in what I have already said.

There is, incidentally, a way in which my own version of utilitarianism can be regarded as Kantian, though straightforward act-utilitarianism cannot be. For my own version of utilitarianism (which I have elsewhere called cumulative-effect utilitarianism, to distinguish it from rule utilitarianism) demands that sometimes I should perform an action, which not everybody (and perhaps not anybody) is going to perform, because good *would* result if everbody *were* to perform it. For example, according to cumulative-effect utilitarianism, even if no-one is keeping his promises, it may be my duty to keep mine, because good *would* result if everybody *were* to keep his promises. Hence sometimes (though not always) I should perform those very actions which it would be my duty to perform if everybody were doing his duty, and performing these actions also. I should, in keeping my promise, behave just as if everybody else were performing his duty by keeping his promises as well as me. In those cases where the goodness or badness of the consequences of the kind of action I am contemplating has a cumulative-effect, and a number of repetitions of an action do good, though one performance of it does no good, or harm, then my duty is to do just what it would be my duty to do if everybody else were doing his duty. One is not necessarily exempted from performing the action on the grounds that no-one else is doing it. My duty is to do just what it would be that I ought to do if the others, as well as I myself were law-abiding members of the Kingdom of Ends.

TELEOLOGICAL ETHICAL THEORIES AND AUTONOMY
OF THE WILL

Kant thought that a good will must be autonomous. That is to say, he believed that an action could be good only if it was performed not from hope of some reward or fear of some punishment, but out of pure respect for the moral law. The reward and punishment in question, are, of course, reward and punishment only in a metaphorical sense. When we are rewarded, we get something that appeals to our inclinations, and when we are punished, we get something to which we are averse, but this does not mean that whenever we get something for which we are inclined this constitutes our being rewarded, or that whenever we get something for which we are disinclined, this constitutes our being punished. Nevertheless, Kant thought that, when we acted upon a maxim from inclination or aversion we were as much subject to that maxim as we would be if we were motivated to obey another human being by the inducement of reward or the sanction of punishment.

There is, however, as we have seen, no reason why our seeking the greatest good should be done only from inclination for good or fear of harm. There is no reason why we should take the slightest interest in the welfare of others. Many do not. Hence there is no reason why we should not seek the greatest good of the greatest number simply because it is our duty. From the fact that what we are aiming at doing is to produce a certain kind of result, it does not follow (as Kant supposed) that we must be acting from a desire for those results. Hence we could try to produce the greatest good of the greatest number purely out of respect for the law that demanded we do so, and not from inclination for the greatest good of all.

Kant thought that, though we were subject to the moral law — for we had a duty to obey it, whether we wanted to or not — our dignity as rational beings was not detracted from thereby because we were subject to a law which we ourselves had a hand in making. Strictly speaking, I cannot make sense of this remark. We not do make the moral law, and not because we do not have the power, but because the expression 'making the moral law' (unlike 'making the positive law') does not have a meaning. There is no operation which these words could possibly describe. If we think that adultery is wrong, and do not like the fact, there are no conceivable steps we can take to make it right, though, if we do not like the fact that paying tithes is legally prescribed, there are conceivable steps we can take to make it so no longer. Since 'making the moral law' does not make sense, 'having a hand in making the moral law' also cannot make sense.

If we could make the moral law, would it be true that we did not lose dignity if we were subject to a law which we had a hand in making, though we would lose this if we did not have a hand in making it? I think it would be true that we did not lose dignity only if at any moment we could change the law to which we were subject. If we can so change it, and at the moment when we are compelled to obey it could change it but do not, then we are forced to obey it only by our consent, much as Christ has been supposed to have been crucified only with his consent. Let us suppose that a minister of transport makes the laws appertaining to motor vehicles which he himself is compelled to obey. In so far as he is compelled to obey them, then he is just as much subject to them as anybody else, and so is not superior in dignity to those who did not have a hand in making them. He is superior to other people only in that he did, but they did not, make them. If, however, he could have changed them at the very moment they were being enforced, but voluntarily chooses not to, then he is, to the extent that he is subject to them, subject to them in such a way that he does not lose dignity thereby.

Sometimes we obey rules because we have to. At other times we obey them because we see the reason for them. It is said of children, rightly or wrongly, that when they are little, they obey rules simply because they are compelled to, but that when they are more mature, they obey them because they see that the reason for having them is a good one. It is possible that the younger children are subject to a law in such a way that they lose dignity by being so subject, but that the more mature children, who obey laws because they see that there are good reasons for having them, are not. It is perhaps something like this that Kant is thinking of when he draws the distinction between being subject to a law which you do, and being subject to a law which you do not, have a hand in making. The latter are not subject to a law which they actually had a hand in making, however, but are subject to one which they would have made (or would have made, if they had the power, and had the proper objects of law-making in view).

It may be that the principle of utilitarianism can comply with this demand Kant makes upon moral principles generally. (It may, indeed, be the *only* moral theory that can comply with it.) If we refrain from eating pork simply because it is a rule that pork is not eaten (and also, perhaps, because sanctions will be applied if we do not), then we are subject to the rule that prohibits eating it. But if we refrain from eating pork because we live in a hot climate, and realise that the practice of pork-eating is harmful to ourselves and others, and so see the reason for it being prohibited, then perhaps we are not merely subject to this rule, but are subject to a rule to which we (metaphorically) consent; hence our will remains autonomous. It would be possible to argue that, whenever we see what harm results from omitting to follow a rule, or what good results from following it, then we see the reason for conforming to the rule, and if we obey it for this reason our wills are autonomous. Since, we then might say, utilitarianism always appeals to the good or harm that our actions do, it always gives a reason for the rules to which we are subject; hence anyone who conforms to these rules because he sees that there is such a reason has a will that is always autonomous.

TELEOLOGICAL ETHICAL THEORIES AND THE FIRST FORMULATION OF THE CATEGORICAL IMPERATIVE

I have kept the first formulation of the categorical imperative to the last because this is the point at which utilitarianism has to be modified in order to fulfill Kant's requirements. There are two versions of the first formulation of the categorical imperative (sometimes known as 'Formula I' and 'Formula Ia'). The first states '*Act only on that maxim through which you can at the same time will that it should become a universal law*' (Kant, 1785, Ak. IV, 421). The second states '*Act as if the maxim of your action were to become through your will a UNIVERSAL LAW OF NATURE*' (Ibid.).

The second of these propositions is easier to understand than the first. It tells you to act as you would act, if as a result of your acting on a given maxim, it were to become a law of nature that everybody else acted on this maxim. For example, if I am considering making a lying promise, I ought to make this promise if and only if I could still make the promise, if I knew that as a result of my acting on my maxim (which we will assume to be to make lying promises if I can further my interest in no other way) everyone else acts on it, and he too makes lying promises when he can further his interest in no other way.

The first proposition, however, is more difficult to interpret. It is sometimes supposed that the law Kant is here referring to is the moral law, as opposed to the law of nature. In this case, he is asking us to act only on maxims which are such that we could will that they should be moral laws. I myself do not know whether by 'universal law' he meant 'universal moral law' or not. If he did, his view has insuperable difficulties. Since there is no such thing as making a moral law, there can be no such thing as willing that something should be a moral law. In any case, there are some moral laws on which nobody acts, many which are acted on but seldom, and none which are acted on all the time. Hence I might not care whether something were a moral law or not, provided no one acted on it, or provided people acted on it but seldom. If I could will that something were a moral law, provided no one acted on it, then there is no reason why the first and second versions of the first formulation of the categorical imperative should be equivalent, for the effects of my willing that something be a universal moral law, and of my willing that something become a universal law of nature, will not be even remotely the same unless the premise is added that everybody acts upon the moral law in question. Perhaps I could will that something be a moral law, provided few people or none acted upon it, although I could not will that it become a law of nature, for in that case everyone would act on it.

It is possible, however, that by 'universal law' in the first version of the first formulation of the categorical imperative Kant meant 'universal positive law'. This positive law would have to be one of a very special kind. There are a large number of things which one regards as being wrong, which one would not wish to be prohibited by any ordinary positive law. The law in question would have to be, so to speak, both ethereal and omniscient. It would need to be able to peep through keyholes to watch me wantoning with my maid, and my inmost thoughts would have to lie open to it. And it could have no means of enforcement more effective than the still small voice which accuses me when I have done wrong, for this is the only sanction which it is universally and always practicable to exact. Indeed, even it may be excessive.

Anyone making laws has to be satisfied on a number of points before he makes them, and this applies even to laws as tenuous as the ones I have imagined. He will naturally ask himself 'How will things stand if (by some miracle) everyone obeys the law I have made?' If the law he is contemplating making is inconsistent with itself or with other laws he is contemplating making, there is a conclusive reason for not making it. Strictly speaking, it is a conclusive reason for a legislator who has in view the proper ends of law-making not to make it. If, for whatever reason, he wanted to undermine the law, then making conflicting laws would be one good way of doing this. If it is logically impossible that everyone should obey it, then it is a bad law, and, provided he has only those motives which are proper to legislators, he will be unable to promulgate it. If it is causally impossible for everyone to act on it, then this is another reason for thinking that the law he is contemplating legislating is a bad one. There is little to be said for laws which cannot be acted upon. But there are many laws, which a good law-giver would not make, which it is neither logically nor causally impossible to act on. In such case, the question I must ask myself is, could I, if I were the maker of universal law, make such laws, or could I not? If I can, then my maxim is a permissible one; if I cannot, it is one on which it is not permissible to act.

The trouble with saying that I should act only on maxims which are such that I can will that they become universal laws is that it introduces an improper (and unKantian) element of subjectivism. What one man can will may not be what another man can will. I, who am rich, might be able to will that no one give to charity, though someone else, who is poor, might not be able to do this. It is quite wrong of Kant to say that the reason why I cannot will that no one should help anyone else in distress is that, in such an event, no one would help me, if I were in distress. Kant's appeal is not exactly to self-interest, for in fact I am not in distress, but when I am invited to consider what my attitude would be to the universalisation of my maxim if I were in a situation other than the one I am in, what psychological effect this has must be from sympathy. Doing so may be some propadeutic against bias, but on the whole it is difficult to see why the poor should be any less biased than the rich, criminals less biased than judges, those who suffer from some measure less biased than those who benefit from it. The position I should put myself in, when I consider whether I could will the universalization of my maxim, is the position of a law-giver, and I should simply forget, except as a means of fully appreciating the consequences my laws would have, what my attitude would be if I were this or that party affected by them.

The question arises, of course, how I know what such a law-giver could or could not do. I think that what a law-giver could do is what he would do, if he were actuated solely by the purposes proper to law-givers, and what he could not do is what he would not do under the same assumption. But what are the proper purposes of law-givers? I myself think that they are to legislate for the welfare of those over whom they have authority (including themselves, if they are a member of the community over which they govern). But such a law-giver will make laws for the greatest benefit of this community. It is arguable that he need only make one law, a law to the effect that everyone should try to produce the greatest happiness of the greatest number. Of course, if such a law were to become part of the normal positive law of a community, it would be impracticable and expensive and meddlesome and unenforceable and subject to continual dispute. But laws as insubstantial as the laws I have argued this law-giver would make would not have these disadvantages.

There are grave difficulties, however, in the way of thinking that such a 'law' would be the one that our legislator would make. Most of these difficulties are extremely well known and it would take me too far from my central topic to discuss them here. I shall content myself with pointing out that there is one difficulty with utilitarianism that Kantian considerations about universalisability enable us to overcome. Sir David Ross once put forward a form of neoKantianism according to which we had a *prima-facie* duty to obey a fairly large number of moral rules, which included rules demanding promise-keeping, truth-telling, non-malevolence, beneficience, etc. Since he thought, rightly, that we might have a duty to depart from any of these rules if the consequences of adhering to them were bad beyond a certain point, he added to this list a *prima-facie* duty to produce good consequences in general. Then if there were a conflict between one of the former rules and our *prima-facie* duty to produce good consequences, he simply said that sometimes the first would override the second, and that sometimes it would be the other way round. Since our *prima-facie* duty to produce good consequences would not *always* override our duty to do such things as tell the truth, his view was not that of a utilitarian. But since, on the other hand, our *prima-facie* duty to produce good consequences would *sometimes* override our *prima-facie* duty to do such things as tell the truth, his theory represented a departure from what used to be known (inappositely, for it is a moral view, not an epistemological one) as intuitionism.

The trouble with this theory (though Ross himself regarded it as a merit) was that it provided no rules for deciding, in the event of a conflict between, say, our *prima-facie* duty to tell the truth and our *prima-facie* duty to pay our debts, which should take precedence over the other. (It would be impossible to put them in an order of preference, for sometimes the first would over-ride the second, but at other times the second would over-ride the first.) There was also no rule for deciding, in the event of a conflict between one of these rules and the *prima-facie* duty to produce good consequences, which should take precedence over the other. It is a further difficulty with the theory, I think, that it makes it just coincidence that it is usually productive of good consequences to observe these rules about debt-paying, truth-telling, promise-keeping, and so on; the rule demanding that we produce good consequences is given no higher status than any of the others, and they are not derived from it. On the other hand, Ross's theory does recognize that the orthodox utilitarian view that we should not pay our debts, tell the truth, keep our promises, etc., whenever we can do more good by not paying our debts, not telling the truth, or by breaking our promises, is just plain wrong, and does not accord with what most people unreflectingly believe.

The clue to finding a form of utilitarianism, if you call it that, which does demand that you ought not to depart from rules demanding truth-telling, etc., whenever you can do more good by breaking them than by keeping them, but that you should depart from them when you can do much more good by breaking them than by keeping them, lies in the fact that acts of departing from these common sense rules have a cumulative effect. Once you realize this, you may find a rationale for Ross's theory which he himself could not provide. Though that they are generally observed is essential to the well-being of society, a few departures can be tolerated without their doing much harm, if any at all; indeed, very often departing from them can do only good. However, since the harm they do is cumulative, a large number of repetitions of infringements, which themselves do no harm, may be very harmful. There is no reason why a large number of repetitions of actions which themselves individually do good should not do a great deal of harm. Individual straws may be quite good for a camel, though their cumulative effect is to break its back.

In circumstances where there is such a cumulative good or ill effect, we might be prepared to will the action, but not to will the universalisation of the action. When we consider telling a lie to help a friend, the good consequences of doing so may outweigh the bad (if it has any bad consequences, which it may not do if the fact that I have lied is never discovered). But if everybody faced with a similar choice were to lie, then the consequences of their collective dishonesty would be bad. Hence the very reasons which would tend to make me decide to break it also tend to make me decide that everybody should keep it, had I the power to decide this. For the same reason, I could not will that it should be a law that everyone should break such promises (at any rate, I could not if I thought that as a result of my willing that this should be a law, everybody would break such promises). Nor could I will that I should break them, if I knew that, as a result of my acting on the maxim prescribing the breaking of such promises, everyone would act on the same maxim. And that is very nearly the same as to say that I could not act on my maxim if I knew that as a result it would become a law of nature that everyone acted on the same maxim.

It is not, as some philosophers have said, that my end in acting on my maxim would be defeated if everybody were to act on it. This, so far as I can see, has no tendency to make my action wrong. If I am at the back row in a football match, and am contemplating standing on my expensive chair to get a better view, my purpose would be defeated if everybody stood on his chair; but it is *not* wrong to stand on your chair if you are on the back row. On the other hand, if my chair is on the front row, my purpose would *not* be defeated by everybody's standing on his chair, though standing on one's chair in such circumstances *is* wrong. In my case, whether my purpose in adopting a maxim is or is not defeated by its universal adoption depends upon what my purpose is, whereas whether my maxim is right or not does not.

If I am right, it follows that utilitarianism, though it survives the other of Kant's criticisms of teleological ethical theories that I have mentioned, does not fulfill those conditions laid down for maxims stipulated by the first version of the first formulation of the categorical imperative. If I am a utilitarian, then, by definition, one of my maxims should be to produce the greatest good of the greatest number. But though if I act on this maxim good will result, if everyone else acts on it also, harm will follow. For the maxim to try to bring about the greatest good of the greatest number will demand that I break my promises, neglect to pay my debts, tell lies, and so on, whenever I can do more good than I can by more conventional behaviour, and though good will result if I alone do this, if everybody follows my example, the result, since the damage I will do will be cumulative, will be harmful. The rules I depart from are essential to the well-being of society, and though they will survive unscathed by a few breaches, a universal policy of breaking them will destroy them completely.

Utilitarianism, therefore, is not universalisable. I have suggested in other places ways in which it can be modified to make it conform to the requirements Kant wants, and it would take me too far afield to go into this complicated problem here. I cannot resist the temptation, however, of raising the question whether morality itself, and not just the utilitarian version of it, can conform to the first formulation of the categorical imperative. To be saintly is doubtless good, when saints are in short supply, but a world in which everyone was a saint might be a little tedious. The world needs, even if one takes a very high-minded view, artists, musicians, writers, scientists and philosophers as well as saints, and people will not make very good artists or scientists if they devote themselves to morality and not to their science or art. To take utilitarianism as an example, even were it not for the cumulative ill effects of utilitarianism which I have already drawn attention to, a world in which everyone devoted themselves to the greatest good of the greatest number, and no one to art, science and literature, would not be as desirable as superficially it might seem.

The distinction Kant draws between perfect and imperfect duties might come to the rescue, though not in the form in which he draws it. There are 'optional duties' — not a happy expression — perhaps, as well as compulsory ones, and I am allowed a choice about whether to devote myself to the latter or alternatively to art, science or literature, or even to some more bizarre form of enterprise such as being the first man to climb Everest on horseback. Much of morality, indeed, is commendable rather than obligatory, and when it is the former I am allowed to act on maxims even though they are such that I would not be prepared to act on them, were it to become a law of nature that everybody does the same. (This is not intended to be criticism of the view that particular moral *judgments* are universalisable, which view I consider to be correct. For whatever particular moral judgments I pass on the actions of a man employed on some supererogatory moral activity, I am logically bound to pass on the similar activity of any similar man.)

TWO KINDS OF TELEOLOGICAL ETHICS

The expression 'teleological ethical theory' may comprehend two quite different kinds of view. The first kind of teleological ethical theory is one which tells you what is the end for man. This is assumed to be some state of affairs in which it is desirable for a man to be, or one which the wise man will aim at, and the rules to which such a theory gives rise are all ones which counsel him how to achieve this end. Such theories hold that the end is happiness, or a life of contemplation, and then go on (if one is lucky) to say how this end may be achieved. However satisfactory they may be as accounts of the good life, and how to live it, they would all be fundamentally unsatisfactory were they theories about what men ought to do or what is man's duty, for they are all primarily egotistical. They tell me to aim at my own happiness, or at my own good, but they do not tell me that I ought to aim at the good for others. For so far as anything they expressly say goes, I do not and cannot have any duties to others, for if my sole occupation is to promote my own happiness, or to secure for myself a life of contemplation, then it logically follows that anyone else's claims on me are of no account whatsoever except indirectly in so far as they bring these admirable conditions about.

Such ethical theories, therefore, are more about what to do in my free time, than they are theories about duty. I should perform my duties and then, with any resources I have left over, seek the end for myself. This may have been disguised from some philosophers because of a logical error. If my only duty is to bring about my own perfection — for I cannot live the *best* possible life if I am short of being perfect — then I may *think* that this duty will comprehend all my duties because, unless I perform all my duties, I will not be perfect. There is, however, an important logical difference between being morally perfect, and being perfect in other ways. One's non-moral perfection may consist in happiness, or in contemplation, and, if so, and my only duty were to make myself perfect, duties could without circularity be derived from these facts. However, the view that I ought to make myself non-morally perfect – from which it follows that I have no duty whatsoever to consider the welfare of others, except in so far as it indirectly leads to my own – is quite preposterous. One may try to defend it by arguing that my own perfection never *can* conflict with that of others, but this kind of per-fectionism nevertheless leads to the conclusion that I would have entirely to ignore the interests of others, *if* there were such a clash, even though in fact there never is one. On the other hand, if included in the idea of the end at which I ought to aim is my own moral perfection, then the theory becomes both circular and covertly non-teleological. It is circular, because I am told that I ought to make myself perfect, as if this were a piece of new infor-mation, and then told that part of my perfection will consist in doing my duty, without being told what these duties are. It is covertly non-teleological because though, when I am told that I ought to realise in myself the end for man, it looks as if my duties are being derived from the end which results from my performing them, I am further told that I will not have achieved this end unless I do my duty, and no further teleological account of these duties is given. Aristotle himself is open to these criticisms. For though he says that what I ought to do is to bring about my own happiness, which is to give a teleological account of ought, it turns out, on closer investigation, that I will not be happy unless I live in accordance with virtue. Aristotle gives no teleological account of that virtue which I must have in order to be happy, and it is fairly clear that the idea of giving such an account has not even occurred to him.

The second kind of teleological theory *is* a theory about duty, rather than a theory about the good life. It maintains, as opposed to theories which have been mis-described as intuitionistic, that whether or not one has a duty to perform any action depends upon the results of that action, for example, that whether or not one has a duty to keep a promise depends upon whether or not doing so will bring about good. The most striking difference between this and the first kind of teleological ethical theory seems to be that, while the former kind is egotistic, and tells you how to obtain a satisfactory form of existence for yourself, the latter is not, and tells you that you have duties to others to bring it about that they, and not just you yourself, are in a certain state. But in fact this difference is really subordinate to the most im-portant difference, which is that one purports to tell you what your duties are, whereas the other simply claims to tell you how to live the good life. It is obvious that Kant's criticisms of teleological ethical theories are much more likely to go home against the first kind of view than against the second. I doubt whether he ever clearly distinguished the two.

CONCLUSION

Kant both put forward a view of the content of the supreme principle of morality, and a number of conditions which he thought any supreme principle of morality must fulfill. (It may be that he believed that the former followed from the latter.) His account of the supreme principle of morality was, I am sure, wrong. But this does not imply that his remarks about the nature of morality were unsound. It is my contention in the foregoing pages that teleological ethical theories in general, and utilitarianism in particular, can by and large conform to Kant's general view of morality to produce a kind of Kantian utilitarianism. The first of two main characteristics of such a theory would be that it held that, though actions are made to be duties by the goodness of their consequences, when someone does an action because he believes it to be a duty for this reason, and does it for duty's sake, he acquires thereby a kind of goodness which is distinct from, and may far outweigh, the goodness of the results of what he does. The second would be that it held that it was not the goodness or badness of the consequences of individual actions that made them right or wrong, but the consequences which would result if everybody performed similar actions. In other words, I should not perform any action unless the very considerations about the goodness of its consequences which led me to think it right to perform it would also lead me to think that it would be right to make the performance of such actions a universal law.

Nottingham University, England

CHARLES M. CORK, III

THE DEONTIC STRUCTURE OF THE GENERALIZATION
ARGUMENT

In this paper I will develop a line of argument which decisively strengthens the argument put forth by Marcus Singer in his book, *Generalization in Ethics*.[1] In accordance with the subtitle of his book, this paper will focus on the logic of ethics and in particular of his argument. To this end, I will first sketch a deontic logic in which the argument is couched. I will then present the logical outline of this version of the generalization argument and an interpretation of its steps which should meet the various criticisms brought against Singer's argument. In the course of the discussion some advantages of the suggested way of analyzing the generalization argument will be detailed.

1. DEONTIC LOGIC

To lay a proper foundation for the argument, a diversion into ordinary deontic logic is in order. What I propose to do is to interpret the terms used by this argument (and, of course, Singer's) and to indicate some of the basic principles used in all deontic systems of which I am aware and which are useful in showing the relations among deontic concepts, so that the following proof (and thus Singer's proof) may be better understood.

1. This deontic system is merely a normatively ethical system: *moral* obligation and permission (indicated by 'O' and 'P' respectively) will, unless otherwise noted, be the only such concepts employed.

2. The *de re–de dicto* distinction should be noted. 'O(a) (Xa)' should indicate that the state of affairs where all agents do X is obligatory (ought to be achieved). This is *de dicto* obligation. On the other hand, '(a) (OXa)' indicates that all agents have an individual obligation to do X. This is *de re* obligation. The two are by no means equivalent. The distinction seems to rest on the different means by which one assesses either modality. For example, in the *de dicto* case of 'O(a) (Xa)' one imagines the state of affairs which '(a) (Xa)' describes and determines its deontic status; here, that state is obligatory. But in the *de re* modality '(a) (OXa)' we, as it were, distribute the obligation to attain the state of affairs by requiring each agent to do his part and hold him accountable for it as well as any undesirable consequences resulting from his failure to do it. Before making the distribution, at most

267

Nelson Potter and Mark Timmons (eds.), Morality and Universality, 267–284.
© 1985 *by D. Reidel Publishing Company.*

only collective responsibility for any undesirable consequences is ascribed to the agents. Another way to put the difference is to adopt the standpoint of an agent, say a_1. To him, the *de dicto* modality indicates that it should be the case that he shares with agents $a_2, \ldots, a_n$ the property of doing X. The *de re* modality, however, tells him that it is in fact the case that he shares the property of having a duty to do X with the other agents, whether they do X or not.

One clear case where the distinction makes a difference is the case where the agents must act in a particular sequence in order to avoid undesirable consequences; every agent is under a *de re* duty to act. But if one imagines that they all act simultaneously (which is one way in which '(a) (Xa)' can be true) and asks what the deontic status *de dicto* of such a state of affairs is, it need not be one of obligation.

3. A word about moral permission: to say that a person is morally permitted to do something is to say that he has a moral right to do it, but it is not necessarily a right in one of the legal senses in which, as a result, others are obliged to refrain from interfering with that person's exercise of those rights. Once more, there is an obvious *de re–de dicto* distinction concerning rights and permissions: a permitted state of affairs might be, for example, that everyone do X, but on the other hand, everyone might have permission or a right to do X. These two, also, are not equivalent, for all of us might be permitted to enter a certain building, but it might not be a permitted state of affairs if all of us tried to enter it simultaneously.

4. 'Permission' and 'obligation' are interdefinable thus: $Pp \equiv {\sim}O{\sim}p$ and $Op \equiv {\sim}P{\sim}p$. That is, it is permitted that p if and only if it is not obligatory that not p, and likewise for 'Op'.

5. A consequence of the fourth note is that the following basic equivalences hold: ${\sim}Pp \equiv O{\sim}p$ and $P{\sim}p \equiv {\sim}Op$. These theorems could be called obligation-permission interchange (OPI).

6. A consequence of the fifth and the laws of quantifier negation is that the following are valid: ${\sim}P(a)\,(Xa) \equiv O(\exists a)\,({\sim}Xa)$; ${\sim}(a)\,(PXa) \equiv (\exists a)\,(O{\sim}Xa)$; etc. In general, the negation sign '${\sim}$' can be "moved" across operators (quantificational and deontic) by replacing the operator with its counterpart, as demonstrated above.

The deontic logic employed here extends beyond a propositional calculus to quantification theory. The system which most closely meets my requirements is Anderson's system OM,[2] although it does not extend to quantification theory. Since I use quantifiers I cannot simply base the argument on OM, but its results are significant and extendable to permit the use of quantifiers. Certain points should be noted by way of comparison: first, all the results mentioned in the fourth and fifth points above are valid theorems in OM. Second, as an analog of Anderson's propositional constant 'S' (Sanction) I will take for the purposes of this paper Singer's "undesirable (or disastrous) consequences" (to be symbolized by the propositional constant 'UC'). Third, given the analog just mentioned, the first two premises of my formulation of the generalization argument are provable in, and are theorems of, OM. So if OM is plausible, this argument is too — at least until quantifiers are employed. At least until then, the logic employed here is not stronger than Anderson's. For the logic used here includes only rules of modal interchange (OPI), and takes as its only "axioms" those two theorems of OM.

2. FORMALIZED VERSION OF THE GENERALIZATION ARGUMENT

I now turn to the formal proof of the generalization argument (GA). I will subsequently interpret each of its steps and consider objections to the argument. The most noticeable thing in the proof will have to be the unusual quantifier in the consequent of Step 9 and in the antecedent of Step 10. It will be defined and explained later, but to give it preliminary intuitive signification it may be compared with the existential quantifier. The latter's normal translation into spoken English is "there is at least one object" meeting some description, and the assertion can be defended by pointing to such an object. The proposed translation for this new quantifier is "there is at least one arbitrary member of a set" (here A) meeting some description, but the assertion can be defended only in ways other than by pointing to an object. Elaborations will follow. As must be obvious, Step 5, the principle of consequences (C), does not play any visible role in the subsequent proof, and is therefore, strictly speaking, eliminable from the proof of GA. Nevertheless, in interpreting the quantifier (яа), it will prove helpful. '*' indicates that this step does not follow from previous steps by logical considerations alone. 'UC' serves formally as a propositional constant and should suggest 'there are undesirable consequences'. 'Xa' is a propositional schema of an act which may be more sufficiently described for certain purposes which are not relevant here by '$X, \ldots, a, \ldots$'. 'X' alone is a constant act-type. 'A' is the set of all relevantly similar agents. 'a' without a subscript ranges over members of A; with a subscript it names some member of the set A.

DLP   (1) $\sim Pq \supset ((p \rightarrow\!\!\!3\ q) \supset \sim Pp)$ * from deontic logic
        (2) $\sim PUC \supset ((p \rightarrow\!\!\!3\ UC) \supset \sim Pp)$ (1), (UC/q)

SEP	(3)	$\sim$PUC	* Assumption
	(4)	$(p \rightarrow\!\!3\ UC) \supset \sim Pp$	(2), (3), M. P.
C	(5)	$(Xa \rightarrow\!\!3\ UC) \supset \sim PXa$	(4), (Xa/p)
	(6)	$((a)(Xa) \rightarrow\!\!3\ UC) \supset \sim P(a)(Xa)$	(4), ((a)(Xa)/p)
GC	(7)	$((a)(Xa) \rightarrow\!\!3\ UC) \supset O \sim (a)(Xa)$	(6), OPI
	(8)	$((a)(Xa) \rightarrow\!\!3\ UC) \supset O(\exists a)(\sim Xa)$	(7), QN
PD	(9)	$O(\exists a)(\sim Xa) \supset (яa)(O \sim Xa)$	* Assumption
GT	(10)	$(яa)(O \sim Xa) \supset (a)(O \sim Xa)$	* Assumption
GP	(11)	$O(\exists a)(\sim Xa) \supset (a)(O \sim Xa)$	(9), (10), Syll.
GA	(12)	$((a)(Xa) \rightarrow\!\!3\ UC) \supset (a)(O \sim Xa)$	(8), (11), Syll.

Step 1: $\sim Pq \supset ((p \rightarrow\!\!3\ q) \supset \sim Pp)$

I call the first formula the "deontic logic principle" (DLP). It holds: "If it is forbidden that q (for my informal purposes this may be rendered by 'q is forbidden'), then if it is necessarily so that if p, then q (informally, p entails q), then it is forbidden that p (p is forbidden)."[3] The strict implication relation has the advantages of material implication (a strict modus ponens and a strict modus tollens) without the disadvantage of allowing either '$q \supset (p \rightarrow\!\!3\ q)$' or '$\sim p \supset (p \rightarrow\!\!3\ q)$' any formal validity. One is permitted to think of the strict implication relation as a kind of causal relation. It is not my purpose to formalize the notion of causal entailment. That project can be accomplished independently of this one and will still not warrant the inference suggested by '$q \supset (p \rightarrow\!\!3\ q)$' and '$\sim p \supset (p \rightarrow\!\!3\ q)$'. Furthermore, since the *prohibitum* is frequently not just doing the act but knowingly doing it, a causal relation, as it is normally understood, may not be the most appropriate one.[4] I am relying on the belief that some such relation can be made intelligible without warranting those inferences.

To illustrate: if it is not permitted that I (knowingly) break a certain window, and if it is necessarily so that if I throw a ball in a certain direction under certain circumstances, then I will (knowingly) break the window, then it is not permitted that I throw the ball under those conditions in that way. Or less formally: if (knowingly) breaking the window is not permitted, then if my throwing the ball in that direction under those circumstances (causally) entails (knowingly) breaking the window, then my throwing the ball then is not permitted. To affirm the antecedent of DLP and to deny its consequent must not be tolerated in a normatively consistent system, even if there are some societies or legal systems in which it is permitted to do something, the result of which, if done, is not permitted. For that would be to tell an agent that he will be blameworthy if he acts so that q obtains, which he will do if he acts so that p, but that he will not be blameworthy if he goes ahead and acts so that p obtains.

Step 2: $\sim PUC \supset ((p \rightarrow UC) \supset \sim Pp)$

Here 'UC' is substituted for 'q'. 'UC', as above mentioned, should suggest the existence of undesirable consequences. 'UC' functions formally as the proposition 'there are undesirable consequences' but informally as an individual constant which denotes a state of affairs which is held to be undesirable. To be sure, there is not merely one such state of affairs, and it would be possible to append subscripts to various occurrences of 'UC' for the purpose of distinguishing among them. For the sake of convenience I will not do so. Singer tells us that 'undesirable' in this formulation is ambiguous: it connotes both 'undesirable on the whole' and 'undesirable' *simpliciter*, and furthermore that no particular standard of what should count as undesirable has been assumed (pp. 64–5). Presumably, what would be required before the generalization argument could be put into operation assessing groups, societies and social institutions is what Nagel calls a "substantive theory of value",[5] the lack of which is no criticism against the generalization argument. At least until one can be formulated, however, disputes about what is and is not undesirable may continue, but need not be inconsistent with the generalization argument (p. 65).

Steps 3 and 4: $\sim PUC$; $(p \rightarrow UC) \supset \sim Pp$

Clearly (4) follows from (2) and (3), so I will concentrate on (3), which is the second premise of this version of the generalization argument, and which provides the substantive force of the argument. Hence I call it "the substantive ethical principle" (SEP). '$\sim PUC$' denotes the single most general prohibition that may be made *a priori*, subject of course to the difficulties of interpretation of 'undesirable consequences' mentioned above.[6] Singer later put the point concerning the force of (3), especially with respect to (5), the principle of consequences, attractively well:

The reasons provided by consequences can vary in force. The force of the reason depends upon how undesirable the consequences are taken to be. They can range all the way from the absolutely disastrous to the mildly undesirable, and the force of this consideration will vary accordingly. Thus let us suppose that the consequences of *as'* doing X would be ABSOLUTELY DISASTROUS. Let us allow our imaginations to run wild, and suppose that they would be such as to preclude the possibility of any further action of any kind by anyone at any time. That would seem to get as close to the conclusive reason for concluding that *a* ought not to do *X* as could be gotten, at least from a consideration of the consequences. But if the consequences of *a*'s doing *X* would be somewhat less horrendous than this, as they almost always are, they will provide no conclusive reason.[7]

Step 5: $(Xa \rightarrow\!\!\!3 \ UC) \supset \sim PXa$

After several steps we finally arrive at Singer's first premise, the principle of consequences (C). Formally, C claims that if *a*'s doing *X* (symbolically: 'Xa') entails undesirable consequences, it is not permitted that *a* do *X* ('~PXa'). Here C is simply a substitution instance of (4), created by replacing '*p*' merely with a different schema 'Xa', which has the advantage of suggesting the relation between the act-type and the agent. There should be no equivocation when the substitution is made since the ordinary and informal mode of talking about 'Xa $\rightarrow\!\!\!3$ UC', e.g., '*a*'s doing *X* entails *UC*' can be restated somewhat more cumbersomely, but with no otherwise undesirable consequences as 'it is necessarily so that if *a* does *X*, then there are (will be) *UC*'.[8]

Step 6: $((a) (Xa) \rightarrow\!\!\!3 \ UC) \supset \sim P(a) (Xa)$

The *same* reasoning by which (5) follows from (4) will guarantee that (6) follows from (4). It would thus appear unlikely that there could be a situation of conflict between C and GA (through GC) where an agent would be called upon to act inconsistently, since both aim at avoiding undesirable consequences. Yet some have claimed that a conflict is possible and have produced purported examples of conflict. Such a claim is either to argue that the premises of the generalization argument are logically false or (more likely) to trade on an ambiguity in '*UC*'. Such ambiguities have been exposed elsewhere.[9]

   (6), (7) and (8) are equivalent formulations, and express what Singer calls the "generalization from the principle of consequences" (GC). The difference between (6) and (4) is that '(a) (Xa)' has replaced each occurrence of '*p*'. The point of course is that, whereas one state of affairs (or act) has been the center of our attention before, various acts ranging both over indefinitely long periods of time and indefinitely many agents can now be talked about. Therefore, I propose to give *in abstracto* to the relevantly similar agents contained in set *A* (now being ranged over by the variable '*a*') the names (or numbers) 'a_1', ..., 'a_n', and to the possible occurrences of the act-type X, which are considered when one says that '(a) (Xa)' is true, the names (or numbers) 'X_a^1', ..., 'X_a^m', where it is not necessary that m = n. These latter names should not be confused with the non-quantified propositional schema of an act denoted by 'Xa'.[10] 'X_a^1' should be read as 'the first act which counts or would count as an occurrence of act-type X by a member of A'. On the other hand, 'Xa' should be read as 'a (a member of A) does X', and could just as well have been the proposition denoted by the variable 'p'. (6) claims that if it is necessary that if all members of the set $\{X_a^1, \ldots, X_a^m\}$ occur or were to occur (so that '(a) (Xa)' is true), then there are or would be undesirable consequences, then in that case it is not permitted that all of those members occur.

Concerning $\{X_a^1, \ldots, X_a^m\}$: whereas it may be helpful to think of the members as beginning with the temporally first occurrence and extending to the temporally last occurrence, this is not necessarily the case, especially where acts occur simultaneously. Officially, no temporal ordering is supposed; it just tells us that m distinct acts are being talked about when '(a) (Xa)' is affirmed. Example: Suppose that there are 10 agents $(a_1, \ldots, a_{10})$, 10 chairs, '(a) (Xa)' is true and the set of acts (sitting on one of the ten chairs) is $\{X_a^1, \ldots, X_a^{10}\}$. The following are not supposed: all agents sit at the same time, or in sequence, or in all ten chairs, or in just one chair, or a_1 sits before a_{10}, etc.[11]

Steps 7 and 8: ((a) (Xa) $\dashv$ UC) $\supset$ O~(a) (Xa); ((a) (Xa) $\dashv$ UC) $\supset$ O($\exists a$) ($\sim Xa$)

(7) involves the use of a theorem of all deontic logics with which I am familiar and which was above called OPI. It would only be possible to affirm (6) and deny (7) (or *vice versa*) if one used either 'permissible' or 'obligatory' in some non-normatively ethical sense. Nonetheless, this has been done:

It has been noted by various critics that, since Singer intends that 'everyone' in 'the consequences of everyone's doing X would be undesirable' *collectively* rather than *distributively*, there is a distinct problem in going from 'not everyone has the right to do X' ($\sim$ (a) (PXa)) to 'there is someone who does not have the right to do X' (($\exists a$) ($\sim$PXa)). Ordinarily, of course, an inference of the sort . . . would be completely proper. But because of the peculiarities of the distinction between the collective and distributive senses of 'everyone', the move is not legitimate in this case. Satisfying the collective maxim merely requires that *some person or other* refrain from doing X. (To break up a no-hit game in baseball, some one person must get a hit. But before the game there is no one person who must get a hit in order to avoid the embarrassment of a no hitter.)[12]

The first point to be made about this argument is that it uses a consequent, which is different from the one which I suggest Singer intended and on which I rest this argument. But the main point is that the argument misunderstands the formal key to the collective-distributive distinction. One determines whether a modality is distributive or collective (*de re* or *de dicto*) by observing whether the modality is within the scope of a quantifier or not. Thus the authors of the last criticism would have seen that the move they discuss is from one distributive modality to another. In the present case the move is from one collective modality to another, and involves no error.

(8) follows from (7) by quantifier negation: if it is obligatory that not all of the acts in $\{X_a^1, \ldots, X_a^m\}$ occur, it is obligatory that at least one of them fails to occur. The same remarks may be made about this step that were made in the case of the previous one.

Step 9: $O(\exists a)\,(\sim Xa) \supset (я a)\,(O \sim Xa)$

Many of Singer's critics have supposed that he implicitly invoked the following conditional: $O(\exists a)\,(\sim Xa) \supset (\exists a)\,(O \sim Xa)$, which changes a collective obligation into a distributive one. That is, if the antecedent is true, out of all members of A, at least one of them, whom we cannot in principle name or indicate (it could be potentially any or all members) ought not do X; or in other words, someone ought to see to it that at least one member of A does not do X. On the other hand, if the consequent is true, it has appeared to some critics that there is some member of A, say a_k, such that '$O \sim Xa_k$' is true. They have advanced plenty of purported counterexamples to the above conditional. For example, if according to Army regulations there ought to be someone on guard duty, it does not follow that there is any particular person who ought to be on guard duty.[13]

What I propose to do is to weaken the consequent by introducing a new quantifier 'я' (only after defining some other terms) to take the place of '$\exists$', e.g., $O(\exists a)\,(\sim Xa) \supset (я a)\,(O \sim Xa)$. Instead of this: there is a particular member of A who ought not do X, the consequent should suggest that there is at least one arbitrary, i.e., unspecified or, in light of our (present) knowledge, unspecifiable member of A who ought not do X. *Arbitrary members* of a set are defined here as those about whom we make no assumptions other than their membership in the set. The "collective-distributive" problem will be solved by *distributing* the collective obligation to avoid undesirable consequences to those arbitrary members of A whose failure to do X is sufficient to avoid such consequences. This approach has the salutary effects of avoiding the embarrassing question, "*who* is forbidden to do X?" and of explaining the exact nature of the *ceteris paribus* restriction on the application of the generalization argument. Thus the name of this formula is the "principle of distribution" (PD).

Let us begin the "deduction" of the use of the new quantifier with the set of occurrences of the act-type in question. As already mentioned under (6), it is:

$$\{X_a^1, \ldots, X_a^m\} \quad \text{which I call: O–X}$$

'O–X' may be read 'the occurrence set of X'.

I now wish to construct a set containing one and only one description for each member of O–X. The description of such an act is a proposition which specifies both which member of A does X on that occasion, and which occurrence for that individual (his first, second, . . .) the act so described is, thus yielding a unique description of each occurrence.

$$\{^1Xa_1, \ldots, ^rXa_1, \ldots, ^1Xa_n, \ldots, ^sXa_n\} \quad \text{Called D–X}$$

'D–X' may be read 'the description set of X'. Although there are many ways to describe any act, it is no objection that D–X does not include all of them. For my purposes, I would use different act-schemas, such as 'Ya' or 'Za', to account for other descriptions, even though for other purposes they may be considered to denote the "same act". Thus, by hypothesis, O–X and D–X are equinumerous.

Now to construct two functions: let f be any arbitrary function mapping D–X onto O–X. By the same hypothesis, f is 1–1. Let g be the function from each member of D–X to its agent variable; g is not necessarily 1–1. Both will be needed later. I now want to introduce the concept of the threshold act by recasting O–X as follows:

$$\{X_a^1, \ldots, X_a^i, \ldots X_a^m\} \quad (O'-X)$$

'i' is defined as the least number of occurrences of act-type X sufficient to entail UC and $1 \leqslant i \leqslant m$.[14] For example, suppose there are ten ticket-holders who enter an auditorium where every chair is taken. In that case, one occurrence of X is the least number to bring about undesirable consequences if X is specified as 'some member of A sits (or tries to sit) in a chair without delay upon entering – preferably a free chair'. If one chair is free, then two occurrences of act-type X is the minimal number. And so on until, if there are nine free chairs, it takes every occurrence of type X to entail undesirable consequences. Of course, in many cases the exact value of i need not be known, but in them even the roughest approximation is normally sufficient. It should be noted that D–X is still equipollent with $O'–X$.

I now construct a subset of $O'–X$:

$$\{X_a^i, \ldots, X_a^m\} \quad (UC–X)$$

'UC–X' may be read 'the undesirable consequences set of $O'–X$'. Since the ith occurrence of act-type X is considered the threshold which causes undesirable consequences, UC–X should be construed to be the subset of $O'–X$ which is composed of all those acts whose individual occurrence entails undesirable consequences. Since $i \leqslant m$, UC–X $\neq \emptyset$ (is non-empty) in all cases where (a) (Xa) $\dashv$ UC. Once more, temporal priority is not necessarily the ordering ground of $O'–X$ and thus not of UC–X. Using f, it is now possible to construct the "description set of UC–X":

$$\{\check{f}(X_a^i), \ldots, \check{f}(X_a^m)\} \quad (DUC–X)$$

which is, of course, equipollent with UC–X and a subset of D–X. It is important here to remember that f was an arbitrary function mapping D–X onto O–X, and thus the actual description of members of UC–X has not been concretely determined to be acts of this or that agent, or this or that time the agent did it. Such a description could be made if one of the possible functions could be singled out as *the* appropriate function. If, for example, the ordering ground of $O'–X$ were temporal priority (as in the common case where a proprietor treats patrons on a "first come, first served" basis), it is not difficult to determine whether an act comes before, at or after the threshold has been reached. *In abstracto* neither f nor the members of DUC–X can be determined.

Finally, the last set I want to construct is:

$$\{g(\check{f}(X_a^i)), \ldots, g(\check{f}(X_a^m))\} \quad (ADUC–X)$$

'ADUC–X' may be read 'the agent set of DUC–X'. Because f is an arbitrary function, and because functions mapping D–X onto $O'–X$ are constructable such that each member of the former set can be related by various functions to 'X_a^i' in the latter, *any* member of A could be a member of ADUC–X. Furthermore, since DUC–X $\neq \emptyset$ in any case where '(a) (Xa) $\dashv$ UC' is true, and each description has an agent variable, ADUC–X $\neq \emptyset$. It follows that if a member of ADUC–X does X (at least, on some occasion), that act will entail undesirable consequences. Since the consequent of GC, namely, '$O(\exists a) (\sim Xa)$', states that it ought to be the case that some member of A refrain from doing X, but it is not able to specify (name) which one(s), now it is possible to "name" them by asserting that, as an implication of C (Step 5), for arbitrary f, each and every member of ADUC–X ought not do X because his doing X is sufficient to entail undesirable consequences.

The only issue now is whether one is a member of ADUC–X. It is here that the collective-distributive shift takes place. *Quid juris*? The distribution of obligation is justified here because 'distribution' is appropriately limited to purely rational constructs: members of ADUC–X; it does not include the imposition of duties upon any concrete individuals and does not run afoul of critics' objections.

The weaker quantifier may now be introduced.

$$\text{'(яа) (O} \sim \text{Xa)' =df '(f) (f maps D–X onto O}'\text{–X} \supset \text{ADUC–X} \neq \emptyset\text{)'.}$$

Thus, the duty of unspecified members of A to refrain from X is defined so as to show that, no matter what function is used to order the acts considered in understanding '(a) (Xa)', there will always be an unspecified member of A who should refrain from doing X. That is, for any such function f, where '(a) (Xa) $\dashv$ UC' is true, it is mathematically demonstrable that there is some member of A who cannot be specified until f is, but who ought not do X. This is because ADUC–X $\neq \emptyset$. To follow up on a prior example, when there are ten ticket-holders, but only one free chair, nine arbitrary members of A are obligated by C not to sit down. If there are only nine chairs, one arbitrary member of A (the sole member of ADUC–X) is obliged to refrain from sitting. In many cases like these two, the correct, tacitly understood function is a "first come, first served" function, when, given a temporal ordering of O$'$–X, the matching members of D–X are related to $\{X_a^1, \ldots X_a^{i-1}\}$, and each remaining member of A (who is thus a member of ADUC–X) has an obligation to refrain from sitting.

To summarize Step 9, it is contended that '(яа) (O $\sim$ Xa)' is a correct analysis of 'O($\exists$ a) ($\sim$ Xa)'. This contention is based on a view that a collective obligation may be seen as distributed, not to those flesh and blood relevantly similar agents who comprise A and to whom we can point, but to logical constructions of agents (blanks, as it were, into which the former can be filled – see Singer, p. 19) who are members of ADUC–X. These constructions are in fact members of A, but they are not considered as empirical objects; rather, they are considered solely as having no properties other than those connoted by membership in ADUC–X.[15] Thus underlying Step 9 is the assumption, analogous to the one discussed in note 11 with reference to "acts" which have not yet occurred, that it is intelligible within limits to talk of "agents" in the constructed sense, even if we will never meet one. The distribution of the obligation in 'O($\exists$a) ($\sim$Xa)' is accomplished by constructing a set ADUC–X so that the collective obligation to avoid doing X can be said to rest on all of its members. Then there is no question about the propriety of distributing the duty to each and every member. So long as there are members of this set, and so long as the only assumption about them is membership in ADUC–X, which is a subset of A, it is appropriate to say that there is at least one arbitrary member of A who ought not do X.

Step 10: ($\textit{я}a$) ($O \sim Xa$) $\supset$ (a) ($O \sim Xa$)

It is the point of universal generalization (UG) in quantification theory to move from a truth about an arbitrary member of a set (whose only qualification is that it is a member of the set) to a truth about each member of the set. For example,

A geometer may begin a proof by saying, 'Let *ABC* be any arbitrarily selected triangle'. Then he may go on to prove that the triangle *ABC* has some specified attribute, and concludes that *all* triangles have that attribute. Now what justifies his final conclusion? Why does it follow from triangle *ABC*'s having a specified attribute that *all* triangles do? The answer is that if no assumption other than its triangularity is made about *ABC*, then the expression '*ABC*' can be taken as denoting any triangle you please. And if the argument has established that *any* triangle must have the attribute in question, then it follows that *all* triangles do.[16]

In fact, I have already employed such an argument: where '(a) (Xa) $\dashv$ UC' is true, for any arbitrary f, ADUC–X $\neq \emptyset$; therefore, for all f, ADUC–X $\neq \emptyset$. Indeed, I am assuming that by using an act-type X, about which all we know is that it is an act-type, I can generalize to any and all act-types. Thus it is not surprising that '(a) ($a \in$ AUDC–X $\supset O \sim Xa$)' follows. But it would be a mistake to generalize to the assertion that (a) ($O \sim Xa$) *solely* on account of the fact that ($\textit{я}a$) ($O \sim Xa$). For in many cases of act-type X there are also arbitrary members of A who are not members of ADUC–X. In that case members of ADUC–X are arbitrary and generalizations about all such members can be made, but they are not arbitrary members of A because there is an assumption about them which is additional to that of membership in A, namely, membership in ADUC–X; and this is true although they are "arbitrary" members of A in the sense that they have not been co-ordinated with the flesh and blood members of A: $a_1, \ldots, a_n$.

What is true, however, of every physical member of A solely by virtue of that membership, is that his every type X act brings the ith act closer to actuality, if it does not actualize it or if the ith act has not already been actualized (in which case C tells the agent not to do X). For example, in case of murder where we may suppose that $i = 1$, C without more tells the agent not to murder. But in the case of sitting in one of nine free seats in a theater when one is a member of a group of ten relevantly similar agents, his act may not seem to entail undesirable consequences if he sits first. Therefore it has seemed appropriate to some to advance this as a counter-example to the generalization argument and to show thereby that GA shows that one should not sit down, while it is obvious (to them) that one may sit down. The "obviousness" of the example is due only to the tacitly understood "first come" function. This is all the more clear when one changes the building from a theater to the Supreme Court, where the seats in question are presumably subject to a "Justices first" function. In this case, even though one's act of sitting first does not immediately entail the undesirable consequence of sitting on top of someone, it does entail leaving only eight seats for nine Justices; thus it entails bringing the ith act one step closer to actuality. Adopting the correct function, it is not difficult to show that the non-Justice is the member of ADUC–X, and it becomes clear that he was under a duty to refrain from X, even if a different result would be reached if a "first come" function were given. Such intuitively obvious counter-examples have not proved to be an objection to the generalization argument because they rely on tacitly understood functions which leave the situation no longer *ceteris paribus*.

Unless a function which would conclusively put the agent within ADUC–X or not has been established, as between the physical agent seeking to except himself from the duty and the hypothesized party who would impose the duty (be it "reason" or the collective responsibility to avoid *UC*), it is reasonable to impose the burden of showing the propriety of a function which puts the agent outside of ADUC–X on the agent rather than to put the burden on the duty-imposer to show that a proper function puts the agent within ADUC–X. This is the same as saying that one should presume that the agent is a member of ADUC–X *ceteris paribus*, i.e., unless the agent rebuts the presumption by showing otherwise, by showing that a proper function excepts him from the duty.[17]

The primary reason for placing the burden on (the presumption against) the agent is that his contention is "disfavored" in comparison with the contrary contention. It is disfavored on account of the policy against allowing undesirable consequences and the fact that there is no *a priori* reason to distinguish any claims he may make from the same claims of all other members, and thus no reason to permit him to "get away with" the act while forbidding other members from doing it in order to avoid undesirable consequences. Professor Singer put the point well when he said:

> What the argument implies is that if *a* has the right to do something, then everyone else, or everyone similar to *a* in certain respects, has this right in a similar situation; and therefore if it would be undesirable for everyone to have this right, then *a* cannot have such a right (p. 90).

The only alternative to this presumption or to distinguishing similar claims without an *a priori* basis is to presume that all agents may do the act unless shown otherwise. But if all the relevantly similar agents chose to exercise this right to do X, that presumption would lead to the dilemma of either allowing undesirable consequences or distinguishing some similar claims from others without a basis. By comparison, to presume rebuttably that the agent, as well as all other agents, are members of ADUC–X is to avoid undesirable consequences to the extent that any argument appealing to reason can do so, even if it goes further than necessary to do so.

But there are more reasons to place the burden on the agent. He is more likely to know of peculiar circumstances which may excuse him from the duty than those who impose the duty are to foresee when they merely determine that everyone's doing the act would be undesirable. Furthermore, because the agent is claiming that he is an exceptional case, it is generally fairer to assume provisionally against him that exceptional conditions do not exist. Then again, in most cases m is large and i is small, so that the probabilities are that a function would be more likely to put him in ADUC–X than to leave him in that portion of A which does not include ADUC–X.

Thus the contention is this: Since we know, on the basis of the fact that $(\text{я}a)\,(O \sim Xa)$, that $(a)\,(a \in \text{ADUC–X} \supset O \sim Xa)$ and that it is reasonable *ceteris paribus* to treat any arbitrary member of A, assuming only that membership, as if he is a member of ADUC–X, we are justified by UG to assert finally that $(a)\,(O \sim Xa)$, subject to the *ceteris paribus* restriction. This constitutes the generalization thesis (GT). Thus GT holds validly, but holds only rebuttably according to the following pattern: if an agent can demonstrate that there is (more than) one correct, appropriate or understood function which does not relate his act from D–X to a member of UC–X, he is justified in disregarding the results of GA. That is, when certain mapping functions for certain acts are preferred or intended, and when others can be disregarded for those acts, the agent is no longer relevantly similar to the others in A, and GA need not restrain him.

To illustrate these points, suppose that someone were to question the propriety of another's sitting in an untaken chair; if the latter could show that the understood policy in effect is defined by, e.g., a "first come, first served" function, he would be justified in disregarding the results of GA.

Or in the guard duty example, where there ought to be one guard on duty and where there are ten privates, any private can justify his not being on guard duty by showing both (1) that there is in effect an "order function" such that a private who is ordered is related to ADUC–X where X is "refrains from guard duty", and by showing (2) that no order was given to him.

The other examples can be handled in the same way.[18] Generally, the *onus probandi* is on the agent seeking to except himself to show that there is a proper function which does so. Thus his statement that "not everyone will" is irrelevant unless a function such as "first come" is in effect (pp. 90f). That one is self-identical, or identical with (fill in here some uniquely denoting expression)[19] in no way demonstrates the existence of such a function. GT claims that unless one can demonstrate the effective existence of such a function, one ought to refrain from doing the act.

Steps 11 and 12: $O(\exists a)\,(\sim Xa) \supset (a)\,(O \sim Xa)$; $((a)\,(Xa) \dashv\!\!3\; UC) \supset$ $(a)\,(O \sim Xa)$

Step 11, the "generalization principle" (GP), follows by hypothetical syllogism from Steps 9 and 10. The "generalization argument" (GA) in Step 12 follows by hypothetical syllogism from Steps 8 and 11. The *ceteris paribus* clause which appends to GP, and thus appears in GA, is explained by being in GT. "[T]he generalization argument ... [b]y reason of the generalization principle ... implies that each and every act of that kind may be presumed to be wrong" (p. 67).

3. CONCLUDING REMARKS

A few remarks on purported counter-examples are in order. First, note that GA does not contradict the possibility of commonsense solutions to the problems which some critics have advanced. I find it plausible that together with a substantive theory of value,[20] GA might even *call for* the same solutions which the critics put forth. For example, assume that undesirable consequences would follow if all camp members refrained from digging latrines, and also if all members dug them.[21] The act-type "digging latrines" is invertible. Invertibility for Singer is simply a recognition that some act-types among the infinite variety of act-types are not suitable for this argument because they are so broadly defined that the opposite act-type also entails undesirable consequences. A more specific act-type such as "agreeing to distribute work assignments equitably among members" may not be invertible. It is only the narrowly mechanical applications of GA which give it the appearance of formalistic nonsense.

Many of the purported counter-examples are likewise baldly invertible and consequently irrelevant to Singer's arguments. On his analysis, such act-types are morally neutral. Despite claims to the contrary, invertibility is not an *ad hoc* restriction. The generalization argument is designed to analyze the concepts of 'duty' and 'right' by showing the *a priori* conditions under which the conclusion is justified *ceteris paribus* that one has a duty or right to act in a certain way. No conclusion is justified *a priori* when *both* the act and its opposite lead to undesirable consequences. Some act-types are clearly suitable for this analysis (e.g., assassination). Others are not because the context is not sufficiently elaborated to permit *a priori* analysis (pp. 72f, 76ff).

Many have tried to refute GA by showing that it entails the questionable 'O($\exists$a) ($\sim$Xa) $\supset$ ($\exists$a) (O $\sim$ Xa)'. Where the examples employed have not been invertible or heedless of the *ceteris paribus* restrictions on GA, they have invoked situations where there is clearly an understood function in effect (e.g., the ticket-holder).

One consequence of the proof above is that what Singer calls the principle of consequences has been shown to be unnecessary for the proof of the "generalization from the principle of consequences" (GC), but it has been shown to be helpful in interpreting the collective-distributive shift that takes place in the principle of distribution. A second consequence, that of multiplying the assumptions twofold from Singer's argument to this one, did not prove to be undesirable because (a) DLP and SEP are, in my opinion, uncontroversial and (b) PD and GT are defensible, though they might be somewhat less than uncontroversial. Indeed, the most significant addition to this argument has been PD, for its use clarifies the *ceteris paribus* quality of GA.

I have tried to provide a minimal logical backbone for GA by using some tools of deontic logic and set theory and discounting various objections registered against it. Nevertheless, concrete applications of the generalization argument may remain exceedingly difficult and require very high aptitudes for practical judgment.[22] But no one ever said that being moral is easy.

Macon, GA 31201, U.S.A.

NOTES

[1] Page references, unless otherwise noted, are to *Generalization in Ethics* (2nd ed., 1971). I have altered the use of variables in this and other sources to present a uniform appearance.

[2] A. Anderson, 'The Formal Analysis of Normative Systems', reprinted in *The Logic of Decision and Action* (N. Rescher ed., 1967). Compare D. Føllesdal and R. Hilpinen, 'Deontic Logic: an Introduction', in *Deontic Logic: Introductory and Systematic Readings* (R. Hilpinen ed., 1970), pp. 13–15, 19–21. I have chosen not to use J. Hintikka's model-theoretic approach, *Models for Modalities* (1970), because the axiomatic approach adopted here is intuitively graspable with less effort than model-theoretic semantical approaches.

[3] DLP is in a form trivially distinct from, but equivalent with, Anderson's OM28, where strict implication (entailment) is also used. On logical grounds, DLP could not have been formulated with material implication thus: '$\sim Pq \supset ((p \supset q) \supset \sim Pp)$' because this is equivalent to '$(p \supset q) \supset (\sim Pq \supset \sim Pp)$', and since '$q \supset (p \supset q)$' is valid, so too would be '$q \supset (\sim Pq \supset \sim Pp)$' and '$\sim Pq \supset (q \supset \sim Pp)$'. The latter are strongly counter-intuitive.

[4] Indeed, it may be that the best understanding of the relation may be found in the legal notion of "proximate cause", if it were suitably unpacked.

[5] T. Nagel, *The Possibility of Altruism* (1970), pp. 97, 126. See also Singer's remarks on "filling in the context of an act" (pp. 79–80).

[6] Replacing 'UC' for 'S', this step is the analog of Anderson's OM48, 'FS'. See n. 2, *supra*, at p. 187. The discerning reader may now understand why I employ only 'P' and 'O' to formulate the deontic components of this argument.

[7] M. Singer, 'The Principle of Consequences Reconsidered', *Philosophical Studies,* **31**, 392, 395 (1977). It should also be noted that (4) is the analog of a conditional constructable from OM8: $Fp \equiv (p \rightarrow S)$. I need not here determine whether (4) can be strengthened into a biconditional.

[8] A criticism of C on the basis of the existence of supererogatory acts has been made by G. Nakhnikian, 'Generalization in Ethics' *Review of Metaphysics,* **XVII**, 436, 456ff (1964). His definition of supererogation leads, however, either to the conclusion that there are no such acts or to a contradiction. I suspect that he has a notion of non-required acts which has not (yet) been formulated in terms of the concepts used here.

[9] See Singer, n. 7 *supra*, 398–402. Generally, such arguments have simply assumed that if the consequences of an act are undesired by the agent, they are undesirable. Repaying debts, paying taxes and voting simply do not produce such undesirable consequences as one would seek to avoid through the institution of ascribing blameworthiness, except in extraordinary cases. If there ever were such a conflict, of which no absolutely clear example has been produced, the 'lesser of evils' approach would probably be the rational means of resolving it. Singer, n. 1 *supra*, 106–7.

[10] This distinction is drawn lest one thinks that 'X_a^1' names some kind of proposition. In that case, it would not name the acts which I desire to name, and the proposition named would not itself name the act, but would be used to describe it. It should be noted additionally that by not limiting those constants to acts to which one could point, it is assured that they exhaust the acts considered when '$(a) (Xa)$' is considered.

[11] I am not concerned here with the question of the "existential import" of deontic sentences such as "trespassing is forbidden". Cf. I. Copi, *Introduction to Logic* (4th

edn., 1972), p. 171. But see W. Quine, 'On What There Is', *From a Logical Point of View* (2nd ed., 1961), p. 4, *inter alia*. Reliance is placed on the belief that a well-founded and limited account can be given of the use to which 'act' is put where one refers to "acts" which have not occurred and which need never occur. Such sentences are intelligible when taken as describing objects of thought which cannot be correlated with objects of experience by pointing.

[12] R. Brockhaus and G. Hochberg, 'The Generalization Argument Revisited', *Philosophical Studies*, 28, 126–7 (1975) (footnotes omitted).

[13] Nakhnikian, n. 8 *supra*, at 443. The assumption that 'there is someone who ought to do X' entails that there is a *particular* person who ought to do X is questionable. If three people are considering entering a two-seat automobile, it is mathematically certain that there is someone who ought not do so, even if there is no particular person who ought not. $3 - 2 = 1$ under any circumstance. But as will appear in the text below, it is not necessary to question this assumption since a weaker 'there is' statement can be used.

[14] I owe this idea to E. Ullman-Margalit, 'The Generalization Argument: Where Does the Obligation Lie?' *Journal of Philosophy*, 73, 511, 520 (1976).

[15] One could thus consider the constructions to be 'problematic concepts' in that they serve to limit the empirical concept of an agent to its appropriate domain. See I. Kant, *Critique of Pure Reason*, B310–315. The suggestion that these constructions are *noumena* is intentional.

[16] I. Copi, *Symbolic Logic* (4th edn., 1973), p. 72.

[17] On the notion of burdens and presumptions, a good source is a text on evidence in law. I have profitted in the following from *McCormick on Evidence* (2nd ed., 1972), sections 337, 343.

[18] Indeed, the "free market" system is also a function. Such a function is justified typically in those cases which Singer calls invertible. That is, although undesirable consequences would result from everyone's entering a certain business, for example, they would also result from nobody's entering the field. It would be justified also only to the extent that not so many, and not so few, do the act as to cause undesirable consequences.

[19] See n. 8 *supra*, pp. 449–53.

[20] See n. 5 *supra*.

[21] E. Ullman-Margalit, n. 14 *supra*, at 515–17.

[22] Judgment and the *use* of moral principles has been a relatively neglected field of philosophical inquiry. Nevertheless, there are indications that greater emphasis will be placed on moral practice in the future. See, e.g., R. Stevens, *Kant on Moral Practice* (1981).

NORMAN GILLESPIE

MORAL REASONS AND THE GENERALIZATION TEST
IN ETHICS

I

In *Forms and Limits of Utilitarianism* (Oxford, 1965), David Lyons argues that for any principle which emphasizes consequences (either the promotion of desirable results or the avoidance of undesirable consequences), it is the *causal properties* of individual acts that are relevant, since it is in virtue of those properties that acts have consequences, and other properties such as 'performed on Tuesday' or 'performed by a red-headed person' are irrelevant.[1] On this view, it matters not *how we describe* or *refer* to individual acts; it is their causal properties, not our description of them, that identify them for purposes of evaluation.

The generalization test, 'What if everyone did that?', applies to individual acts with specific threshold-related effects.[2] We are asked to consider *everyone's* doing an act with *that* threshold-related effect — in effect, to use the formula $T = n \times e$, in which the number of persons included within the scope of 'everyone' provides the value for n, and the threshold-related effect of the particular act in question supplies the value for e. If T (the total effect) is undesirable, the generalization test concludes that the individual act with *that* threshold-related effect ought not to be done. When the product of $n \times e$ is not undesirable, the act in question is morally permissible. In a community suffering a water-shortage, drinking a glass of water would have a *smaller* threshold-related effect than taking a bath. Both acts (would) contribute to the production of the same threshold effect (in this case, the disappearance of the available water), but if the *generalized* threshold-related effect of drinking a glass of water (in these circumstances) is not undesirable, while the *generalized* threshold-related effect of taking a bath (in those circumstances) is undesirable, then the former is permissible and the latter is not according to this argument, *and* the two acts are relevantly different.

This disparity in judgment is sufficient to indicate that in some cases at least a shared contribution to a common threshold effect is insufficient to render two acts relevantly similar as far as the generalization test (GT) is concerned. So, to be relevantly similar for that test, two acts' individual threshold-related effects must not only *contribute* to the production of the

285

Nelson Potter and Mark Timmons (eds.), Morality and Universality, 285–295.
© 1985 *by D. Reidel Publishing Company.*

same threshold effect, they must also be *similar* in magnitude, i.e. either sufficient, when generalized, to produce that collective consequence, or insufficient to do so. Thus, two individual acts are relevantly similar for generalization in ethics when:

(i)   both acts contribute, or would contribute if performed, to the production of the same threshold effect; and

(ii)   each act, if generalized, would produce (or would fail to produce) that threshold effect.

This criterion of relevant similarity is specific, and it deliberately does not speak to the issue of whether individual acts that satisfy these two conditions can have other morally relevant features. If an act's undesirable generalized threshold-related effect is *one* of its morally significant properties, it need not be its *only* such property. An act prescribed by the generalization test may have sufficient morally redeeming features on other grounds to warrant making an exception to the *prima facie* conclusion supported by the application of the generalization test to this act. The generalization test provides one reason why a certain act ought not to be done, but that reason can be outweighed by other morally relevant considerations.

II

Many apparent counter-examples result from applying the generalization test to acts and activities that we normally regard as permissible, i.e. acts which everyone has the right to engage in or not, as he chooses. The obvious move, then, is to substitute 'What if everyone had the right to do that?' for the question 'What if everyone did not?' Or, to put it another way, we can ask "What if a relevantly specified type of act, A, were permissible?" The significant difference between these generalization tests is that everyone can *have the right* to do something without *exercising* that right, while the standard generalization test envisions *everyone's doing* the type of act in question. The standard version is ineffective when the number of persons likely to engage in a certain type of activity or perform a specific type of act is so small that undesirable consequences are not going to result from everyone's being permitted to do such things. Thus, if everyone *refrained* from having children, the consequences would be undesirable; but they would not be so, if everyone has the *right* to so act, since relatively few people will exercise that right. And the same is true of being a student, teaching philosophy and taking books out of the library (although here, an upper limit may be required). So, as far as the revised generalization test is concerned, everyone should have those rights, and individuals who exercise them are not acting wrongly. One important step, therefore, in reformulating the generalization test in ethics is to note that: If the collective consequences of A's being permitted (or of everyone's having the right to do A) would not be undesirable, then A is not impermissible as far as the revised generalization test is concerned.[3] And the basic principle for the revised generalization test is:

(RGT)   If the collective consequences of A's being permissible would be undesirable, then A ought not to be permissible.

With this principle in hand, we can return to the formula $T = n \times e$, and appreciate that what this revision accomplishes is to alter the way in which the value of n is determined. The ordinary language version of GT either does not take into account the *frequency* with which people do the act in question, or it simply assumes that each person will so act just once. In any case, the frequency with which e-type acts would be performed in the absence of any (or further) restrictions is causally relevant since if the incidence of e is less than k, the total required to produce an undesirable collective consequence, then that collective consequence will not result. So this factor is causally relevant for the generalization test and should be taken into account. This point has seemed controversial to many writers on the subject, but it is indisputable that n is really the *incidence* of the act in question, and simply using the *number* of persons included within the scope of 'everyone' as the indication of its value generates numerous counterexamples. The revised generalization test uses the likely incidence of e-type acts in the absence of any rules or restrictions limiting or prohibiting such acts as the source of the value of n, and thus avoids several standard counterexamples to generalization arguments.

III

The most common response to the question 'What if everyone did that?' is that 'Not everyone *will* do it.' Some philosophers believe that if the actions of others are taken into account, the generalization test collapses into simple act utilitarianism, and many rely upon Lyons' argument in *Forms and Limits* to support this view. In that book, Lyons' purpose is to demonstrate on strictly utilitarian grounds that analogous versions of act utilitarianism and utilitarian generalization are extensionally equivalent. In the following passage, however, it is not that overall strategy and its consequences that are in question, only the issue of how including the actions of others in the relevant description for the generalization test affects or limits the conclusions one obtains in employing that test. This, I should emphasize, is the only point at issue in this passage and in my subsequent remarks. Lyons writes:

> It may appear that adding predicates like 'performed when the practice of A is not general' is logically unacceptable, a paradoxical condition. Perhaps it seems as if the test we employ, in taking others' behavior into acount in the way I have proposed, is 'What would happen if everyone did A when the practice of A is not general?' Or to put it more sharply: 'What would happen if the practice of A were general when in fact the practice of A is not general?' – 'What would happen if everyone did A when in fact not everyone does A?'
>
> These certainly sound paradoxical – the suppositions seem self-contradictory. But the foregoing questions are not accurate renderings of the test I propose to make, which is 'What would happen if everyone *who had occasion to do so* did A *under these circumstances*, when not everyone is doing A (when the practice of A is not general)?' The supposition is, not that everyone will do A, for that everyone who has occasion to do A will do A, but rather that everyone who has occasion to do $A\overline{C}$ will do $A\overline{C}$. The condition $\overline{C}$, that A is not generally performed, rules out the possibility that everyone who has occasion to do A will have occasion to do $A\overline{C}$. This is precisely the sort of condition we require – and there is nothing paradoxical about it.[4]

This distinction between AC and $A\overline{C}$ can be made: the issue is whether it is relevant for the generalization test. The normal cases in which one employs that test are those in which there is *not* a general practice of similar acts, and the question asks us to consider what is only a hypothetical general practice of such acts. So the addition of $\overline{C}$ to A does indicate the context in which one would normally employ the generalization test; and Lyons contends that this fact limits its scope and force. His basic idea is that only a limited number of acts can be performed which are accurately described as $A\overline{C}$, so that if $A\overline{C}$ is the true description of an individual act, then if everyone who could were to do an act so described, the consequences could not be undesirable. He says, " . . . the effective scope of the term 'everyone' depends upon the given description of the act: it is restricted to that class of persons each of whom will have occasion to do the sort of thing specified, to each of whom such a course of action is or will be a practical possibility".[5] Yet, the number of persons for whom $A\overline{C}$ is a practical possibility is not limited simply to those persons who perform such an act; it includes, as well, all those persons who *fail* to do it. Take a simple case: suppose 2,000 persons pass the local courthouse lawn, and could cross it directly from point *a* to point *b*. Suppose also that 500 do so, and that number is insufficient to produce a threshold effect. So there is not a general practice of such crossings, and $A\overline{C}$ is the accurate description of each of them. For how many persons, then, is $A\overline{C}$ a practical possibility? The answer is obviously 2,000, and if all of them *were* to do it, C, instead of $\overline{C}$, *would* be true. The fact that $\overline{C}$ obtains does not limit what *could*, and *would*, be true, if everyone for whom $A\overline{C}$ is a practical possibility were to realize that possibility. So, adding $\overline{C}$ to A in no way seems to limit the scope of 'everyone' or the force of the generalization test. Lyons' relevant description would have that effect only if the number of persons who could do $A\overline{C}$ is always less than the total required to produce a threshold effect. Since $\overline{C}$ indicates what people *will* do and not what they *could* do, there will be many cases in which more than that many persons could (but do not) do $A\overline{C}$.

In this challenge to Lyons' argument, I agree with him that the question to be considered is: 'What if everyone who could were to do $A\overline{C}$?' and that the pivotal issue is his contention that the presence of $\overline{C}$ in that question effectively limits its scope to those possible worlds that share $\overline{C}$ with the actual world. Yet three essential issues remain to be resolved: (i) How does the *relevance* of $\overline{C}$ for the generalization test *restrict*, if at all, the possible worlds to which it appeals? (ii) Are the *unperformed* possible instances of A in this world C or $\overline{C}$? and (iii) Should the generalization test be read *de re* or *de dicto*? I shall consider each of these questions, and argue that the correct answer to each undermine Lyons' argument.

The answer to the question: are the *unperformed* possible instances of A, C or $\overline{C}$? should be straightforward given Lyons' reliance upon objective utilitarianism in making his argument. We are dealing in each case either with a C-world or with a $\overline{C}$-world, and only one of those predicates, never both, is true of any particular world. Yet, Lyons says explicitly that " ... even if the threshold (effect) is not produced, C will be true of a sufficient number of acts which could be performed but are not performed".[6] He makes this claim without considering the possible worlds appealed to in that contention. Under what conditions, then, is C true of the unperformed possible instances of A? In a world in which sufficient instances of A occur, C is true; and in a world with less than that total, $\overline{C}$ obtains. And one would think that it obtains for all possible instances of A, performed and unperformed, in that world. The only problematical case for this thesis – that $\overline{C}$ (or C, if it is true in the actual world) holds uniformly for *all* the possible instance of A – arises when there is an act that would be, if performed, the threshold instance of A, so that its being done would make C true of all the acts that are $\overline{C}$. But this case is not problematic once one specifies the world under consideration and whether the act in question is A or $\overline{A}$ (i.e. performed or unperformed) in that world. If it is $\overline{A}$, it is also $\overline{C}$; if it is A, it is also C; and this is true of each act in such a pivotal position.

Lyons' assumption of objective utilitarianism grounds his use of C and $\overline{C}$, and once it is determined that the actual world is a C-world, or that it is $\overline{C}$-world, the ascription of that predicate to all its A and $\overline{A}$ acts is straightforward. Lyons is simply mistaken, therefore, if he thinks that 'even if the threshold effect is not produced, C is true of a sufficient number of acts which could be performed but are not performed in this world". The uniformity thesis precludes that result. What Lyons may believe is that "if a sufficient number of acts which could be performed but are not performed *were to be performed*, then C would be true of each of them in that world W_2". That is true, but it has no bearing on whether $\overline{A}$ acts in a $\overline{C}$-world are C: they are not. So the answer to our question is that *all* the *possible* instances of A in any particular world share the predicate $\overline{C}$ (or C when it obtains): if the performed acts are $\overline{C}$, so are the unperformed ones.

How one should read the generalization test is equally straightforward, once one realizes that there are two ways to read it.[7] Lyons' interpretation is the equivalent of asking 'How many bachelors can be married?' and interpreting that question as asking: How many individuals can simultaneously be bachelors and married? Lyons' version of the generalization test is: How many possible instances of A can simultaneously be $\overline{C}$ and performed? The answer to the first of these questions is none; and the answer to the second is less than K. The *de re* reading of the bachelor question, however, is: What if all the individuals, who are bachelors, were to marry? And the *de re* reading of the generalization test is: What if all the possible instances of A, which are $\overline{C}$, were to be performed? The answer to each of these questions is that there would be no bachelors left, and that all those acts would be C.

The generalization test does not propose to consider how many individual acts can simultaneously be performed and $\overline{C}$, since it would be pointless for it to do so. Indeed, the use of 'that' (one of Russell's "logically proper names") in GT is manifestly a *de re* reference to the act in question; and if the generalization test proposes to consider all the *unperformed* possible instances of A (in this world) as being *performed* in W_2, why can it not do the same with $\overline{C}$, i.e. consider all the possible instances of A that are $\overline{C}$ (in this world) as being C in W_2? If Lyons' *de dicto* reading of the generalization test precludes that result, the obvious solution is to jettison that reading, not the generalization test itself. Hence the answer to this question is that all versions of the generalization test in ethics should be read *de re*.

Lyons' attempt to hold $\overline{C}$ rigid stems from his having argued that the actions and inactions of others are morally relevant for act utilitarianism and for the generalization test. He believes that on strictly utilitarian grounds the relevance for each is the same, which as we shall see, it is not; and he never considers how questions such as GT normally function, e.g. whether the use of $\overline{C}$ as a *relevant* identifying property of the individual acts in question entails hold $\overline{C}$ *constant* in the possible world invoked by that test. Lyons proposes to use $A\overline{C}$ to determine the scope of 'everyone', just as one would use 'the Queen of England' in the question "What if the Queen of England were not the Queen of England?" to select the individual in question, and the property of being six feet tall in selecting the subjects of "What if everyone six feet tall were ten feet tall?" Yet, with the latter questions, one does not hold *constant* in the envisioned possible worlds the *relevant properties* for identifying the individual(s) in question, since those are the very properties the questions ask us to consider changed. So the relevance of a particular property, p, for such a question does not entail holding it constant in the possible world postulated by that question.[8] And the same is true of $\overline{C}$.

Lyons' method is most transparent when he considers the property 'knowing that less than K instances of A will occur'. He says, "The condition that one knows that the practice of A is not (and will not be) general precludes that it become general. . . . "[9] Once again, reference to possible worlds blunts Lyons' use of this claim. Suppose 5,000 persons know that less than 2,000 instances of A will occur in W_1. What if all these knowledgeable persons were to do A? The question envisions a world, W_2, in which those 5,000 persons do A, and the knowledge used to identify those individuals in W_1 is not maintained as one of the properties of those agents in W_2. So while that knowledge may preclude A's being general in W_1, it has no such effect in W_2, and the appeal of the generalization test to W_2 is not precluded by the fact that in W_1 all the individuals in question know that the undesirable collective consequences will not ensue there.

An act utilitarian would consider only those "near" possible worlds in which the actions of others are held constant; but the generalization test explicitly invokes the relatively "distant" possible world in which all the possible unperformed instances of A that are $\overline{C}$ in the actual world are performed. The advocate of utilitarian generalization cites those hypothetical consequences as the basis for concluding that one should not perform the act in question. And there is nothing about $\overline{C}$ that prevents him from doing so. In the next and concluding section of this paper, I shall distinguish utilitarian generalization from what I take to be a morally sound interpretation of the generalization test. But since the appeal of the former to a possible world in which all the $\overline{C}$ acts (here) are C (there) is a part of that sound interpretation, it is important to see that simply including $\overline{C}$ in the relevant description of the act in question does not, by itself, reduce the generalization test to its act utilitarian analogue. Only the *de dicto* reading of the resulting question provides that impression; and as we have seen, a utilitarian generalizer can and should eschew that reading. Contrary to Lyons' conclusions in the passage cited earlier, the number of possible instances of $A\overline{C}$ in a $\overline{C}$ world is the same as the number of possible instances of A; the relevance of $\overline{C}$ for the generalization test does not preclude its being false in the possible world that test invokes; and the *de re* reading of the generalization test is the appropriate one for capturing its sense and moral force.

IV

C or $\overline{C}$ indicates the context in which one acts, while A or $\overline{A}$ indicates how you perform in that context. $\overline{C}$ indicates that less than the requisite number of persons are doing (or will do) A, so that if undesirable consequences would result if everyone who could were to do $A\overline{C}$, then we know that in the actual world those consequences are merely hypothetical. C. D. Broad rejects the generalization test for this reason, on the grounds that it is insufficiently utilitarian,[10] but it turns out to be one of its most noteworthy features.

In *Catch-22*, when Yossarian refuses to fly additional combat missions, someone asks him " . . . suppose everybody of our side felt that way?" He replies, "Then I'd be a damn fool to feel any other way, wouldn't I?"[11] Yossarian interprets the question 'What if everyone did that?' as postulating his act taking place in a context in which everyone else is acting as he is. But of course he is not so situated – in his world everyone else is flying their missions – and his questioner knows that as well as Yossarian. So the point of the generalization test is not what Yossarian would have us think it is. That test postulates a world in which everyone acts in a certain way, not to ask how one would or should act in that world, but to contrast that world with this world to make several points: (i) This world is preferable to that hypothetical world; (ii) it is the general practice of individuals acting in a certain way that creates this desirable set of circumstances; and (iii) Yossarian's conduct is contrary to this desirable general practice. If we distinguish the question: What should the general practice be? from the question: what are the moral duties and obligations of individuals in relation to the general practice? then we can begin to realize that the answer to the former does not settle the latter,[12] and that it is the *contrast* between A and $\overline{C}$ (or between $\overline{A}$ and C) that is essential for GT. For, as we shall see, it is this contrast that explains why in some cases individuals are morally obligated not to act contrary to the general practice.

The desirable and undesirable consequences that the generalization test contrasts are not any set of consequences; they involve, instead, the actions and related consequences of a group of individuals. Rousseau claimed that: "The undertakings which bind us to the social body are obligatory only because they are mutual; and their nature is such that in fulfilling them we cannot work for others without working for ourselves."[13] The generalization test, unlike generalized utilitarianism, morally *obligates* individuals to perform *only* those acts that satisfy Rousseau's *mutuality* requirement *for obligations*. In this respect, it is quite distinct from any form of utilitarianism that fails to appreciate that not just any set of desirable consequences give rise to moral obligations. The distinctive ·feature of the generalization test in ethics is that when the collective consequences it seeks to avoid are merely hypothetical (or will remain so if one does his part), then, "one cannot work for others without working for himself".

There are three conditions for such an obligation:

(i)   One's act has an undesirable generalized threshold-related effect.
(ii) There is a general practice of not doing such acts.
(iii) That general practice is due to the restraint of others.

With the reformulated generalization test, conditions (i) and (ii) ensure (iii) because of how that test determines whether condition (i) is satisfied. Recall that with that test the value of n is determined by how many people would act in a certain way in the absence of restrictions on their doing so, so that one's act has an undesirable generalized threshold-related effect, according to the principle RGT, only when the number of people who would exercise the right to act in a certain way is sufficient to produce a threshold effect. Hence whenever condition (i) is met, some restraints will be in effect if condition (ii) is also true. Thus conditions (i) and (ii) entail (iii), and when all three obtain, one's acting contrary to the general practice in those circumstances would be unfair in that it takes advantage of the restraint of others. This unfairness is not present when others are not restraining themselves, e.g. when C is true.

So while the context in which one acts, i.e. C or $\overline{C}$, is morally relevant for generalization in ethics, its significance is not what it is for act utilitarianism. The *moral* point of the generalization test in ethics is *not* that your act will, either individually or as part of a general practice, produce undesirable consequences, but that it is unfair. Postulating a possible world in which A is generally done, or generally permitted, is only the initial part of that test. The second step involves the realization that those undesirable consequences are *merely hypothetical* because of the restraint of others. The generalization test reminds you of what would be true without those restraints to suggest that your act may be exploiting them unfairly.

The four elements, then, required to transform a natural fact into a moral property via the generalization test are: (1) the act in question has an undesirable generalized threshold-related effect, (2) other acts of that type are not being generally performed, (3) people are restraining themselves or being restrained, and (4) you fail to exercise similar restraint. There is, in this analysis, no single natural fact that is identical with wrongness. But items (2)–(4) are empirically ascertainable; the generalized threshold-related effect of an act is a natural fact (even if its undesirability is not); and the unfairness which makes the act *prima facie* wrong emerges in the relation between (3) and (4). So the act's moral property is not simply the result of its having an undesirable generalized threshold-related effect, as a utilitarian generalizer would allege. Instead, the full argument for that moral property relies not only upon the principle RGT to indicate both what the general practice should be and whether condition (1) is met, but also upon conditions (2), (3) and (4) as well. So the generalization test in ethics is not simply nor strictly utilitarian. If it were, there would be no moral point to it.[14]

Department of Philosophy,
Memphis State University

NOTES

[1] David Lyons, *Forms and Limits of Utilitarianism* (Oxford, 1965), pp. 57–61.
[2] A threshold-related effect is the contribution an act makes to the production of a threshold effect. The latter is the cumulative effect, such as a path in the grass, produced by many individual acts. Lyons seems to require that the threshold effect be produced for individual acts to have a threshold-related effect (cf. pp. 72–77). As I am using the term 'threshold-related effect', individual acts have such effects, i.e. contribute toward the production of a threshold effect, whether the latter is realized or not.
[3] In "Moral Rules and the Generalization Argument", *American Philosophical Quarterly*, 1966, pp. 282–90), Alexander Sesonske notes that Marcus Singer relies upon the idea that 'if the consequences of everyone's doing x would not be undesirable, then x is not wrong' (*Generalization in Ethics* (New York, 1961), p. 284). Singer would insist that this inference holds only as far as his generalization argument is concerned, intending to

leave open whether x might still be wrong on some other grounds. However, if you also claim, as Singer does, that one's principle is *the* fundamental principle for *all* moral reasoning, then Sesonske is right: if, according to the fundamental principle of morality, x is not wrong, then it is not wrong. On my analysis, GT is one test of an act's morality, but not the only one, nor the fundamental one. So when I say that something is not wrong as far as RGT is concerned, I deliberately leave open whether it might be wrong on other grounds.

4 Lyons, *op. cit.*, p. 107. This, of course, is not Lyons' entire argument. It is only that portion which contains the conclusion that I wish to challenge in this paper.

5 *Ibid.*, p. 31.

6 *Ibid.*, p. 93.

7 In a *de dicto* reading, one focuses on the predicate ('bachelor' and '$\overline{C}$' in these examples) and asks: how many other predicates are compatible with it? With a *de re* reading, one focuses on the individual and asks: can *it* be, say, C instead of $\overline{C}$, or married instead of unmarried?

8 Cf. Saul Kripke, "Naming and Necessity", in *Semantics and Natural Languages*, ed. by Donald Davidson and Gilbert Harman (Dordrecht Holland, 1972), pp. 270–79, where Kripke discusses questions of this kind.

9 Lyons, *op. cit.*, p. 112.

10 C. D. Broad, "On the Function of False Hypotheses in Ethics", *The International Journal of Ethics*, 1915–16, p. 378.

11 Joseph Heller, *Catch-22* (New York, 1961), Ch. ix.

12 Richard Brandt's "Ideal Rule Utilitarianism" seems to assume the contrary: that the answer to the former question does determine what individuals are morally obligated to do. (See his *A Theory of the Good and the Right*.)

13 Jean-Jacques Rousseau, *The Social Contract*, Book II, Ch. 4, para. 5.

14 There are complications involving the comparative benefits and costs in restricting individual behavior to create a desirable general practice, which I have not discussed. For a partial discussion – especially regarding the fairness of such restrictions – see Robert Nozick, *Anarchy, State and Utopia* (New York, 1974), pp. 90–95; and Brian Barry, "The Public Interest", in *Political Philosophy* (Oxford, 1967), ed. by Anthony Quinton. Nozick's counterexample in that section to Hart's "fairness argument" depends crucially upon the relative insignificance of the "good" created by the cooperative practice (consider what we would say of his example if it were the daily water supply instead of daily incidental public amusement that were at issue).

There are also cases in which both the collective consequences of A's being permitted and of its being prohibited would be undesirable, and this may seem to pose a problem for RGT. One has only to remember, however, that RGT supports *prima facie* conclusions to realize that here, too, one is faced with two *prima facie* indications of what ought not to be done. So "invertibility" is not a sign that the revised generalization test is inapplicable; one is simply confronted with a special case of conflicting *prima facie* conclusions. A generalized version of RGT in which 'prohibited' is substitutable for 'permissible' supports the conclusion that a solution be found that avoids *both sets* of undesirable consequences. So distributional arrangements that permit some but not all to do x need not be counterexamples to RGT, and typically "first come, first served" is used to handle such cases.

SELECT BIBLIOGRAPHY

PART I: BOOKS

Austin, J.: 1832, *The Province of Jurisprudence Determined*, H. L. A. Hart, ed., reprinted by Weidenfelt and Nicholson, London, 1954 (Lecture II).

Baier, K.: 1958, *The Moral Point of View: A Rational Basis of Ethics*, Cornell University Press, Ithaca, New York.

Becker, L.: 1973, *On Justifying Moral Judgments*, Routledge & Kegan Paul, London (Ch. 11).

Bedau, H. (ed.): 1971, *Justice and Equality*, Prentice Hall, Inc., Englewood Cliffs, New Jersey.

Blum, L. A.: 1980, *Friendship, Altruism and Morality*, Routledge & Kegan Paul, London (Ch. 5).

Brandt, Richard B.: 1979, *A Theory of the Good and the Right*, Clarendon Press, Oxford (pp. 278–85).

—: 1959, *Ethical Theory*, Englewood Cliffs, N. J., Prentice-Hall, Inc. (Ch. 2).

Dihle, Albrecht: 1962, *Die Goldene Regel. Eine Einfuhrung in die Geschichte der antiken und fruhchristlichen Vulgarethic*. Göttingen.

Donagan, A.: 1977, *The Theory of Morality*, The University of Chicago Press, Chicago (pp. 57–66).

Dorman, Neil A.: 1967, *Generalization in Ethics*, doctoral dissertation, Xerox, University Microfilms, Ann Arbor, Michigan, Order No. 67-12418.

Emmet, Dorothy: 1966, *Rules, Roles and Relations*, St. Martin's Press, New York (pp. 59ff., 75ff.).

Ewing, A. C.: 1959, *Second Thoughts in Moral Philosophy*, The Macmillan Company, New York (pp. 145–49).

Flathman, Richard E.: 1966, *The Public Interest*, John Wiley & Sons, New York (Ch. 8).

Fowler, Thomas: 1884, *Progressive Morality*, Macmillan and Co., London (pp. 75ff. passim).

—: 1887, *The Principles of Morals*, Part II, Clarendon Press, Oxford (pp. 244–59).

Gewirth, A.: 1978, *Reason and Morality*, The University of Chicago Press, Chicago.

Gillespie, Norman: 1970, *Fundamental Moral Principles*, doctoral dissertation, Xerox University Microfilms, Ann Arbor, Michigan, Order No. 75-03458.

Goldman (Smith), Holly: 1972, *The Generalization Principle in Ethics*, doctoral dissertation, Xerox University Microfilms, Ann Arbor, Michigan, Order No. 73-11125.

Hancock, R. N.: 1974, *Twentieth Century Ethics*, Columbia University Press, New York and London (Chs. 5 & 7).

Hare, R. M.: 1952, *The Language of Morals*, Oxford University Press, London.

—: 1963, *Freedom and Reason*, Oxford University Press, Oxford.

—: 1981, *Moral Thinking: Its Levels, Method and Point*, The Clarendon Press, Oxford (see esp. Ch. 6).

Nelson Potter and Mark Timmons (eds.), Morality and Universality, 297–306.

Harrison, J.: 1971, *Our Knowledge of Right and Wrong*, Allen and Unwin, Ltd., The Humanities Press, London (Ch. 8 and pp. 158ff., 327ff., 369ff.).

Hartland-Swann, J.: 1960, *An Analysis of Morals*, Allen and Unwin, London (pp. 39–42, and Ch. 4, Sec. 4, pp. 84–9).

Hospers, John: 1982, *Human Conduct*, Second Edition, Harcourt Brace Jovanovich, New York (Ch. 6, Sec. 2, pp. 212–16).

Kampe, C.: 1974, *Universalizability in Ethics*, doctoral dissertation, Queen's University, Ontario, Canada.

Kant, I.: 1785, *Groundwork to the Metaphysics of Morals*, Trans. H. J. Paton, Harper & Row, 1956, New York.

—: 1797, *The Metaphysical Elements of Virtue*, Part II of *The Metaphysics of Morals*, Trans. Mary Gregor, Harper & Row, 1964, New York.

Lyons, D.: 1965, *Forms and Limits of Utilitarianism*, The Clarendon Press, Oxford.

Mackie, J. L.: 1977, *Ethics: Inventing Right and Wrong*, Penguin Books, Ltd., Harmodsworth, Middlesex, England (Ch. 4).

Mayo, B.: 1958, *Ethics and the Moral Life*, Macmillan, New York.

Monro, D. H.: 1977, *Empiricism and Ethics*, Cambridge University Press, London (Chs. 13–16).

Nagel, T.: 1970, *The Possibility of Altruism*, Clarendon Press, Oxford.

Narveson, J.: 1967, *Morality and Utility*, The Johns Hopkins Press, Baltimore, Maryland (Ch. 5, esp. pp. 129–40).

O'Neill (Nell), O.: 1975, *Acting on Principle: An Essay on Kantian Ethics*, Columbia University Press, New York and London.

Paley, William: 1785, *The Principles of Moral and Political Philosophy*, 7th ed., 1790, R. Faulder, London (Vol. I. Bk. II, Chs. VI, VII, VIII).

Pollock, Lansing: 1971, *Reciprocity in Moral Theory*, doctoral dissertation, University of Chicago.

Potter, N. T. and Timmons, M., eds.: 1985, *Morality and Universality*, D. Reidel, Dordrecht, Holland.

Rabinowicz, W.: 1979, *Universalizability: A Study in Morals and Metaphysics*, D. Reidel, Dordrecht, Holland.

Rawls, John: 1971, *A Theory of Justice*, Harvard University Press, Cambridge, Massachusetts.

Schrag, B. E.: 1975, *Universalizability and the Concept of Morality*, doctoral dissertation, Xerox University Microfilms, Ann Arbor, Michigan, Order No. 76-119.

Sidgwick, H.: 1907, *Methods of Ethics* (7th edition), Macmillan and Co., Ltd., London (Bk. III, Ch. I, Sec. 3; Ch. V, Secs. 1 and 2; Ch. VII, Sec. 3, Ch. XIII, Sec. 3 and 4; Bk. IV, Ch. III, Sec. 4; Ch. 5, Sec. 3).

Singer, M. G.: 1961, *Generalization in Ethics: An Essay in the Logic of Ethics with the Rudiments of a System of Moral Philosophy*, Alfred Knopf, Inc., New York.

Sobel, J. H.: 1961, *What If Everyone Did That?*, doctoral dissertation, Xerox University Microfilms, An Arbor, Michigan, Order No. 61-02796.

Taylor, P. W.: 1975, *Principles of Ethics: An Introduction*, Dickenson Publishing Co., Inc., Encino, California (Ch. 5).

Wimmer, R.: *Universalisierung in der Ethik: Analyse, Kritik and Rekonstruktion ethischer Rationalitatsanspruche*, Suhrkamp Verlag, Frankfurt am Main.

Winch, P.: 1972, *Ethics and Action*, Routledge & Kegan Paul, London (Ch. 8).

PART II. ARTICLES AND REVIEWS

Adams, E. M.: 1980, 'Gewirth on Reason and Morality', *Review of Metaphysics* **33**, 579–92.

Agrawal, M. M.: 1976, 'Universalizability and Argument in Morals', *Second Order* **5**, 67–74.

Atwell, J.: 1967, 'A Note on Decisions, Judgments and Universalizability', *Ethics* **77**, 130–34.

—: 1969, 'Are Kant's First Two Moral Principles Equivalent?', *Journal of the History of Philosophy* **7**, 273–84.

Bach, Kent: 1976–77, 'When to Ask, "What if Everyone Did That?"', *Philosophy and Phenomenological Research* **37**, 464–81.

Baier, Kurt: 1954, 'The Point of View of Morality', *Australasian Journal of Philosophy* **32**, 104–35.

—: 1978, 'Moral Reasons', in French, P. A., *et. al.*, eds., *Midwest Studies in Philosophy*, 62–74.

Blackstone, W. T.: 1965, 'The Golden Rule: A Defense', *Southern Journal of Philosophy*, Winter, 172–77.

—: 1966–67, 'On the Meaning and Justification of the Equality Principle', *Ethics* **77**, 239–53.

Blegvad, Mogens: 1964, 'Equality, Utility, and Moral Rules', *Danish Yearbook of Philosophy* **1**, 23–36.

Blum, R. P.: 1970, 'Review of *Forms and Limits of Utilitarianism*', *Journal of Value Inquiry* **4**, 140–52.

—: 1970, 'The True Function of the Generalization Argument', *Inquiry* **13**, 274–88.

Bond, E. J.: 1980, 'Gewirth on Reason and Morality', *Metaphilosophy* **11**, 36–53.

Braybrooke, David: 1962, 'Collective and Distributive Generalization in Ethics', *Analysis* **23**, 45–8.

Broad, C. D.: 1916, 'On the Function of False Hypotheses in Ethics', *International Journal of Ethics* **26**, 377–97.

Brock, Dan W.: 1973, 'Recent Work in Utilitarianism', *American Philosophical Quarterly* **10**, 241–76 at 258–62.

Brockhaus, Richard R. and Hochberg, Gary M.: 1975, 'The Generalization Argument Revisited', *Philosophical Studies* **28**, 123–29.

Brody, Baruch.: 1967, 'The Equivalence of Act and Rule Utilitarianism', *Philosophical Studies* **18**, 81–7.

Brunton, J. A.: 1966, 'Restricted Moralities', *Philosophy* **41**, 113–26.

Buchanan, James W. and Tullock, Gordon: 1964, 'Economic Analogues of the Generalization Argument', *Ethics* **74**, 300–01.

Cadoux, A. T.: 1912, 'The Implications of the Golden Rule', *The International Journal of Ethics* **22**, 272–87.

Cargile, James: 1965, 'The Universalizability of Lying', *Australasian Journal of Philosophy* **43**, 229–31.

Castaneda, H-N.: 1966, 'Imperatives, Oughts, and Moral Oughts', *Australasian Journal of Philosophy* **44**, 277–300.

Caton, C. E.: 1963, 'In What Sense and Why "Ought" Judgments are Universalizable', *Philosophical Quarterly* **13**, 48–55.

Cohen, Brenda: 1967, 'An Ethical Paradox', *Mind* 76, 250–59.
Cottingham, J.: 1983, 'Ethics and Impartiality', *Philosophical Studies* 43, 83–99.
Curtler, Hugh M.: 1971, 'What Kant Might Say to Hare', *Mind* 80, 295–97.
Dietrichson, P.: 1964, 'Kant's Criteria of Universalizability', *Kant-Studien* 55, 143–70.
—: 1964, 'When Is a Maxim Fully Universalizable?', *Kant-Studien* 55, 143–70.
Dorman, Neil A.: 1964, 'The Refutation of the Generalization Argument', *Ethics* 74, 150–54.
Duncan-Jones, A. E.: 1955, 'Kant and Universalization', *Analysis* 16, 12–14.
Dworkin, Gerald: 1974, 'Non-Neutral Principles', *Journal of Philosophy* 71, 491–506.
Edgely, R.: 1962, 'Impartiality and Consistency', *Philosophy* 37, 158–63.
—: 1965, 'Practical Reasons', *Mind* 74, 174–91.
Eggerman, Richard W.: 1972, 'Invertibility Revisited', *Philosophical Studies* 23, 424–26.
—: 1972, 'The Normative Significance of Moral Universalization', *Southwestern Journal of Philosophy* 3, 141–47.
Ehring, D.: 1977, 'A Defence of Lyons' Reductive Thesis', *Kinesis* 8, 26–43.
Ellett, Jr., Frederick S., *et. al.*: 1978–79, 'Moral Reasoning, Needs Assessment and Universalizability', *Philosophical Education Proceedings*, 199–207.
Emmet, Dorothy: 1963, 'Universalisability and Moral Judgment', *Philosophical Quarterly* 13, 214–28.
Ezorsky, Gertrude: 1963, 'Review of *Generalization in Ethics*', *Journal of Philosophy* 60, 12.
—: 1968, 'A Defence of Rule Utilitarianism Against David Lyons who insists on tieing it to Act Utilitarianism, plus a brand new way of checking out General Utilitarian Properties', *Journal of Philosophy* 65, 553–54.
—: 1974, 'It's Mine', *Philosophy and Public Affairs* 3, 327–30.
Ewing, A. C.: 1953, 'What Would Happen if Everybody Acted Like Me?', *Philosophy* 28, 16–29.
—: 1964, 'Hare and the Universalization Principle', *Philosophy* 39, 71–4.
Feinberg, Joel: 1967, 'The Forms and Limits of Utilitarianism', *Philosophical Review* 76, 368–81.
Feldman, Fred: 1974, 'On the Extensional Equivalence of Simple and General Utilitarianism', *Nous* 8, 185–94.
Fisher, John.: 1974, 'Universalizability and Judgments of Taste', *American Philosophical Quarterly* 11, 219–25.
Flathman, Richard E.: 1967, 'Equality and Generalization: A Formal Analysis', *Equality*, J. R. Pennock & J. W. Chapman, eds., *Nomos IX*, Atherton Press, New York, pp. 38–60.
Fowley, H. H.: 1951, 'The Chinese Sages and the Golden Rule', *Submission in Suffering and other Essays on Eastern Thought*, University of Wales Press, Cardiff, pp. 74–107.
Frohock, Fred M.: 1975, 'Individuals and Aggregates: The Generalization Argument Reconsidered', *Social Theory and Practice* 3, 343–66.
Fullinwinder, R.: 1977, 'Fanaticism and Hare's Moral Theory', *Ethics* 87, 165–81.
Garnett, A. Campbell: 1963, 'Virtues, Rules, and Good Reasons', *Monist* 47, 545–62.
—: 1964, 'A New Look at the Categorical Imperative', *Ethics* 74, 295–99.
Gellner, E. A.: 1954–55, 'Ethics and Logic', *Aristotelian Society Proceedings* 55, 157–78.
—: 1956, 'Morality and *Je Ne Sais Quoi* Concepts', *Analysis* 16, 97–103.

Gewirth, Alan: 1964, 'The Generalization Principle', *Philosophical Review* 73, 229–42.
—: 1967, 'Categorial Consistency in Ethics', *Philosophical Quarterly* 17, 289–99.
—: 1969, 'The Non-Trivializability of Universalizability', *Australasian Journal of Philosophy* 47, 123–31.
—: 1978, 'The Golden Rule Rationalized', *Midwest Studies in Philosophy* III, 133–47.
—: 1980, 'Reason and Morality: Rejoinder to E. J. Bond', *Metaphilosophy* 11, 138–42.
Gilbert, Joseph.: 1968, 'Interests, Role Reversal, Universalizability, and the Principle of Mutual Acknowledgement', in Kiefer and Munitz, eds., *Ethics and Social Justice* (Contemporary Philosophic Thought, Vol. IV), Albany, N. Y.
—: 1970, 'Features of Morality', *Personalist* 51, 470–76.
—: 1972, 'Neutrality and Universalizability', *Personalist* 53, 438–41.
Gillespie, Norman C.: 1974, 'A Valid Deduction of the Generalization Argument', *Ethics* 86, 87–91.
—: 1974, 'Exceptions to the Categorical Imperative', *Proceedings of the Fourth International Kant Congress, Mainz, Germany,* 2, 525–33.
—: 1975, 'On Treating Like Cases Differently', *Philosophical Quarterly* 25, 151–58.
—: 1977, 'Abortion and Human Rights', *Ethics* 87, 237–43.
Glass, Ronald: 1971, 'The Contradictions in Kant's Example', *Philosophical Studies* 22, 65–70.
Goldman, Holly, S.: 1974, 'David Lyons on Utilitarian Generalization', *Philosophical Studies* 26, 77–95.
—: 1978, 'The "Collective" Interpretation of Utilitarian Generalization', *Philosophical Studies* 34, 207–09.
Gould, James A.: 1963, 'The Not-So-Golden Rule', *Southern Journal of Philosophy* 1, 10–14.
—: 1981, 'Blackstone's Meta-Not-So-Golden Rule', *Southern Journal of Philosophy* 18, 509–13.
Gram, M. S.: 1967, 'Kant and Universalizability Once More and Again', *Kant-Studien* 58, 301–12.
Greenlee, Douglas: 1969, 'Oldenquist on Moral Judgments and Moral Principles', *Journal of Value Inquiry* 3, 49–51.
Griffiths, A. Phillips: 1962, 'Review of *Generalization in Ethics*', *Philosophical Books* 3, 18–21.
—: 1963, 'The Generalization Argument: A Reply to Mr. Braybrooke', *Analysis* 23, 113–15.
Gruzalski, Bart: 1981, 'Utilitarian Generalization, Competing Descriptions, and the Behavior of Others', *Canadian Journal of Philosophy* 11, 487–504.
—: 1982, 'The Defeat of Utilitarian Generalization', *Ethics* 93, 22–38.
Hare, R. M.: 1954–55, 'Universalisability', *Proceedings of the Aristotelian Society* 55, 295–312. Reprinted R. M. Hare: 1972, *Essays on the Moral Concepts*, University of California Press, Berkeley and Los Angeles.
—: 1962, 'Critical Study of *Generalization in Ethics*', *Philosophical Quarterly* 12, 351–55.
—: 1973, 'Principles', *Proceedings of the Aristotelian Society* 73, 1–18.
—: 1975, 'Abortion and the Golden Rule', *Philosophy and Public Affairs* 4, 201–22.
—: 1976, 'Ethical Theory and Utilitarianism', H. D. Lewis, ed., *Contemporary British Philosophy*, Vol. 4, Allen & Unwin, London.

—: 1978, 'Relevance', Goldman and Kim, eds., *Values and Morals*, D. Reidel, Dordrecht, Holland, pp. 73–90.

—: 1979, 'Universal and Past-tense Prescription: A Reply to Mr. Ibberson', *Analysis* **39**, 161–65.

Harman, G.: 1978, 'What is Moral Relativism?', *Values and Morals*, A. I. Goldman and J. Kim, eds., D. Reidel, Dordrecht, Holland, pp. 143–61.

Harrison, J.: 1952–53, 'Utilitarianism, Universalization, and Our Duty to be Just', *Proceedings of the Aristotelian Society* **53**, 105–34.

—: 1957, 'Kant's Examples of the First Formulation of the Categorical Imperative', *Philosophical Quarterly* **7**, 50–62.

—: 1958, 'The Categorical Imperative', *Philosophical Quarterly* **8**, 360–64.

—: 1979, 'Rule Utilitarianism and Cumulative-Effect Utilitarianism', *Canadian Journal of Philosophy* **5**, 21–45.

Harrod, R. F.: 1936, 'Utilitarianism Revised', *Mind* **14**, 137–56.

Hertzler, J. O.: 1934, 'On Golden Rules', *The International Journal of Ethics* **44**, 418–36.

Hochberg, G. M.: 1973, 'A Re-Examination of the Contradictions in Kant's Examples', *Philosophical Studies* **24**, 264–67.

Hoche, Hans-Ulrich: 1982, 'The Golden Rule: New Aspects of an Old Moral Principle', trans. by J. Claude Evans, *Contemporary German Philosophy*, Vol. I., D. E. Christensen, M. Riedel, R. Spaemann, R. Wiehl and W. Wieland, eds., The Pennsylvania University State Press, University Park and London.

Höffe, Otfried: 1977, 'Kants kategorischer Imperativ als Kriterium des Sittlichen', *Zeitschrift fur Philosophische Forschung* **31**, 354–84.

Holmes, Robert J.: 1963, 'On Generalization', *Journal of Philosophy* **60**, 317–22.

—: 1966, 'Descriptivism, Supervenience, and Universalizability', *Journal of Philosophy* **63**, 113–19.

Ibberson, John: 1979, 'A Doubt About Universal Prescriptivism', *Analysis* **39**, 153–58.

James, Edward W.: 1972, 'Working In And Working to Principles: Penn's Lie and Hare's Myth of Universalizability', *Ethics* **83**, 51–7.

Kalin, Jesse: 1968, 'A Note on Singer and Kant', *Ethics* **78**, 234–36.

Kavka, Gregory S.: 1975, 'Extensional Equivalence and Utilitarian Generalization', *Theoria* **41**, 125–47.

Kemp, J.: 1959, 'Kant's Examples of the Categorical Imperative', *Philosophical Quarterly* **8**, 63–71.

Kekes, J.: 1981, 'Morality and Impartiality', *American Philosophical Quarterly* **18**, 295–303.

Keyt, David: 1963, 'Singer's Generalization Argument', *Philosophical Review* **72**, 466–76.

King, George Brockwell: 1928, 'The "Negative" Golden Rule', *Journal of Religion* **8**, 268–79.

—: 1935, 'The "Negative" Golden Rule: Additional Note', *Journal of Religion* **15**, 59–62.

Kohlberg, L.: 1979, 'Justice As Reversibility', *Philosophy, Politics and Society*, Laslett, P., ed., Yale University Press, New Haven.

Kolenda, Konstantin: 1975, 'Moral Conflicts and Universalizability', *Philosophy* **50**, 460–65.

Kucheman, Clark: 1968, 'Towards a Theory of Normative Economics', *Social Ethics*, Gibson Winter, ed., Harper & Row, New York, pp. 83–103.

Kupfer, Joseph: 1974, 'Universalization in Berkeley's Rule-Utilitarianism', *Review of International Philosophy* 28, 511–31.

Lang, Berel: 1969, 'Ordinary Language and the Principle of Generalizability: A Note', *Journal of Value Inquiry* 3, 217–20.

Lappin, Shalon: 1978, 'Moral Judgments and Identity Across Possible Worlds', *Ratio* 20, 69–74.

Laymon, R. E. and Machamer, P. K.: 1970, 'Personal Decisions and Universalizability', *Mind* 79, 425–26.

Levin, Michael E.: 1979, 'The Universalizability of Moral Judgments Revisited', *Mind* 88, 115–19.

Lipkin, Robert: 1967, 'In Defense of Sidgwick', *Philosophical Studies* 18, 70–2.

—: 1977, 'Universalizability and Prescriptivity in Practical Reasoning', *Southwestern Journal of Philosophy* 15, 67–79.

Locke, D.: 1968, 'The Trivializability of Universalizability', *Philosophical Review* 77, 25–44.

—: 1981, 'The Principle of Equal Interests', *Philosophical Review* 90, 531–559.

Lutz, Adolf: 1964, 'Die Goldene Regel', *Zeitschrift fur Philosophische Forschung* 18, 467–75.

Lycan, William G. and Oldenquist, Andrew: 1972, 'Can the Generalization Argument be Reinstated?', *Analysis* 32, 76–81.

Lycan, William: 1969, 'Hare, Singer, and Gewirth on Universalizability', *Philosophical Quarterly* 19, 135–44.

MacIntyre, A.: 1957, 'What Morality is Not', *Philosophy* 32, 325–35.

MacNiven, C. D.: 1964–65, 'Hare's Universal Prescriptivism', *Dialogue* 3, 191–98.

Margolis, Joseph: 1963, 'Generalization and Moral Principles', *Personalist* 44, 364–75.

—: 1970, 'Review of *Freedom and Reason*', *Journal of Value Inquiry* 5, 57–64.

McCloskey, H. J.: 1966, 'Suppose Everyone Did the Same', *Mind* 75, 432–33.

—: 1979, 'Universalized Prescriptivism and Utilitarianism: Hare's Attempted Forced Marriage', *Journal of Value Inquiry* 13, 63–76.

Meilander, Gilbert: 1980, 'Is What is Right For Me Right For All Persons Similarly Situated?', *Journal of Religious Ethics* 8, 125–34.

Mew, Peter: 1975, 'Doubts About Moral Principles', *Inquiry* 18, 289–308.

Milkman, Kenneth A.: 1982, 'Hare, Universalizability and the Problem of Relevant Act Descriptions', *Canadian Journal of Philosophy* 12, 19–32.

Mitchell, Dorothy: 1963, 'Are Moral Principles Really Necessary?', *Australasian Journal of Philosophy* 41, 163–81.

Monro, D. H.: 1961, 'Impartiality and Consistency', *Philosophy* 36, 161–76.

—: 1964, 'Critical Notice of *Freedom and Reason*', *Australasian Journal of Philosophy* 42, 120–34.

Montague, Roger: 1965, 'Universalizability', *Analysis* 25, 189–202.

—: 1972–73, 'Justice, Reasonableness, and the Similar Handling of Similar Cases', *Philosophy and Phenomenological Research* 33, 90–99.

—: 1974, 'Winch on Agent's Judgments', *Analysis* 34, 161–66.

Morris, Donald: 1976, 'Evaluative Meaning and Universalizability', *Midwest Journal of Philosophy* 4, 44–7.

Mounce, J. O. and Philips, D. Z.: 1965, 'On Morality's Having a Point', *Philosophy* **40**, 308–19.

Mulholland, Leslie: 1978, 'Kant: On Willing Maxims to Become Laws of Nature', *Dialogue* (Canada) **17**, 92–105.

Nakhnikian, George: 1964, 'Generalization in Ethics', *Review of Metaphysics* **17**, 436–61.

Narveson, Jan: 1969, 'Silverstein on Egoism and Universalizability', *Australasian Journal of Philosophy* **47**, 356–66.

—: 1980, 'Review of *Reason and Morality*', *Dialogue* (Canada) **19**, 651–74.

Nielsen, Kai: 1984, 'Against Ethical Rationalism', *Gewirth's Ethical Rationalism*, Edward Regis, Jr., ed., The University of Chicago Press, Chicago, Illinois.

Nelson, William N.: 1974, 'Special Rights, General Rights, and Social Justice', *Philosophy and Public Affairs* **3**, 410–30.

Norton, David L.: 1980, 'On An Internal Disparity in Universalizability-Criterion Formulations', *Review of Metaphysics* **33**, 519–29.

Nute, Donald: 1979, 'Extensional Equivalence of Simple and General Utilitarian Principles', *Notre Dame Journal of Formal Logic* **20**, 32–6.

Oldenquist, Andrew: 'Universalizability and the Advantages of Nondescriptivism', *Journal of Philosophy* **65**, 57–79.

—: 1969, 'The Good Reasons Paradox', *Journal of Value Inquiry* **3**, 52–4.

Panaccio, Claude: 1973, 'Hare *et al*. Universalisation des Jugments Moraux', *Canadian Journal of Philosophy* **2**, 345–61.

Persson, I.: 1983, 'Hare on Universal Prescriptivism and Utilitarianism', *Analysis* **43**, 43–9.

Pollock, Lansing: 1972, 'Formal Moral Arguments', *Personalist* **53**, 25–42.

—: 1973, 'Freedom and Universalizability', *Mind* **82**, 234–48.

—: 1977, 'The Principle of Consequences', *Philosophical Studies* **31**, 385–90.

—: 1978, 'A Dilemma for Singer', *Philosophical Studies* **33**, 425–26.

Postow, B. C.: 1977, 'Generalized Act Utilitarianism', *Analysis* **37**, 49–52.

Potter, N. T.: 1973, 'Paton on the Application of the Categorical Imperative', *Kant-Studien* **64**, 411–22.

—: 1975, 'How to Apply the Categorical Imperative', *Philosophia* **5**, 395–416.

Quinton, Anthony: 1970, 'The Bounds of Morality', *Metaphilosophy* **1**, 202–22.

Rees, D. A.: 1970–71, 'Some Problems of Universalization', *Proceedings of the Aristotelian Society* **71**, 243–57.

Reeve, E. G.: 1969, ' "Suppose Everyone Did the Same" – A Note', *Mind* **78**, 280.

Reiner, H.: 1948, 'Die Goldene Regel', *Zeitschrift fur Philosophische Forschung* **3**, 74–105.

Robins, Michael, H.: 1974, 'Hare's Golden-Rule Argument: A Reply to Silverstein', *Mind* **81**, 578–81.

—: 1975, 'The Fallacy of "What Would Happen if Everybody Did That?" ', *Southwestern Journal of Philosophy* **6**, 89–108.

Robinson, H. M.: 1982, 'Is Hare a Naturalist?', *Philosophical Review* **91**, 73–86.

Robinson, Richard: 1981, 'Imagination, Desire, and Prescription', *Analysis* **41**, 55–9.

Ross, Alf: 1964, 'On Moral Reasoning', *Danish Yearbook of Philosophy* **1**, 120–32.

Ryan, Alan: 1964, 'Universalisability', *Analysis* **25**, 44–8.

Schlecht, Jr., L. F.: 1970–71, 'Universalizability and the Impartiality of Brandt's Ideal Observer', *Philosophical Forum* 2, 396–401.

Scott-Taggart, M. J.: 1966, 'Recent Work in the Philosophy of Kant', *American Philosophical Quarterly* 3, 171–209 at 194–200.

—: 1974, 'Kant, Conduct, and Consistency', Stephan Korner, ed., *Practical Reason*, Oxford.

Sesonske, Alexander: 1966, 'Moral Rules and the Generalization Argument', *American Philosophical Quarterly* 3, 282–90.

Shaida, S. A.: 1976, 'Nature of Ethical Statements', *Indian Philosophical Quarterly* 3, 335–43.

Sher, George: 1977, 'Hare, Abortion and the Golden Rule', *Philosophy and Public Affairs* 6, 185–90.

Silverstein, Harry: 1968, 'Universalizability and Egoism', *Australasian Journal of Philosophy* 46, 242–64.

—: 1972, 'A Note on Hare on Imagining Oneself in the Place of Others', *Mind* 81, 448–50.

—: 1974, 'Practical Reasons and Universalizability', *Australasian Journal of Philosophy* 52, 146–53.

—: 1974, 'Universality and Treating Persons as Persons', *Journal of Philosophy* 71, 57–71.

—: 1974, 'Simple and General Utilitarianism', *Philosophical Review* 83, 339–63.

—: 1976, 'Goldman's "Level-2" Act Descriptions and Utilitarian Generalization', *Philosophical Studies* 30, 45–55.

Singer, Marcus G.: 1954, 'The Categorical Imperative', *Philosophical Review* 63, 577–91.

—: 1955, 'Generalization in Ethics', *Mind* 54, 361–65.

—: 1958, 'Moral Rules and Principles', *Essays in Moral Philosophy*, A. I. Melden, ed., Washington University Press, Seattle, pp. 160–97.

—: 1963, 'The Golden Rule', *Philosophy* 38, 293–314.

—: 1967, 'Golden Rule', *The Encyclopedia of Philosophy*, Paul Edwards, Ed., Vol. III, London/New York, PP. 365–67.

—: 1977, 'The Principle of Consequences Reconsidered', *Philosophical Studies* 31, 391–410.

—: 1980, 'On Pollock's Dilemma for Singer', *Philosophical Studies* 38, 107–10.

—: 1984, 'Gewirth's Ethical Monism', *Gewirth's Ethical Rationalism*, Edward Regis, Jr., ed., University of Chicago Press, Chicago, Illinois.

Snare, Frank: 1972, 'Wants and Reasons', *Personalist* 53, 395–407.

Sobel, J. Howard: 1962, 'Review of *Generalization in Ethics*', *Harvard Educational Review* 32, 357–61.

—: 1965, 'Generalization Arguments', *Theoria* 31, 32–60.

—: 1967, 'Everyone, Consequences, and Generalization Arguments', *Inquiry* 10, 373–404.

—: 1970, 'Utilitarianisms: Simple and General', *Inquiry* 13, 394–449.

Sparshott, F. E.: 1963, 'Review of *Generalization in Ethics*', *Philosophical Review* 72, 97–9.

—: 'Critical Study of R. M. Hare, *Freedom and Reason*', *Philosophical Quarterly* 14, 358–67.

Spendel, Gunter: 1967, 'Die Goldene Regel als Rechtsprinzip', *Festschrift fur Fritz von Hippel*, J. Esser and H. Thieme, eds., Turingen, pp. 491–516.

Spooner, W. A.: 1941, 'Golden Rule', *The Encyclopedia of Religion and Ethics* 6, 310–12.

Stocker, Michael: 1965, 'Consistency in Ethics', *Analysis* 25, 116–22.

Stout, A. K.: 1954, 'But Suppose Everyone Did the Same?', *The Australasian Journal of Philosophy* 32, 1–29.

Strang, C.: 1960, 'What if Everyone Did That?', *Durham University Journal* 23, 5–10.

Taylor, C. C. W.: 1964, 'Review of *Generalization in Ethics*', *Mind* 73, 296–98.

—: 1965, 'Critical Notice of *Freedom and Reason*', *Mind* 74, 280–98.

Taylor, P.: 1968, 'Universalizability and Justice', *Ethics and Social Justice*, Kiefer, H. E. and Munitz, M. K., eds., State University of New York Press, Albany, New York, pp. 142–63.

—: 1978, 'On Taking the Moral Point of View', in French, P. A., *et. al.*, eds., *Midwest Studies in Philosophy* 3, 35–61.

Thomas, Jr., Sid B.: 1968, 'The Status of the Generalization Principle', *American Philosophical Quarterly* 5, 174–82.

Timmons, Mark: 1984, 'Contradictions and the Categorical Imperative', *Archiv fur Geschichte der Philosophie* 66, 294–312.

Ullman-Margalit, Edna: 1976, 'The Generalization Argument: Where Does the Obligation Lie?', *Journal of Philosophy* 73, 511–22.

Veatch, Henry B.: 1970–71, 'Language and Ethics: "What's Hecuba to Him, or He to Hecuba?"', *Proceedings of the American Philosophical Association* 44, 45–62.

—: 1977, 'On the Use and Abuse of the Principle of Universalizability', *Proceedings of the Catholic Philosophical Association* 51, 162–70.

Verdi, John J.: 1977, 'In Defence of Marcus Singer', *Personalist* 58, 208–20.

Versenyi, Laszlo.: 1972, 'Prescription and Universalizability', *Journal of Value Inquiry* 6, 22–36.

Wallace, James D.: 1968, 'The Duty to Help People in Distress', *Analysis* 29, 33–8.

Ward, Andrew: 1973, 'Morality and the Thesis of Universalizability', *Mind* 82, 289–91.

Weiler, Gershon: 1960, 'Universalizability by Me', *Philosophical Quarterly* 10, 167–70.

Werner, Richard: 1976, 'Hare on Abortion', *Analysis* 36, 177–81.

Whiteley, C. H.: 1966, 'Universalisability', *Analysis* 27, 45–9.

—: 1976, 'Morality and Egoism', *Mind* 85, 90–6.

White, Harold J.: 1969, 'An Analysis of Hare's Application of the Thesis of Universalizability in his Moral Arguments', *Australasian Journal of Philosophy* 47, 174–83.

Wick, Warner: 1962, 'Generalization and the Basis of Ethics', *Ethics* 72, 288–98.

Williams, B. A. O.: 1965, 'Ethical Consistency', *Proceedings of the Aristotelian Society* Suppl. 39, 103–24.

Winch, Peter: 1965, 'The Universalizability of Moral Judgments', *Monist* 49, 196–214.

[Note: A complete bibliography of articles on Gewirth's theory antecedent to the publication of *Reason and Morality* can be found in that book, Ch. 1 (Chicago: University of Chicago Press, 1978). Gewirth's moral theory is the main topic of a collection of essays, *Gewirth's Ethical Rationalism*, Edward Regis Jr., ed., The University of Chicago Press, Chicago.]

INDEX OF NAMES

307

INDEX OF SUBJECTS